EDENS ZERO

17

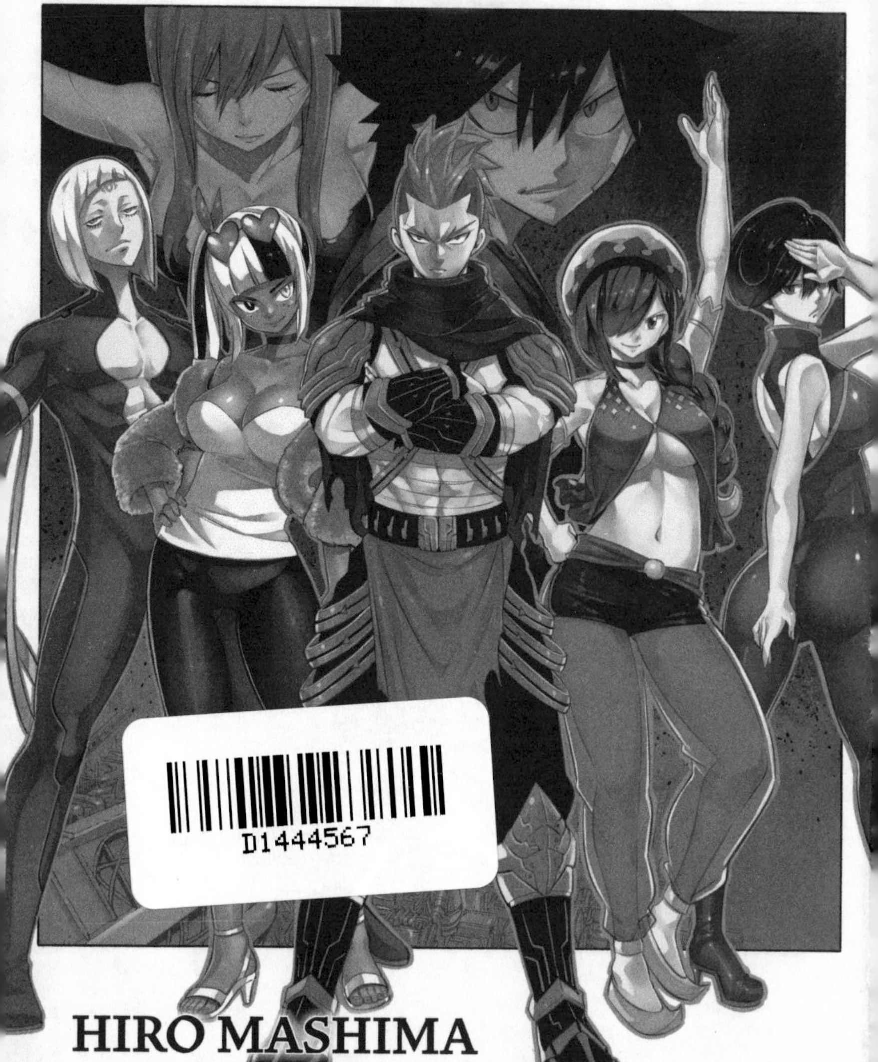

HIRO MASHIMA

EDENS ZERO 17 contents

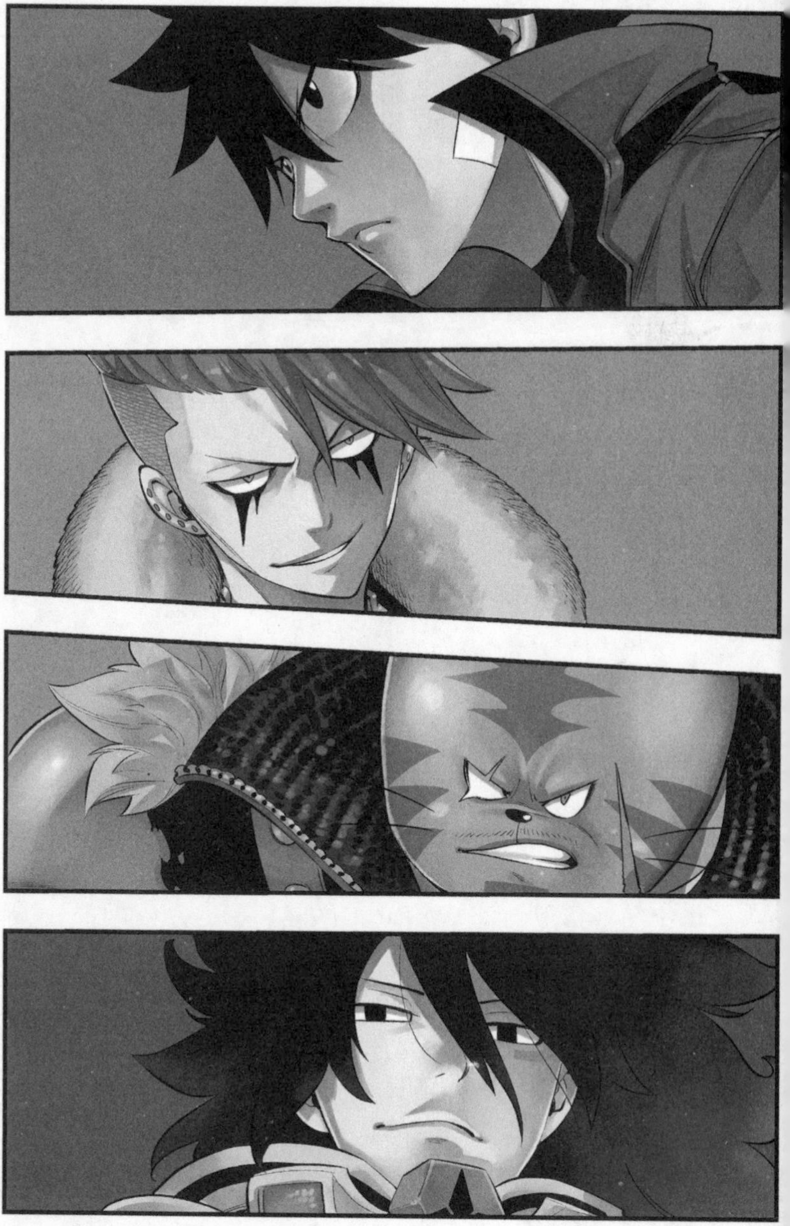

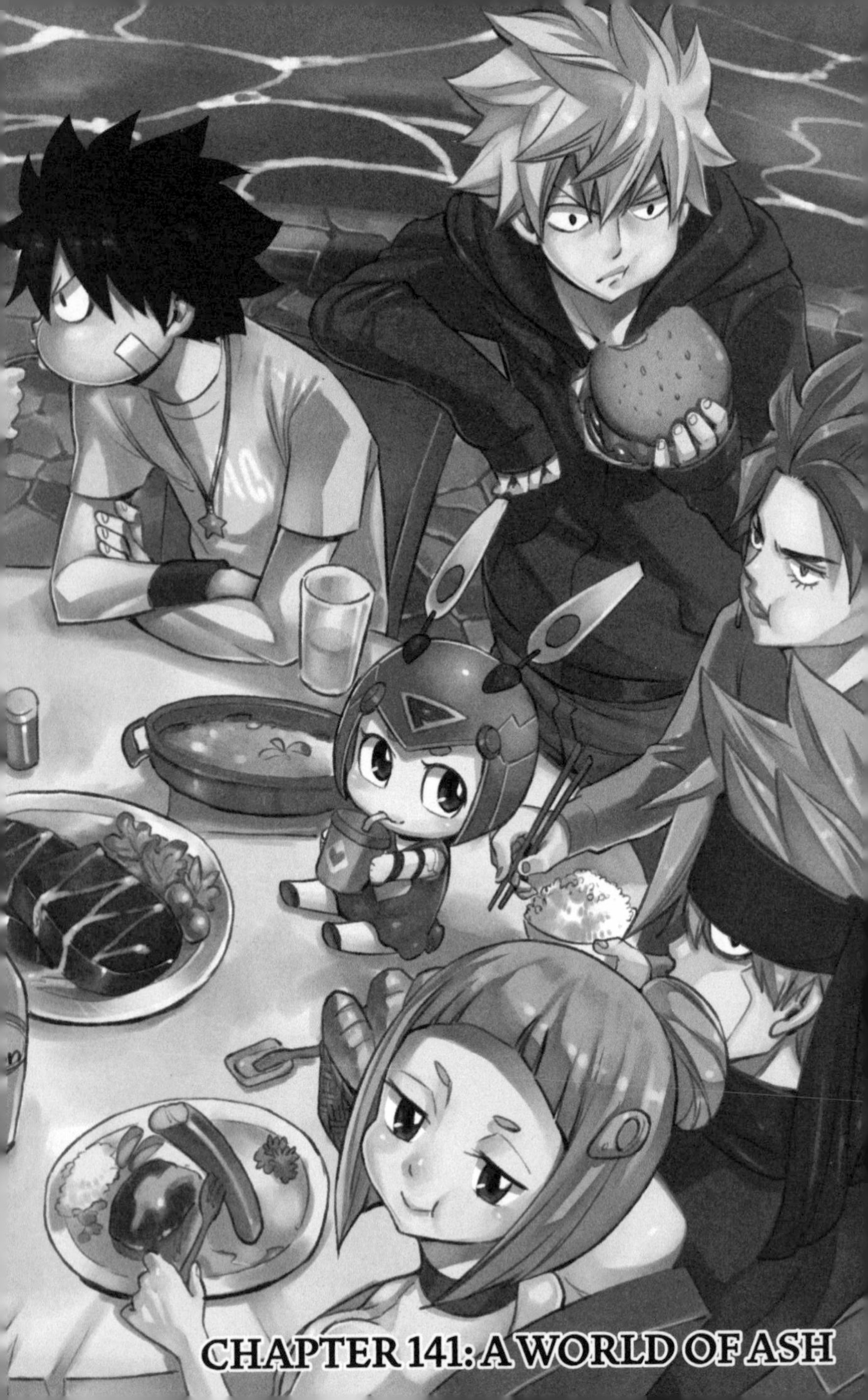

CHAPTER 141: A WORLD OF ASH

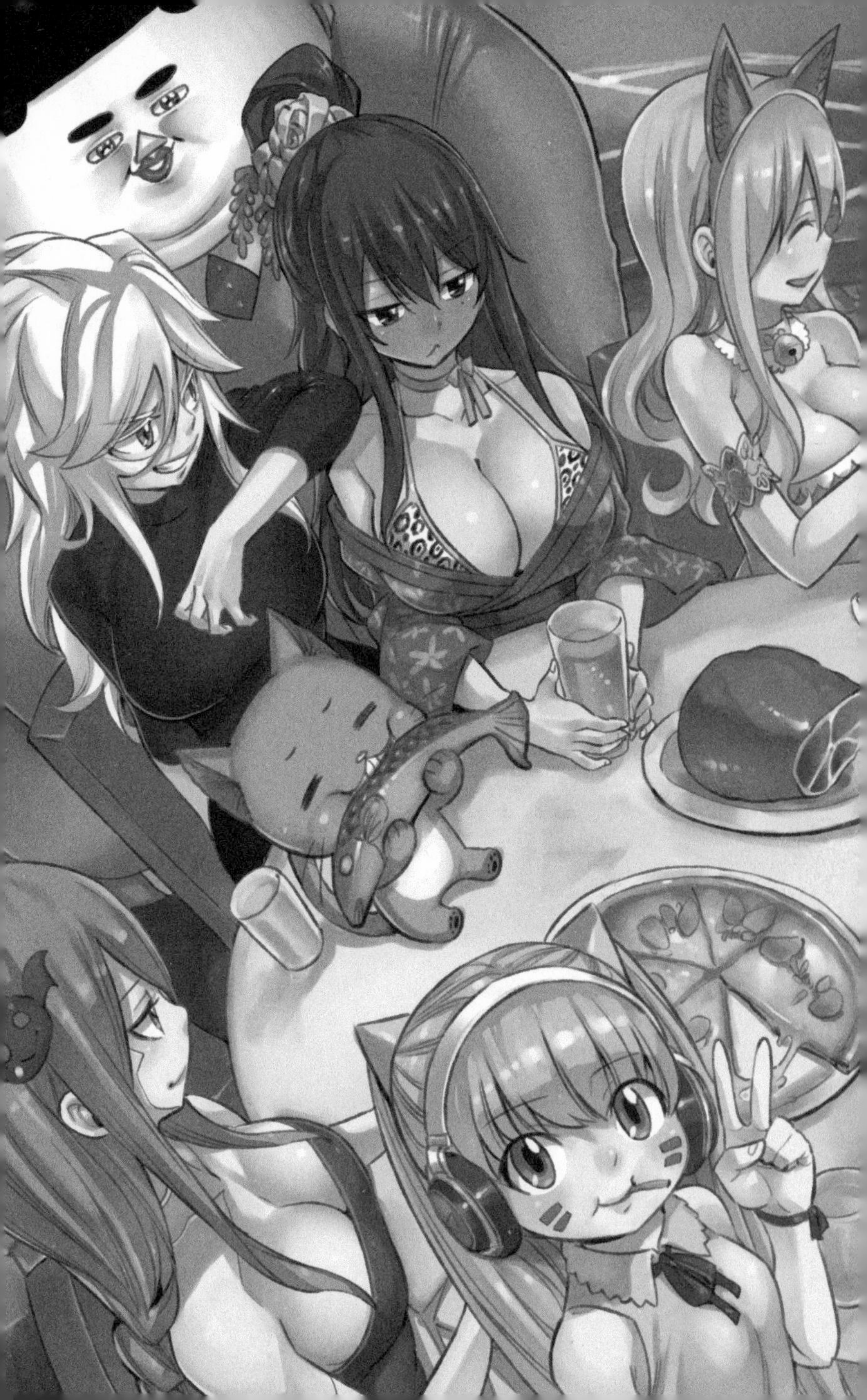

EDENSZERO

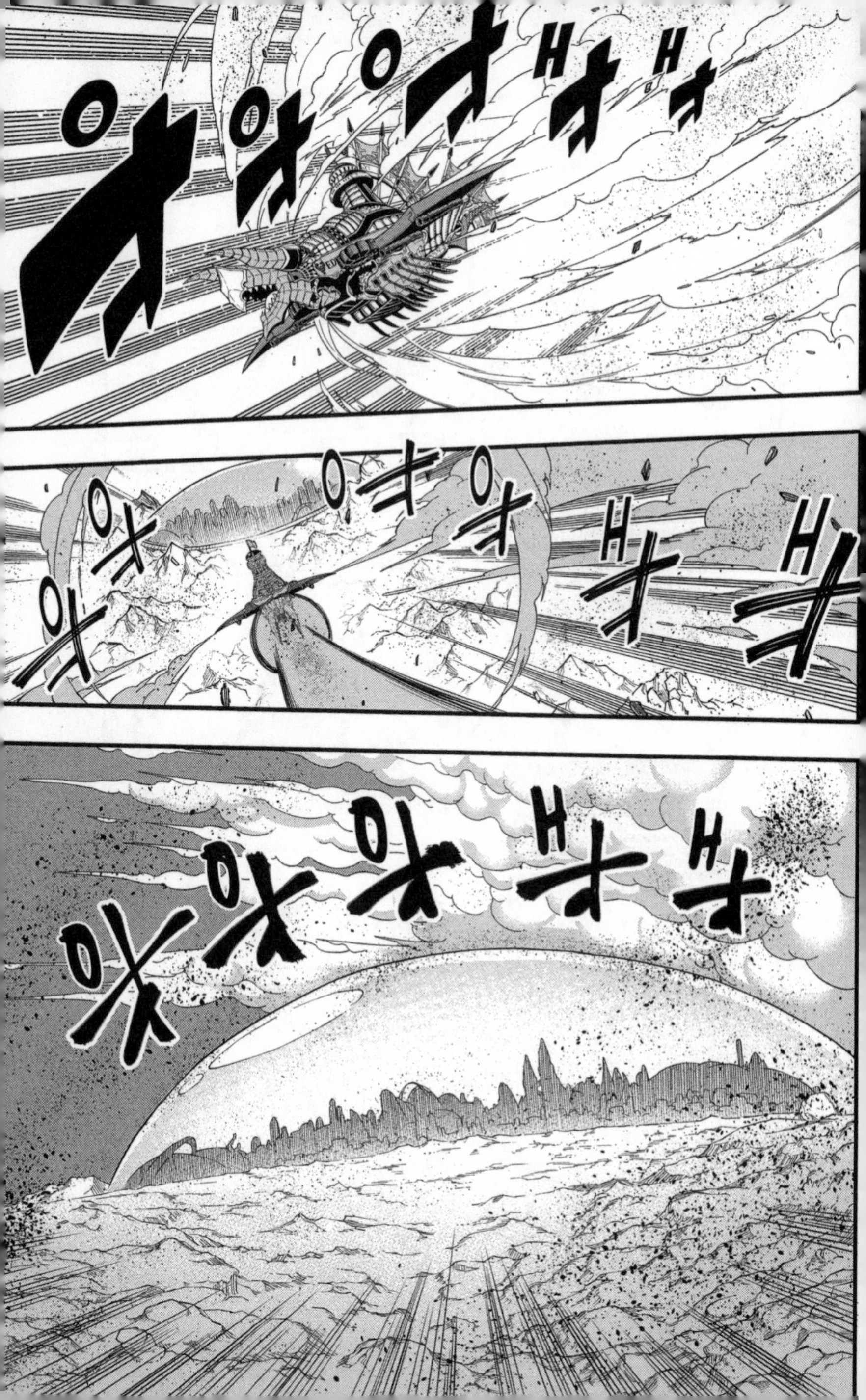

THERE'S A DOME OVER THE CITY.
YEAH, BECAUSE THIS PLACE IS KNOWN AS THE PLANET OF ASH.
DOES THIS ASH IN THE AIR AFFECT THE HUMAN BODY?
I WOULD NOT RECOMMEND LONG-TERM ACTIVITY OUTSIDE THE DOME.
BUT I'M SURE A *LITTLE* ASH WON'T HURT ANYBODY.
OH, GEE, *THAT'S* REASSURING.
IF ANYTHING HAPPENS, I'LL FIX YOU RIGHT UP.
I ATTEMPTED TO ANALYZE ITS COMPOSITION, BUT I COULD NOT IDENTIFY ALL OF ITS COMPONENTS.
AND THIS TOWN IS WHERE WE'LL FIND THE WHATSIT SYSTEM?
THE ALL-LINK SYSTEM.
ARE WE GOING TO BREAK THROUGH THE DOME?
THAT'S HOW THEY GOT IN ON THE BELIAL GORE, SO...

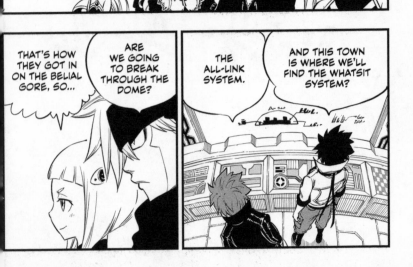

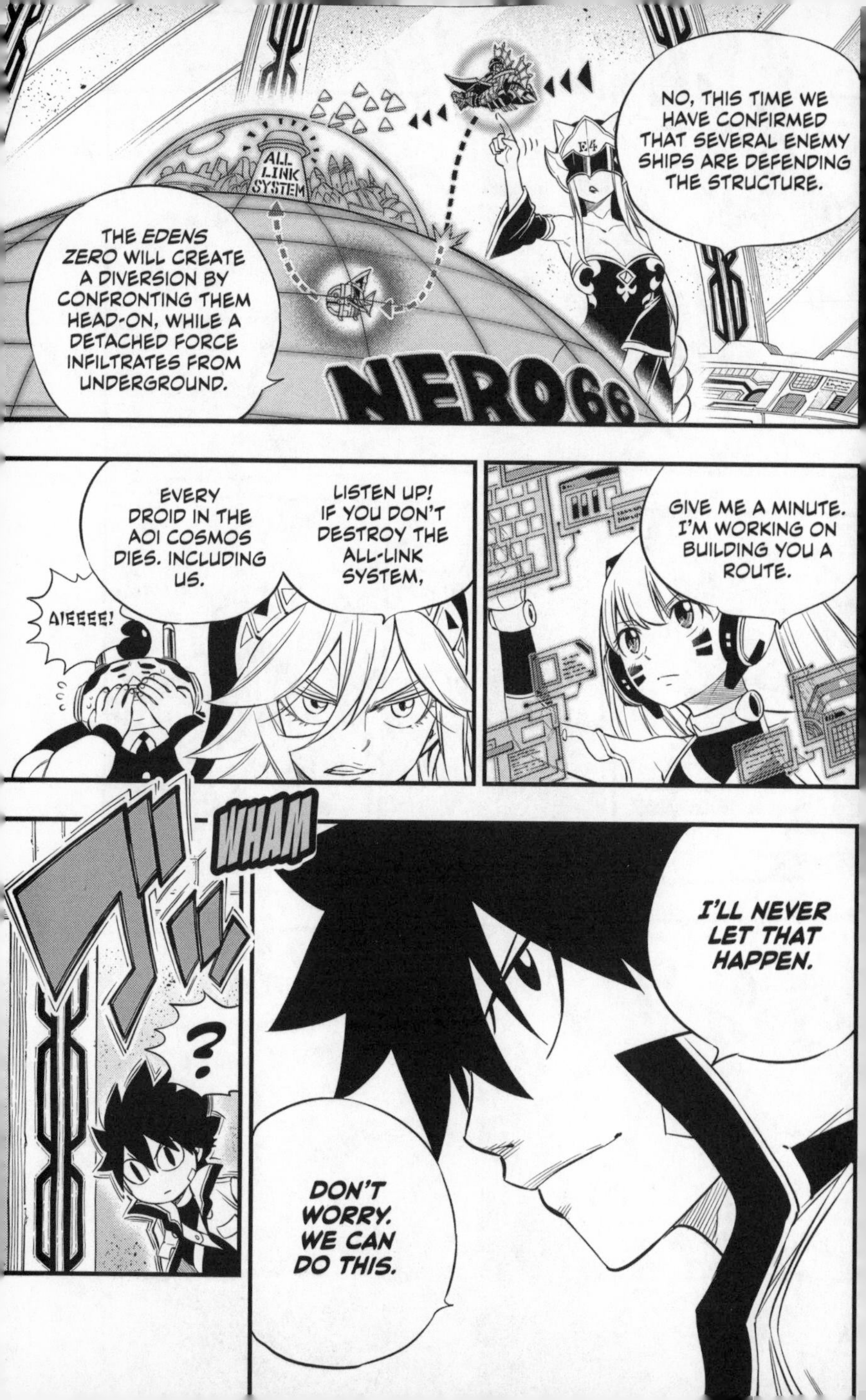
NO, THIS TIME WE HAVE CONFIRMED THAT SEVERAL ENEMY SHIPS ARE DEFENDING THE STRUCTURE.
ALL LINK SYSTEM
THE *EDENS ZERO* WILL CREATE A DIVERSION BY CONFRONTING THEM HEAD-ON, WHILE A DETACHED FORCE INFILTRATES FROM UNDERGROUND.
NERO66
GIVE ME A MINUTE. I'M WORKING ON BUILDING YOU A ROUTE.
LISTEN UP! IF YOU DON'T DESTROY THE ALL-LINK SYSTEM,
EVERY DROID IN THE AOI COSMOS DIES. INCLUDING US.
AIEEEE!
I'LL NEVER LET THAT HAPPEN.
DON'T WORRY. WE CAN DO THIS.
WHAM
?

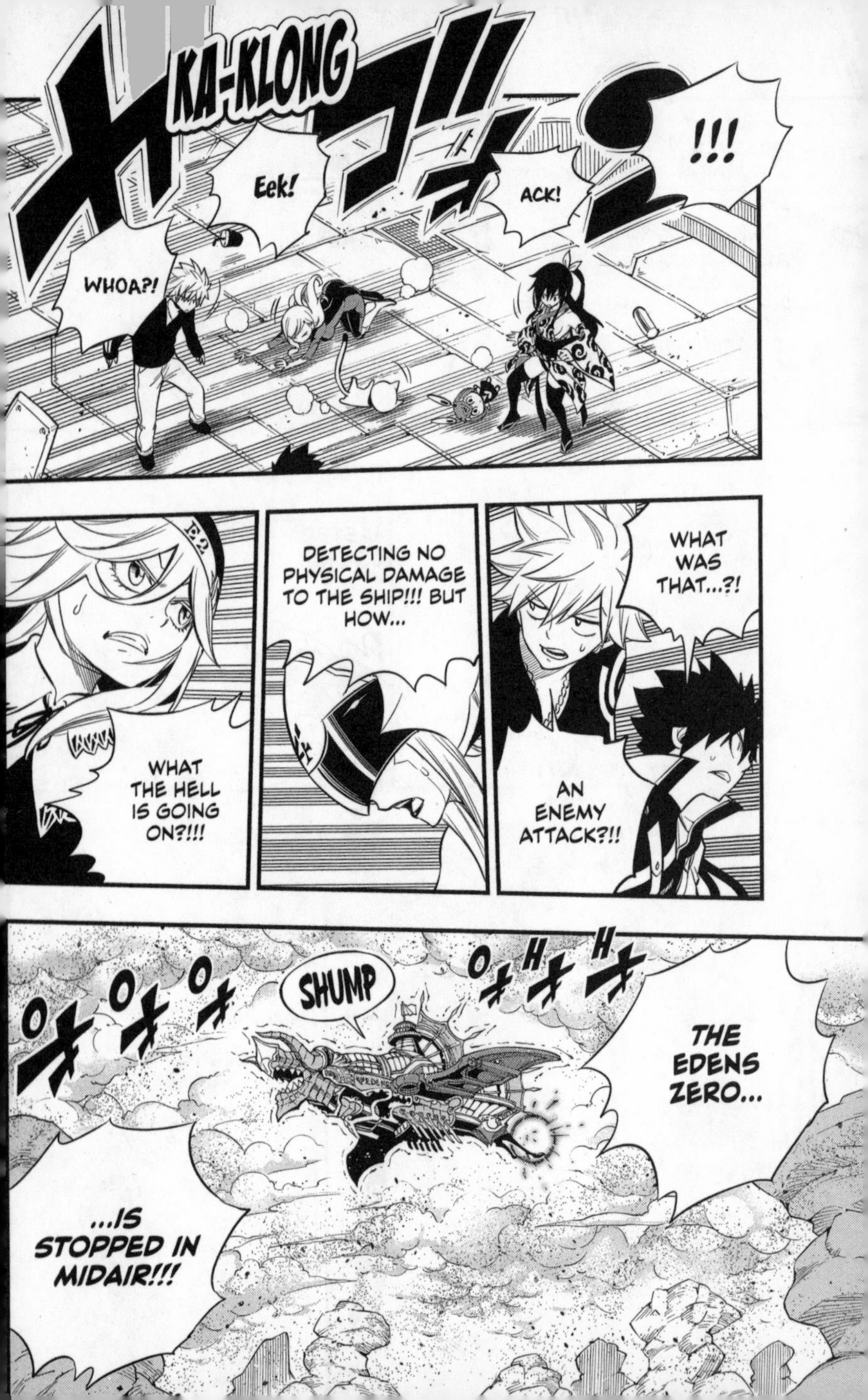
KA-KLONG
!!!
ACK!
Eek!
WHOA?!
WHAT WAS THAT...?!
AN ENEMY ATTACK?!!
DETECTING NO PHYSICAL DAMAGE TO THE SHIP!!! BUT HOW...
WHAT THE HELL IS GOING ON?!!!
THE EDENS ZERO...
SHUMP
...IS STOPPED IN MIDAIR!!!

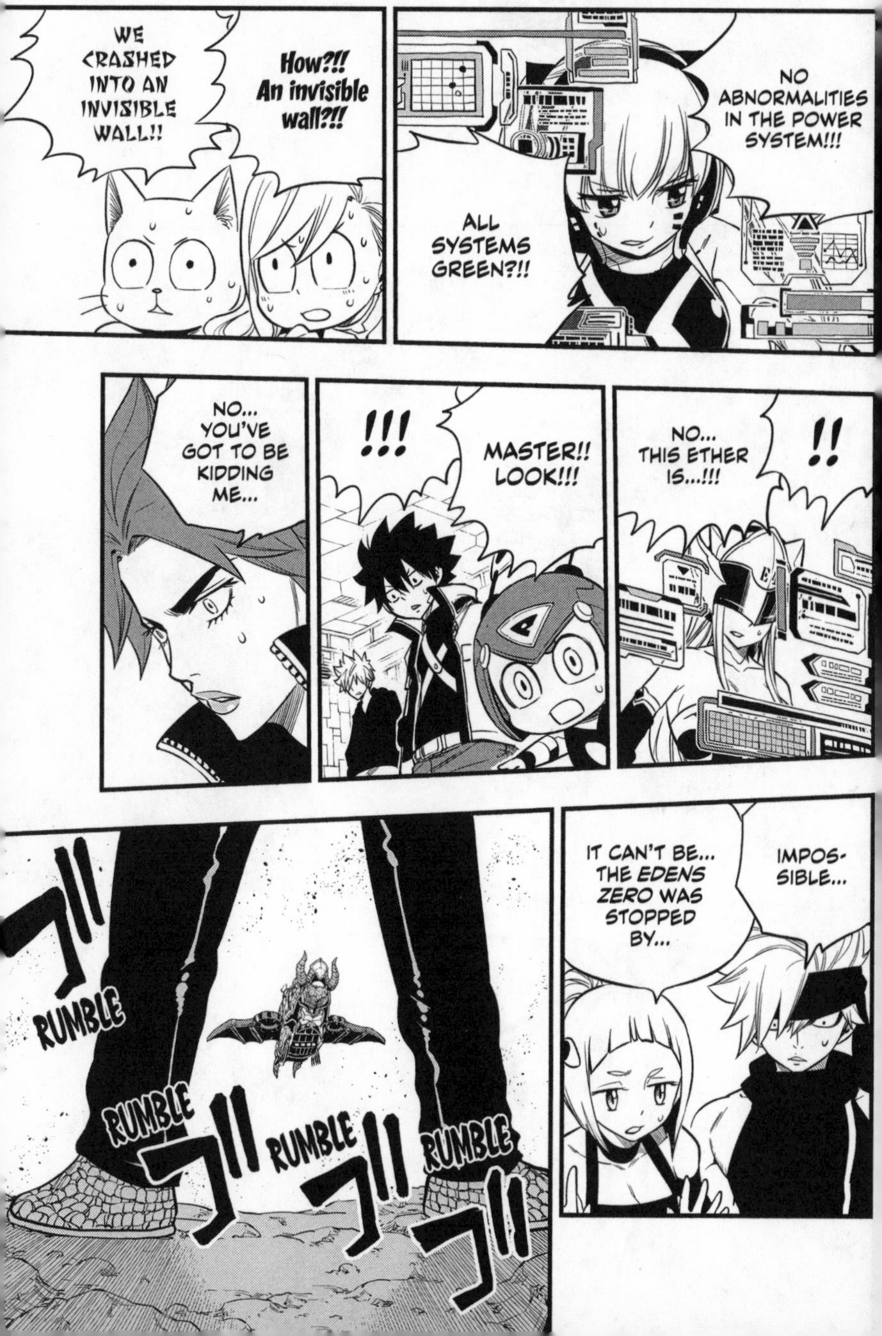
NO ABNORMALITIES IN THE POWER SYSTEM!!!
ALL SYSTEMS GREEN?!!
WE CRASHED INTO AN INVISIBLE WALL!!
How?!! An invisible wall?!!
!!
NO... THIS ETHER IS...!!!
!!!
MASTER!! LOOK!!!
NO... YOU'VE GOT TO BE KIDDING ME...
IMPOS-SIBLE...
IT CAN'T BE... THE *EDENS ZERO* WAS STOPPED BY...
RUMBLE
RUMBLE
RUMBLE
RUMBLE

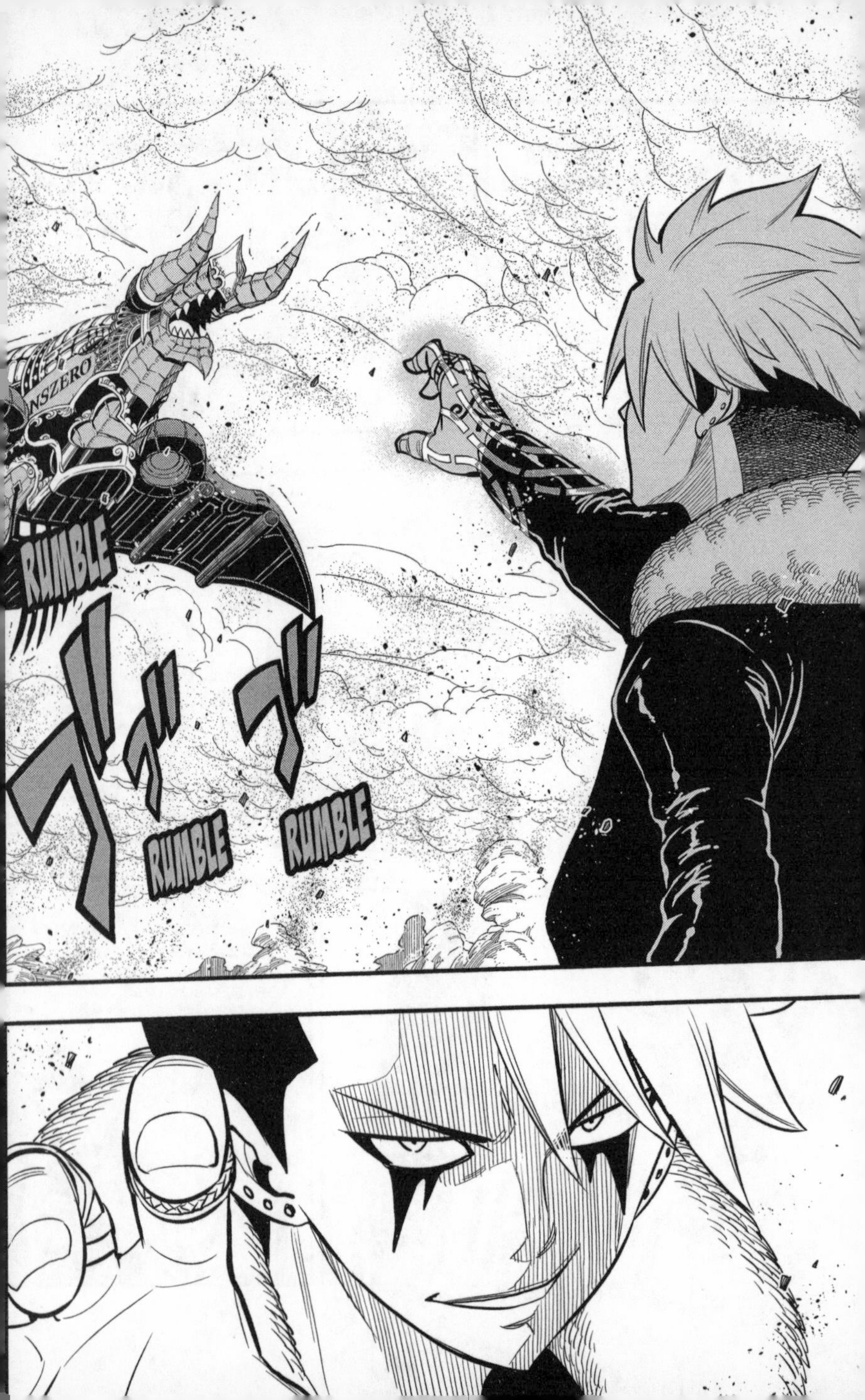
NSZERO
RUMBLE
ゴゴゴ
RUMBLE
RUMBLE

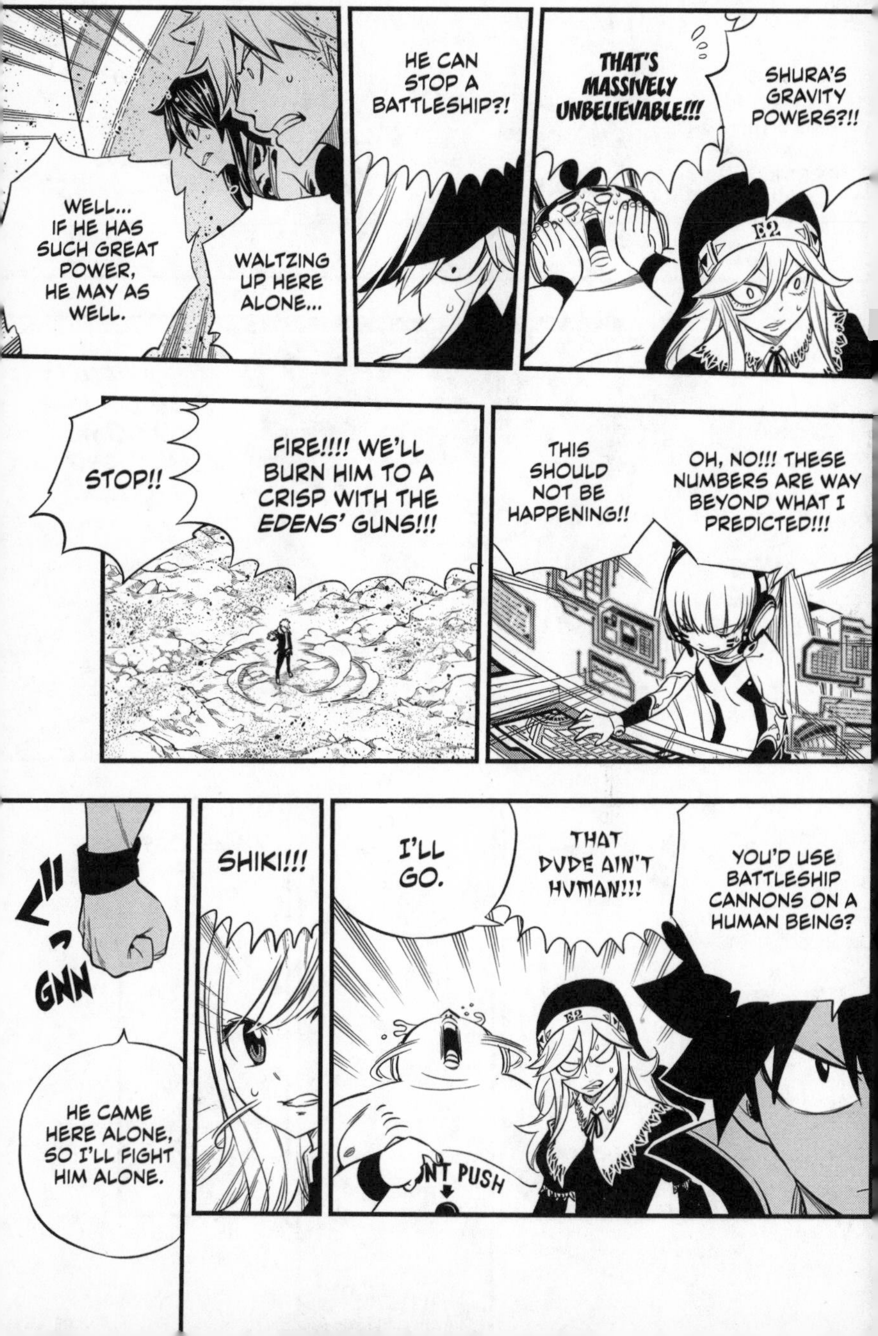
SHURA'S GRAVITY POWERS?!!
THAT'S MASSIVELY UNBELIEVABLE!!!
HE CAN STOP A BATTLESHIP?!
WALTZING UP HERE ALONE...
WELL... IF HE HAS SUCH GREAT POWER, HE MAY AS WELL.
OH, NO!!! THESE NUMBERS ARE WAY BEYOND WHAT I PREDICTED!!!
THIS SHOULD NOT BE HAPPENING!!
FIRE!!!! WE'LL BURN HIM TO A CRISP WITH THE *EDENS'* GUNS!!!
STOP!!
YOU'D USE BATTLESHIP CANNONS ON A HUMAN BEING?
THAT DUDE AIN'T HUMAN!!!
I'LL GO.
NT PUSH
SHIKI!!!
GNN
HE CAME HERE ALONE, SO I'LL FIGHT HIM ALONE.

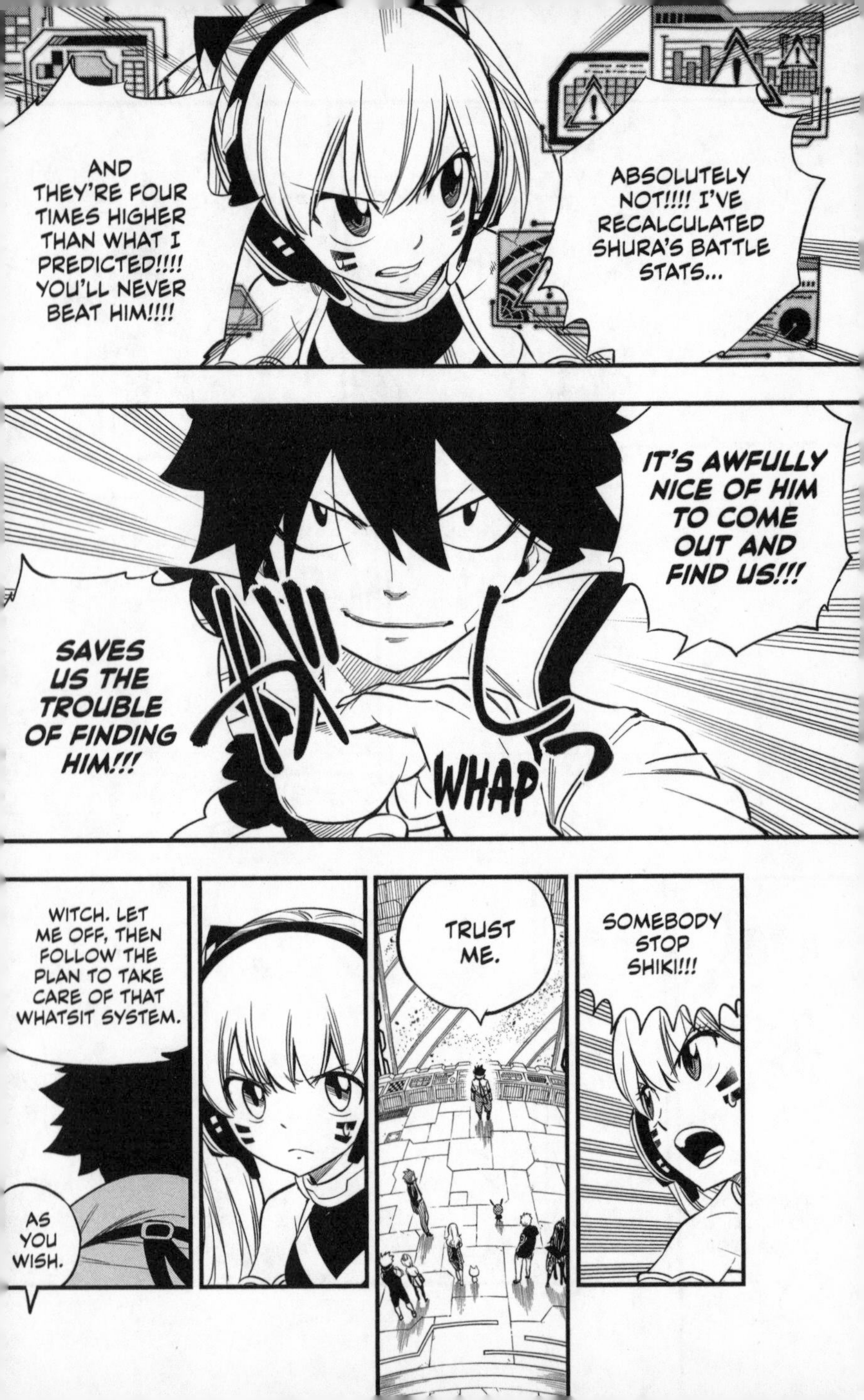
ABSOLUTELY NOT!!!! I'VE RECALCULATED SHURA'S BATTLE STATS...
AND THEY'RE FOUR TIMES HIGHER THAN WHAT I PREDICTED!!!! YOU'LL NEVER BEAT HIM!!!!
IT'S AWFULLY NICE OF HIM TO COME OUT AND FIND US!!!
SAVES US THE TROUBLE OF FINDING HIM!!!
WHAP
SOMEBODY STOP SHIKI!!!
TRUST ME.
WITCH. LET ME OFF, THEN FOLLOW THE PLAN TO TAKE CARE OF THAT WHATSIT SYSTEM.
AS YOU WISH.

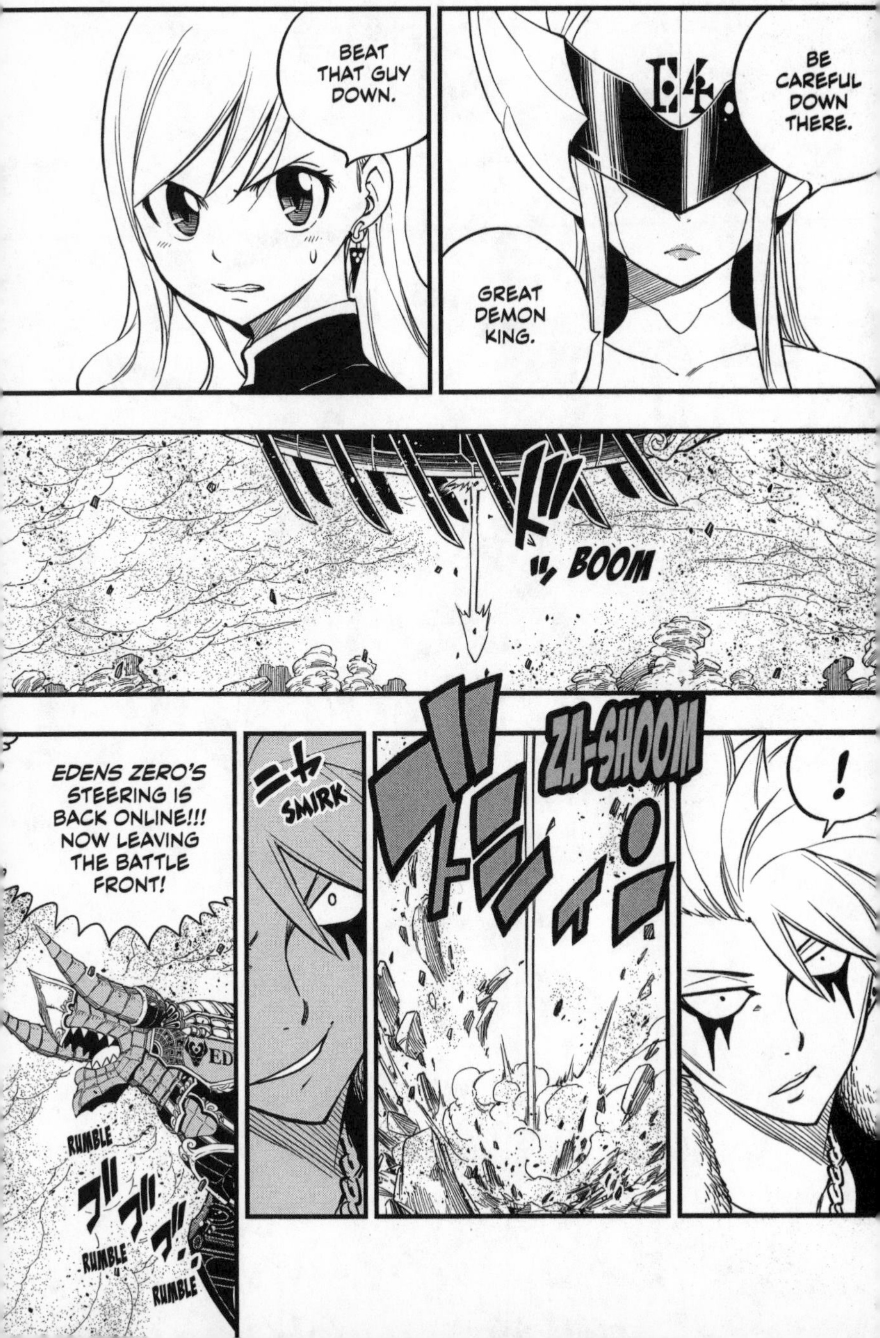
BE CAREFUL DOWN THERE.
GREAT DEMON KING.
BEAT THAT GUY DOWN.
BOOM
!
ZA-SHOOM
ニヤ
SMIRK
EDENS ZERO'S STEERING IS BACK ONLINE!!! NOW LEAVING THE BATTLE FRONT!
RUMBLE
RUMBLE
RUMBLE

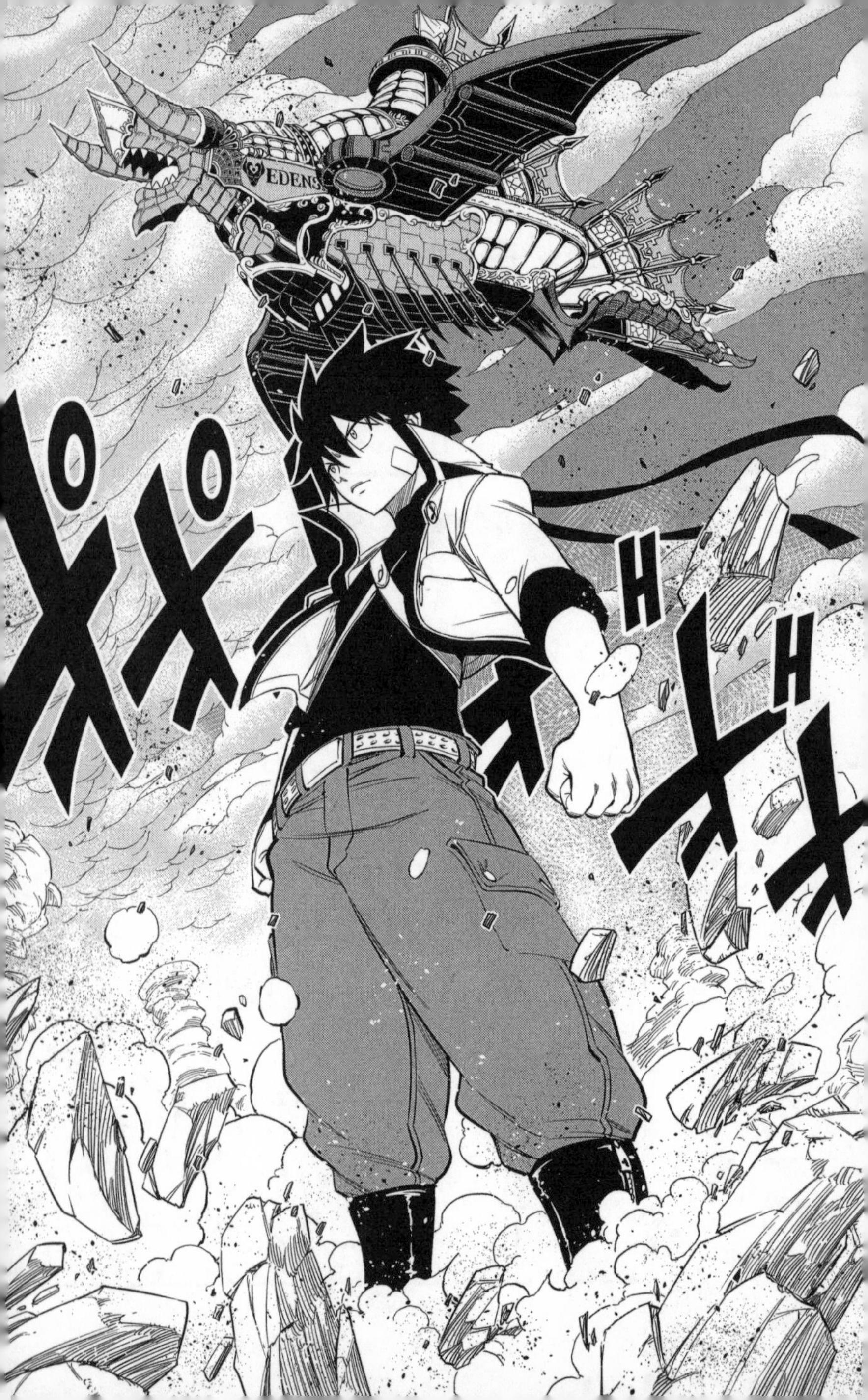
EDENS

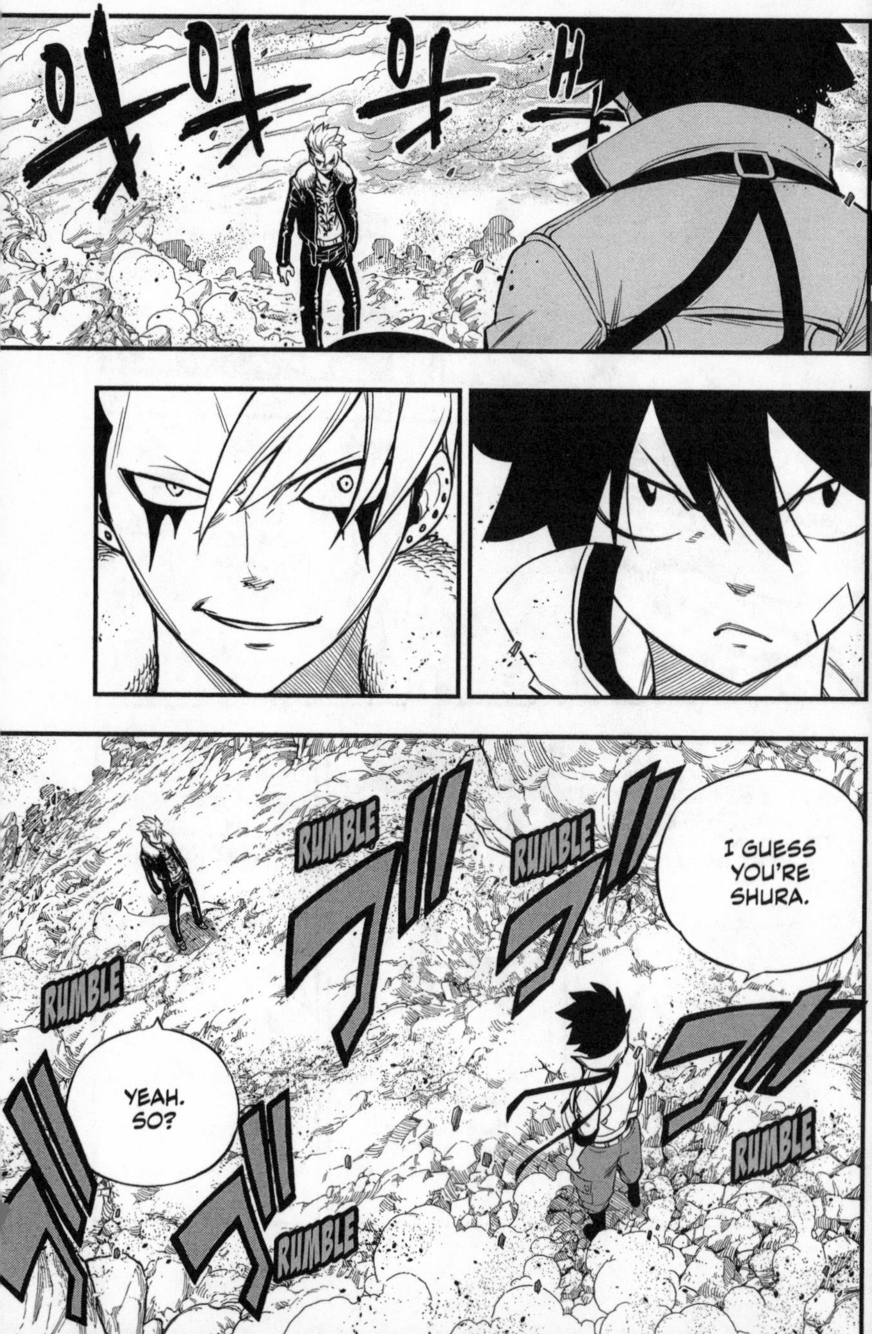
RUMBLE
I GUESS YOU'RE SHURA.
RUMBLE
RUMBLE
RUMBLE
YEAH. SO?
RUMBLE

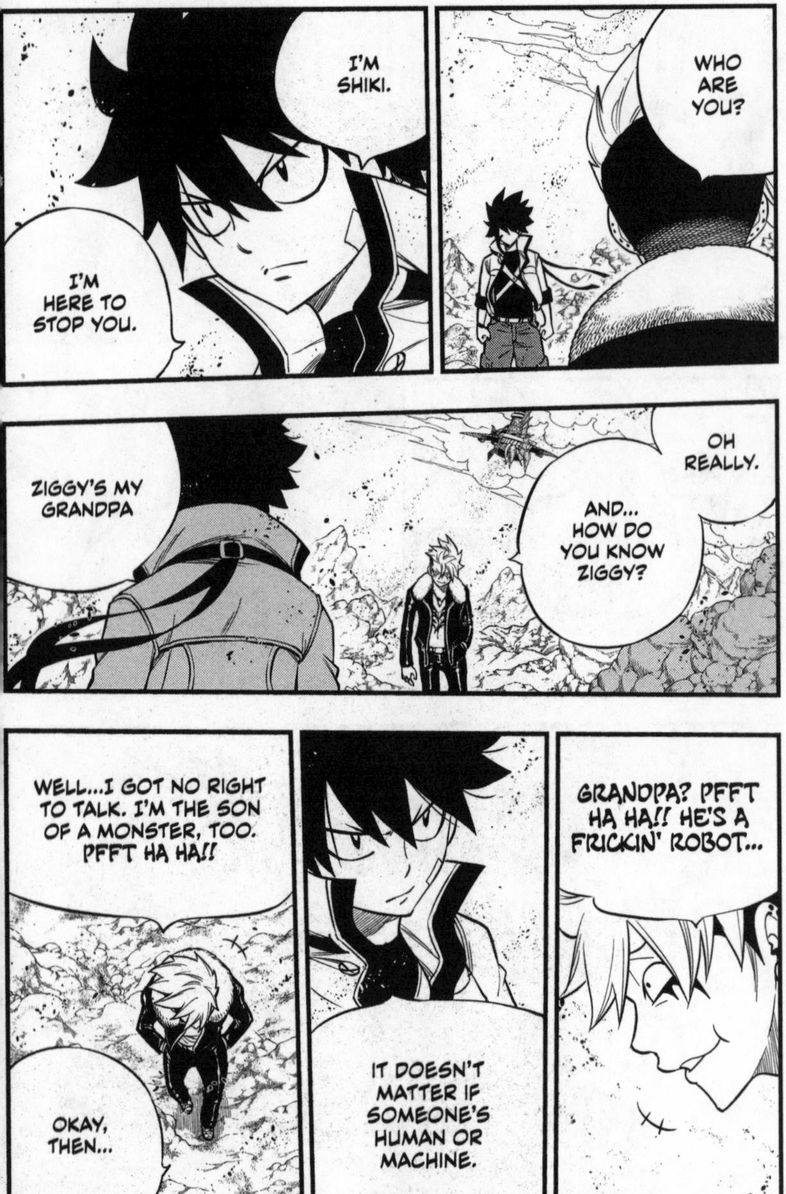
WHO ARE YOU?
I'M SHIKI.
I'M HERE TO STOP YOU.
OH REALLY.
AND... HOW DO YOU KNOW ZIGGY?
ZIGGY'S MY GRANDPA
GRANDPA? PFFT HA HA!! HE'S A FRICKIN' ROBOT...
IT DOESN'T MATTER IF SOMEONE'S HUMAN OR MACHINE.
WELL...I GOT NO RIGHT TO TALK. I'M THE SON OF A MONSTER, TOO. PFFT HA HA!!
OKAY, THEN...

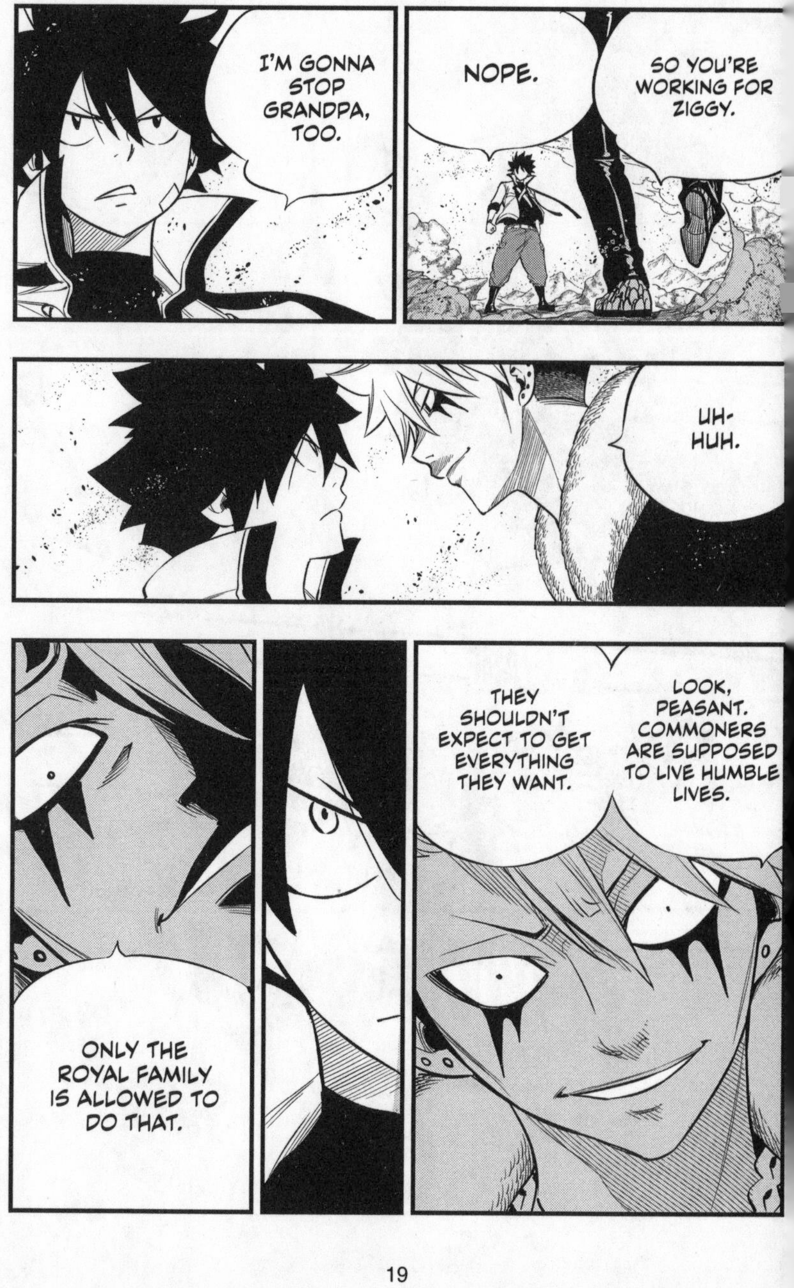
SO YOU'RE WORKING FOR ZIGGY.
NOPE.
I'M GONNA STOP GRANDPA, TOO.
UH-HUH.
LOOK, PEASANT. COMMONERS ARE SUPPOSED TO LIVE HUMBLE LIVES.
THEY SHOULDN'T EXPECT TO GET EVERYTHING THEY WANT.
ONLY THE ROYAL FAMILY IS ALLOWED TO DO THAT.

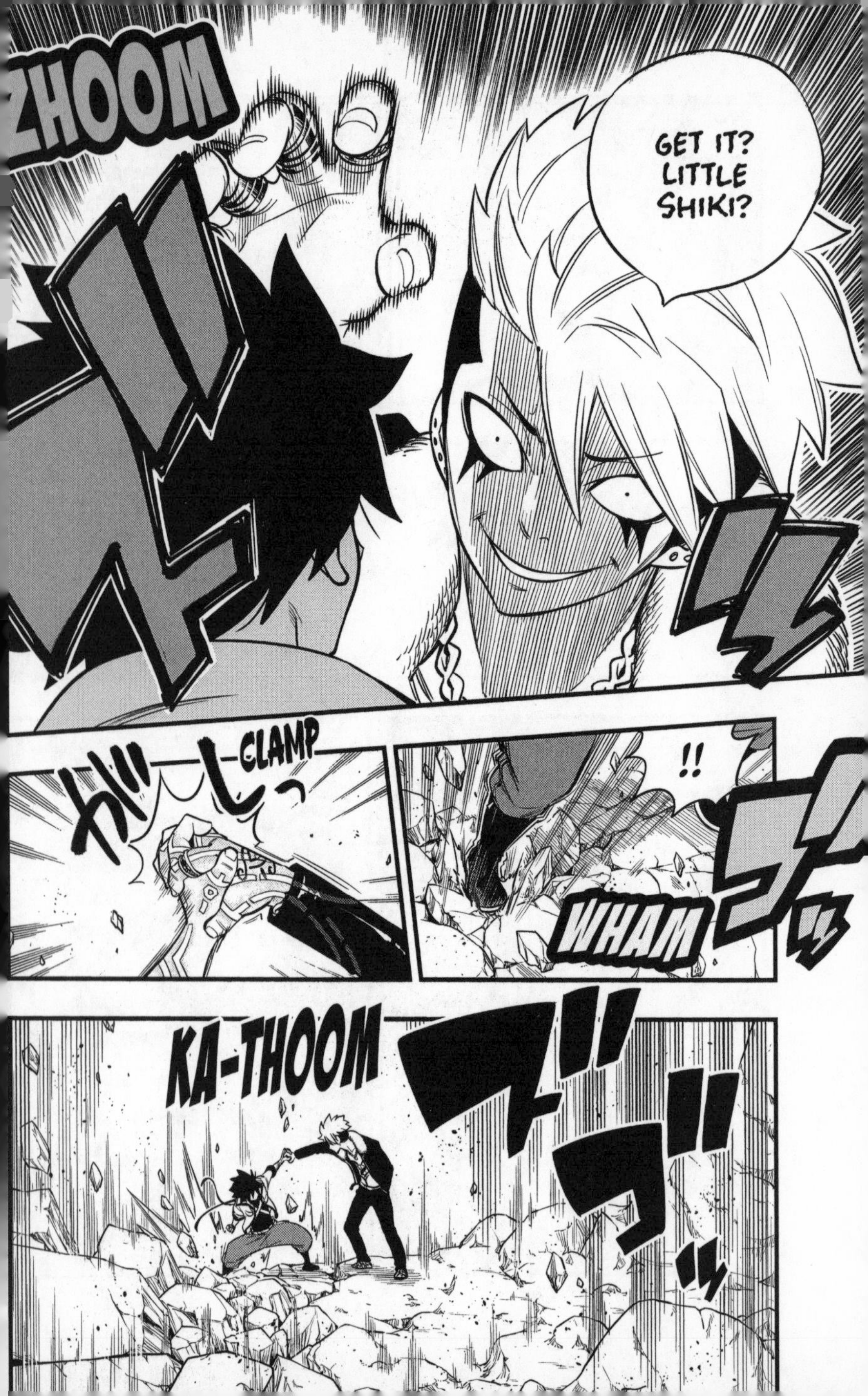
GET IT? LITTLE SHIKI?
ZHOOM
!!
WHAM
CLAMP
KA-THOOM

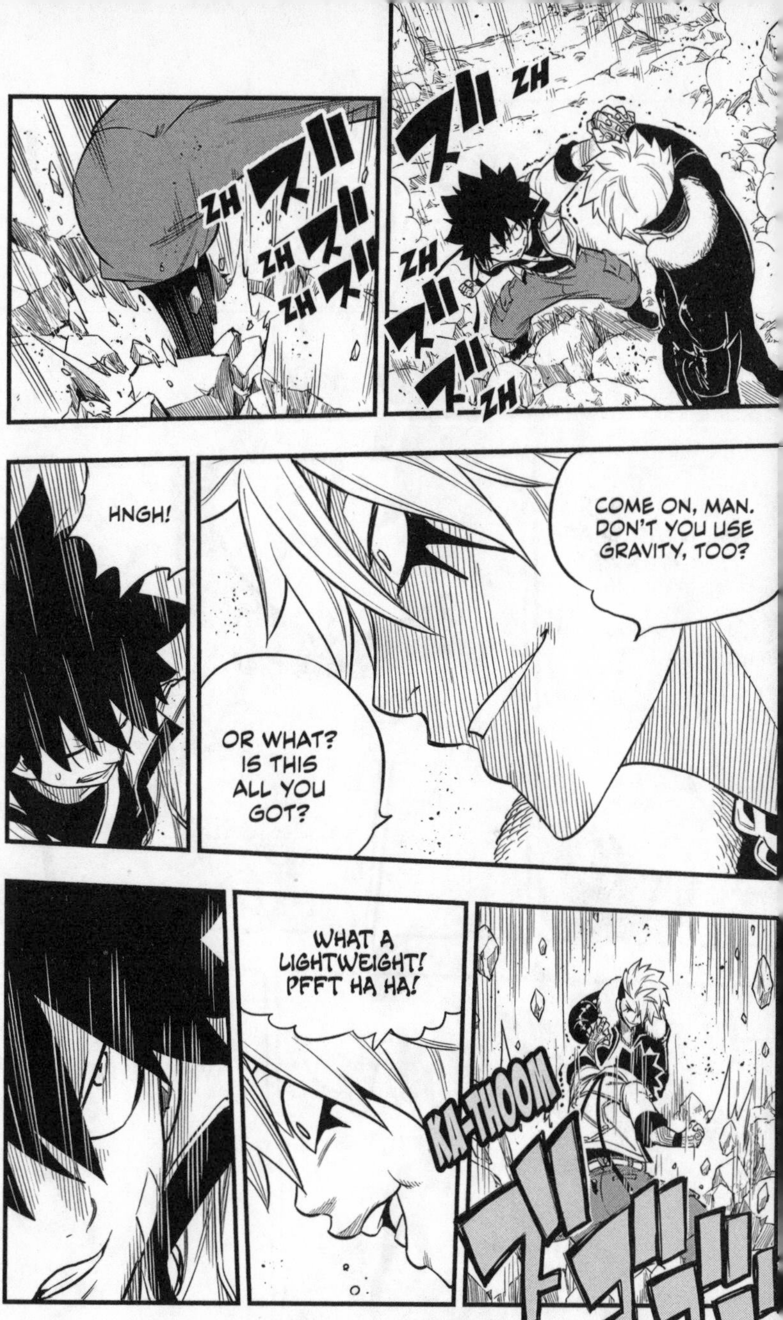
ZH
ZH
ZH
ZH
ZH
ZH
ZH
COME ON, MAN. DON'T YOU USE GRAVITY, TOO?
OR WHAT? IS THIS ALL YOU GOT?
HNGH!
KA-THOOM
WHAT A LIGHTWEIGHT! PFFT HA HA!

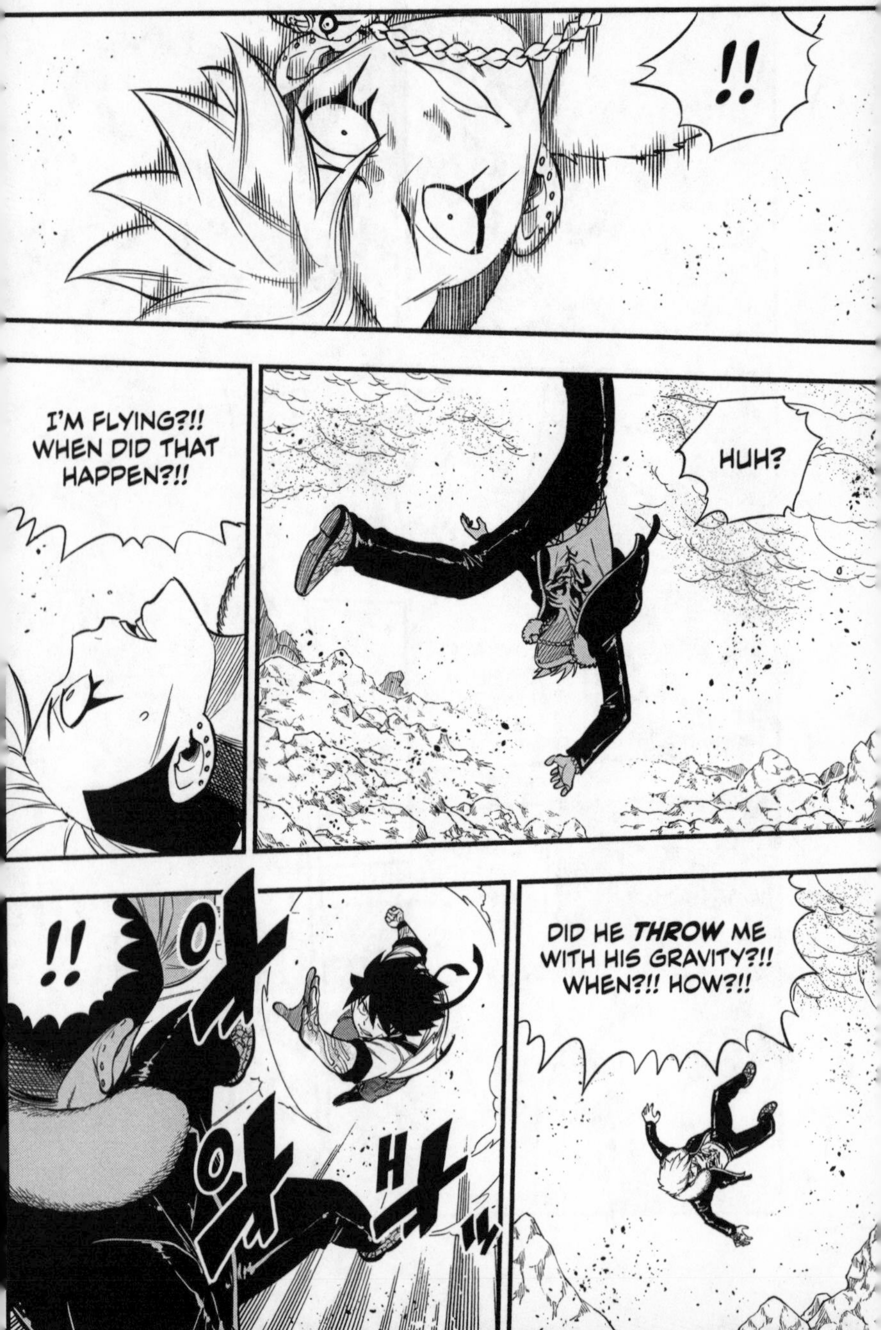
!!
HUH?
I'M FLYING?!! WHEN DID THAT HAPPEN?!!
DID HE *THROW* ME WITH HIS GRAVITY?!! WHEN?!! HOW?!!
!!

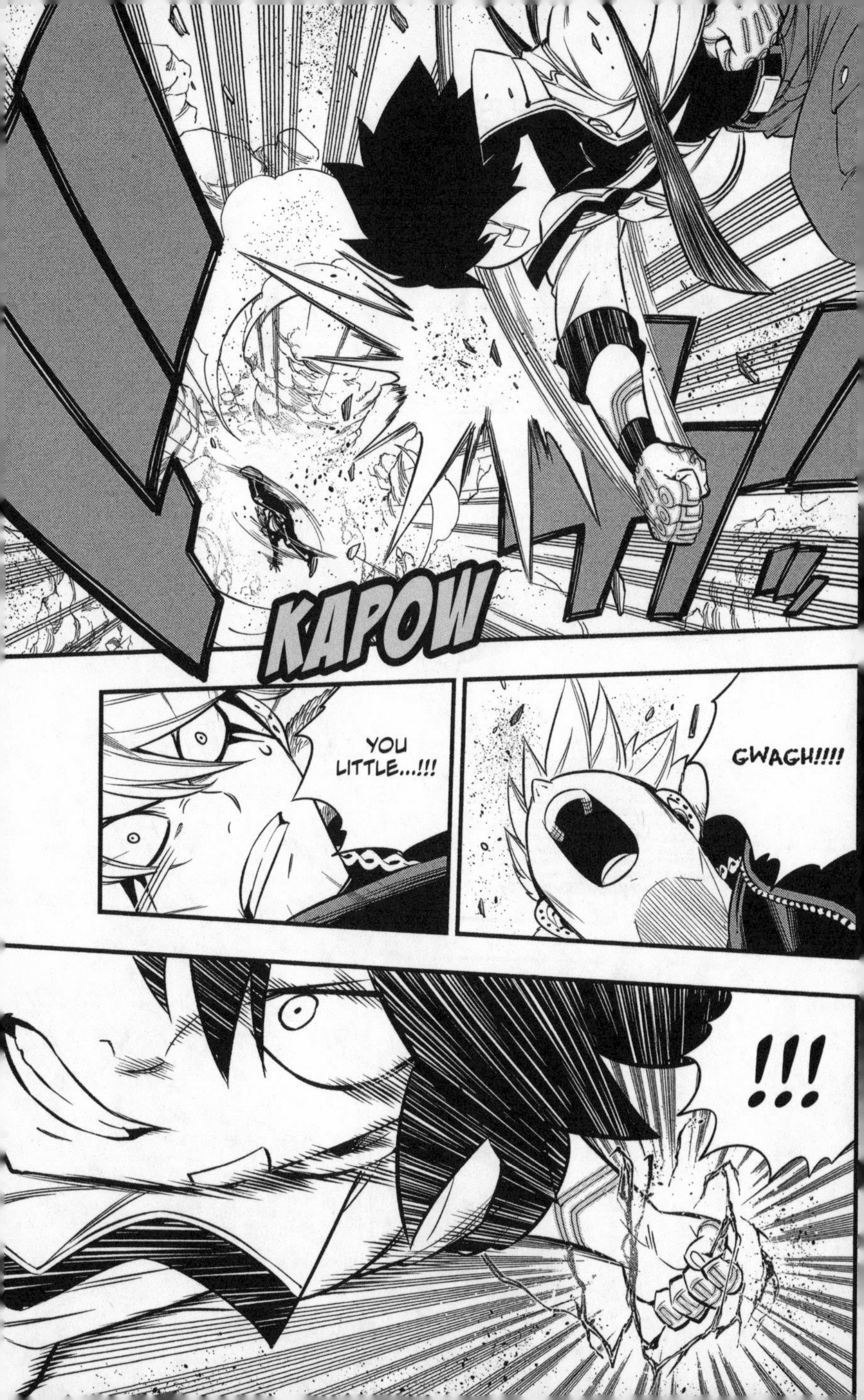
KAPOW
GWAGH!!!!
YOU LITTLE...!!!
!!!

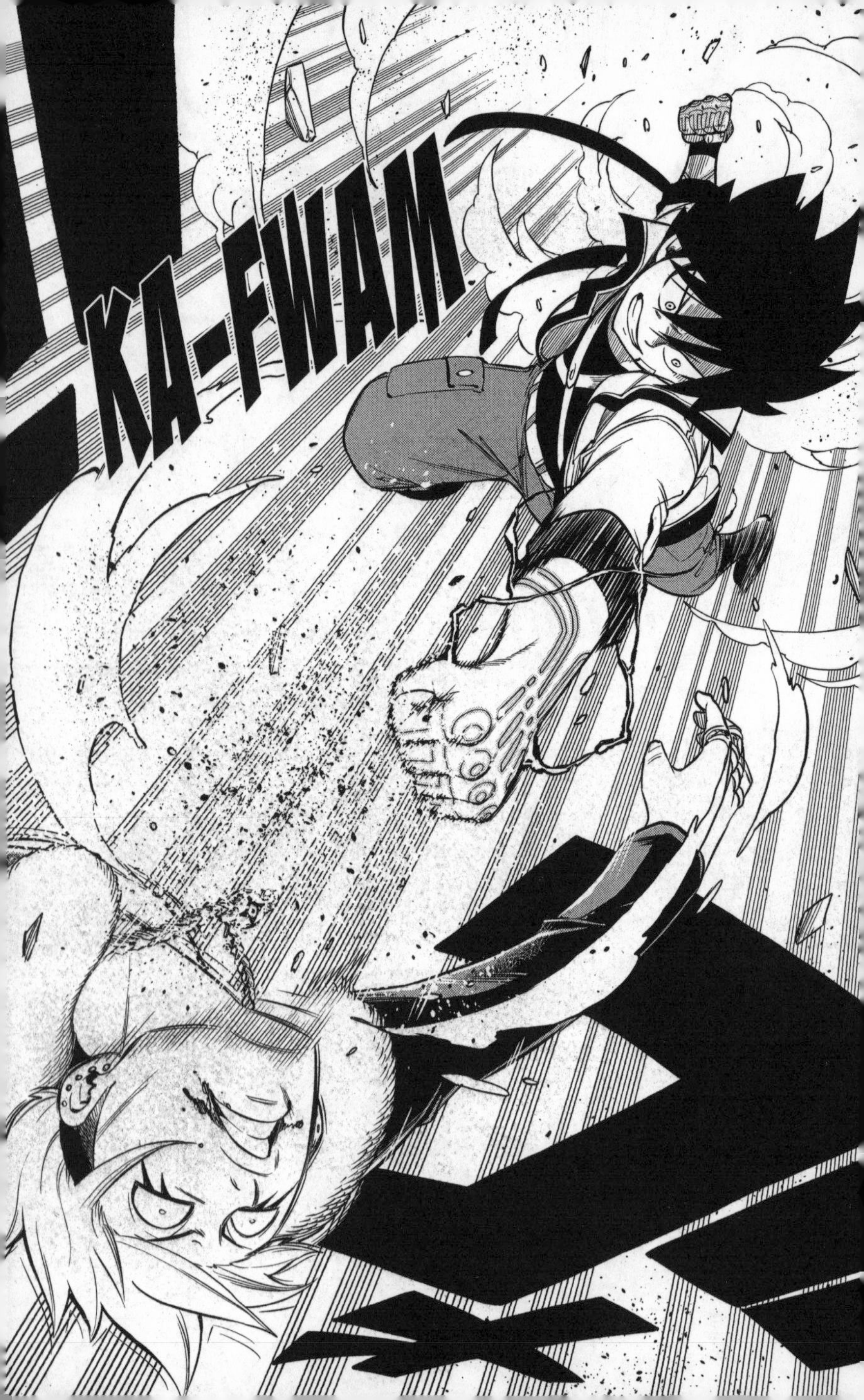
KA-FWAM

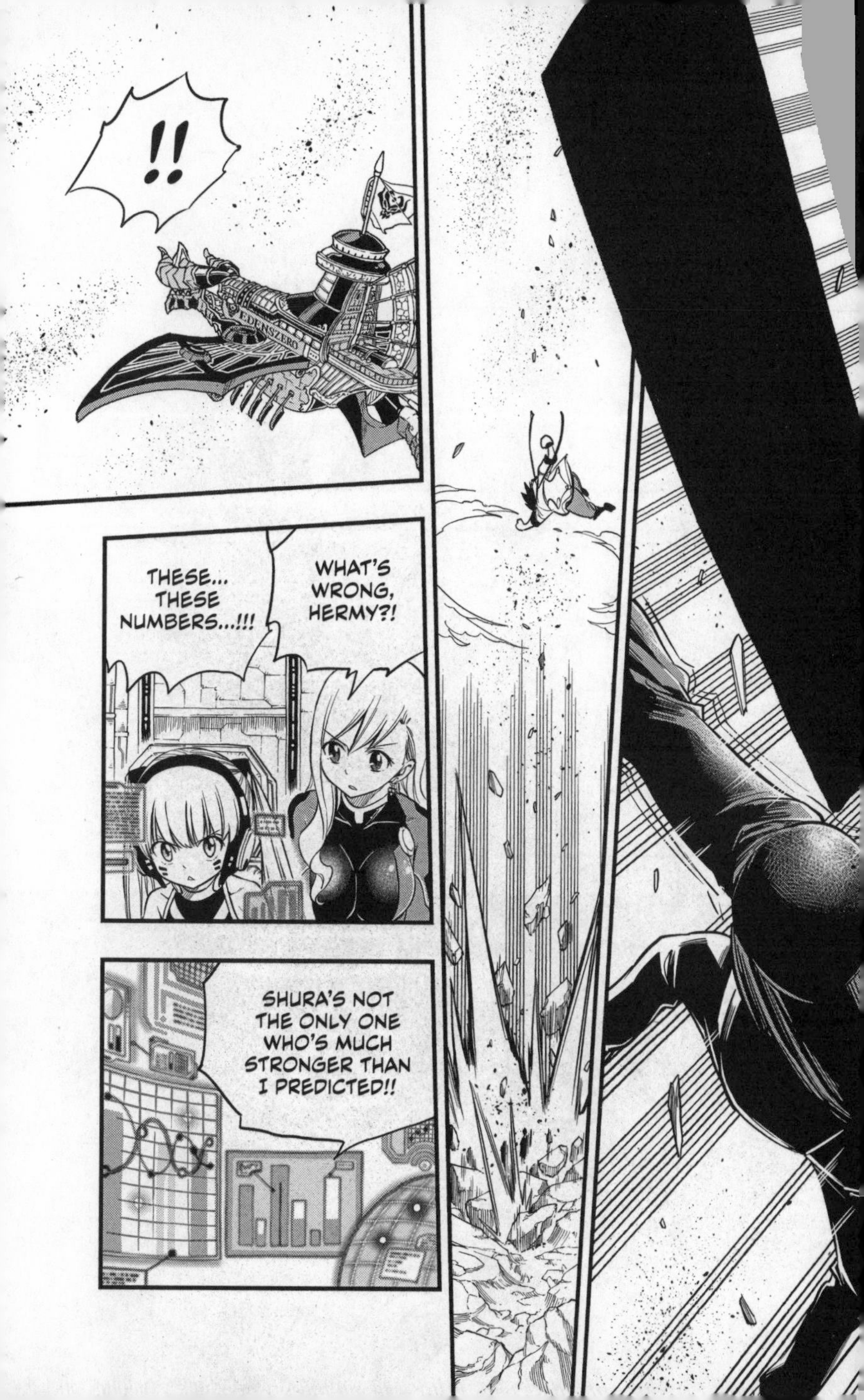
!!
EDENSZERO
WHAT'S WRONG, HERMY?!
THESE... THESE NUMBERS...!!!
SHURA'S NOT THE ONLY ONE WHO'S MUCH STRONGER THAN I PREDICTED!!

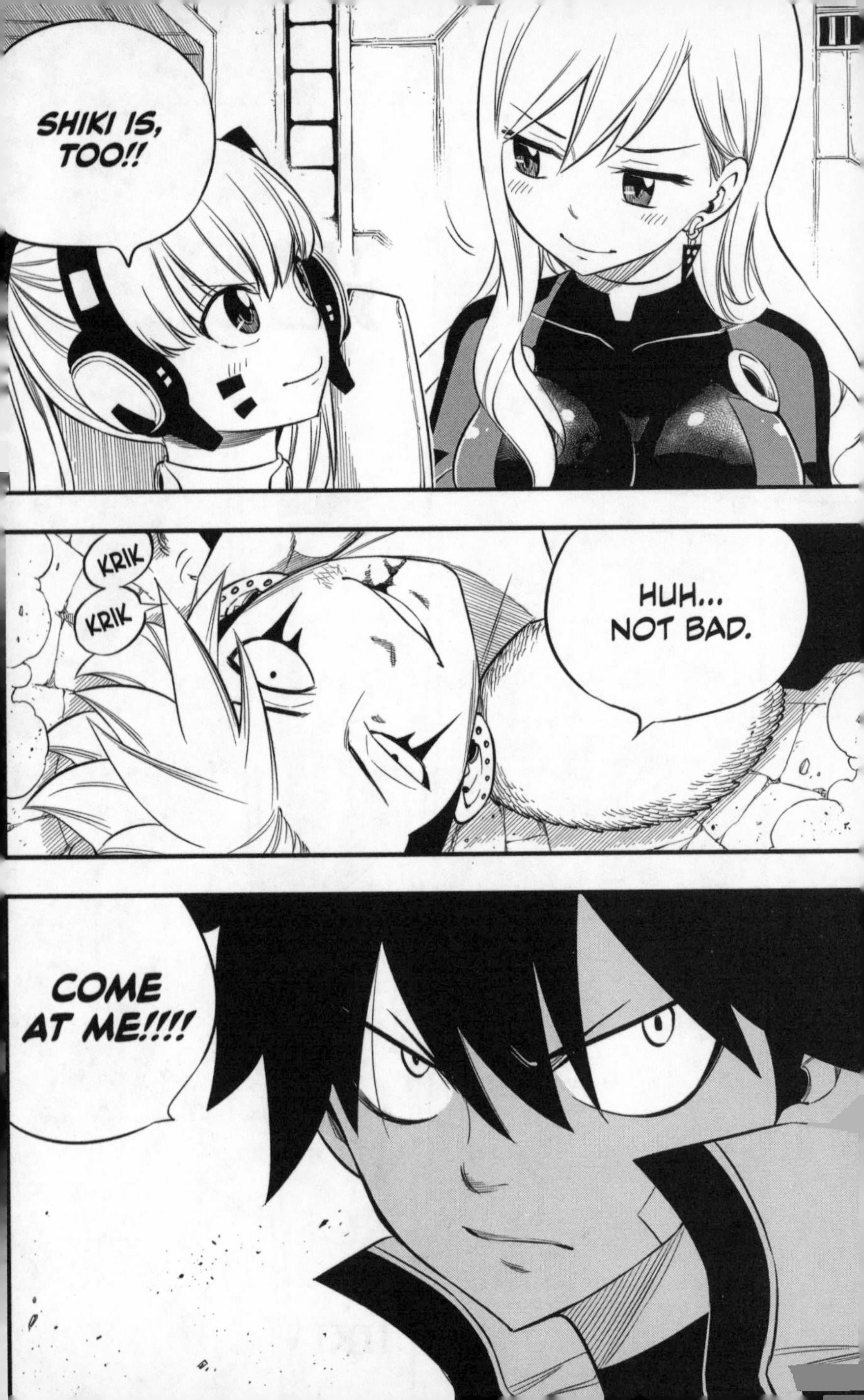
SHIKI IS, TOO!!
HUH... NOT BAD.
KRIK
KRIK
COME AT ME!!!!

EDENS ZERO

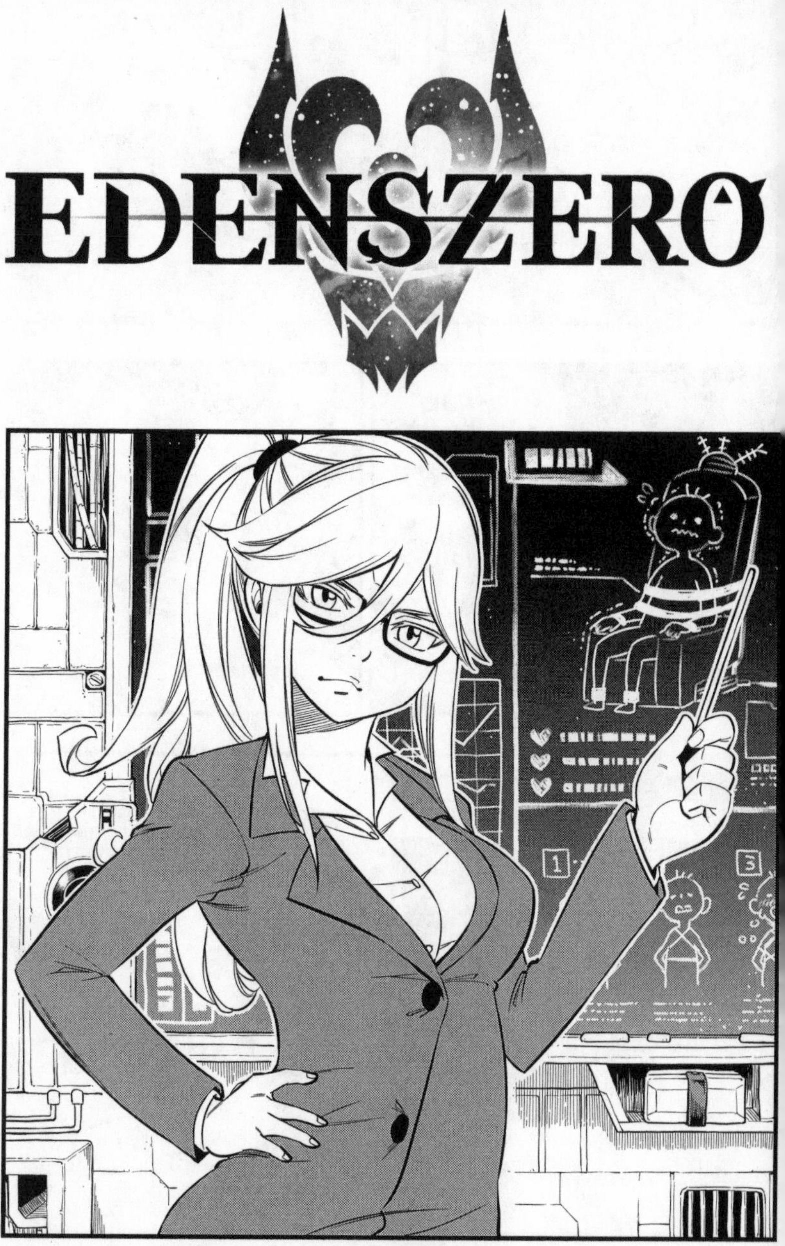

CHAPTER 142: SHIKI VS. SHURA

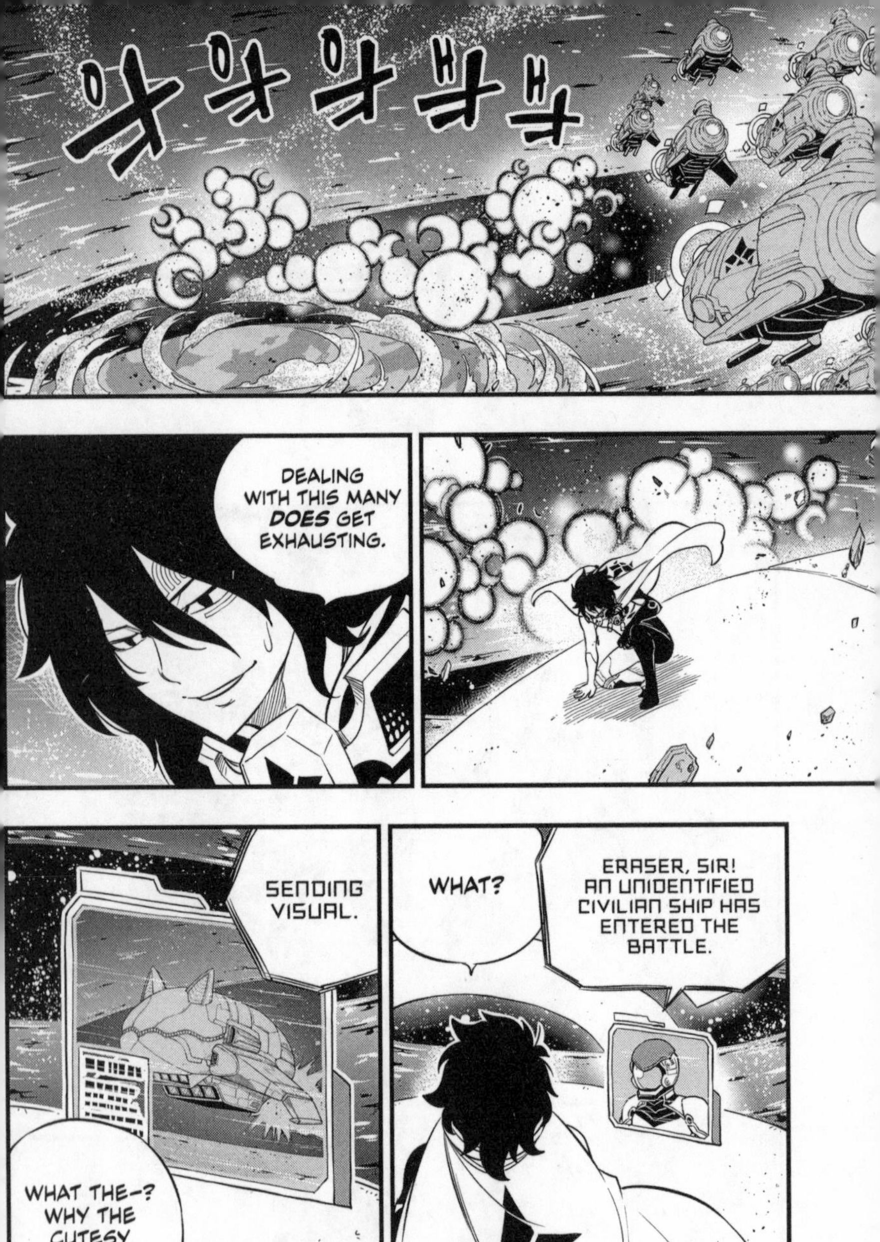
DEALING WITH THIS MANY *DOES* GET EXHAUSTING.
ERASER, SIR! AN UNIDENTIFIED CIVILIAN SHIP HAS ENTERED THE BATTLE.
WHAT?
SENDING VISUAL.
WHAT THE–? WHY THE CUTESY SHIP?

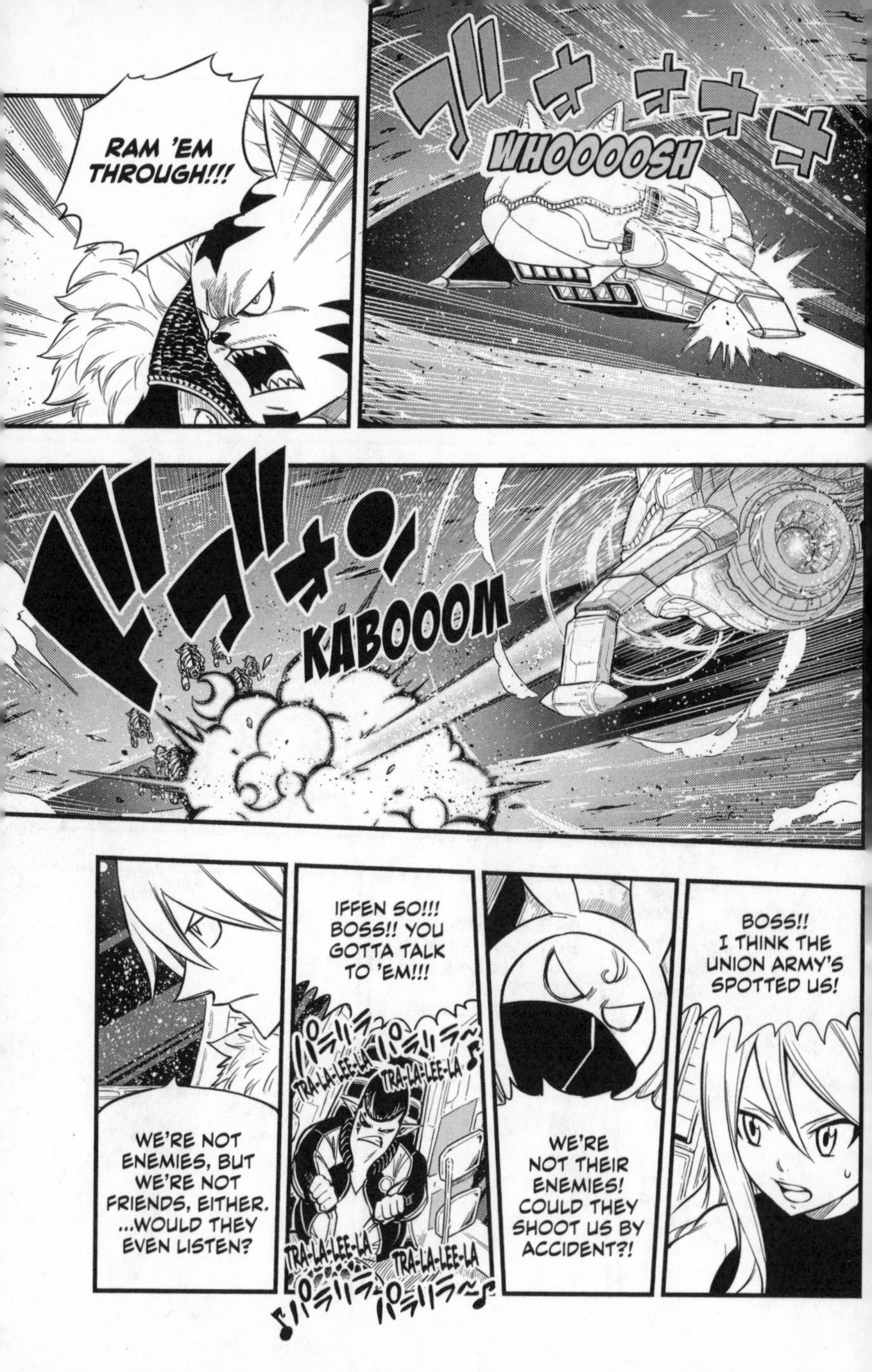
WHOOOOSH
RAM 'EM THROUGH!!!
KABOOOM
BOSS!! I THINK THE UNION ARMY'S SPOTTED US!
WE'RE NOT THEIR ENEMIES! COULD THEY SHOOT US BY ACCIDENT?!
IFFEN SO!!! BOSS!! YOU GOTTA TALK TO 'EM!!!
TRA-LA-LEE-LA
TRA-LA-LEE-LA
TRA-LA-LEE-LA
TRA-LA-LEE-LA
WE'RE NOT ENEMIES, BUT WE'RE NOT FRIENDS, EITHER. ...WOULD THEY EVEN LISTEN?

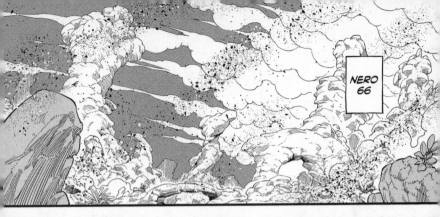

SKFF

THAT'S INTERESTING... WE BOTH USE GRAVITY, BUT IT LOOKS LIKE OUR POWERS ARE A LITTLE DIFFERENT.

YOUR POWERS FOCUS ON ALTERING YOUR OWN PERSONAL GRAVITY.

SWOOO

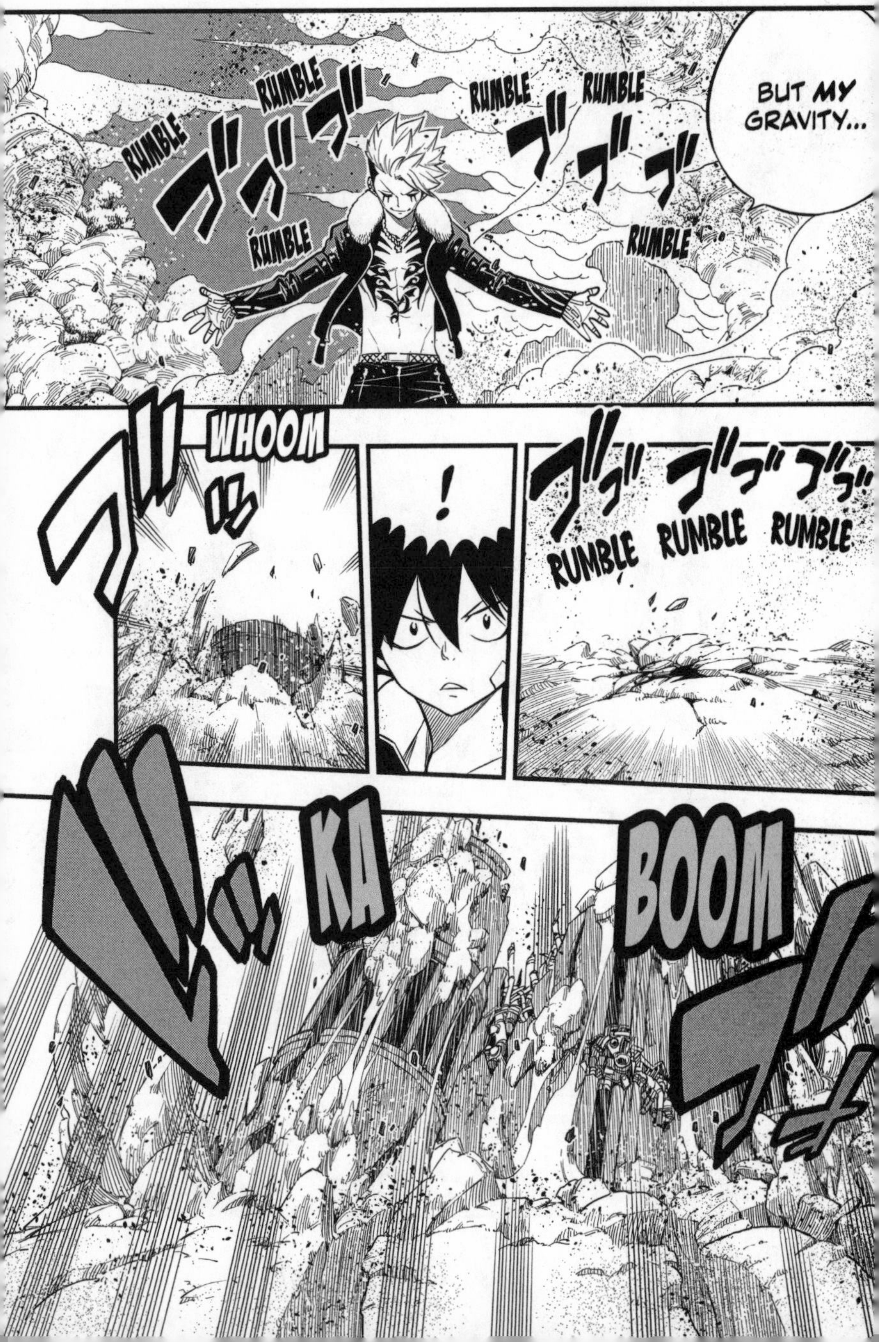
BUT MY GRAVITY...
RUMBLE
RUMBLE
RUMBLE
RUMBLE
RUMBLE
RUMBLE
RUMBLE RUMBLE RUMBLE
!
WHOOM
KA
BOOM

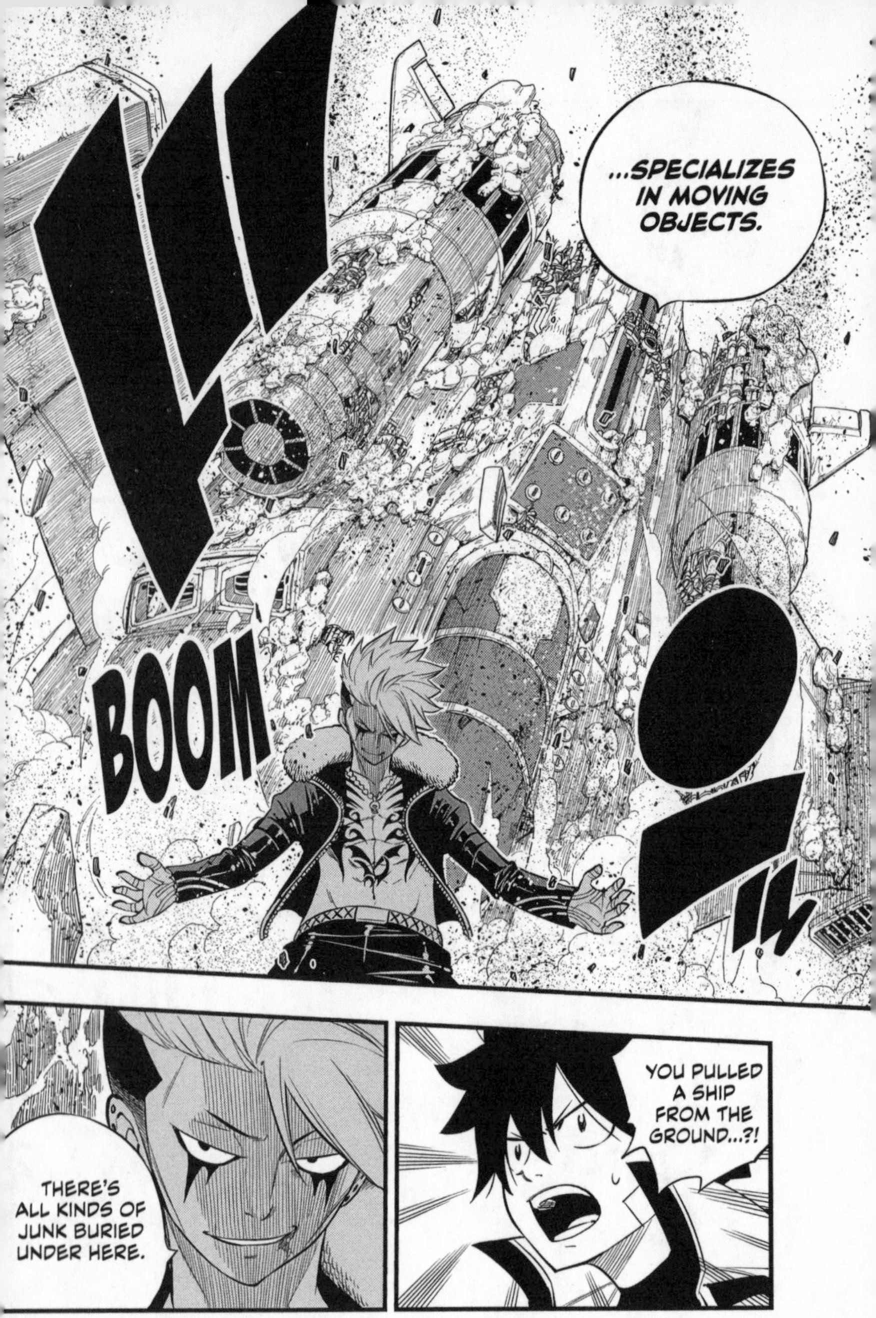
...SPECIALIZES IN MOVING OBJECTS.
BOOM
YOU PULLED A SHIP FROM THE GROUND...?!
THERE'S ALL KINDS OF JUNK BURIED UNDER HERE.

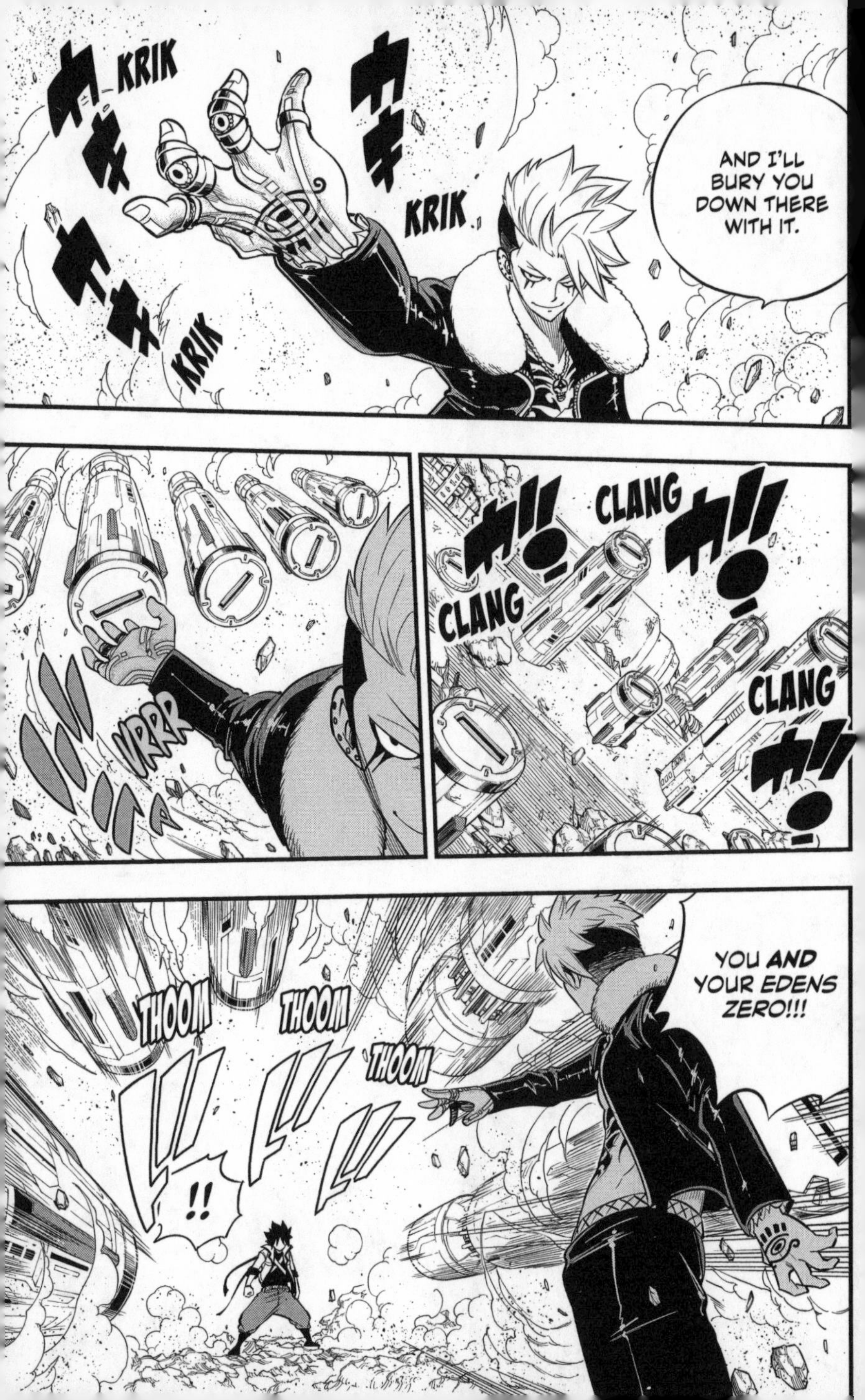
AND I'LL BURY YOU DOWN THERE WITH IT.
KRIK
KRIK
KRIK
CLANG
CLANG
CLANG
VRRR
YOU AND YOUR EDENS ZERO!!!
THOOM
THOOM
THOOM
!!

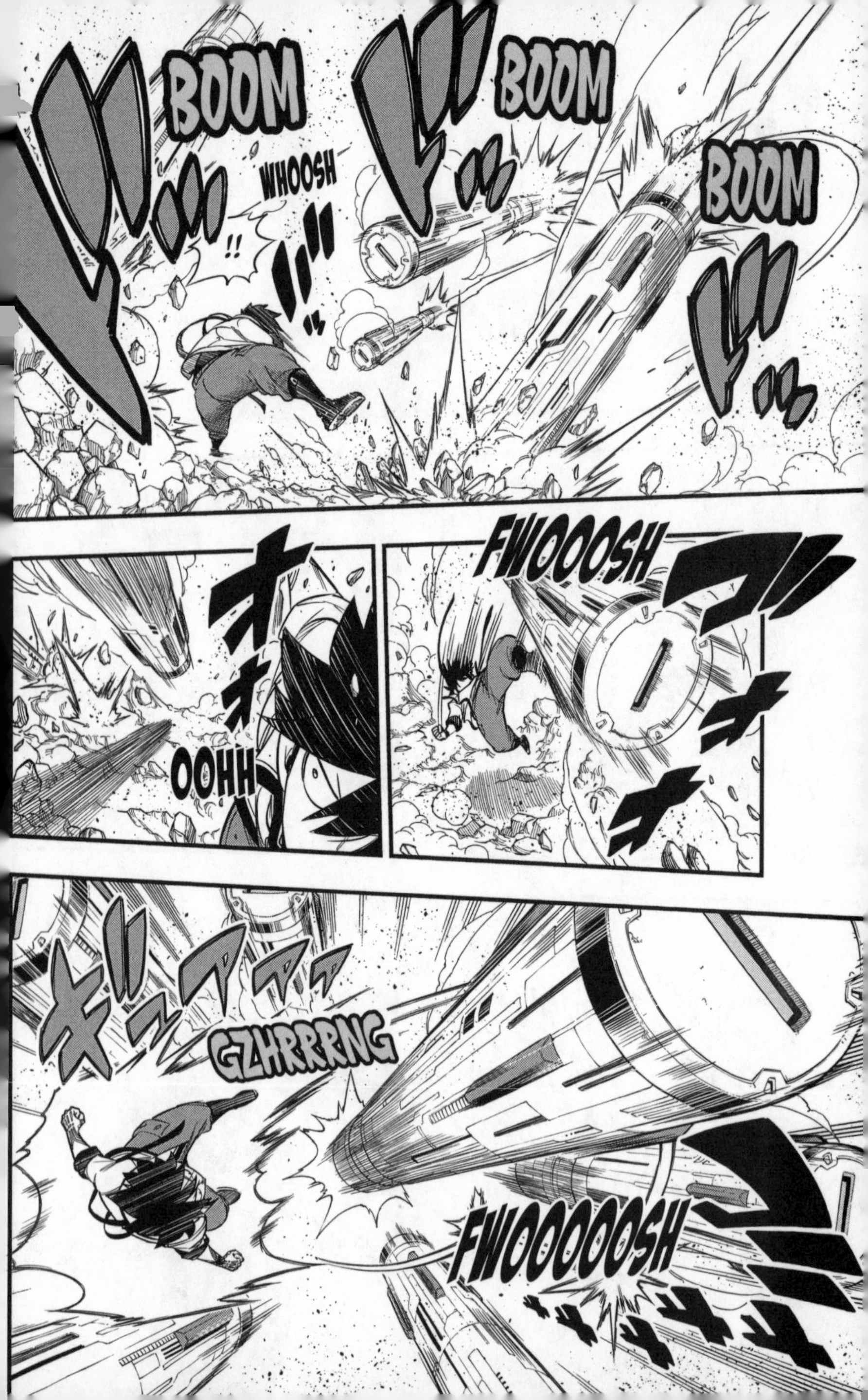
BOOM
BOOM
BOOM
WHOOSH
!!
FWOOOSH
OOHH
GZHRRRNG
FWOOOOOSH

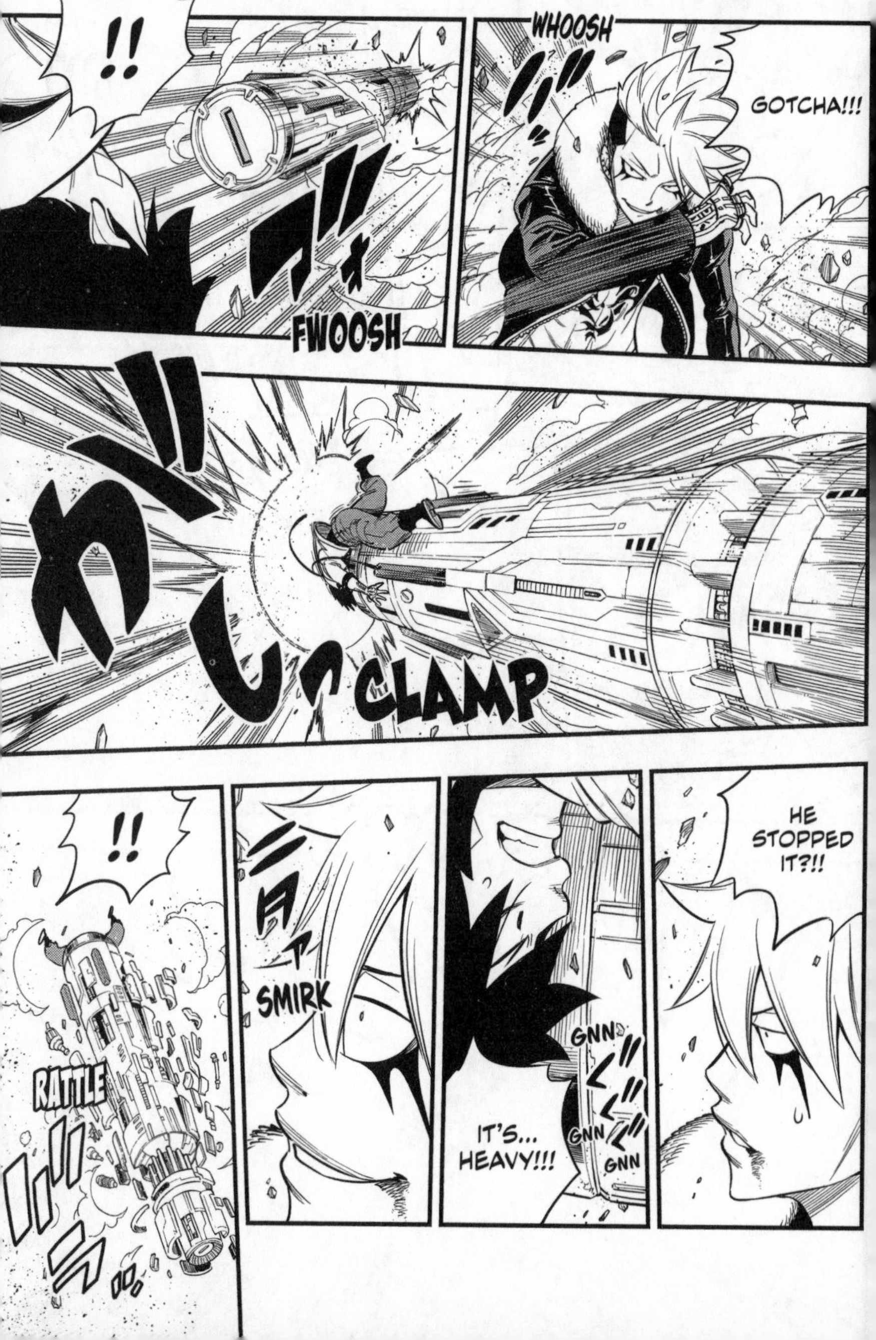
WHOOSH
GOTCHA!!!
!!
FWOOSH
CLAMP
HE STOPPED IT?!!
GNN
GNN
GNN
IT'S... HEAVY!!!
SMIRK
!!
RATTLE

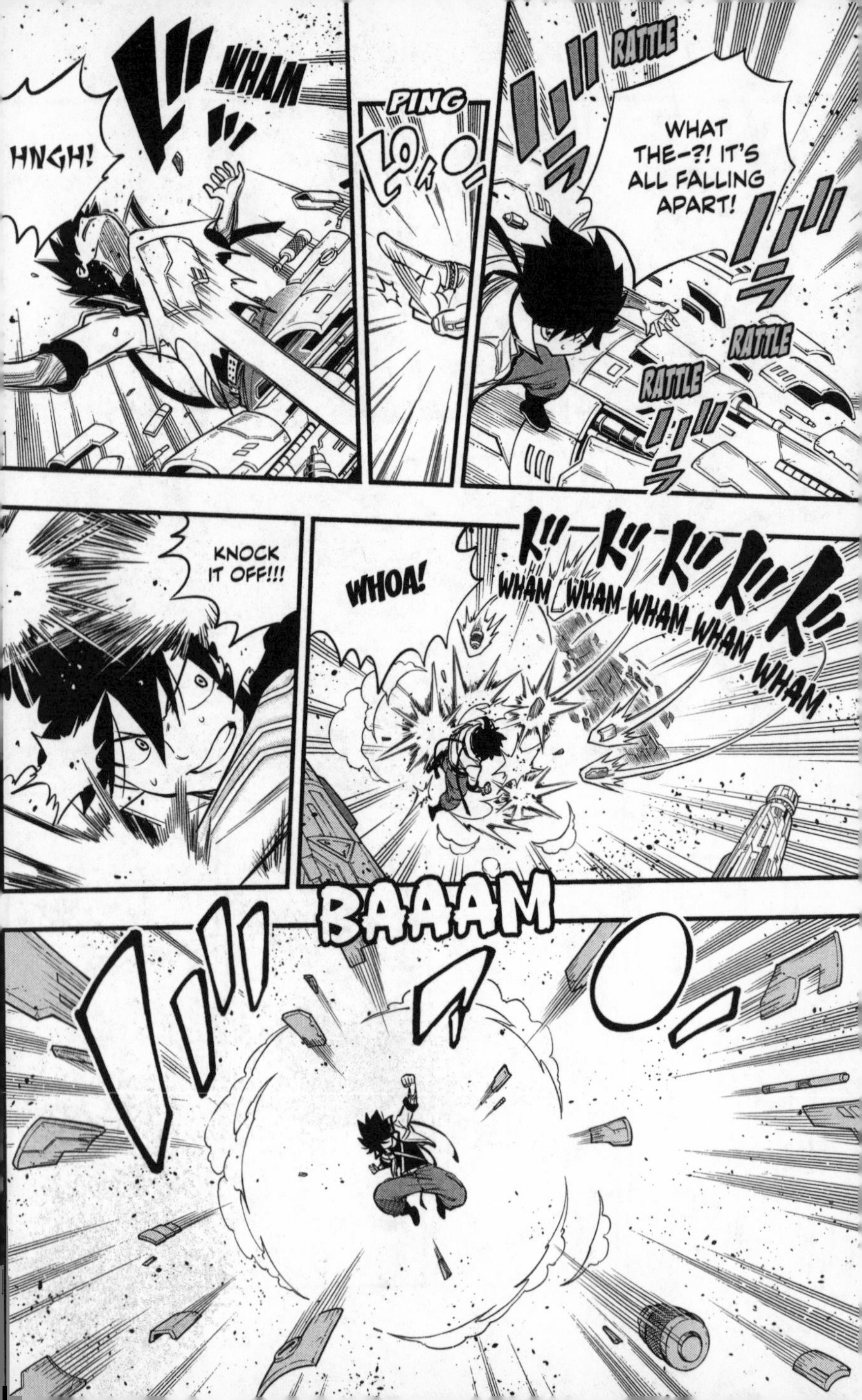
RATTLE
WHAT THE-?! IT'S ALL FALLING APART!
RATTLE
RATTLE
PING
WHAM
HNGH!
WHOA!
WHAM WHAM WHAM WHAM WHAM
KNOCK IT OFF!!!
BAAAM

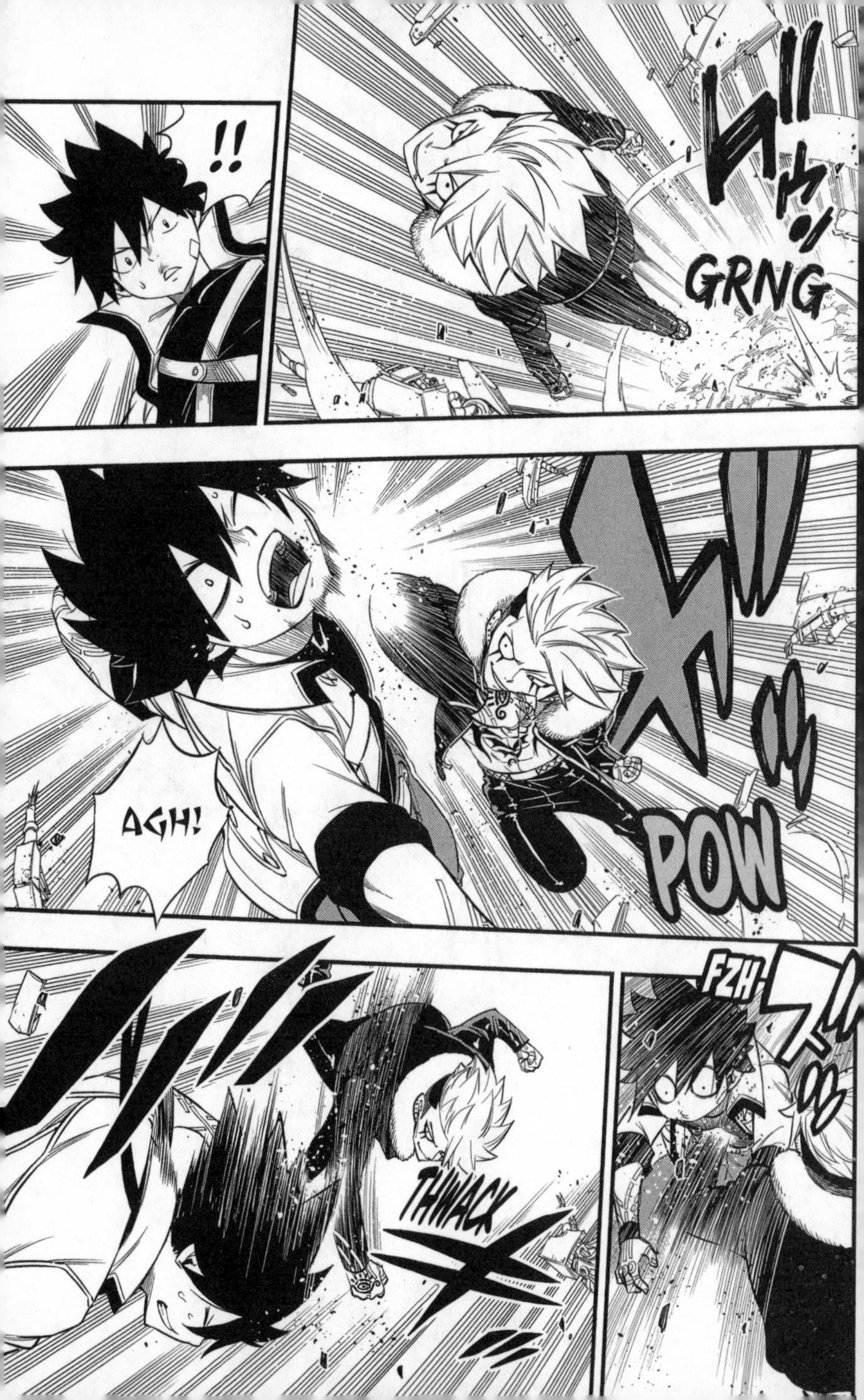
GRNG
!!
POW
AGH!
FZH
THWACK

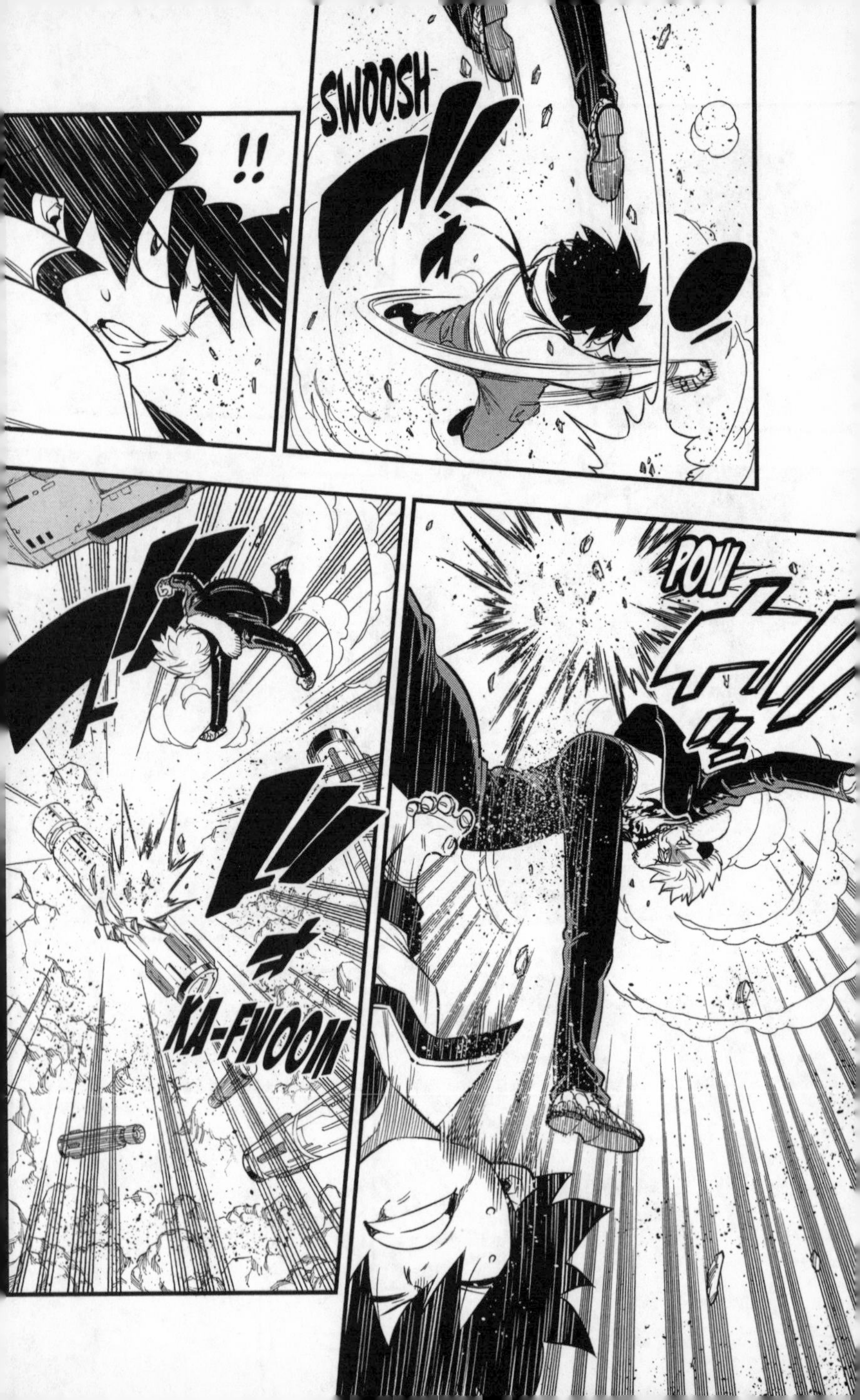
SWOOSH
!!
POW
KA-FWOOM

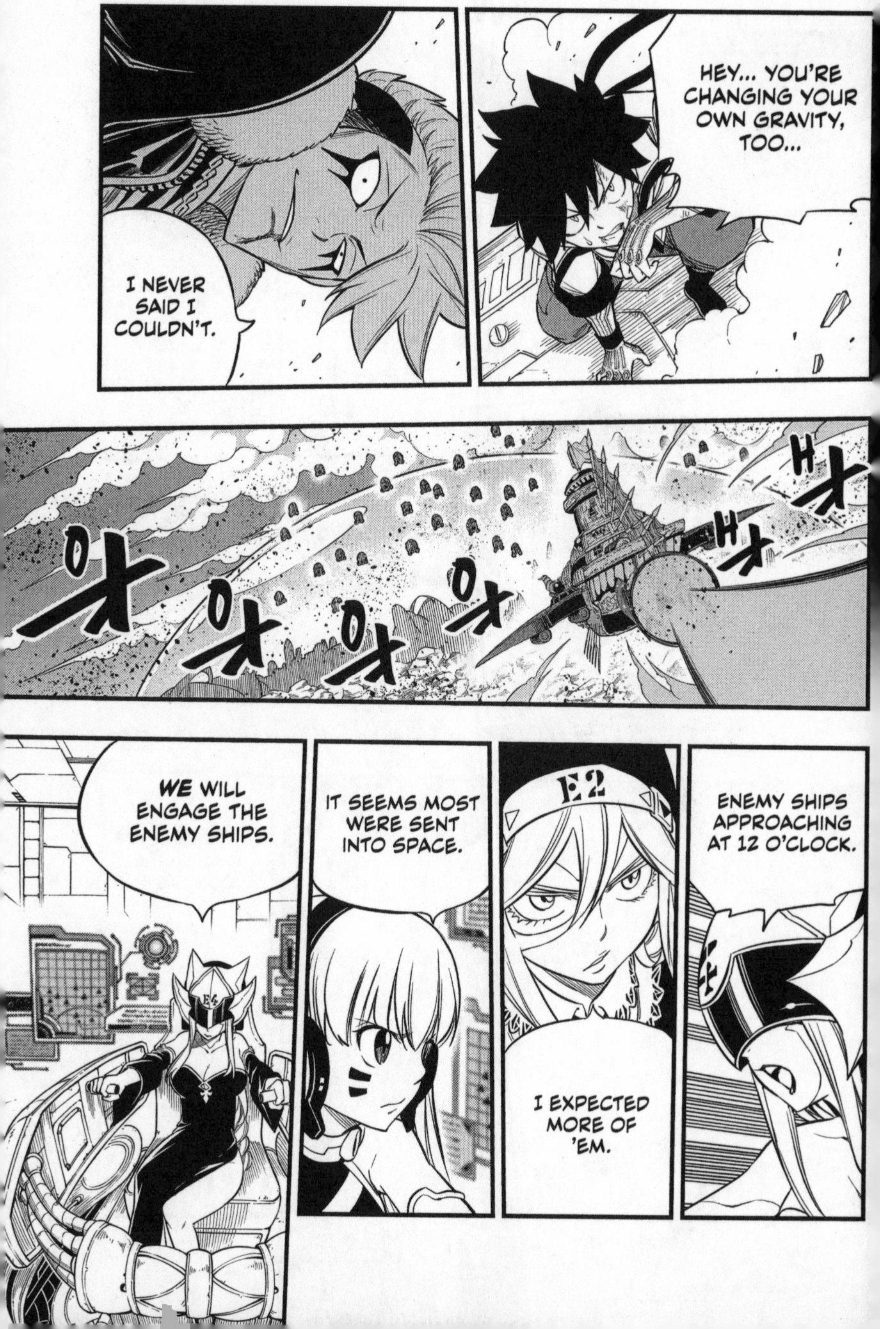
HEY... YOU'RE CHANGING YOUR OWN GRAVITY, TOO...
I NEVER SAID I COULDN'T.
ENEMY SHIPS APPROACHING AT 12 O'CLOCK.
E2
I EXPECTED MORE OF 'EM.
IT SEEMS MOST WERE SENT INTO SPACE.
WE WILL ENGAGE THE ENEMY SHIPS.

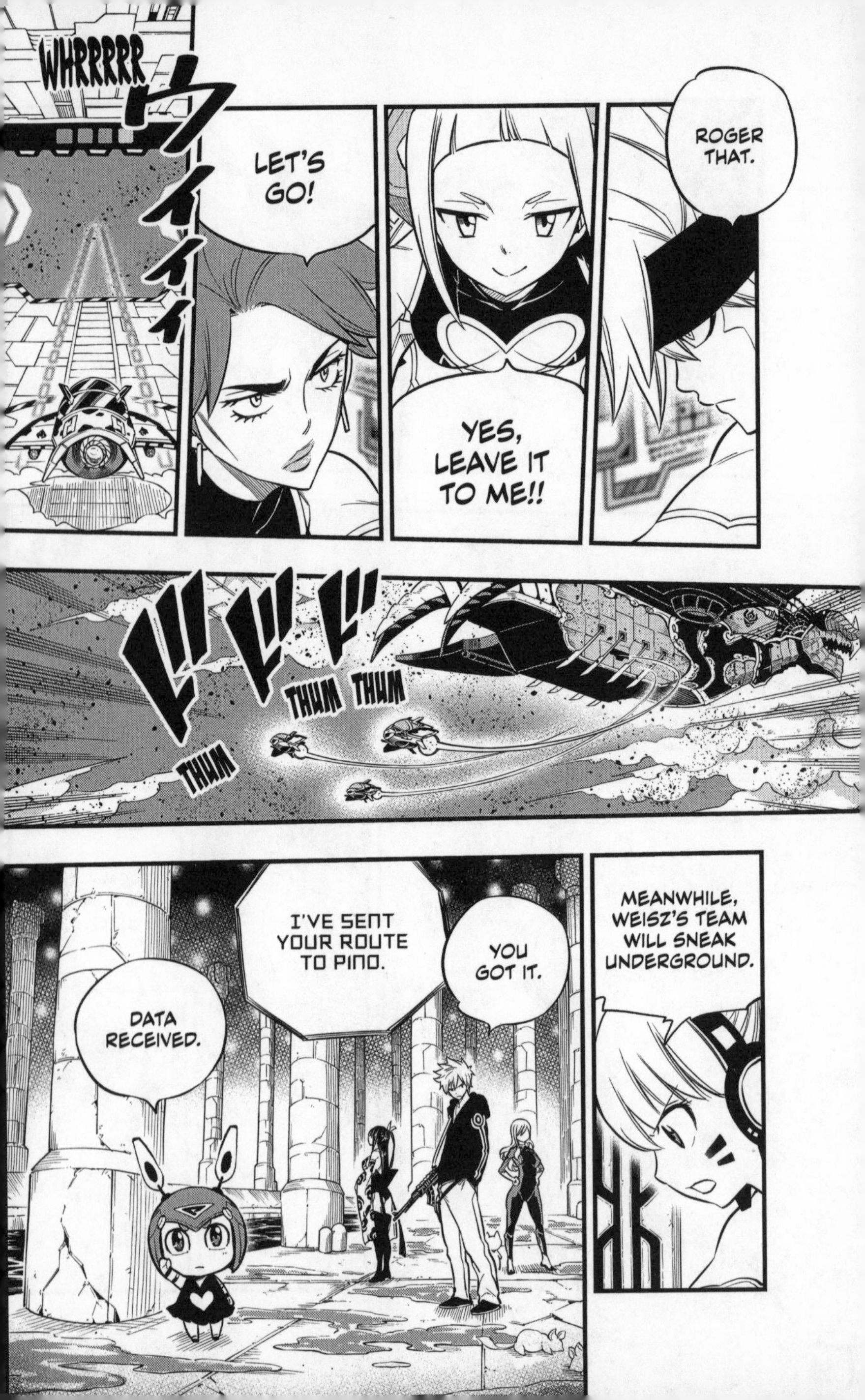
ROGER THAT.
YES, LEAVE IT TO ME!!
LET'S GO!
WHRRRRR
THUM THUM
THUM
MEANWHILE, WEISZ'S TEAM WILL SNEAK UNDERGROUND.
I'VE SENT YOUR ROUTE TO PINO.
YOU GOT IT.
DATA RECEIVED.

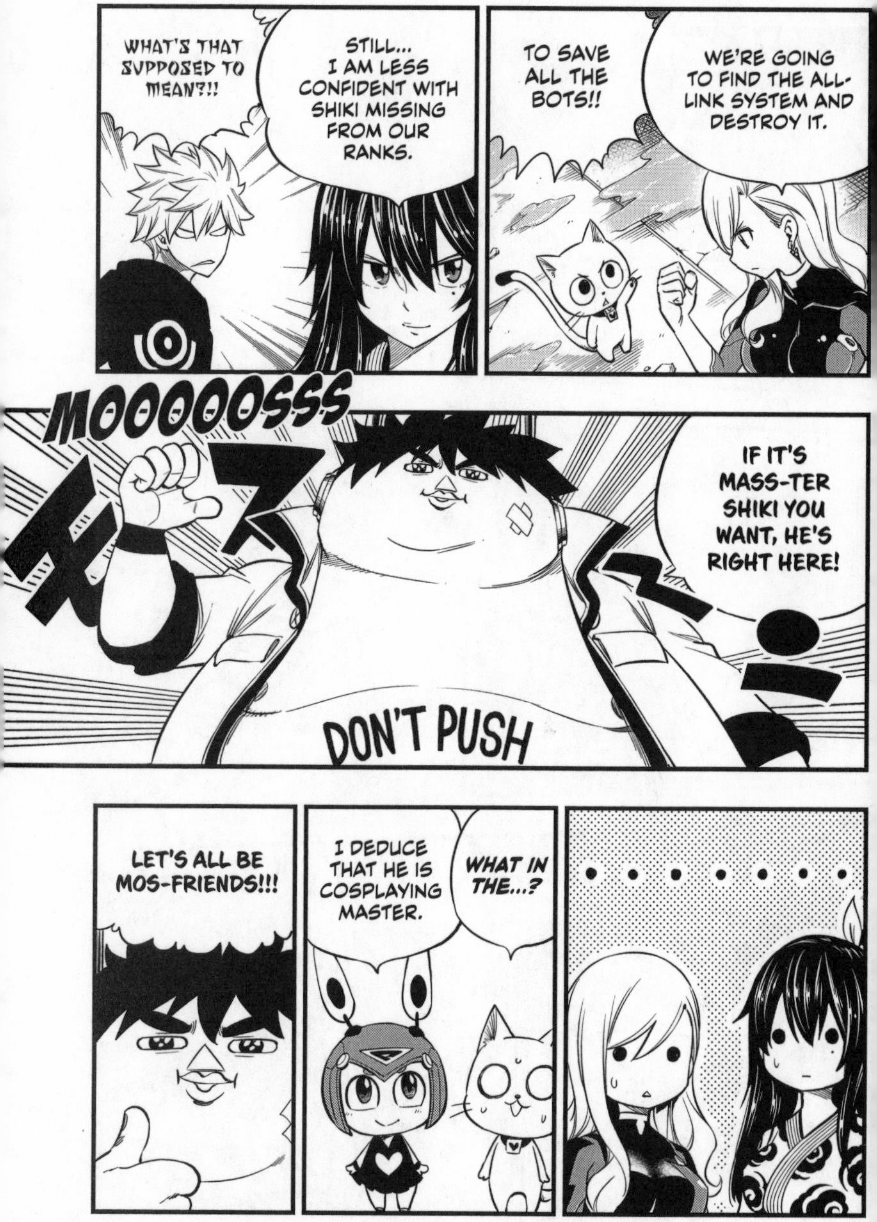
WE'RE GOING TO FIND THE ALL-LINK SYSTEM AND DESTROY IT.
TO SAVE ALL THE BOTS!!
STILL... I AM LESS CONFIDENT WITH SHIKI MISSING FROM OUR RANKS.
WHAT'S THAT SUPPOSED TO MEAN?!!
IF IT'S MASS-TER SHIKI YOU WANT, HE'S RIGHT HERE!
MOOOOOSSS
DON'T PUSH
....
WHAT IN THE...?
I DEDUCE THAT HE IS COSPLAYING MASTER.
LET'S ALL BE MOS-FRIENDS!!!

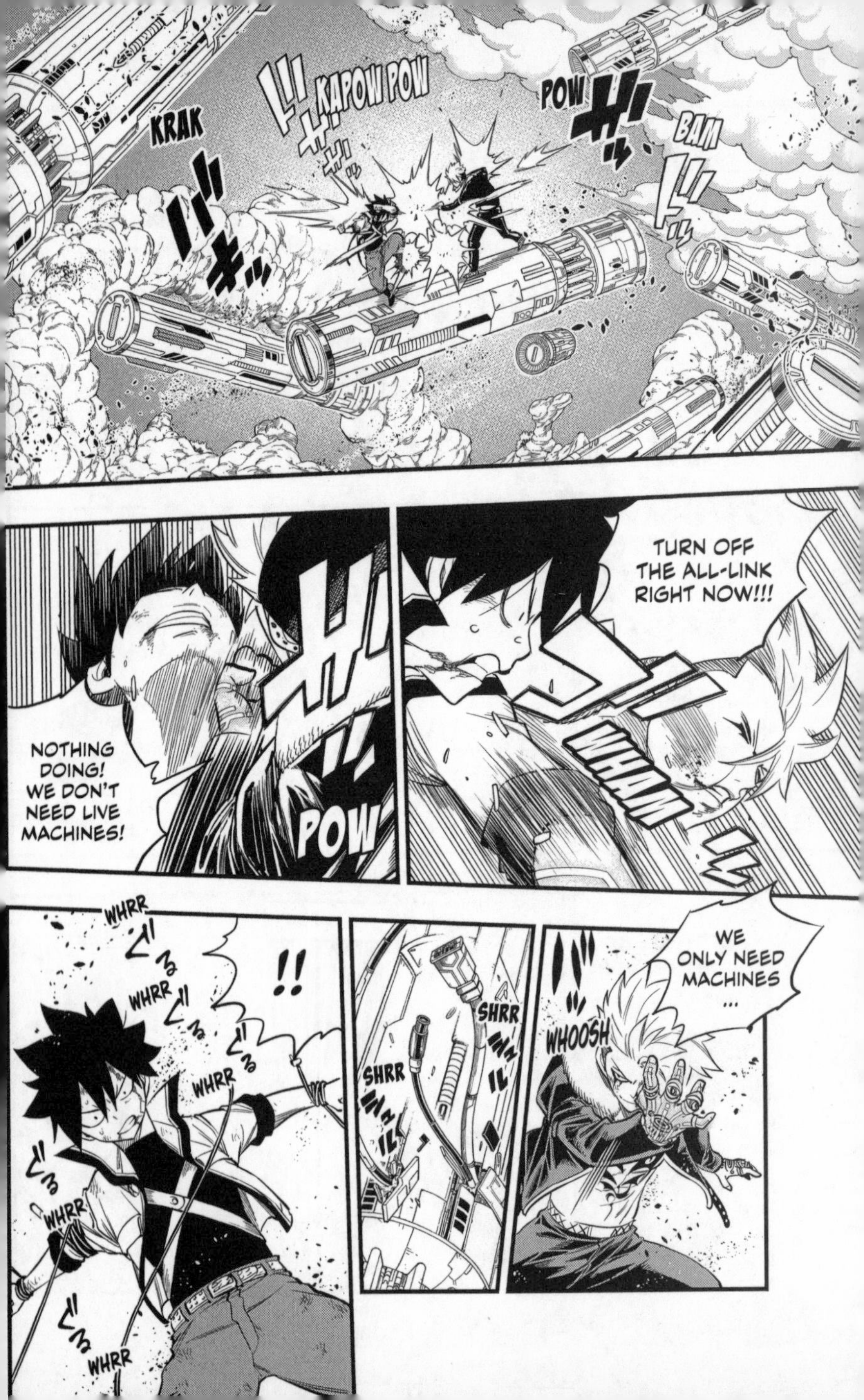

POW
BAM
KAPOW POW
KRAK
TURN OFF THE ALL-LINK RIGHT NOW!!!
WHAM
POW
NOTHING DOING! WE DON'T NEED LIVE MACHINES!
WE ONLY NEED MACHINES ...
WHOOSH
SHRR
SHRR
!!
WHRR
WHRR
WHRR
WHRR
WHRR

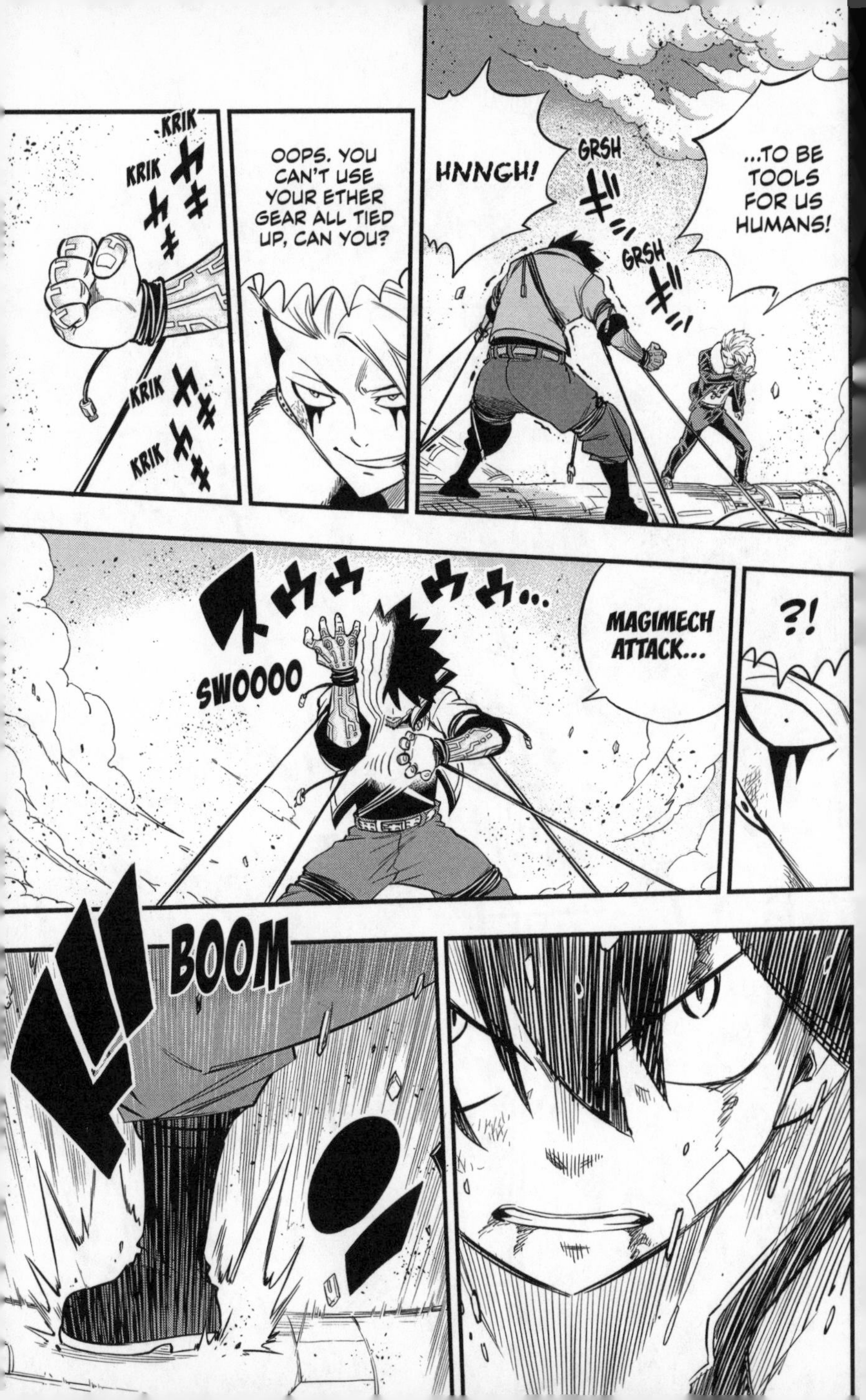
...TO BE TOOLS FOR US HUMANS!
GRSH
HNNGH!
GRSH
OOPS. YOU CAN'T USE YOUR ETHER GEAR ALL TIED UP, CAN YOU?
KRIK
KRIK
KRIK
KRIK
?!
MAGIMECH ATTACK...
SWOOOO
BOOM

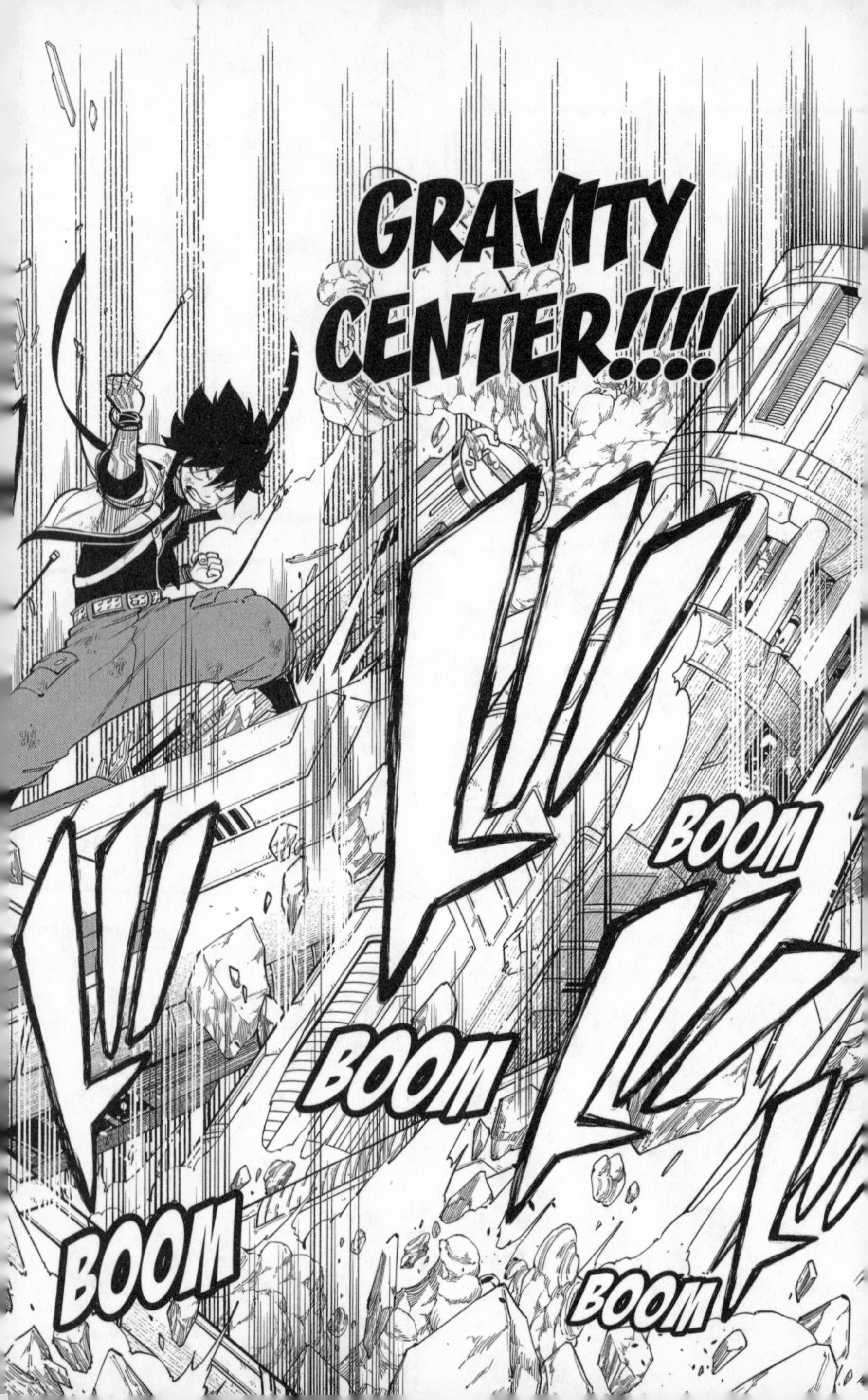
GRAVITY CENTER!!!!
BOOM
BOOM
BOOM
BOOM

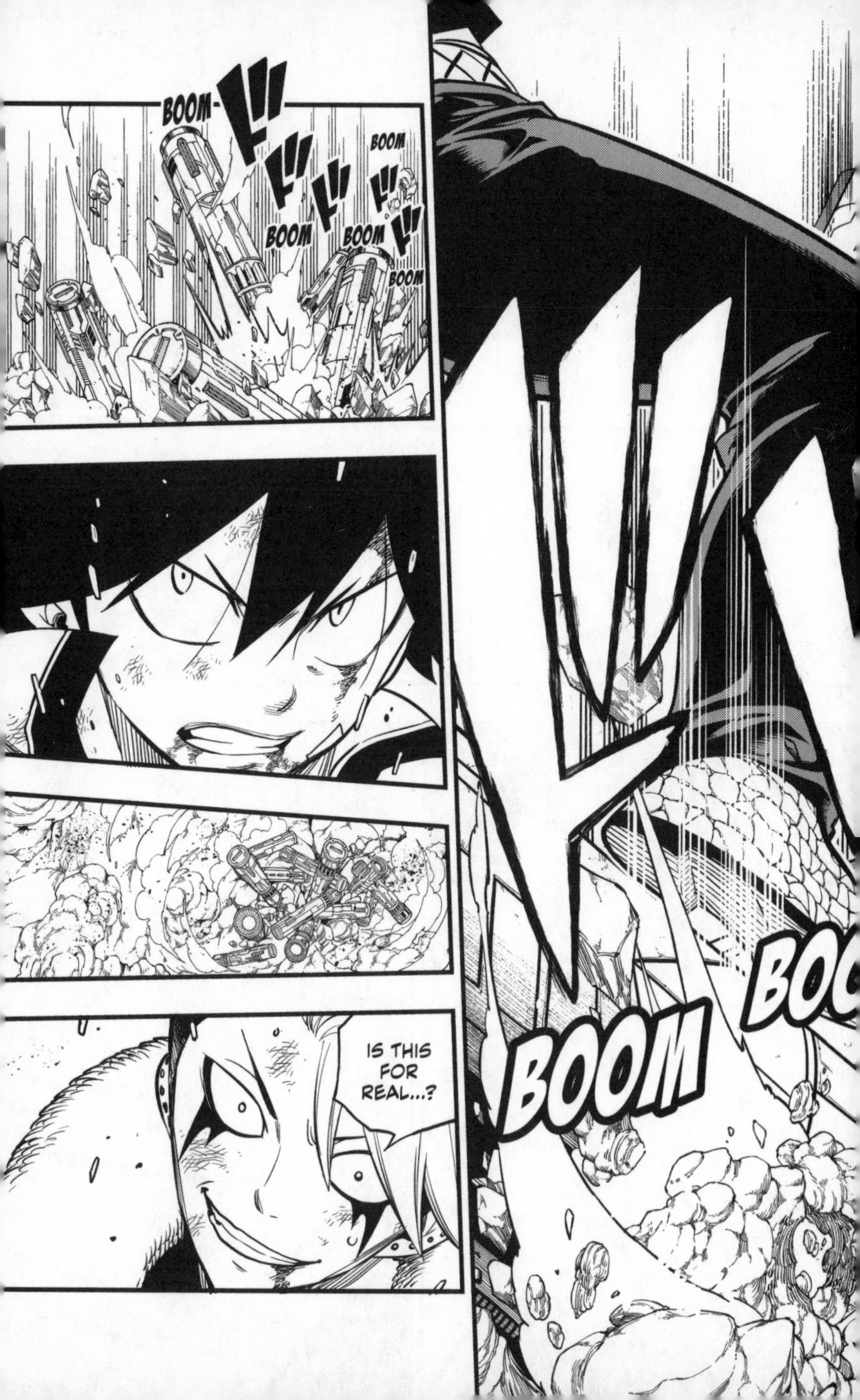
BO
BOOM
BOOM-
ドドド
BOOM
ドド
BOOM
BOOM
BOOM
IS THIS FOR REAL...?

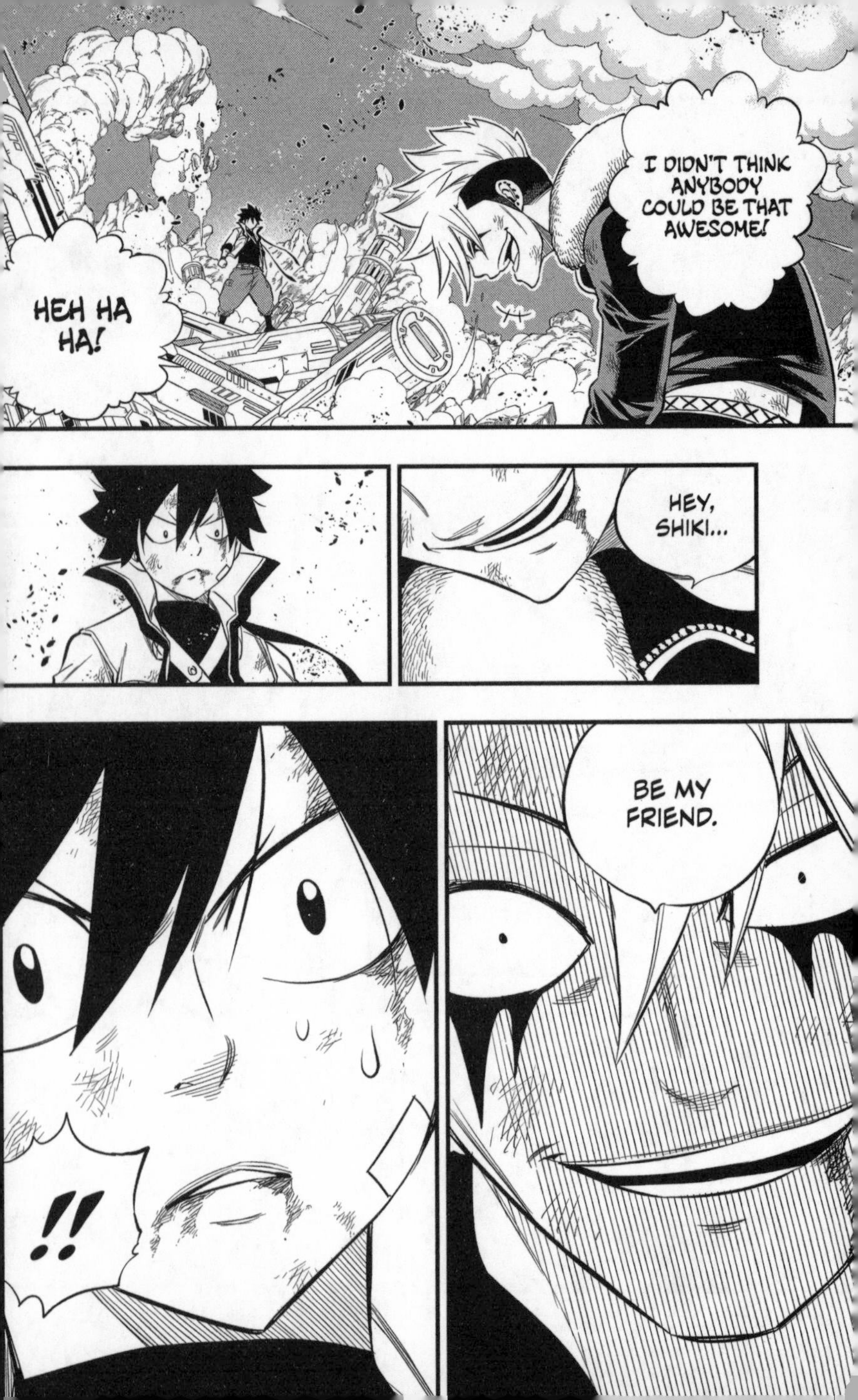
I DIDN'T THINK ANYBODY COULD BE THAT AWESOME!
HEH HA HA!
HEY, SHIKI...
BE MY FRIEND.
!!

EDENS ZERO

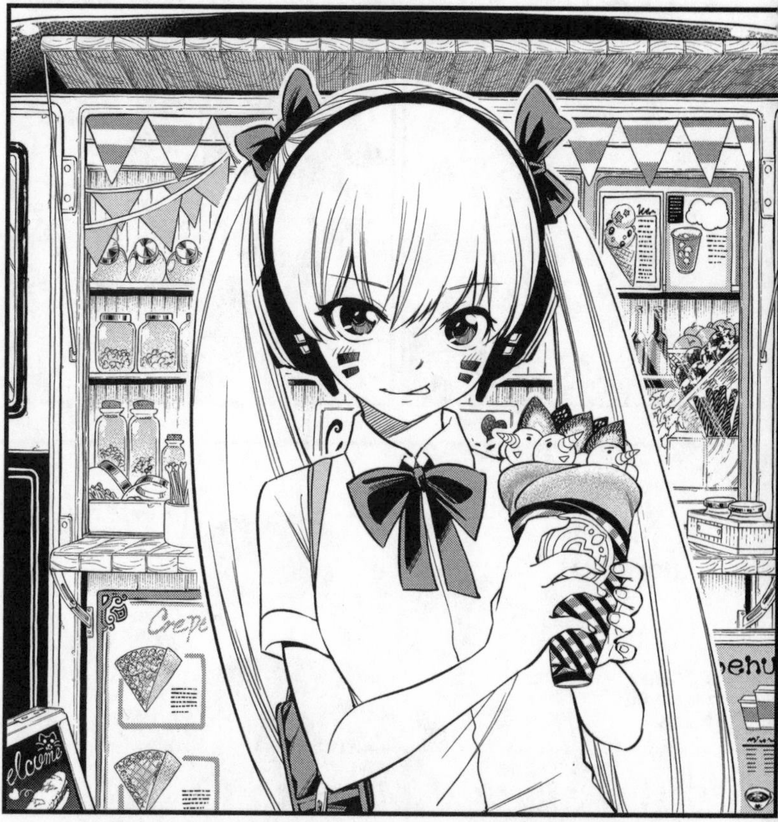
Crepe

CHAPTER 143: YOU DIDN'T DO ANYTHING TO DESERVE THIS

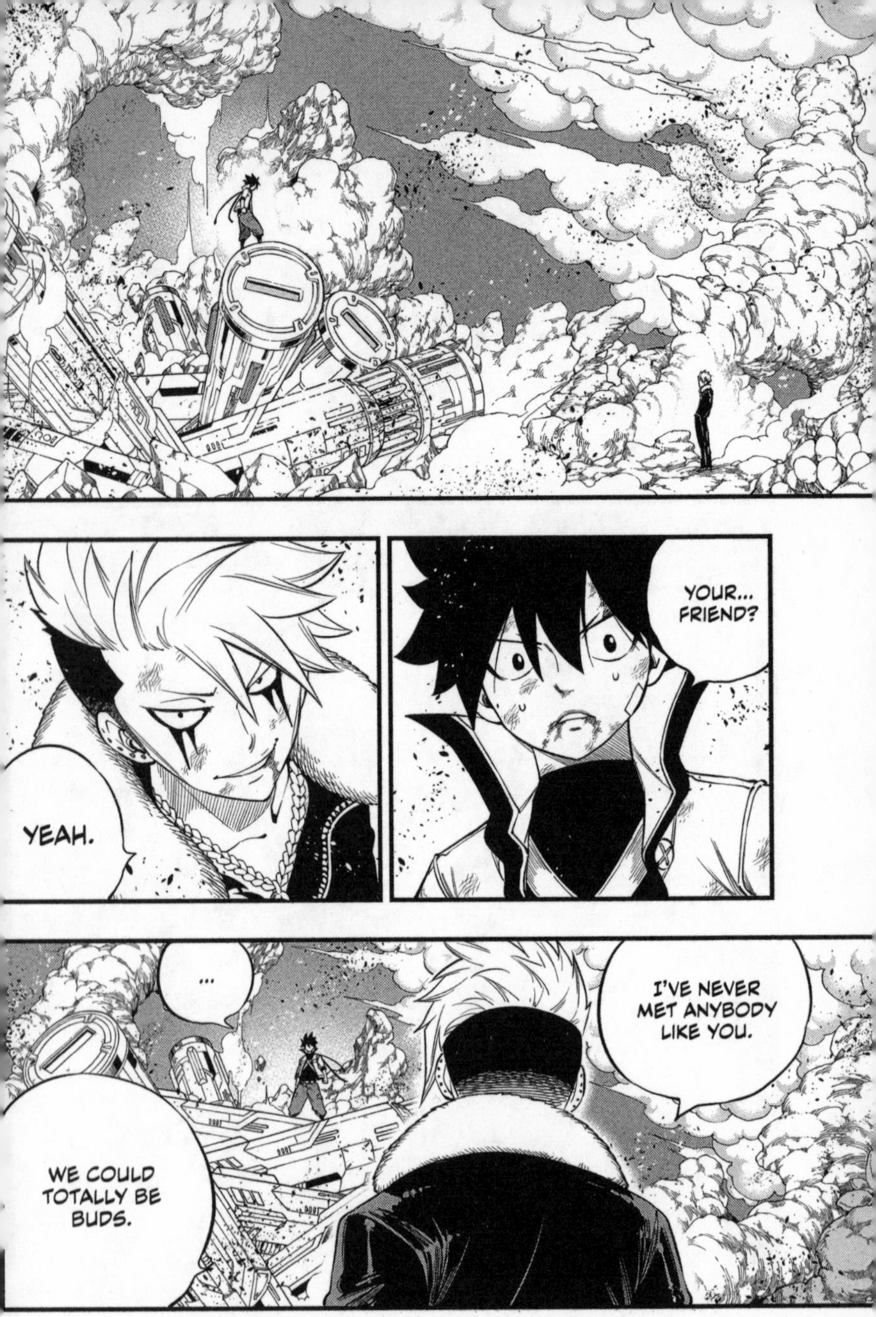
YOUR... FRIEND?
YEAH.
I'VE NEVER MET ANYBODY LIKE YOU.
...
WE COULD TOTALLY BE BUDS.

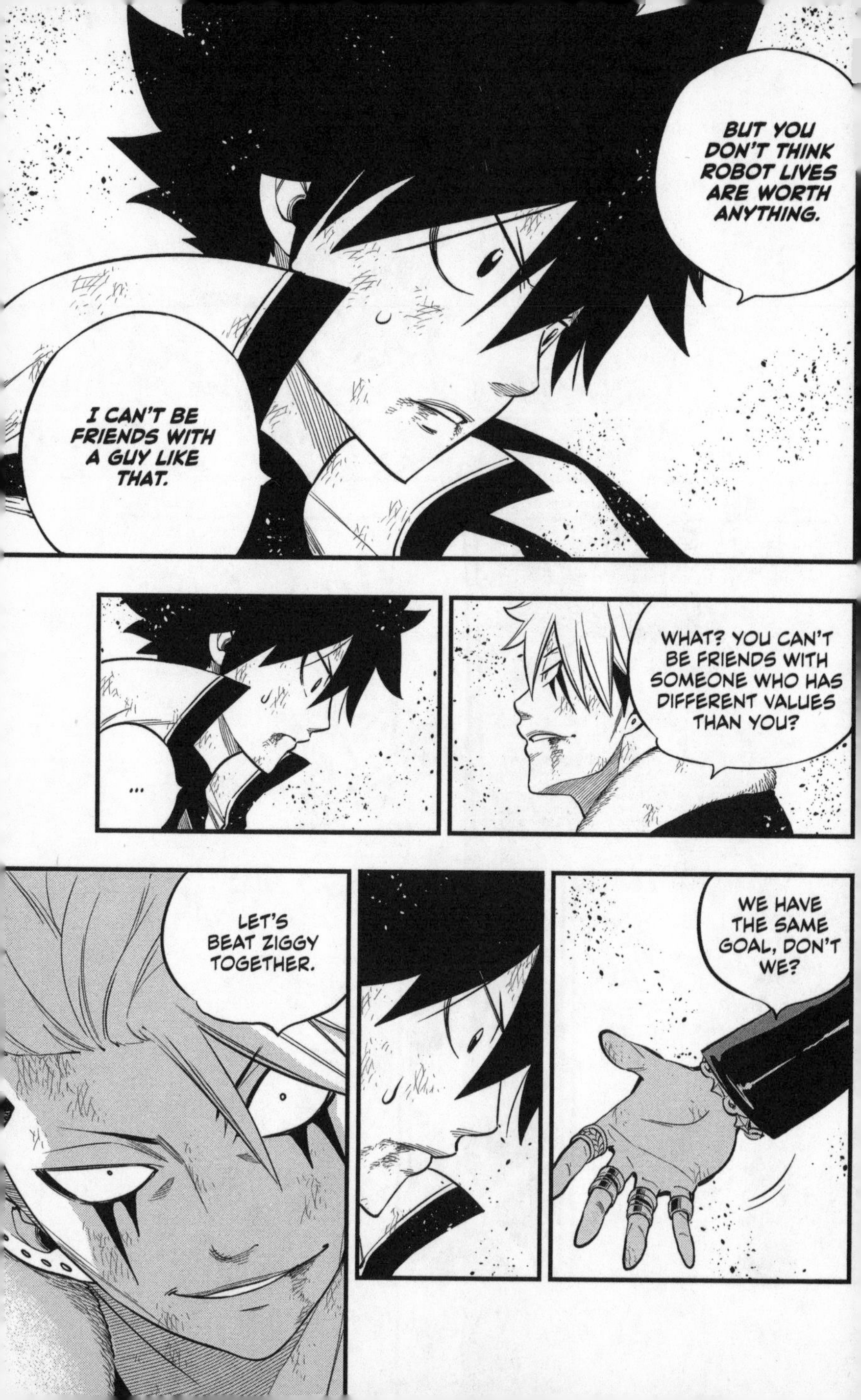
BUT YOU DON'T THINK ROBOT LIVES ARE WORTH ANYTHING.
I CAN'T BE FRIENDS WITH A GUY LIKE THAT.
WHAT? YOU CAN'T BE FRIENDS WITH SOMEONE WHO HAS DIFFERENT VALUES THAN YOU?
...
WE HAVE THE SAME GOAL, DON'T WE?
LET'S BEAT ZIGGY TOGETHER.

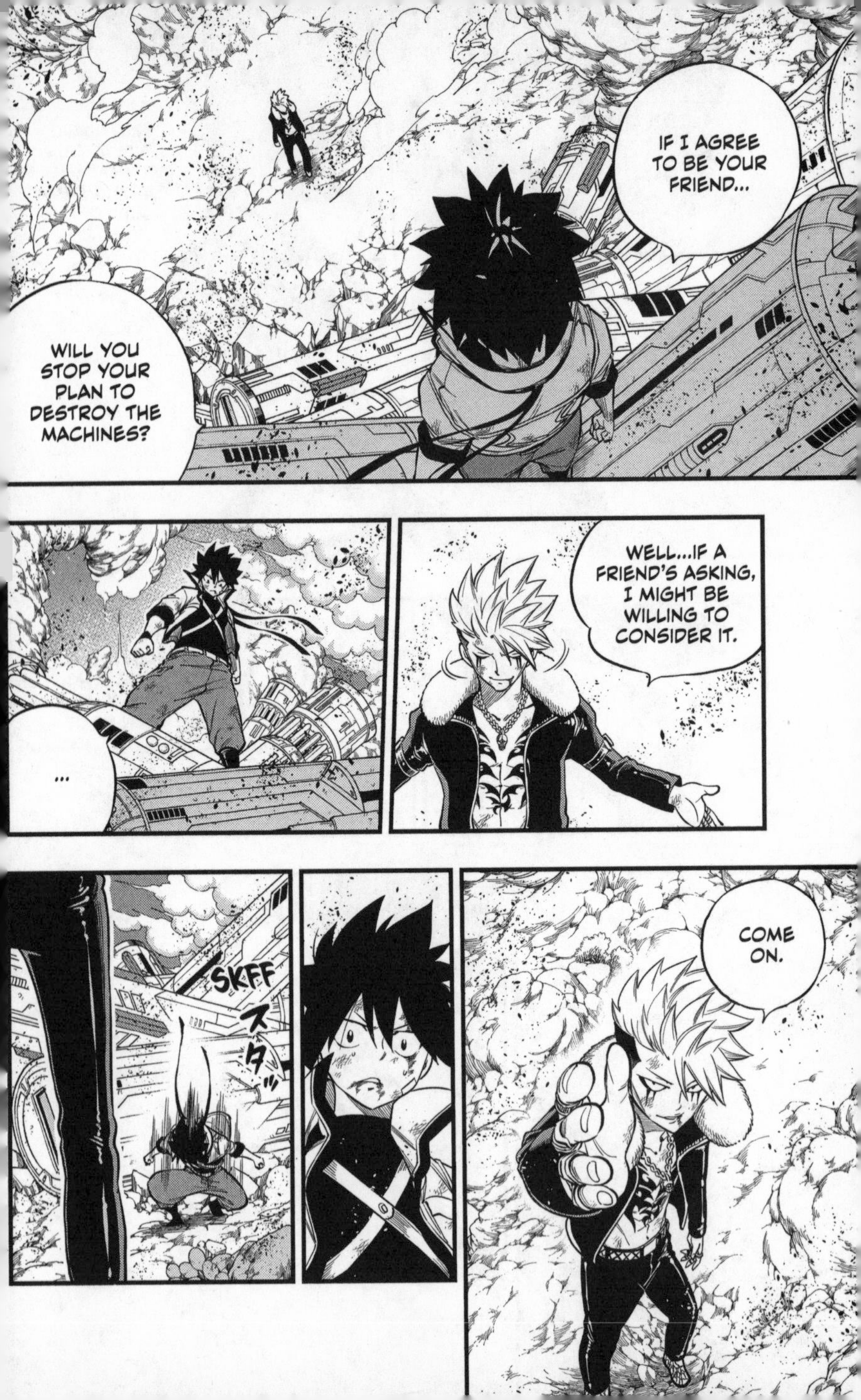
IF I AGREE TO BE YOUR FRIEND...
WILL YOU STOP YOUR PLAN TO DESTROY THE MACHINES?
WELL...IF A FRIEND'S ASKING, I MIGHT BE WILLING TO CONSIDER IT.
...
COME ON.
SKFF
スタッ

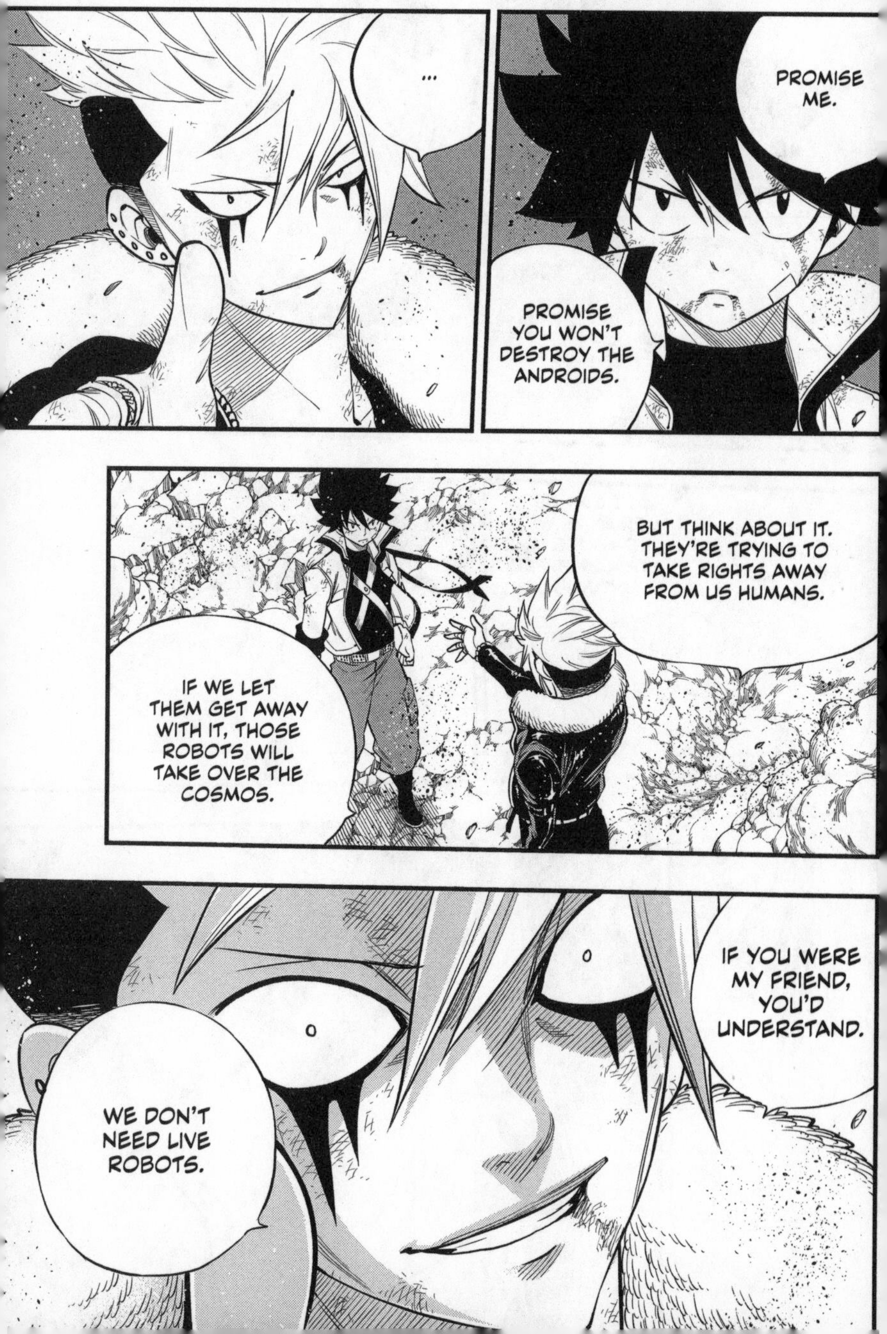
PROMISE ME.
PROMISE YOU WON'T DESTROY THE ANDROIDS.
...
BUT THINK ABOUT IT. THEY'RE TRYING TO TAKE RIGHTS AWAY FROM US HUMANS.
IF WE LET THEM GET AWAY WITH IT, THOSE ROBOTS WILL TAKE OVER THE COSMOS.
IF YOU WERE MY FRIEND, YOU'D UNDERSTAND.
WE DON'T NEED LIVE ROBOTS.

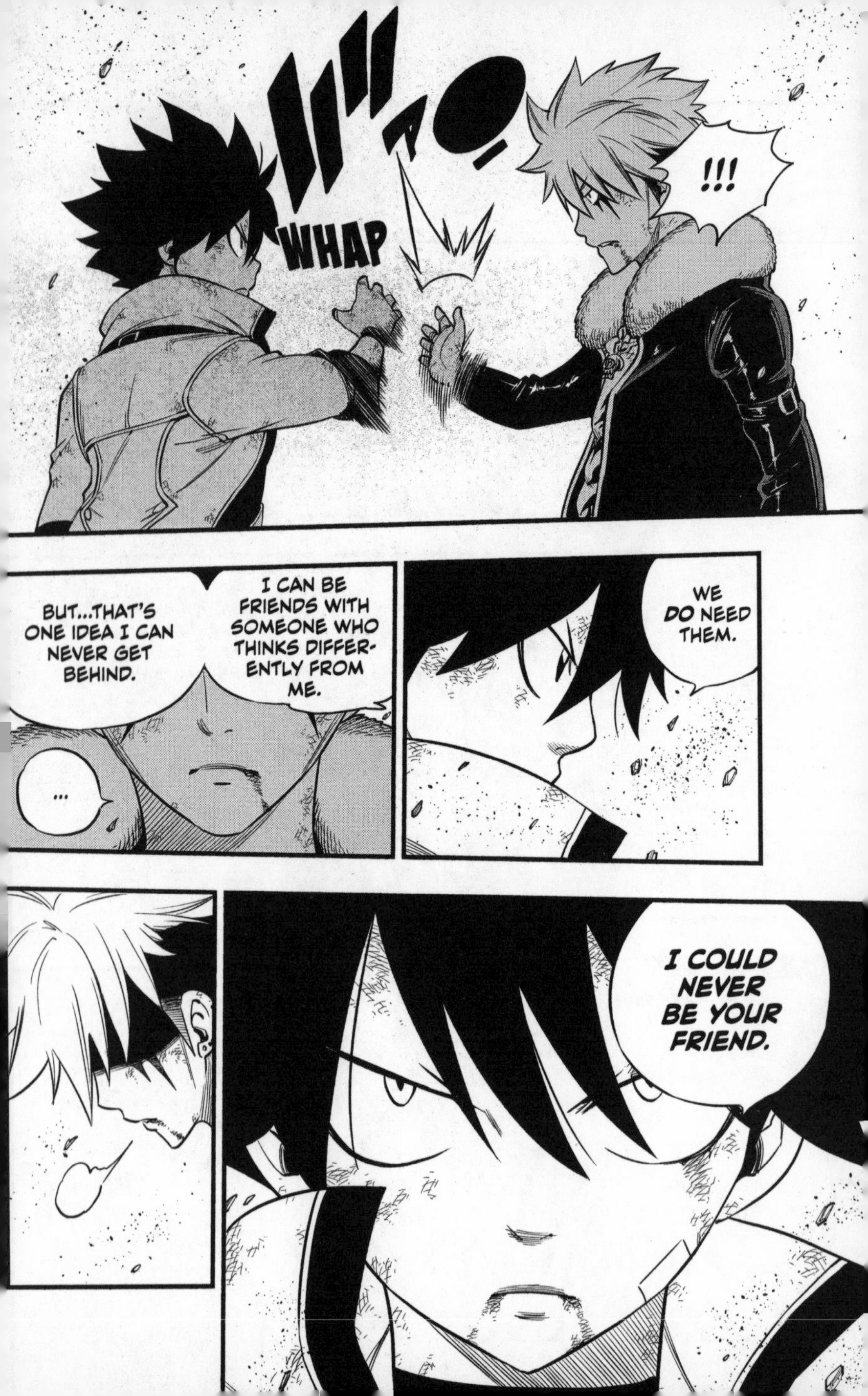
!!!
WHAP
WE DO NEED THEM.
I CAN BE FRIENDS WITH SOMEONE WHO THINKS DIFFERENTLY FROM ME.
BUT...THAT'S ONE IDEA I CAN NEVER GET BEHIND.
...
I COULD NEVER BE YOUR FRIEND.

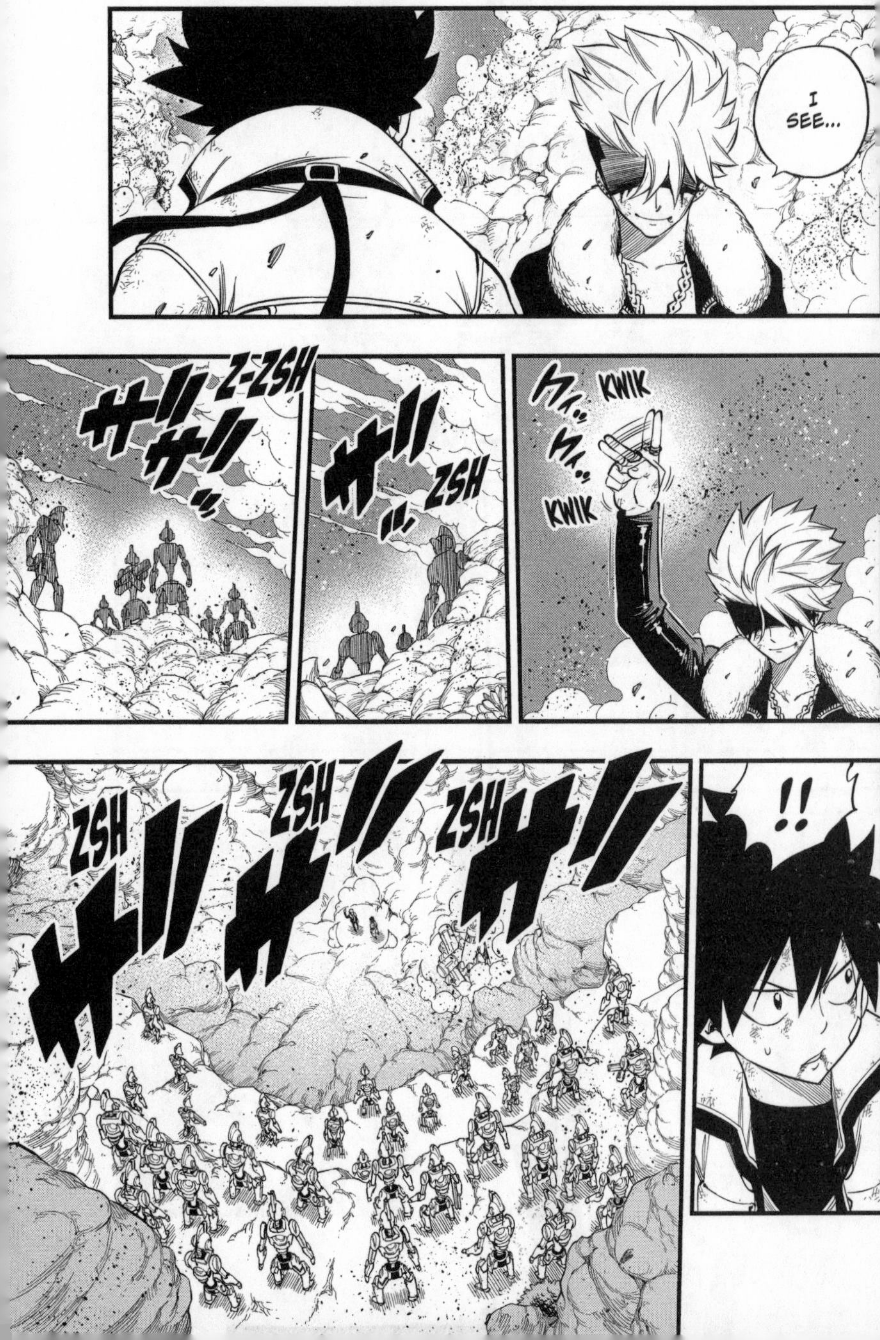
I SEE...
KWIK
KWIK
ZSH
Z-ZSH
!!
ZSH
ZSH
ZSH

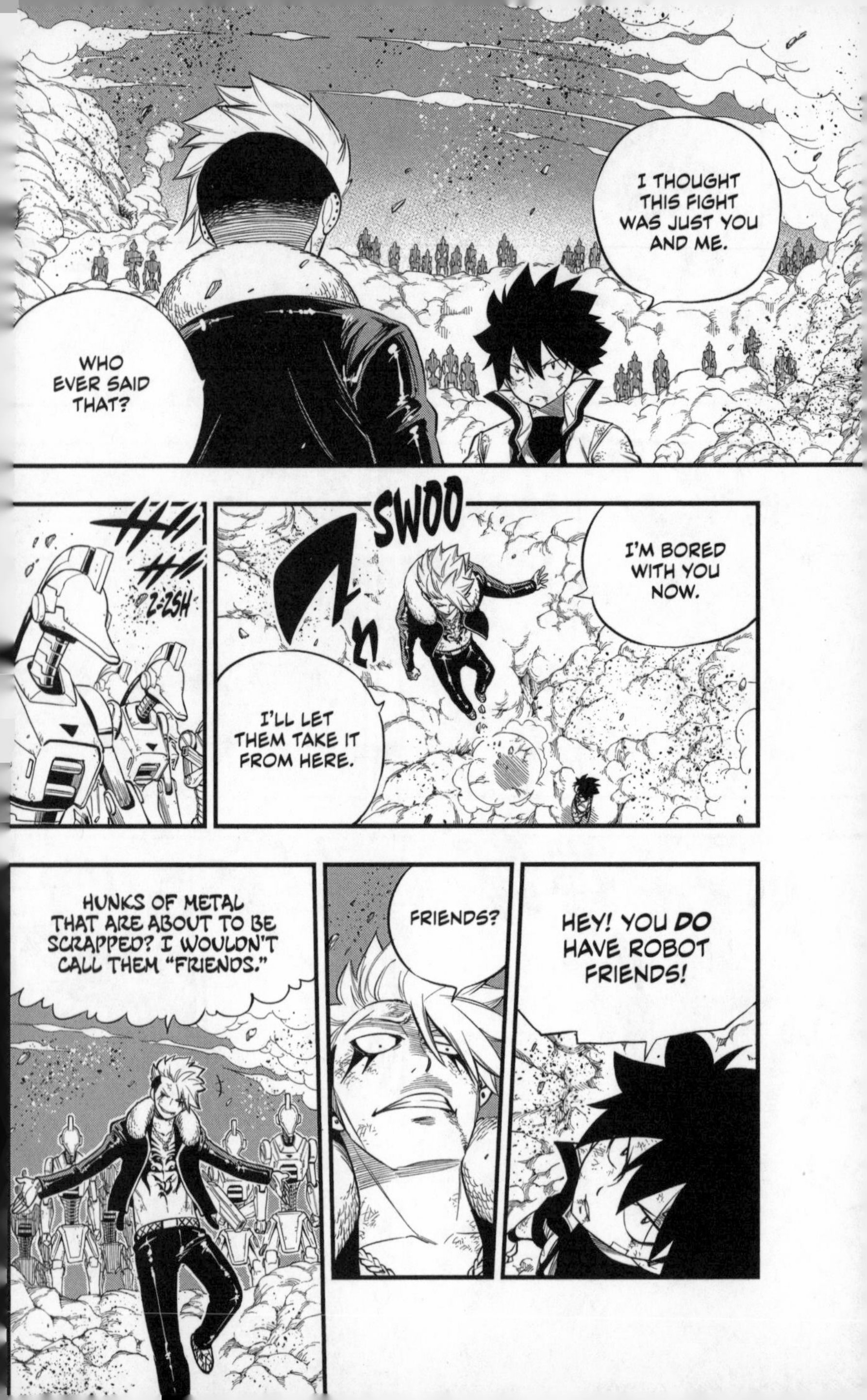
I THOUGHT THIS FIGHT WAS JUST YOU AND ME.
WHO EVER SAID THAT?
SWOO
I'M BORED WITH YOU NOW.
I'LL LET THEM TAKE IT FROM HERE.
Z-ZSH
HEY! YOU *DO* HAVE ROBOT FRIENDS!
FRIENDS?
HUNKS OF METAL THAT ARE ABOUT TO BE SCRAPPED? I WOULDN'T CALL THEM "FRIENDS."

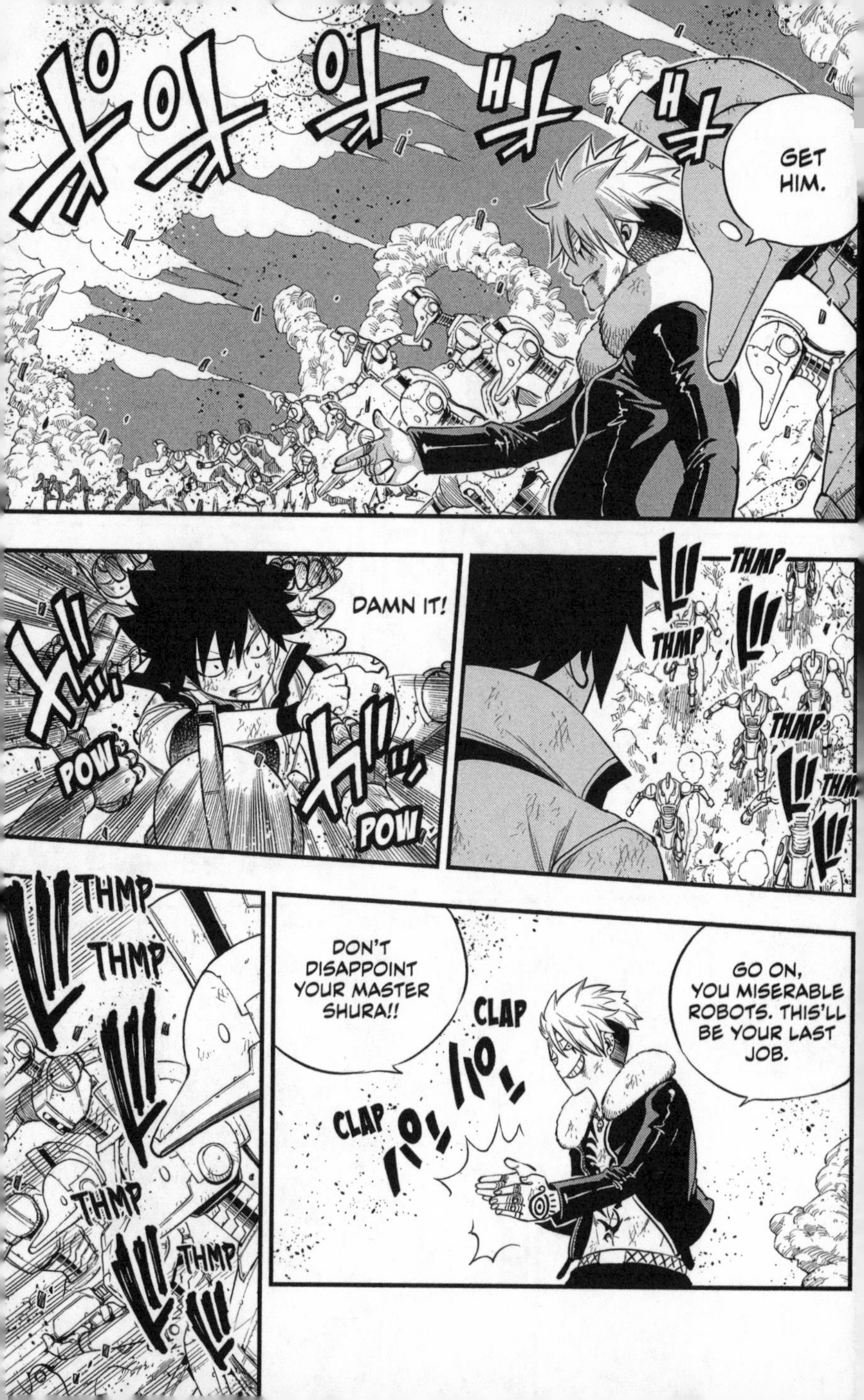
GET HIM.
THMP
THMP
THMP
THM
DAMN IT!
POW
POW
GO ON, YOU MISERABLE ROBOTS. THIS'LL BE YOUR LAST JOB.
DON'T DISAPPOINT YOUR MASTER SHURA!!
CLAP
CLAP
THMP
THMP
THMP
THMP

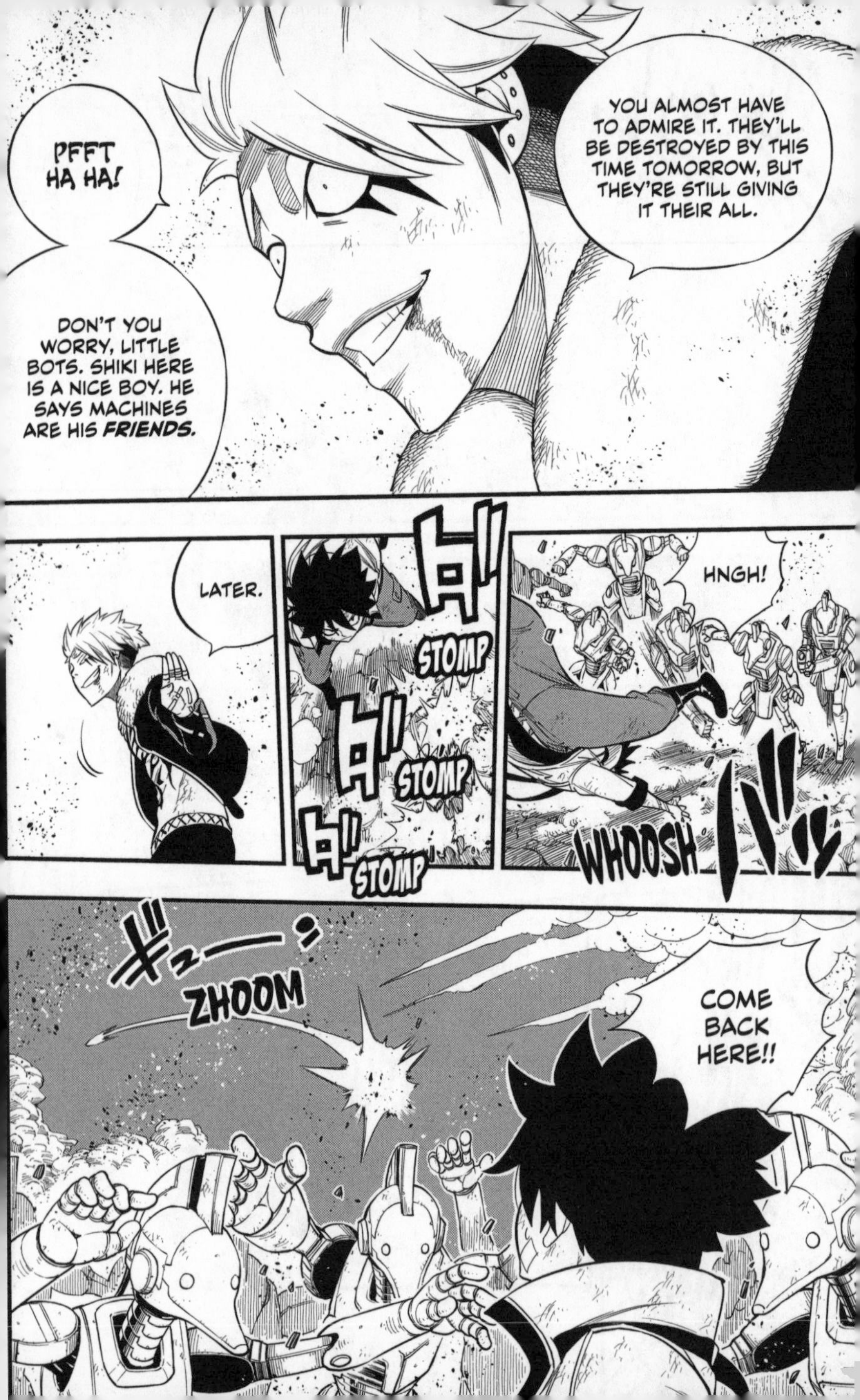
YOU ALMOST HAVE TO ADMIRE IT. THEY'LL BE DESTROYED BY THIS TIME TOMORROW, BUT THEY'RE STILL GIVING IT THEIR ALL.
PFFT HA HA!
DON'T YOU WORRY, LITTLE BOTS. SHIKI HERE IS A NICE BOY. HE SAYS MACHINES ARE HIS *FRIENDS.*
HNGH!
WHOOSH
STOMP
STOMP
STOMP
LATER.
COME BACK HERE!!
ZHOOM

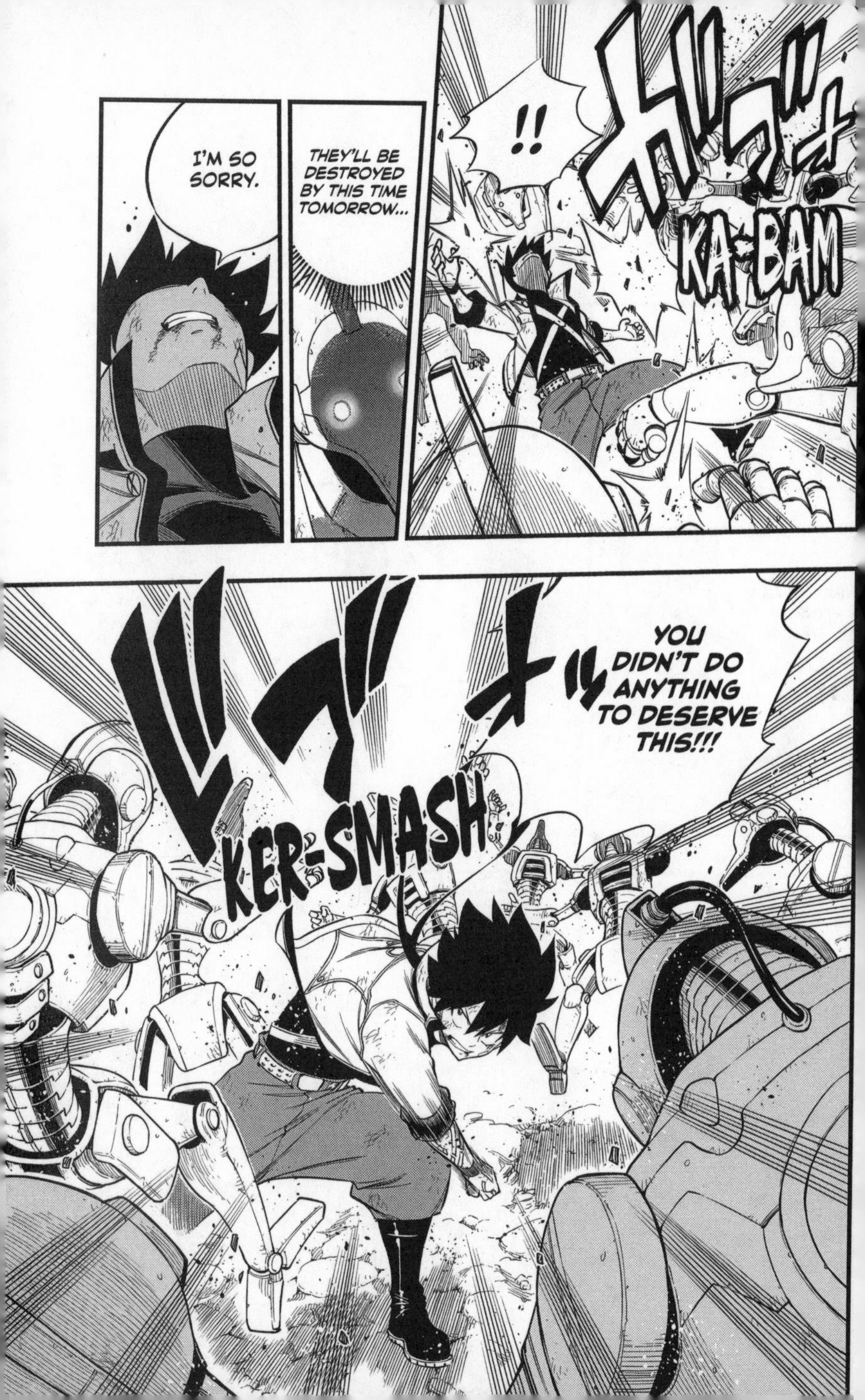
!!
KA-BAM
THEY'LL BE DESTROYED BY THIS TIME TOMORROW...
I'M SO SORRY.
YOU DIDN'T DO ANYTHING TO DESERVE THIS!!!
KER-SMASH

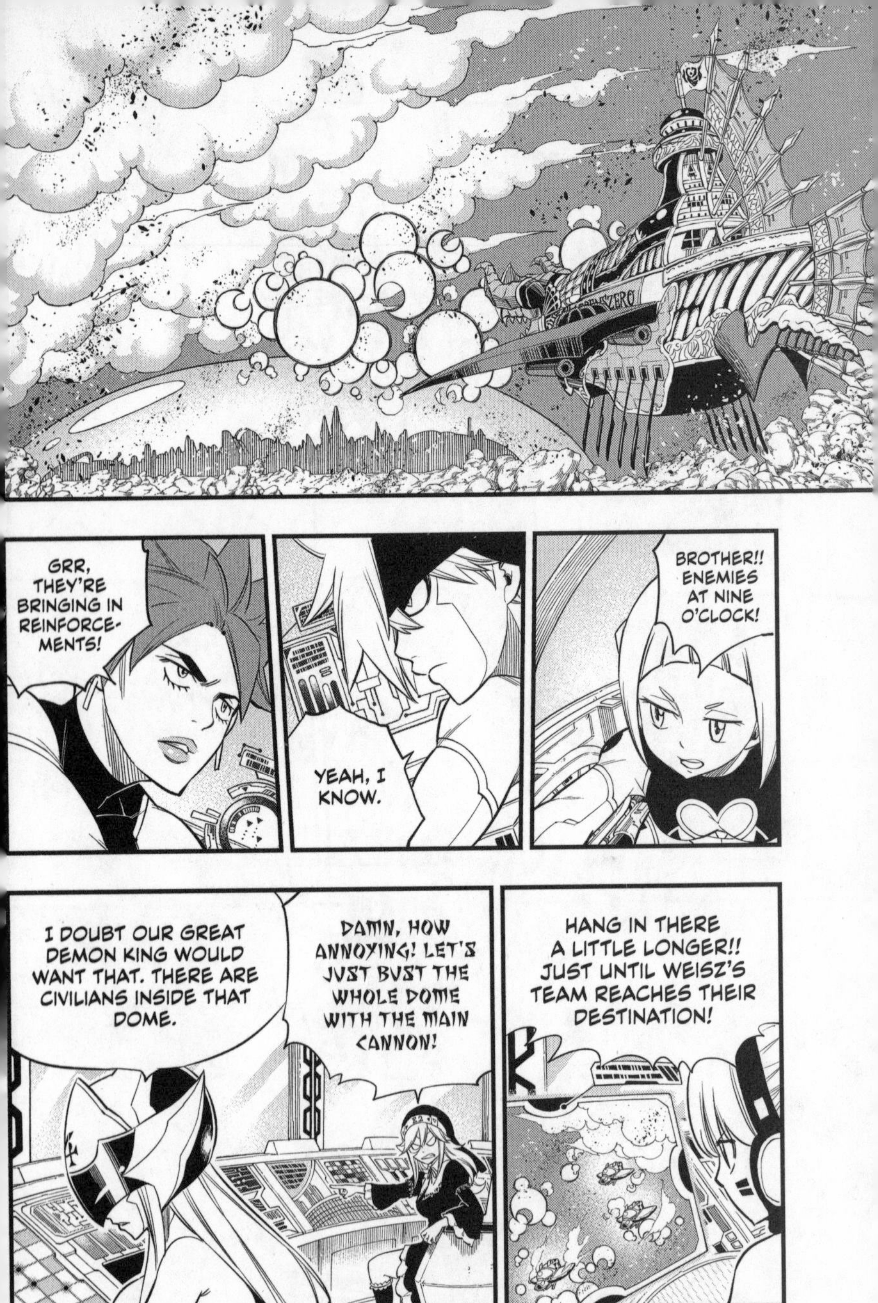
BROTHER!! ENEMIES AT NINE O'CLOCK!
YEAH, I KNOW.
GRR, THEY'RE BRINGING IN REINFORCE-MENTS!
HANG IN THERE A LITTLE LONGER!! JUST UNTIL WEISZ'S TEAM REACHES THEIR DESTINATION!
DAMN, HOW ANNOYING! LET'S JUST BUST THE WHOLE DOME WITH THE MAIN CANNON!
I DOUBT OUR GREAT DEMON KING WOULD WANT THAT. THERE ARE CIVILIANS INSIDE THAT DOME.

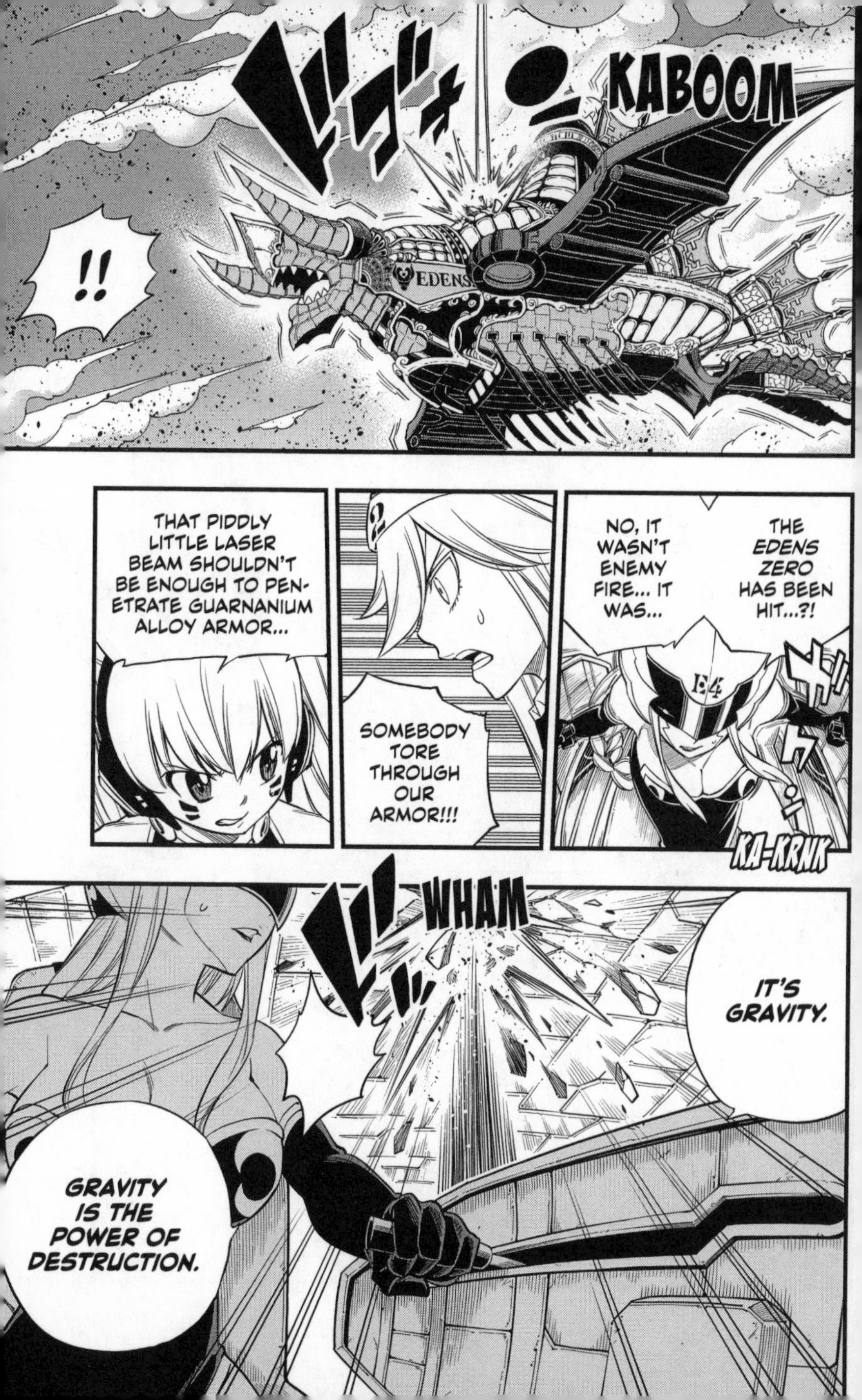
KABOOM
!!
THE EDENS ZERO HAS BEEN HIT...?!
NO, IT WASN'T ENEMY FIRE... IT WAS...
KA-KRNK
SOMEBODY TORE THROUGH OUR ARMOR!!!
THAT PIDDLY LITTLE LASER BEAM SHOULDN'T BE ENOUGH TO PEN-ETRATE GUARNANIUM ALLOY ARMOR...
WHAM
IT'S GRAVITY.
GRAVITY IS THE POWER OF DESTRUCTION.

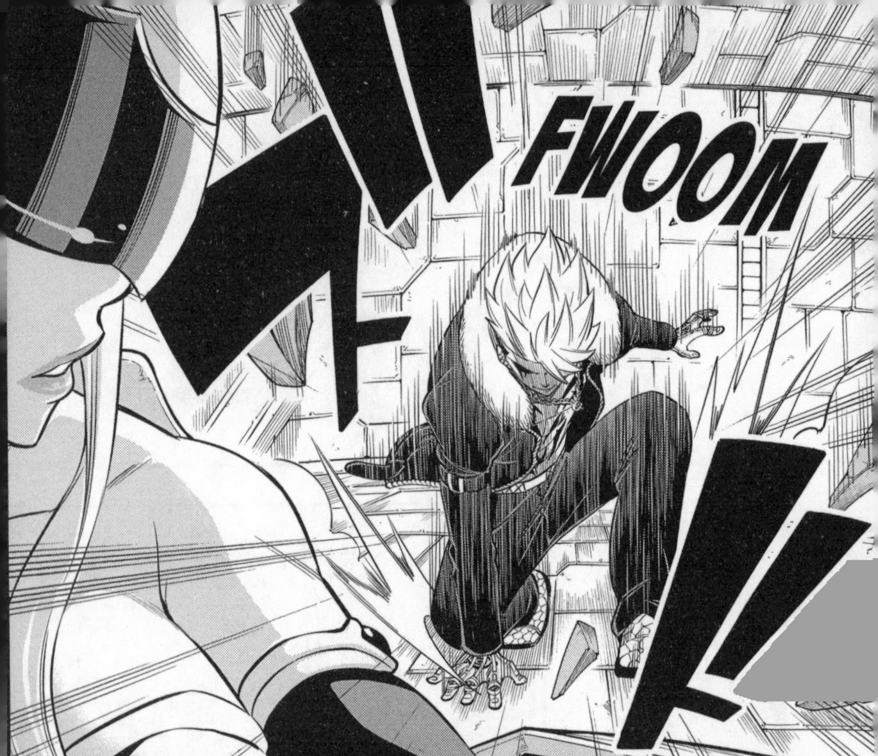
FWOOM
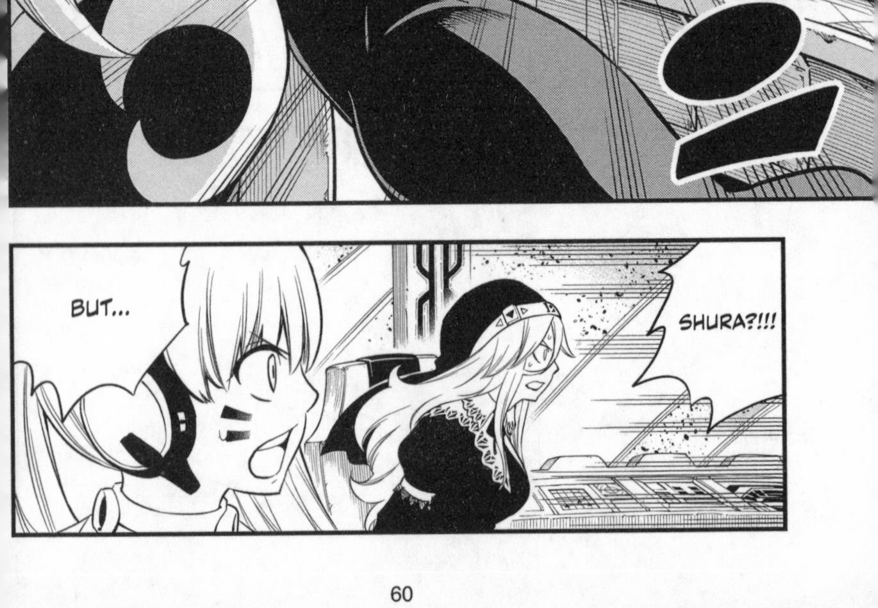
SHURA?!!!
BUT...

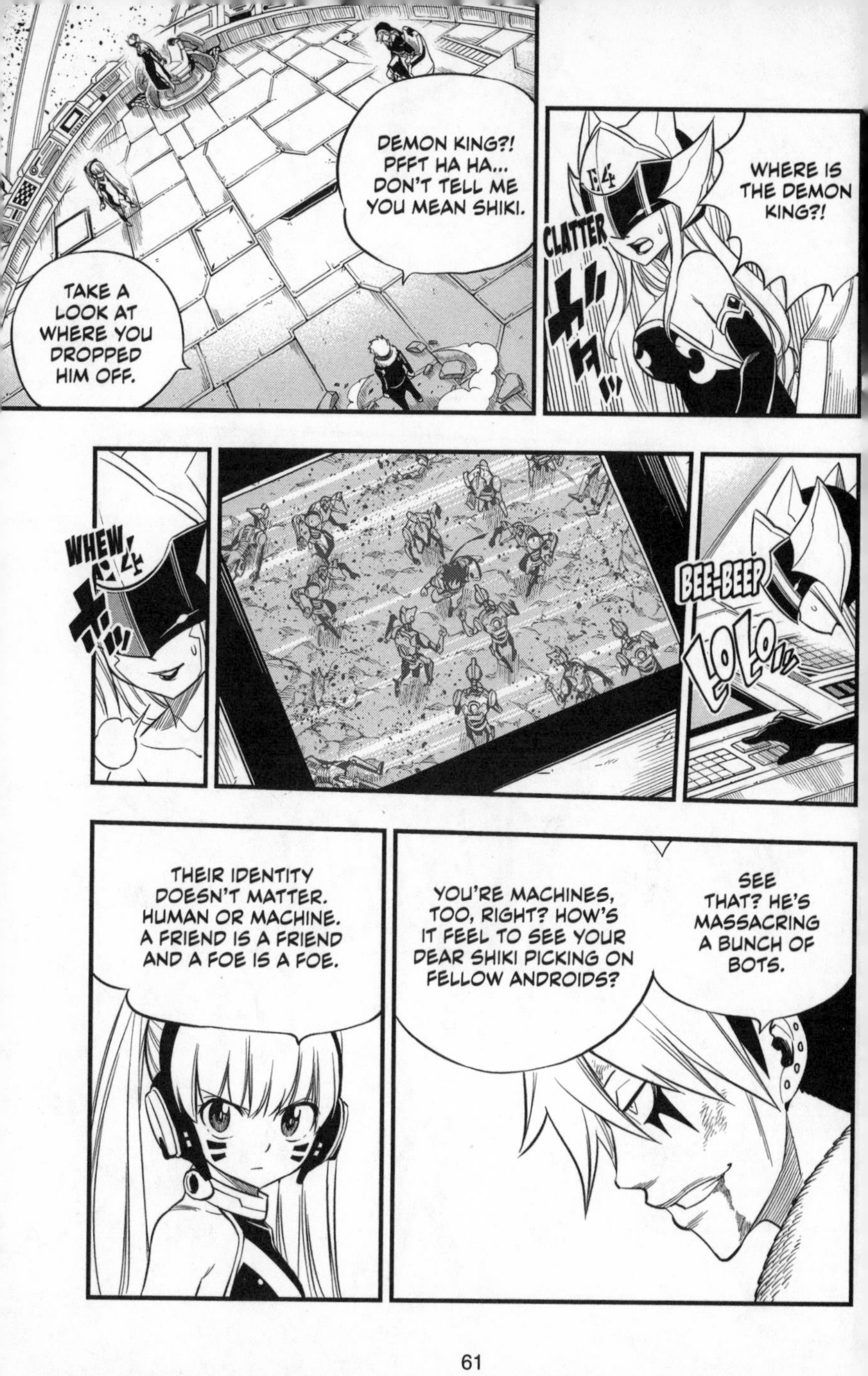
WHERE IS THE DEMON KING?!
CLATTER
DEMON KING?! PFFT HA HA... DON'T TELL ME YOU MEAN SHIKI.
TAKE A LOOK AT WHERE YOU DROPPED HIM OFF.
BEE-BEEP
WHEW
SEE THAT? HE'S MASSACRING A BUNCH OF BOTS.
YOU'RE MACHINES, TOO, RIGHT? HOW'S IT FEEL TO SEE YOUR DEAR SHIKI PICKING ON FELLOW ANDROIDS?
THEIR IDENTITY DOESN'T MATTER. HUMAN OR MACHINE. A FRIEND IS A FRIEND AND A FOE IS A FOE.

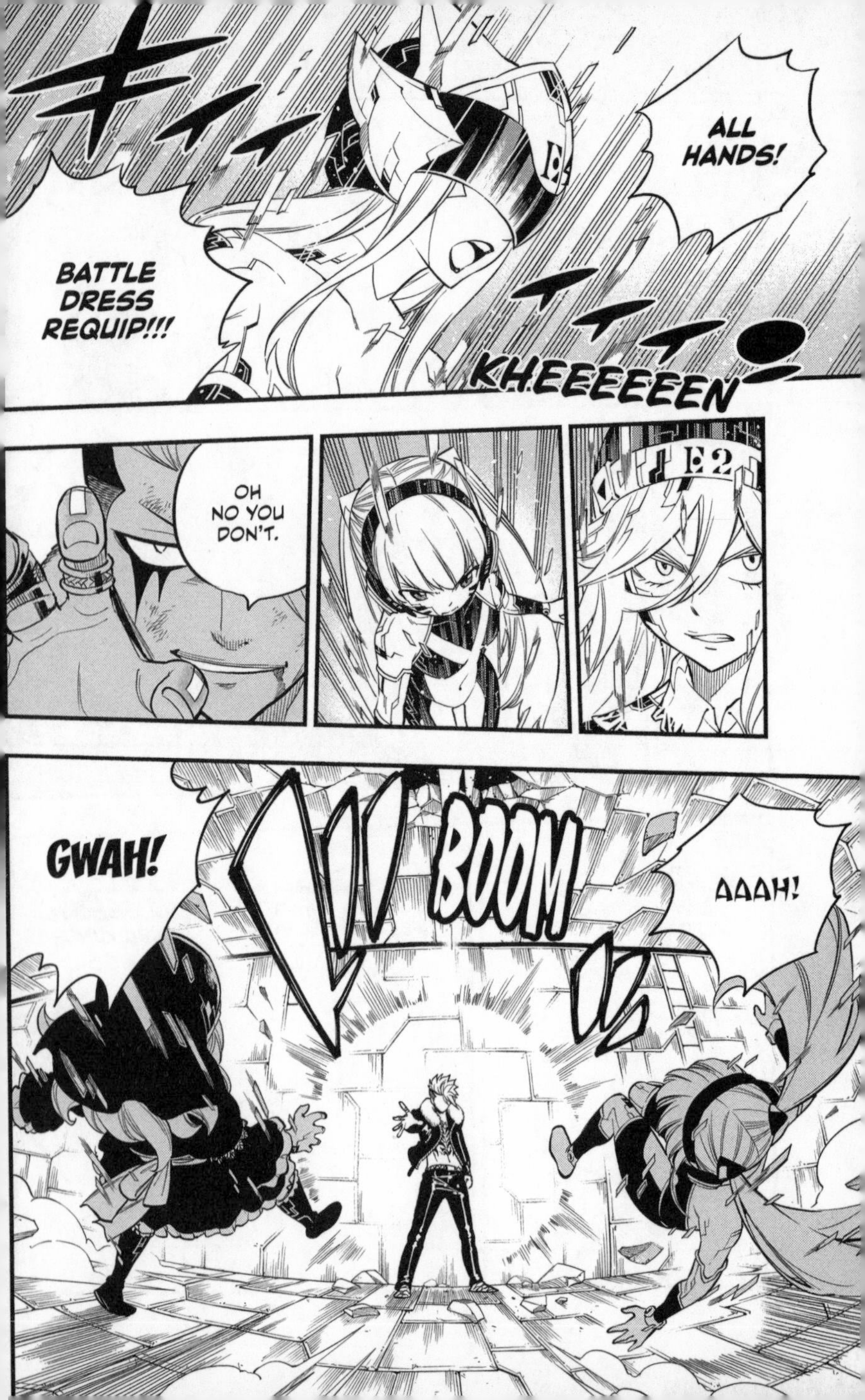
ALL HANDS!
BATTLE DRESS REQUIP!!!
KHEEEEEEN
OH NO YOU DON'T.
AAAH!
BOOM
GWAH!

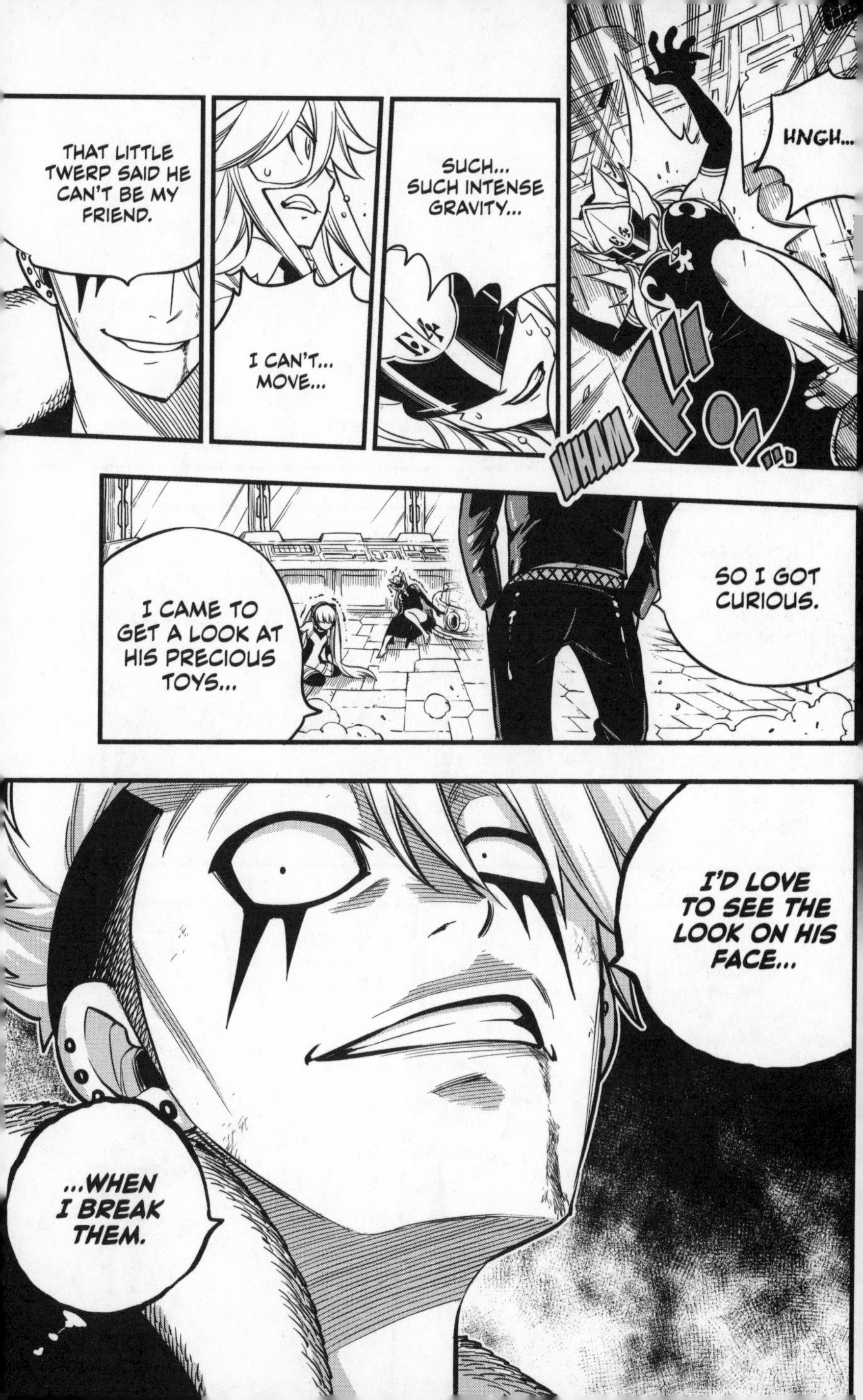
HNGH...
WHAM
SUCH... SUCH INTENSE GRAVITY...
I CAN'T... MOVE...
THAT LITTLE TWERP SAID HE CAN'T BE MY FRIEND.
SO I GOT CURIOUS.
I CAME TO GET A LOOK AT HIS PRECIOUS TOYS...
I'D LOVE TO SEE THE LOOK ON HIS FACE...
...WHEN I BREAK THEM.

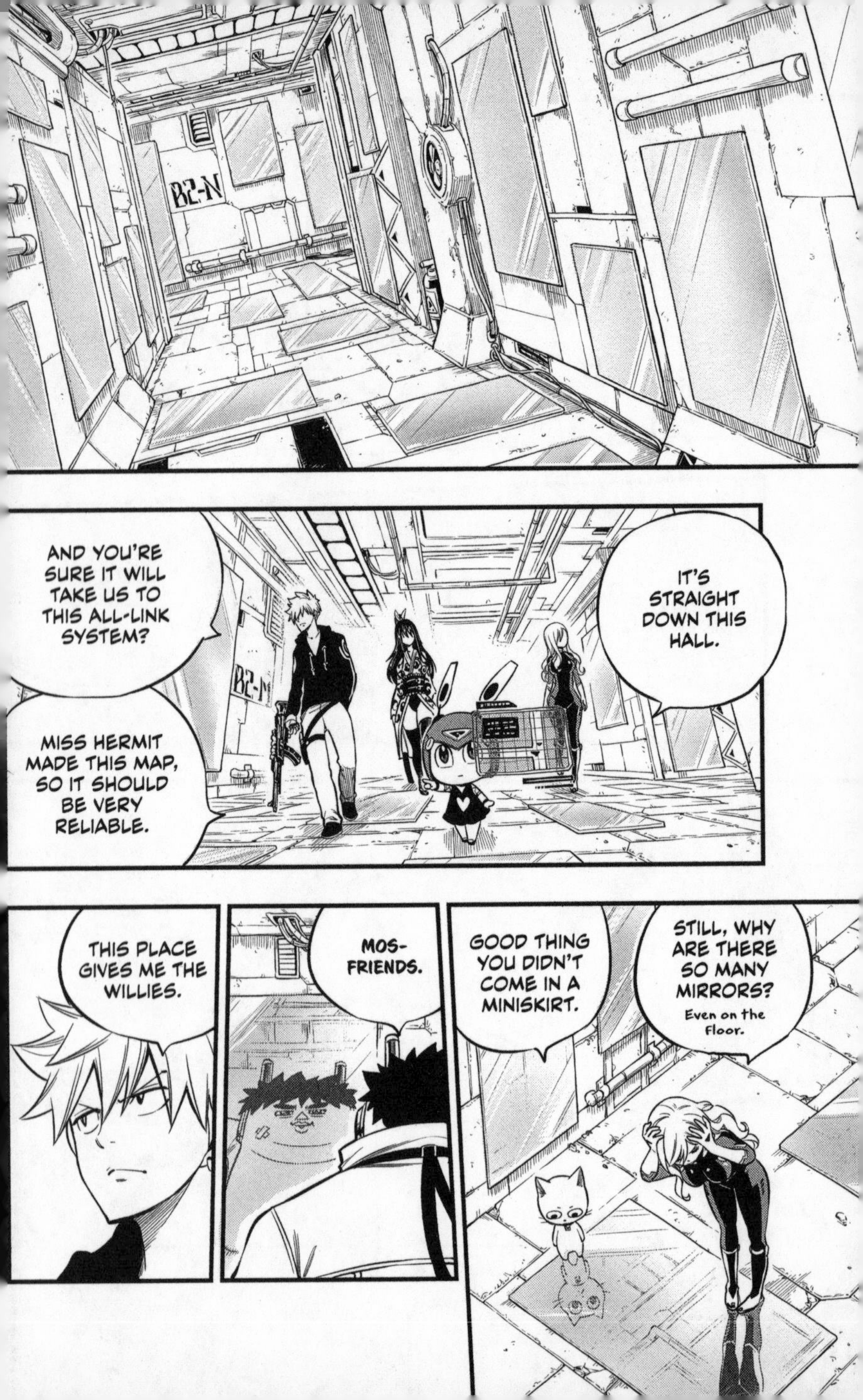
B2-N
IT'S STRAIGHT DOWN THIS HALL.
AND YOU'RE SURE IT WILL TAKE US TO THIS ALL-LINK SYSTEM?
MISS HERMIT MADE THIS MAP, SO IT SHOULD BE VERY RELIABLE.
STILL, WHY ARE THERE SO MANY MIRRORS? Even on the Floor.
GOOD THING YOU DIDN'T COME IN A MINISKIRT.
MOS-FRIENDS.
THIS PLACE GIVES ME THE WILLIES.

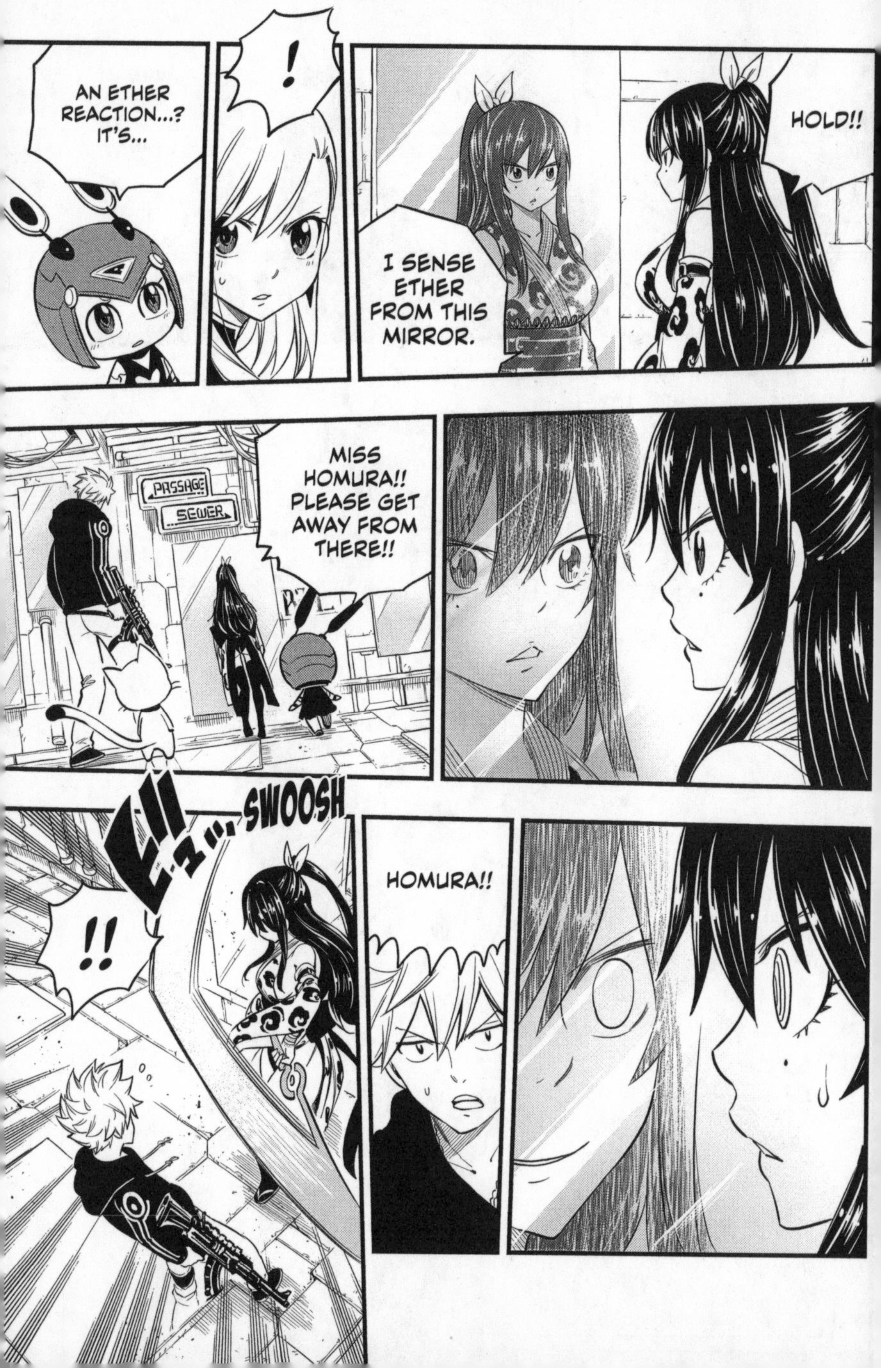
HOLD!!
I SENSE ETHER FROM THIS MIRROR.
!
AN ETHER REACTION...? IT'S...
MISS HOMURA!! PLEASE GET AWAY FROM THERE!!
PASSAGE
SEWER
HOMURA!!
SWOOSH
!!

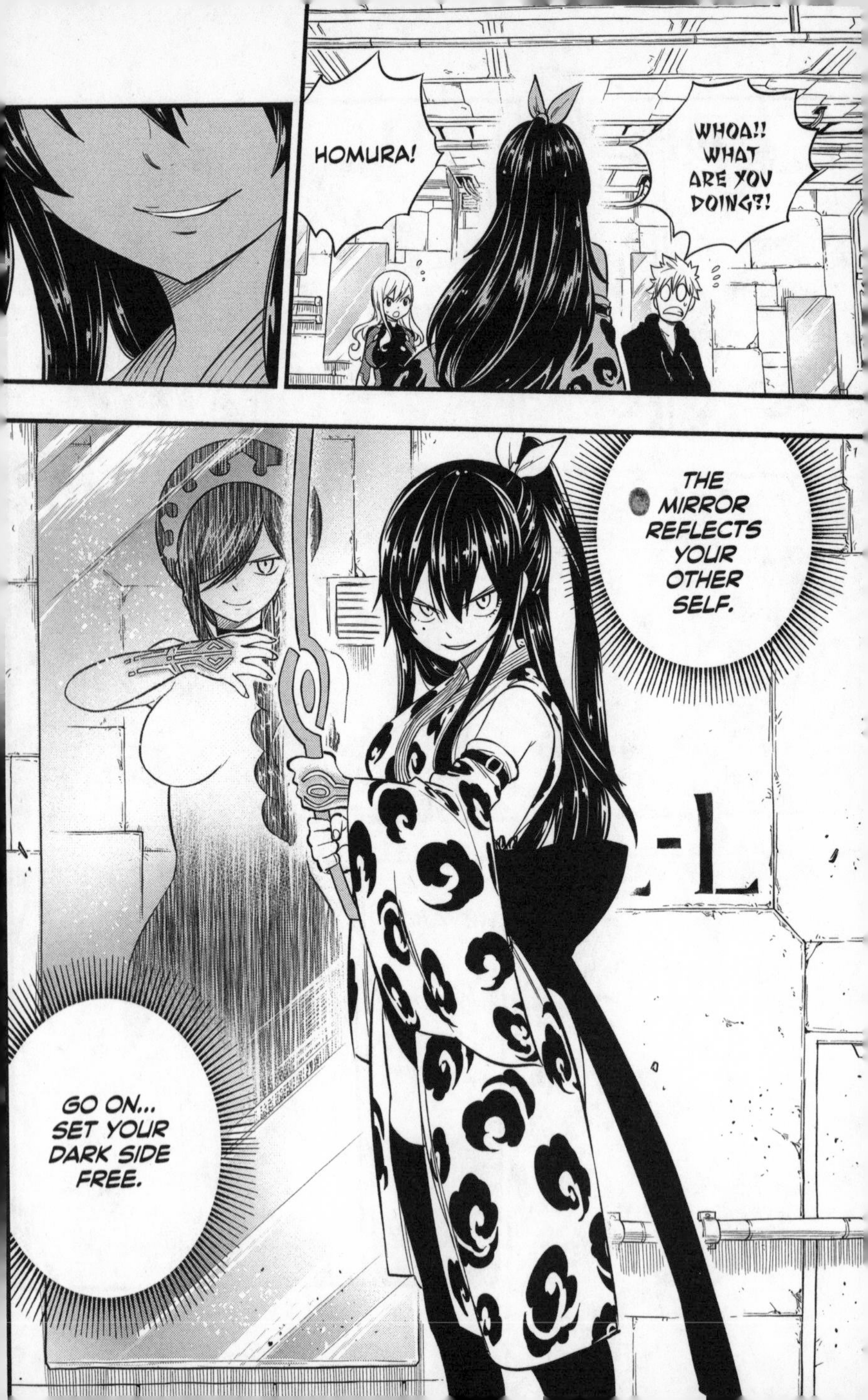
WHOA!! WHAT ARE YOU DOING?!
HOMURA!
THE MIRROR REFLECTS YOUR OTHER SELF.
GO ON... SET YOUR DARK SIDE FREE.

EDENSZERO

Edens Zero
In-Depth Character File 12

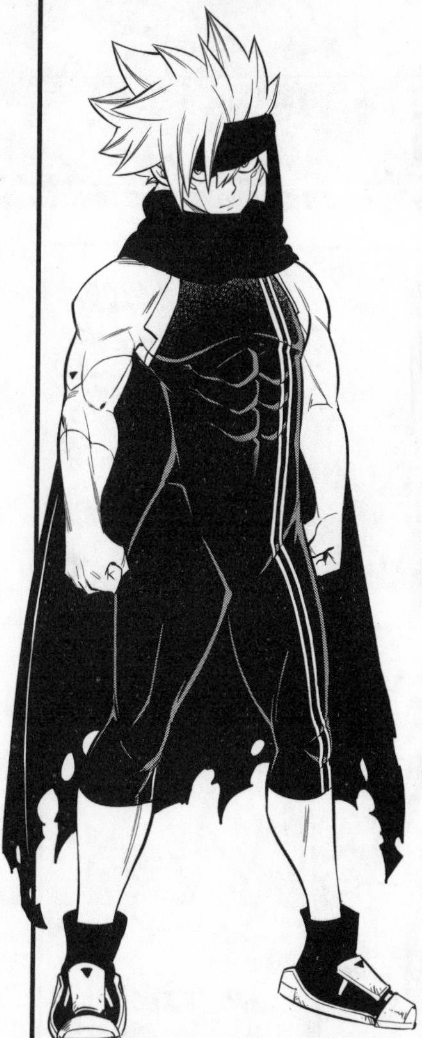

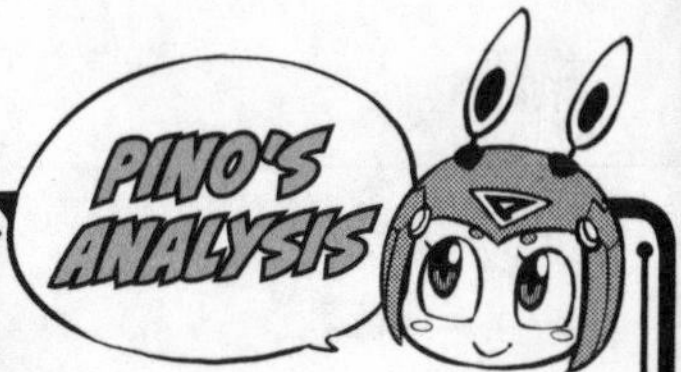
PINO'S ANALYSIS

Name: Jinn
(né Kris Rutherford)
Powers: Wind Ether Gear
(Wind Rage)
Likes: Kleene
Dislikes: Any man who approaches Kleene

Attack: ☆☆☆☆☆
Defense: ☆☆☆
Marksmanship: ☆☆☆
Ether Power: ☆☆☆
Intelligence: ☆☆☆
Loves His Sister: ☆☆☆☆☆

Memo

Has a tragic past in which he was made into a cyborg at a young age. He initially refused to open his heart to anyone, but I think that his sister Miss Kleene has helped him warm up to Master and the crew. Mr. Jinn's wind Ether Gear has such tremendous power, it's like a typhoon.

CHAPTER 144: THROUGH THE LOOKING GLASS

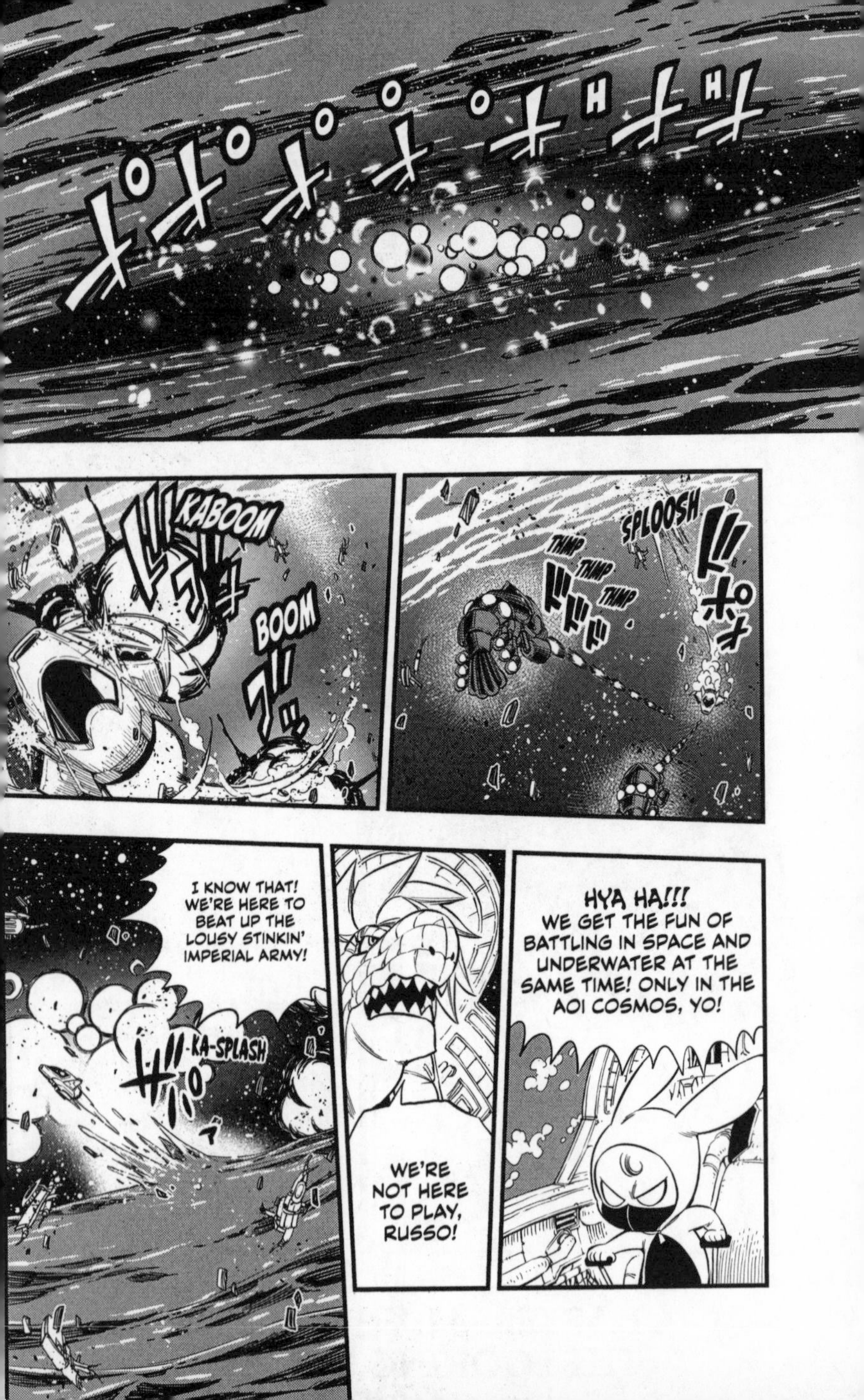
SPLOOSH
THMP
THMP
THMP
KABOOM
BOOM
HYA HA!!!
WE GET THE FUN OF BATTLING IN SPACE AND UNDERWATER AT THE SAME TIME! ONLY IN THE AOI COSMOS, YO!
WE'RE NOT HERE TO PLAY, RUSSO!
I KNOW THAT! WE'RE HERE TO BEAT UP THE LOUSY STINKIN' IMPERIAL ARMY!
KA-SPLASH

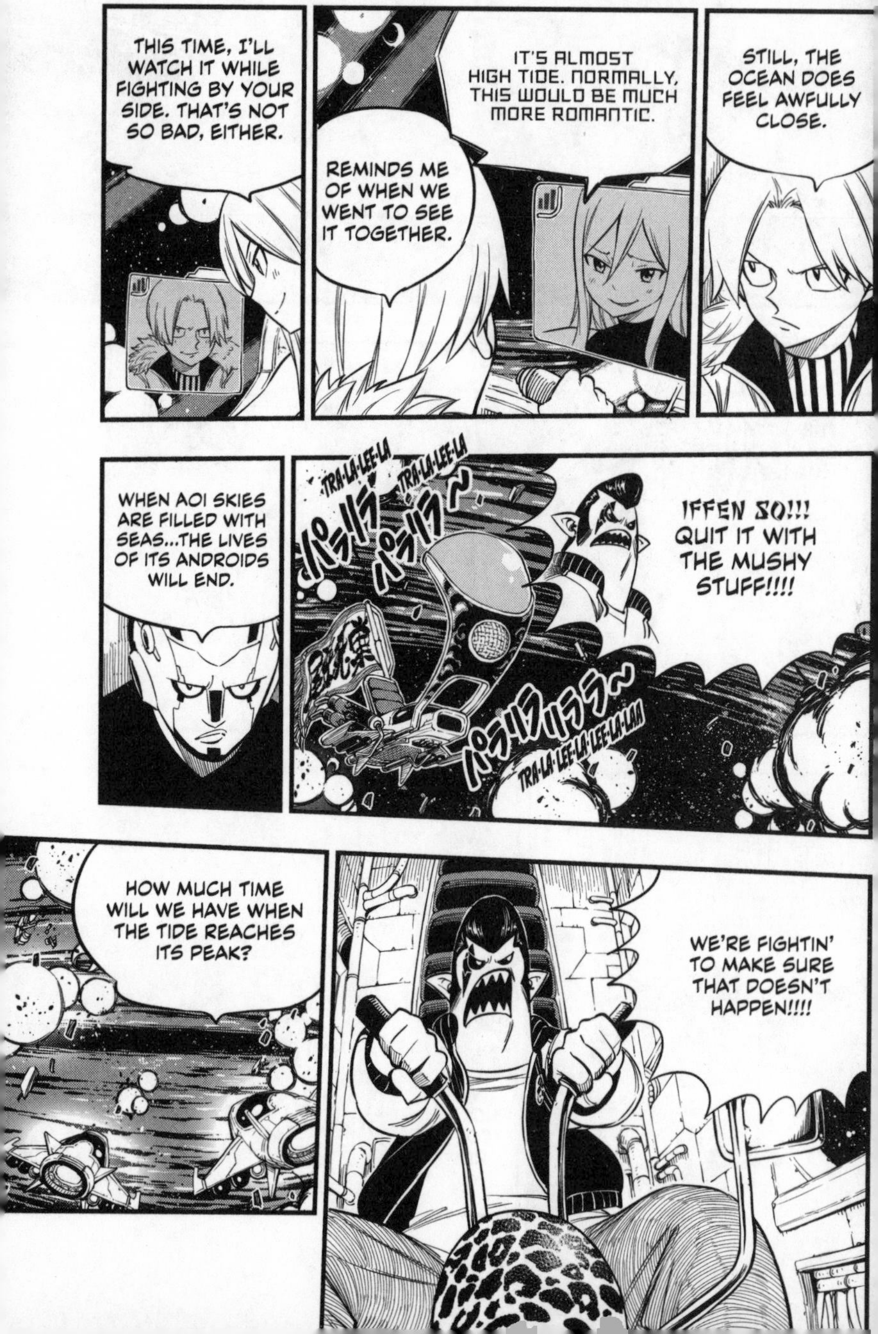
STILL, THE OCEAN DOES FEEL AWFULLY CLOSE.
IT'S ALMOST HIGH TIDE. NORMALLY, THIS WOULD BE MUCH MORE ROMANTIC.
REMINDS ME OF WHEN WE WENT TO SEE IT TOGETHER.
THIS TIME, I'LL WATCH IT WHILE FIGHTING BY YOUR SIDE. THAT'S NOT SO BAD, EITHER.
TRA-LA-LEE-LA
TRA-LA-LEE-LA
IFFEN SO!!! QUIT IT WITH THE MUSHY STUFF!!!!
TRA-LA-LEE-LA-LEE-LA-LAA
WHEN AOI SKIES ARE FILLED WITH SEAS...THE LIVES OF ITS ANDROIDS WILL END.
WE'RE FIGHTIN' TO MAKE SURE THAT DOESN'T HAPPEN!!!!
HOW MUCH TIME WILL WE HAVE WHEN THE TIDE REACHES ITS PEAK?

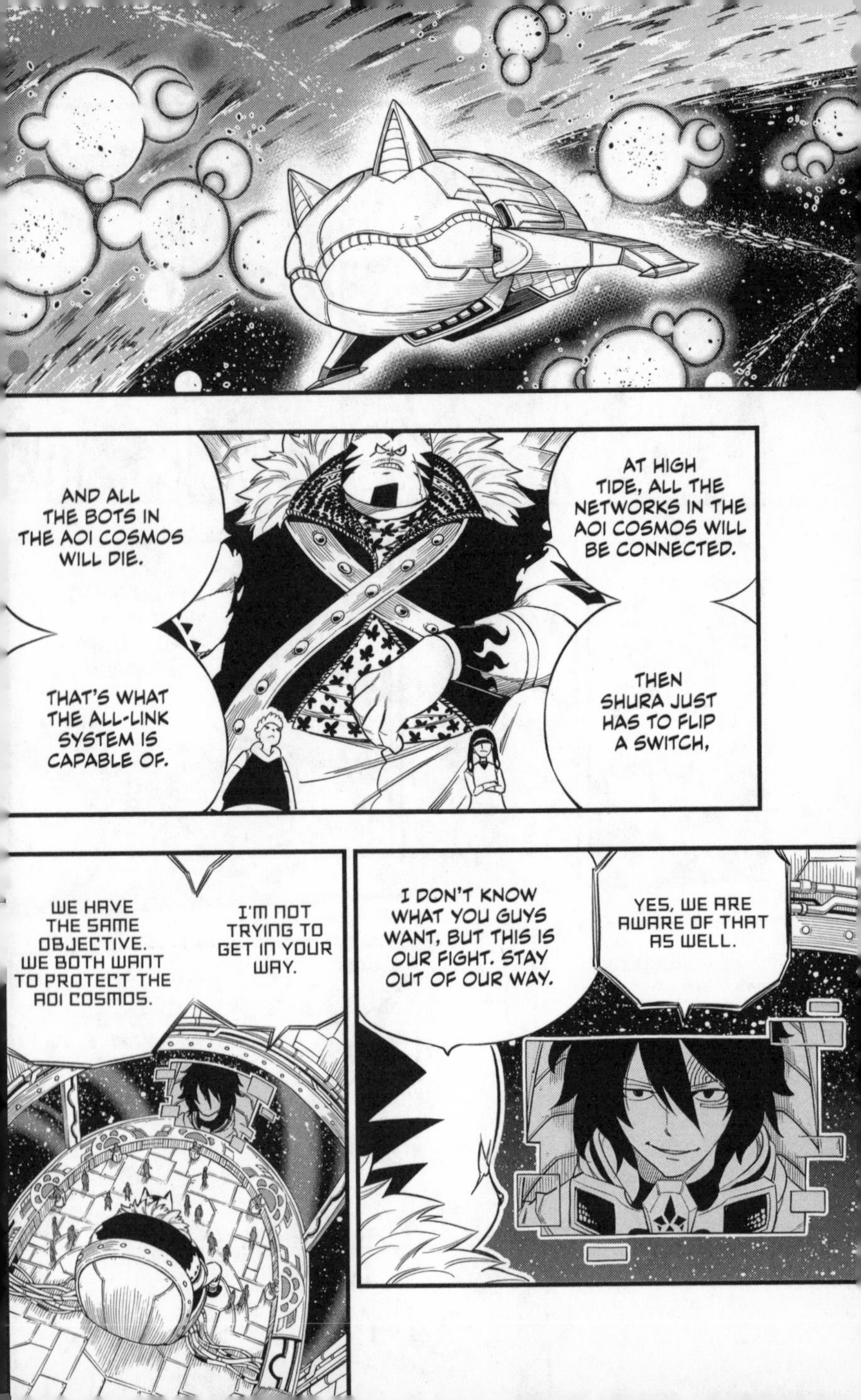
AT HIGH TIDE, ALL THE NETWORKS IN THE AOI COSMOS WILL BE CONNECTED.
THEN SHURA JUST HAS TO FLIP A SWITCH,
AND ALL THE BOTS IN THE AOI COSMOS WILL DIE.
THAT'S WHAT THE ALL-LINK SYSTEM IS CAPABLE OF.
YES, WE ARE AWARE OF THAT AS WELL.
I DON'T KNOW WHAT YOU GUYS WANT, BUT THIS IS OUR FIGHT. STAY OUT OF OUR WAY.
I'M NOT TRYING TO GET IN YOUR WAY.
WE HAVE THE SAME OBJECTIVE. WE BOTH WANT TO PROTECT THE AOI COSMOS.

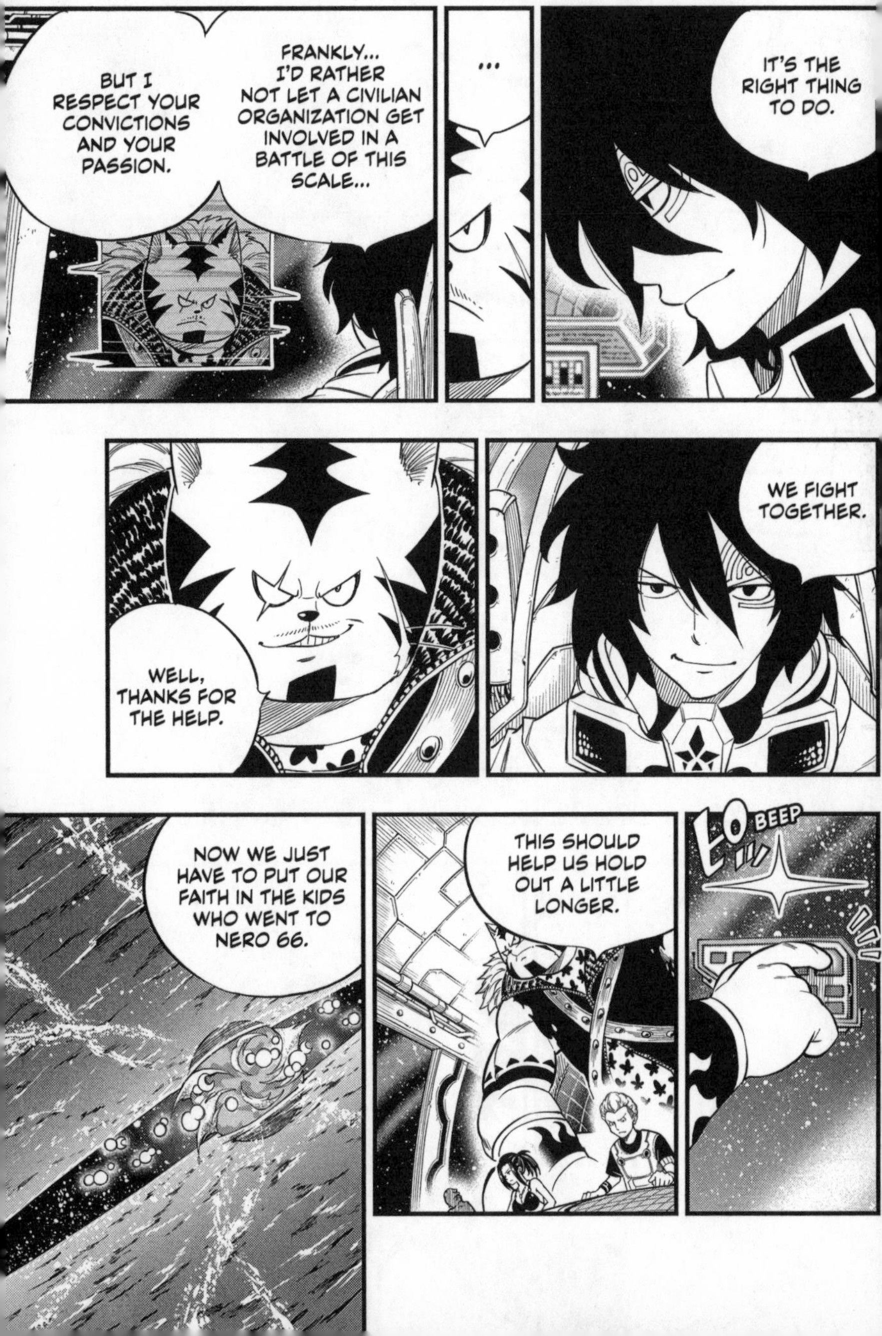
IT'S THE RIGHT THING TO DO.
...
FRANKLY... I'D RATHER NOT LET A CIVILIAN ORGANIZATION GET INVOLVED IN A BATTLE OF THIS SCALE...
BUT I RESPECT YOUR CONVICTIONS AND YOUR PASSION.
WE FIGHT TOGETHER.
WELL, THANKS FOR THE HELP.
BEEP
THIS SHOULD HELP US HOLD OUT A LITTLE LONGER.
NOW WE JUST HAVE TO PUT OUR FAITH IN THE KIDS WHO WENT TO NERO 66.

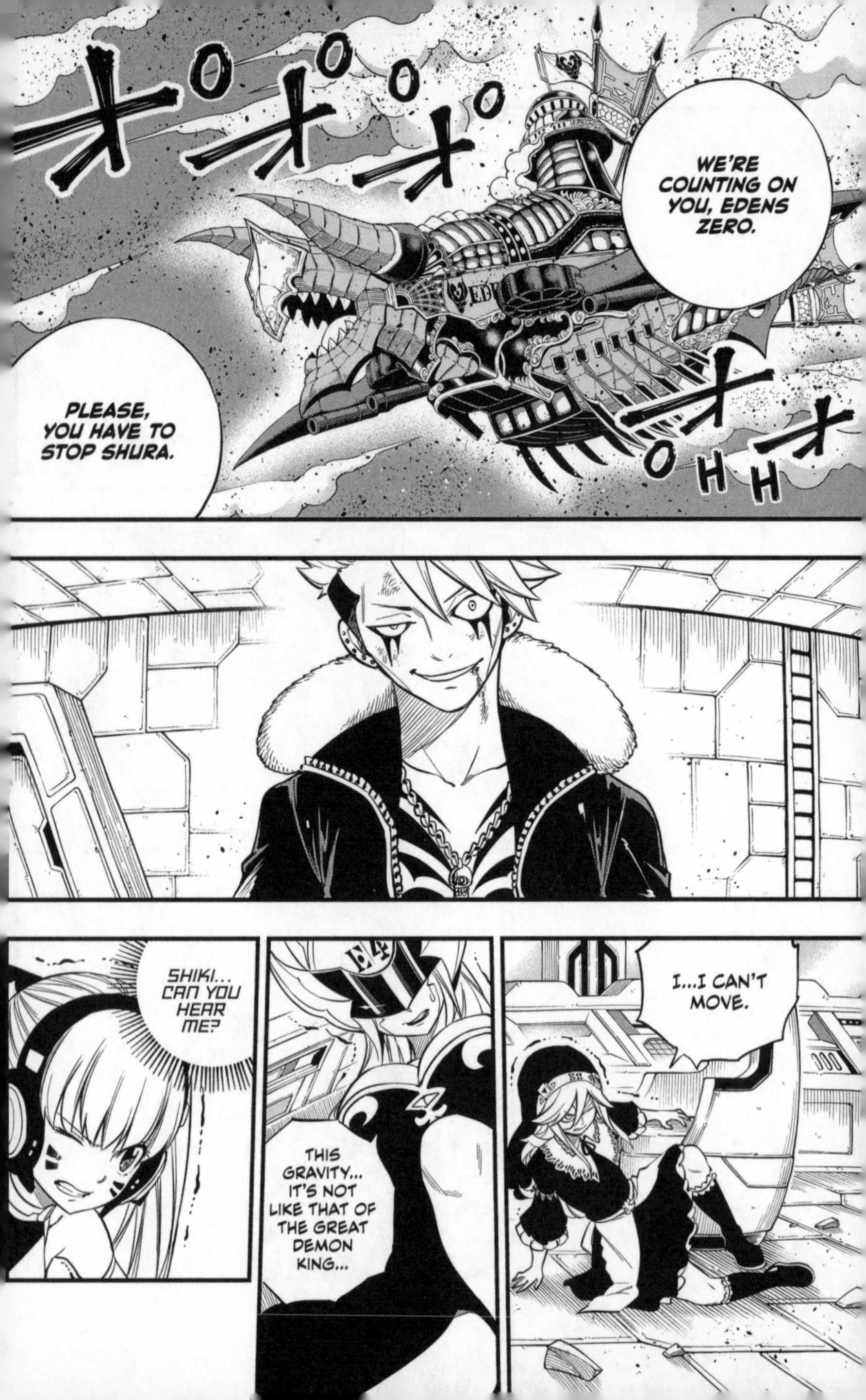
WE'RE COUNTING ON YOU, EDENS ZERO.
OOOOO
OHH
PLEASE, YOU HAVE TO STOP SHURA.
I...I CAN'T MOVE.
THIS GRAVITY... IT'S NOT LIKE THAT OF THE GREAT DEMON KING...
SHIKI... CAN YOU HEAR ME?

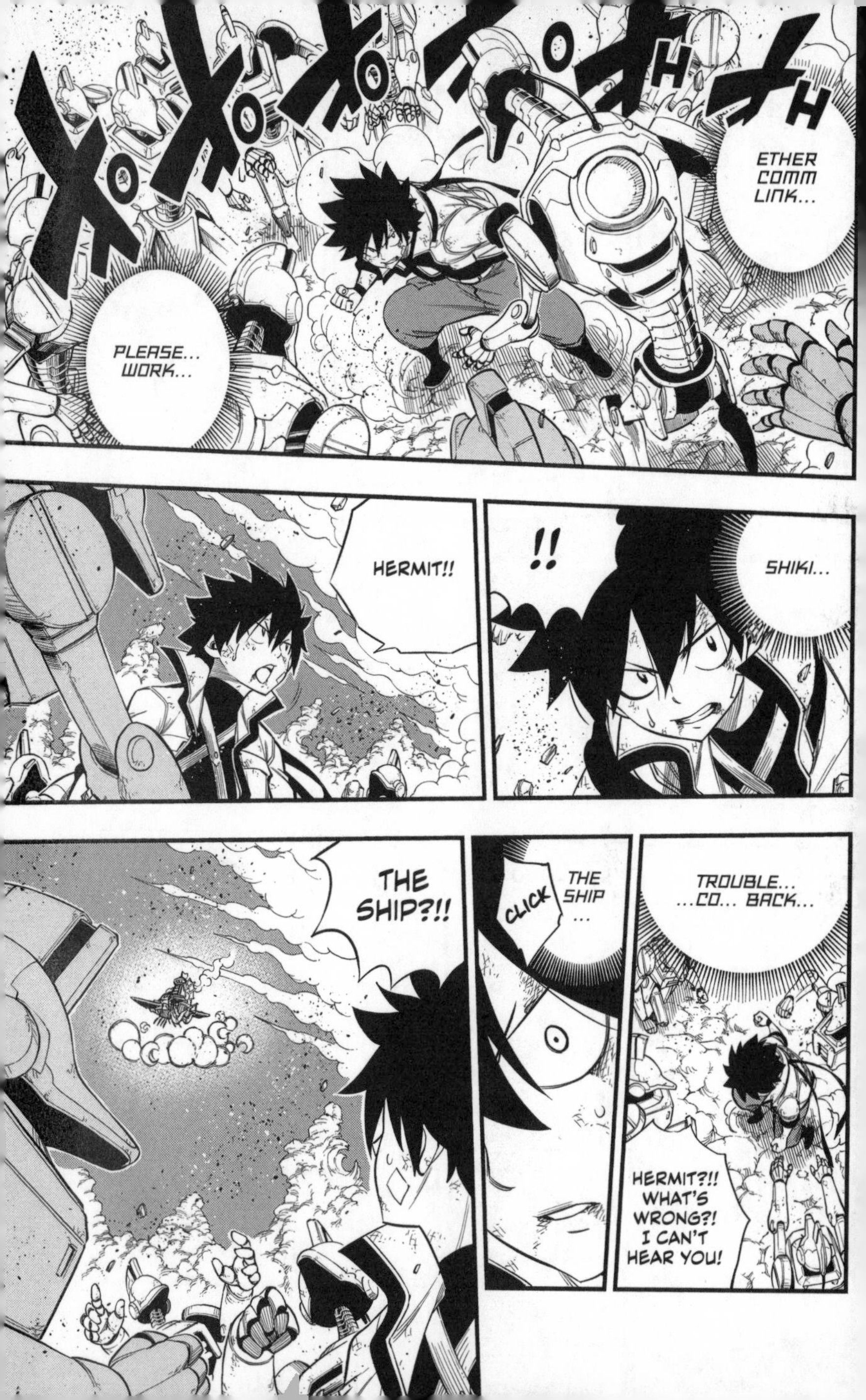
ETHER COMM LINK...
PLEASE... WORK...
SHIKI...
!!
HERMIT!!
TROUBLE... ...CO... BACK...
HERMIT?!! WHAT'S WRONG?! I CAN'T HEAR YOU!
THE SHIP ...
CLICK
THE SHIP?!!

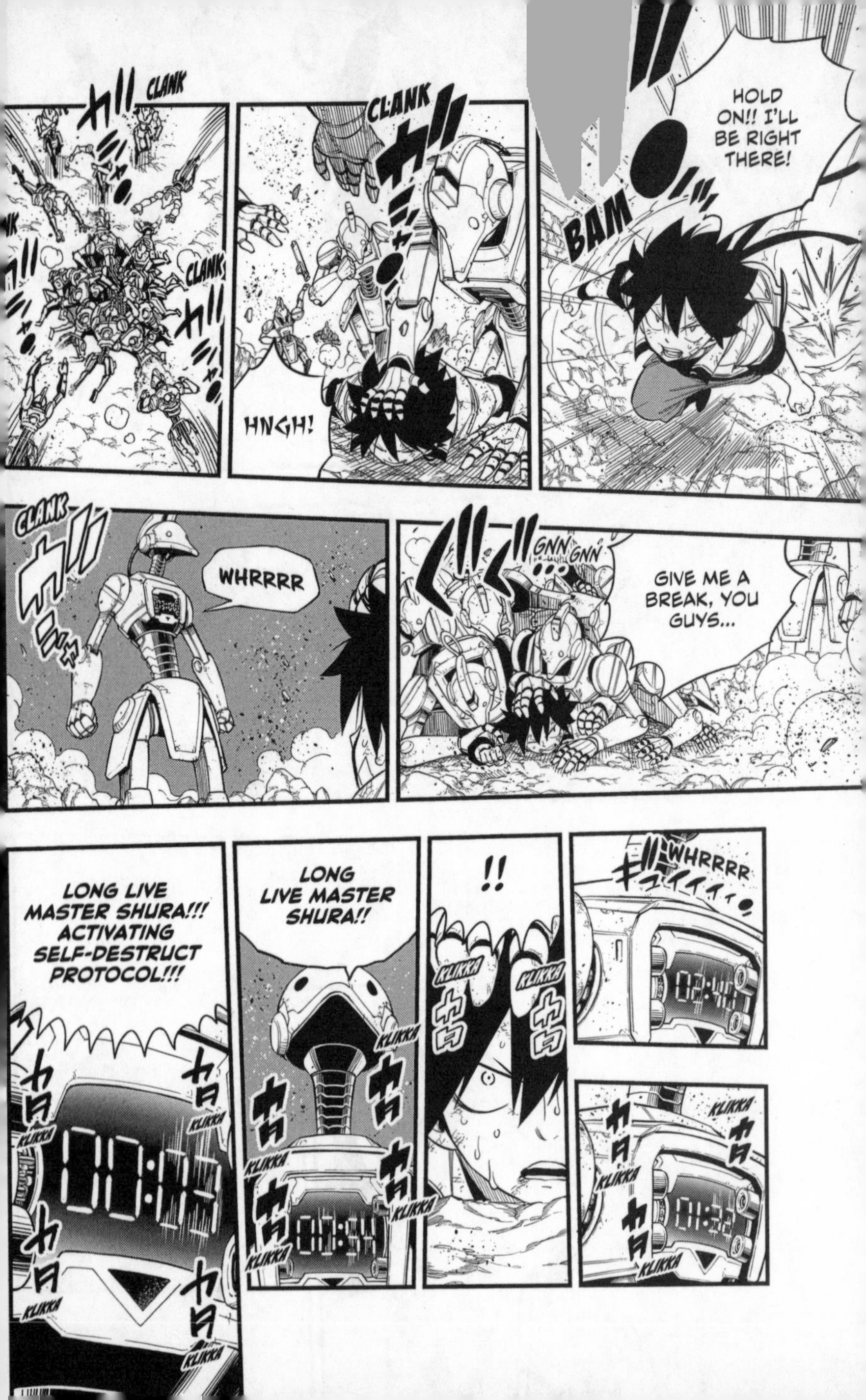
HOLD ON!! I'LL BE RIGHT THERE!
BAM
CLANK
HNGH!
CLANK
CLANK
GNN GNN
GIVE ME A BREAK, YOU GUYS...
CLANK
WHRRRR
WHRRRR
KLIKKA
KLIKKA
KLIKKA
!!
KLIKKA
KLIKKA
LONG LIVE MASTER SHURA!!
KLIKKA
KLIKKA
KLIKKA
KLIKKA
LONG LIVE MASTER SHURA!!! ACTIVATING SELF-DESTRUCT PROTOCOL!!!
KLIKKA
KLIKKA
KLIKKA
KLIKKA

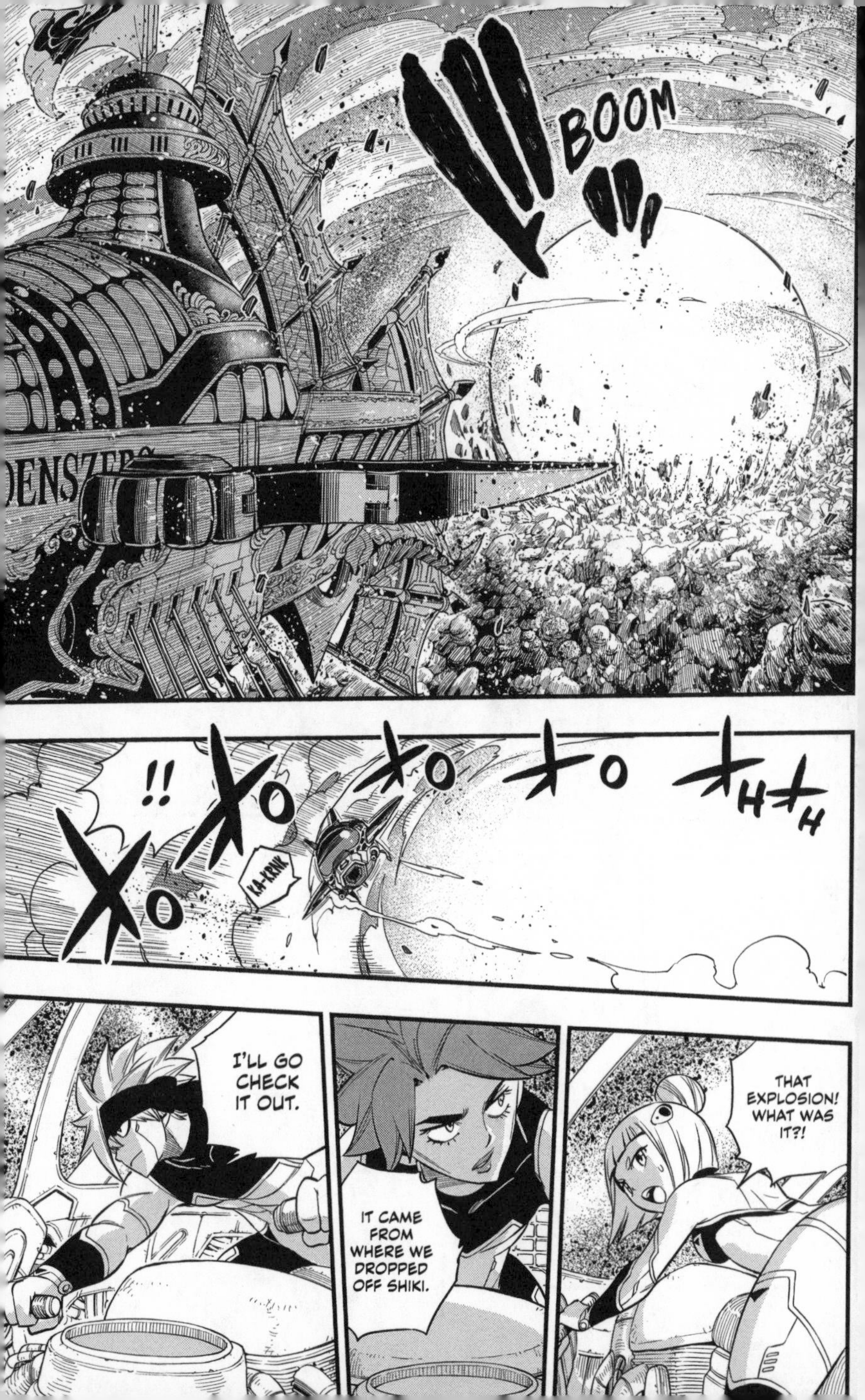
BOOM
!!
KA-KRNK
THAT EXPLOSION! WHAT WAS IT?!
IT CAME FROM WHERE WE DROPPED OFF SHIKI.
I'LL GO CHECK IT OUT.

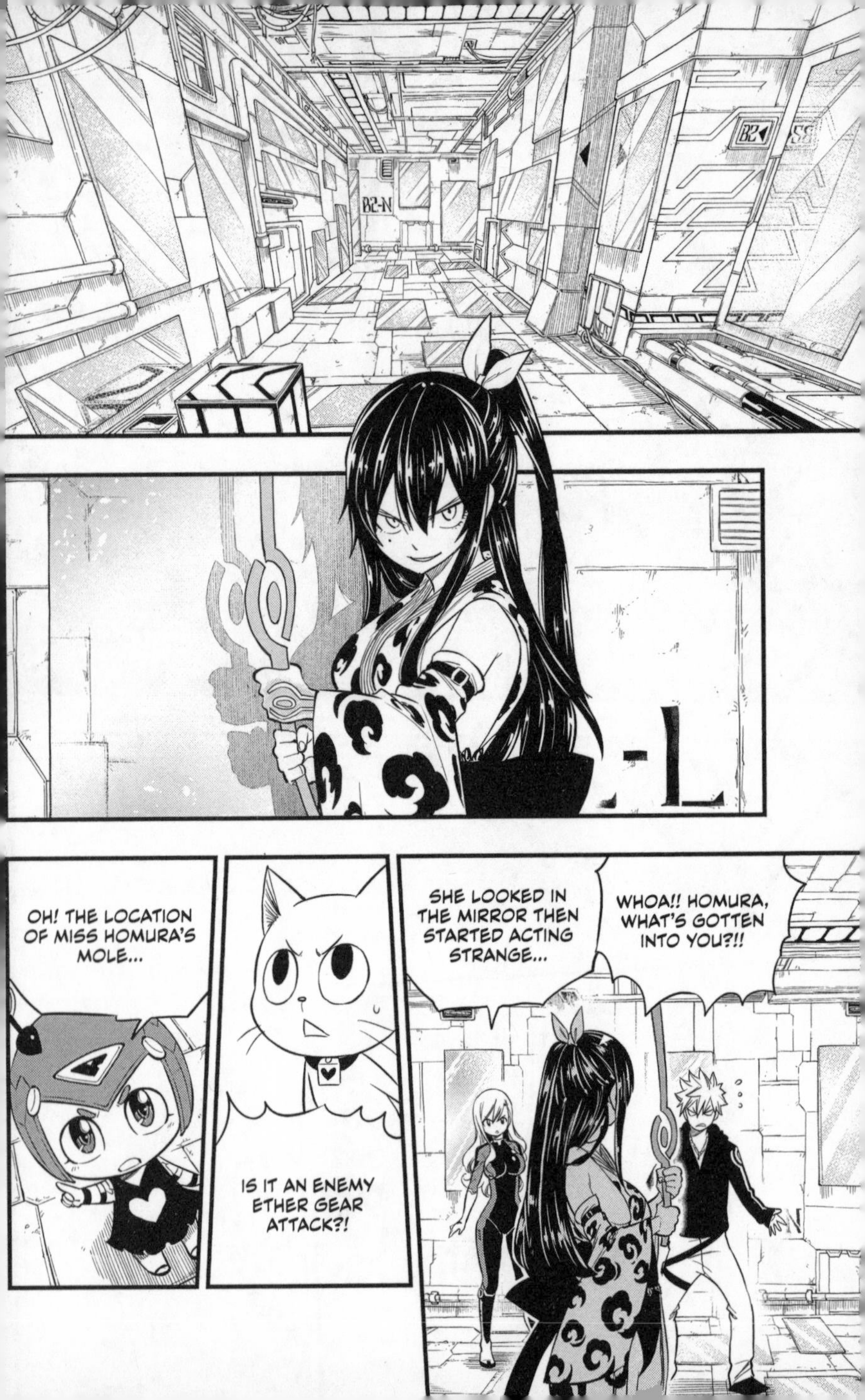
B2
B2-N
WHOA!! HOMURA, WHAT'S GOTTEN INTO YOU?!!
SHE LOOKED IN THE MIRROR THEN STARTED ACTING STRANGE...
IS IT AN ENEMY ETHER GEAR ATTACK?!
OH! THE LOCATION OF MISS HOMURA'S MOLE...

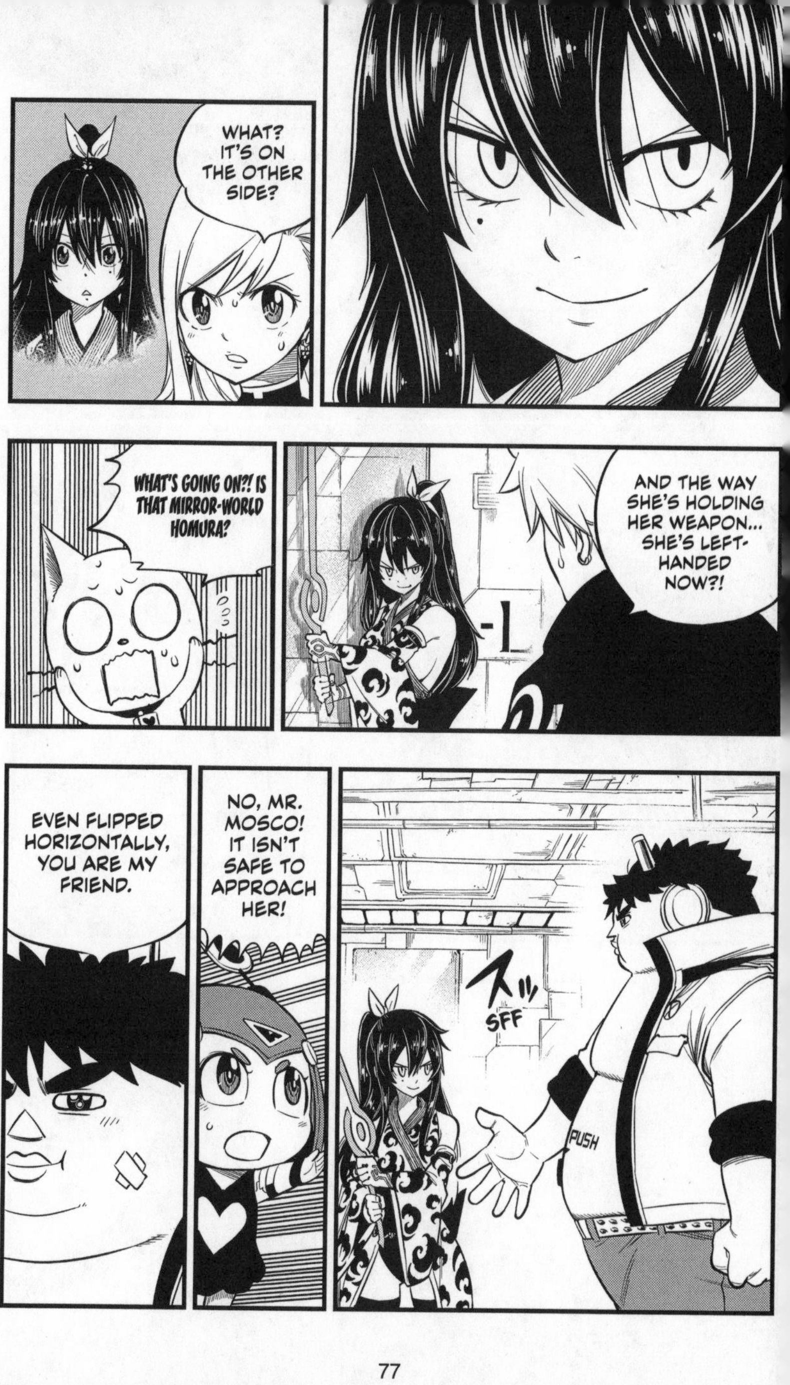
WHAT? IT'S ON THE OTHER SIDE?
AND THE WAY SHE'S HOLDING HER WEAPON... SHE'S LEFT-HANDED NOW?!
WHAT'S GOING ON?! IS THAT MIRROR-WORLD HOMURA?
SFF
PUSH
NO, MR. MOSCO! IT ISN'T SAFE TO APPROACH HER!
EVEN FLIPPED HORIZONTALLY, YOU ARE MY FRIEND.

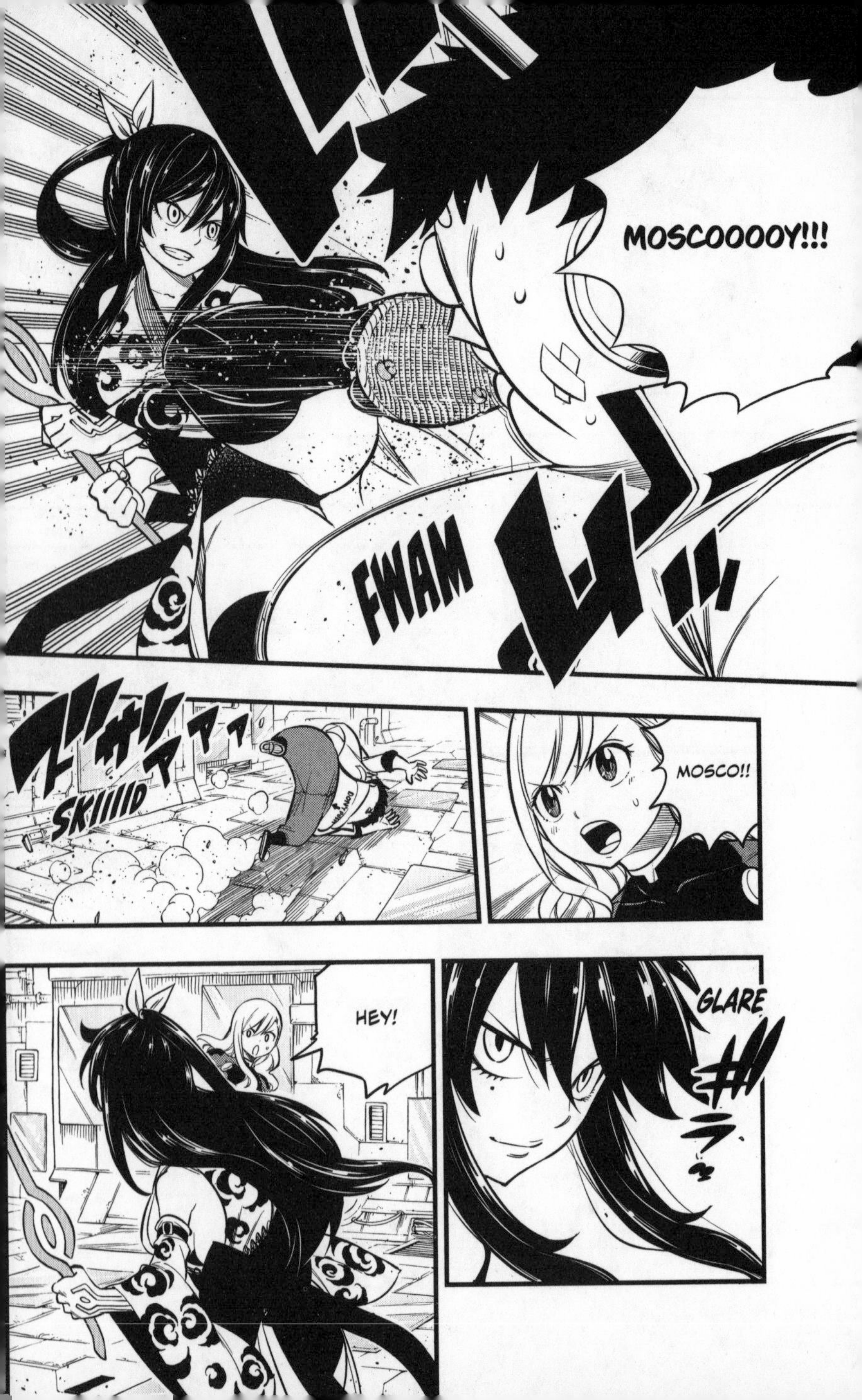
MOSCOOOOY!!!
FWAM
MOSCO!!
SKIIIID
GLARE
HEY!

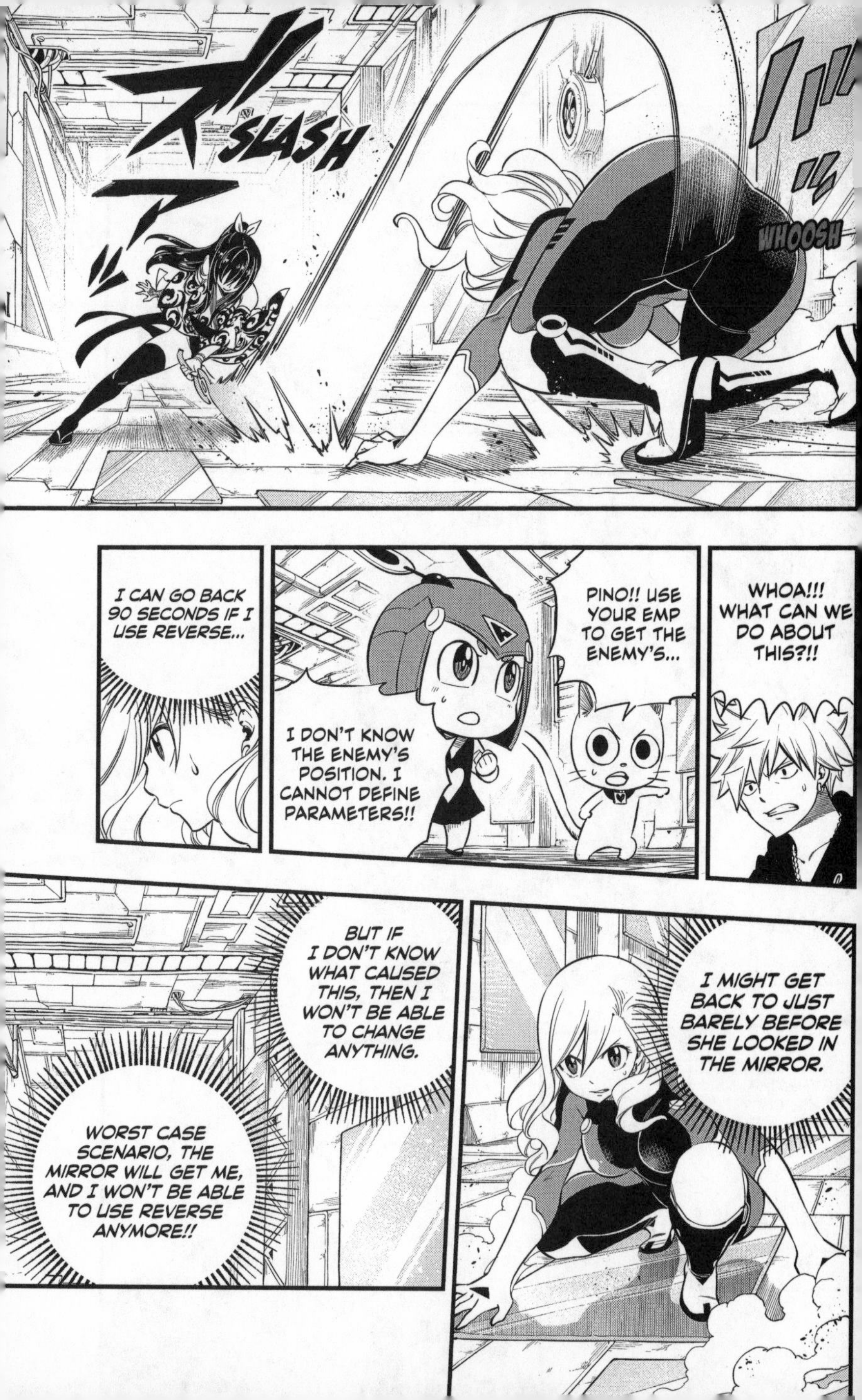
WHOOSH
SLASH
WHOA!!! WHAT CAN WE DO ABOUT THIS?!!
PINO!! USE YOUR EMP TO GET THE ENEMY'S...
I DON'T KNOW THE ENEMY'S POSITION. I CANNOT DEFINE PARAMETERS!!
I CAN GO BACK 90 SECONDS IF I USE REVERSE...
I MIGHT GET BACK TO JUST BARELY BEFORE SHE LOOKED IN THE MIRROR.
BUT IF I DON'T KNOW WHAT CAUSED THIS, THEN I WON'T BE ABLE TO CHANGE ANYTHING.
WORST CASE SCENARIO, THE MIRROR WILL GET ME, AND I WON'T BE ABLE TO USE REVERSE ANYMORE!!

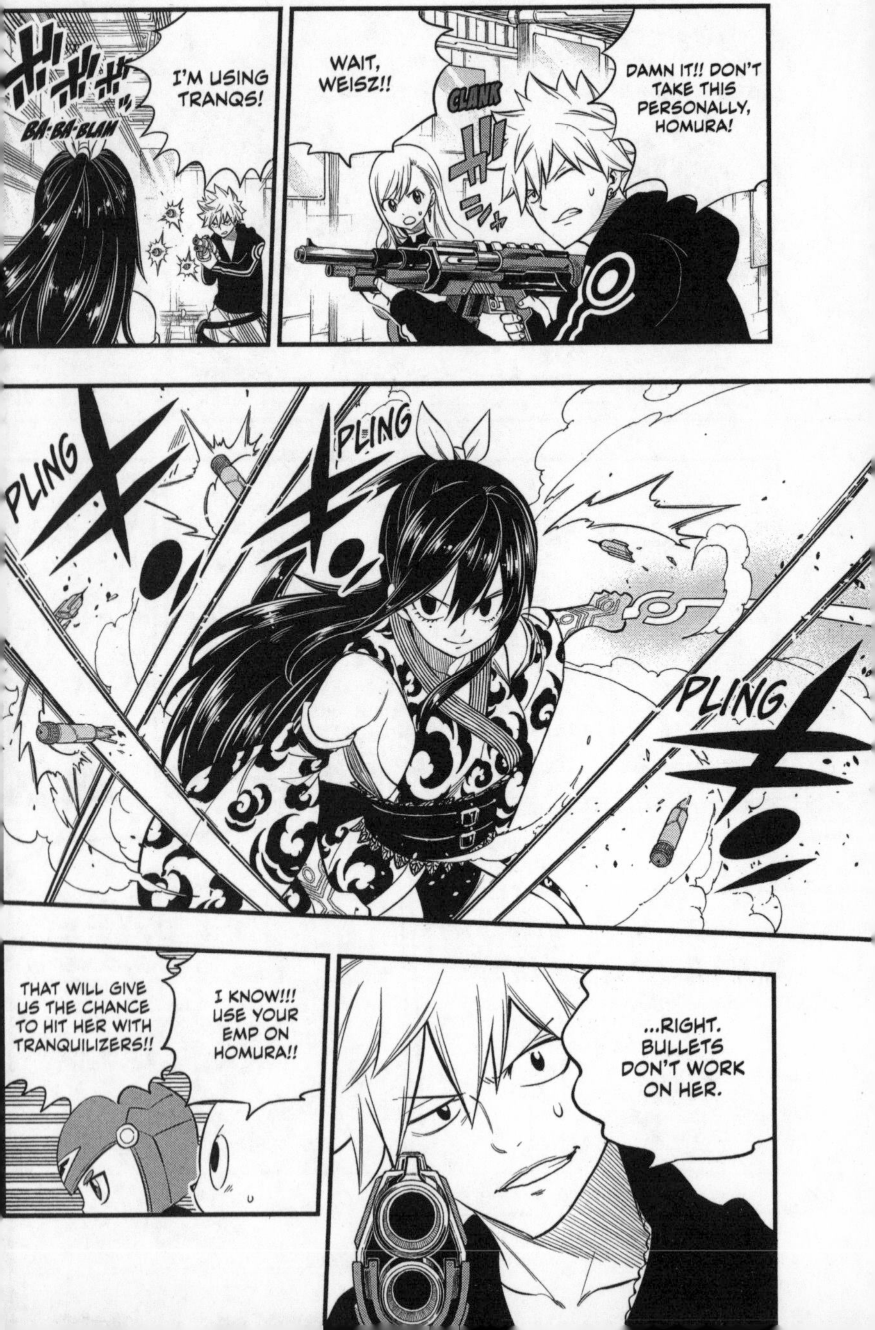
DAMN IT!! DON'T TAKE THIS PERSONALLY, HOMURA!
CLANK
WAIT, WEISZ!!
I'M USING TRANQS!
BA-BA-BLAM
PLING
PLING
PLING
...RIGHT. BULLETS DON'T WORK ON HER.
I KNOW!!! USE YOUR EMP ON HOMURA!!
THAT WILL GIVE US THE CHANCE TO HIT HER WITH TRANQUILIZERS!!

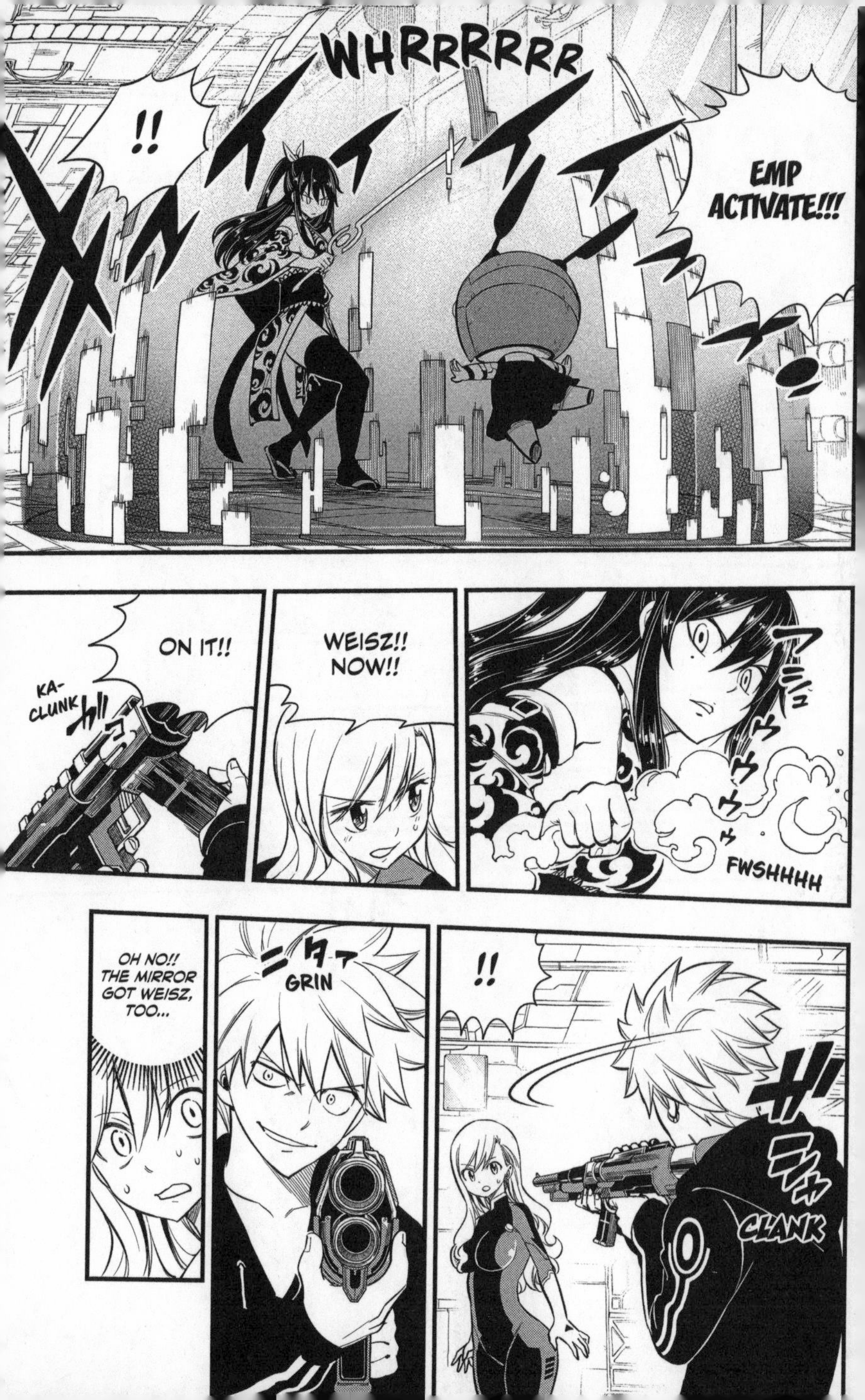
EMP ACTIVATE!!!
WHRRRRRRR
!!
FWSHHHH
WEISZ!! NOW!!
ON IT!!
KA-CLUNK
!!
CLANK
GRIN
OH NO!! THE MIRROR GOT WEISZ, TOO...

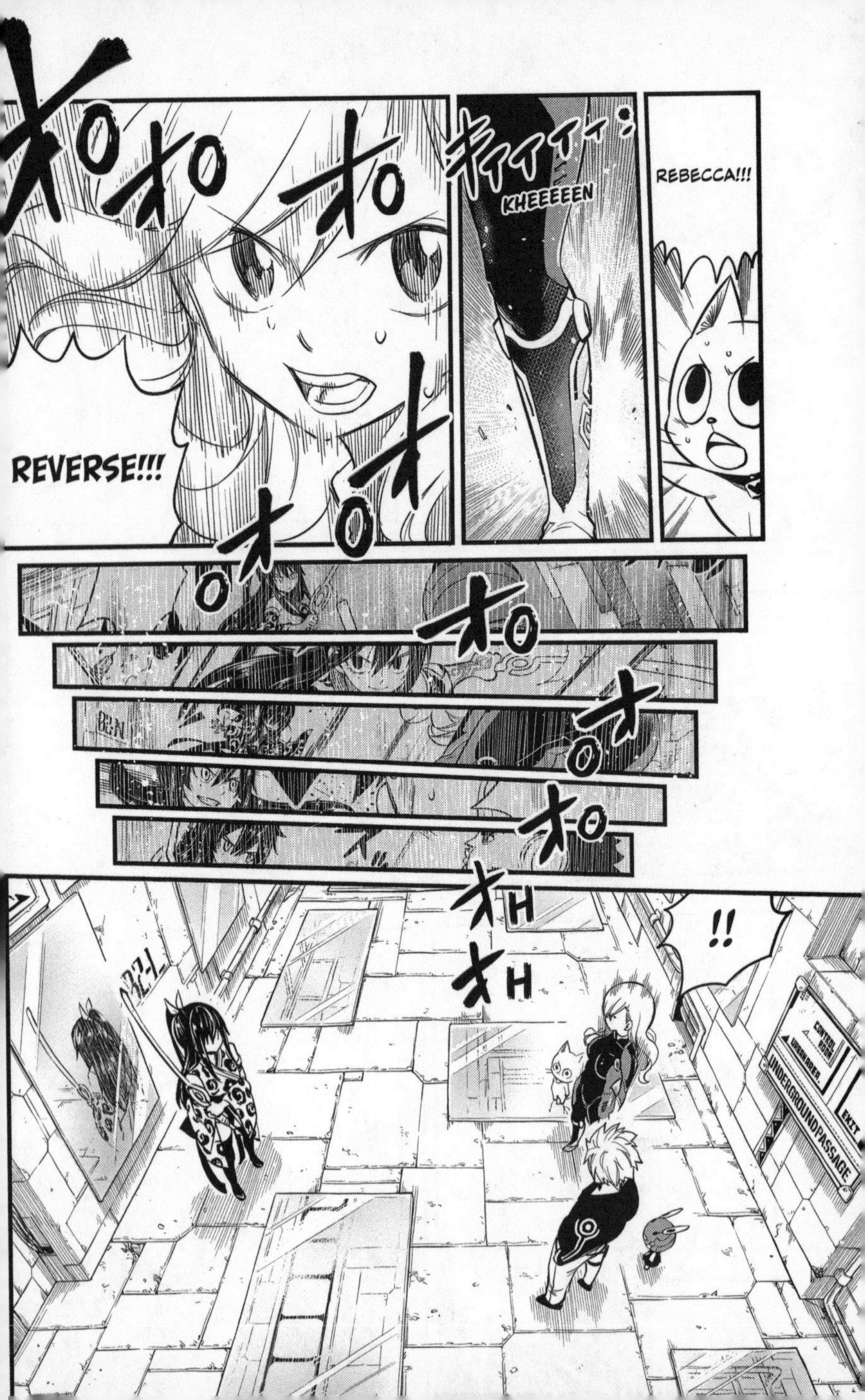
REBECCA!!!
KHEEEEEN
REVERSE!!!
!!
UNDERGROUNDPASSAGE
EXIT

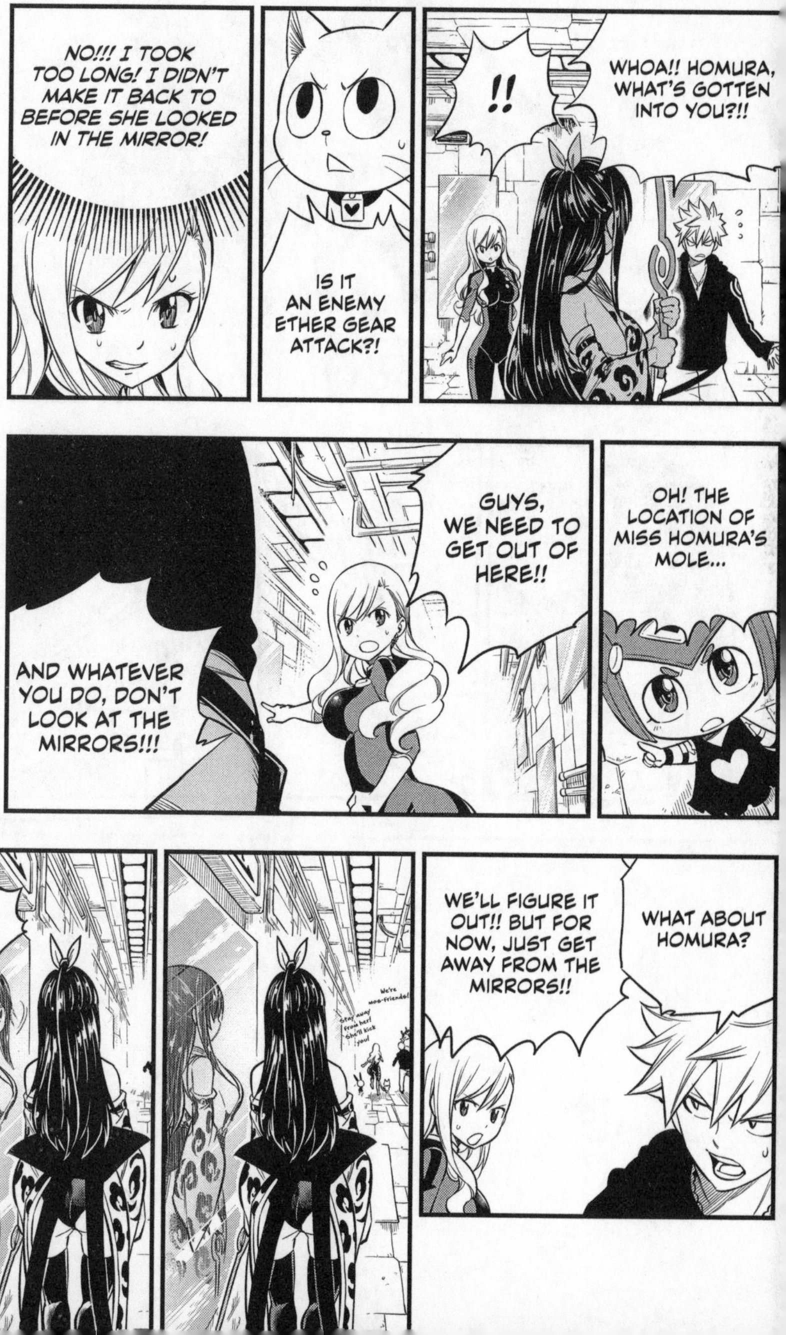
WHOA!! HOMURA, WHAT'S GOTTEN INTO YOU?!!
!!
IS IT AN ENEMY ETHER GEAR ATTACK?!
NO!!! I TOOK TOO LONG! I DIDN'T MAKE IT BACK TO BEFORE SHE LOOKED IN THE MIRROR!
OH! THE LOCATION OF MISS HOMURA'S MOLE...
GUYS, WE NEED TO GET OUT OF HERE!!
AND WHATEVER YOU DO, DON'T LOOK AT THE MIRRORS!!!
WHAT ABOUT HOMURA?
WE'LL FIGURE IT OUT!! BUT FOR NOW, JUST GET AWAY FROM THE MIRRORS!!
We're moo-friends!
Stay away from her! She'll kick you!
!!

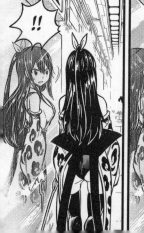

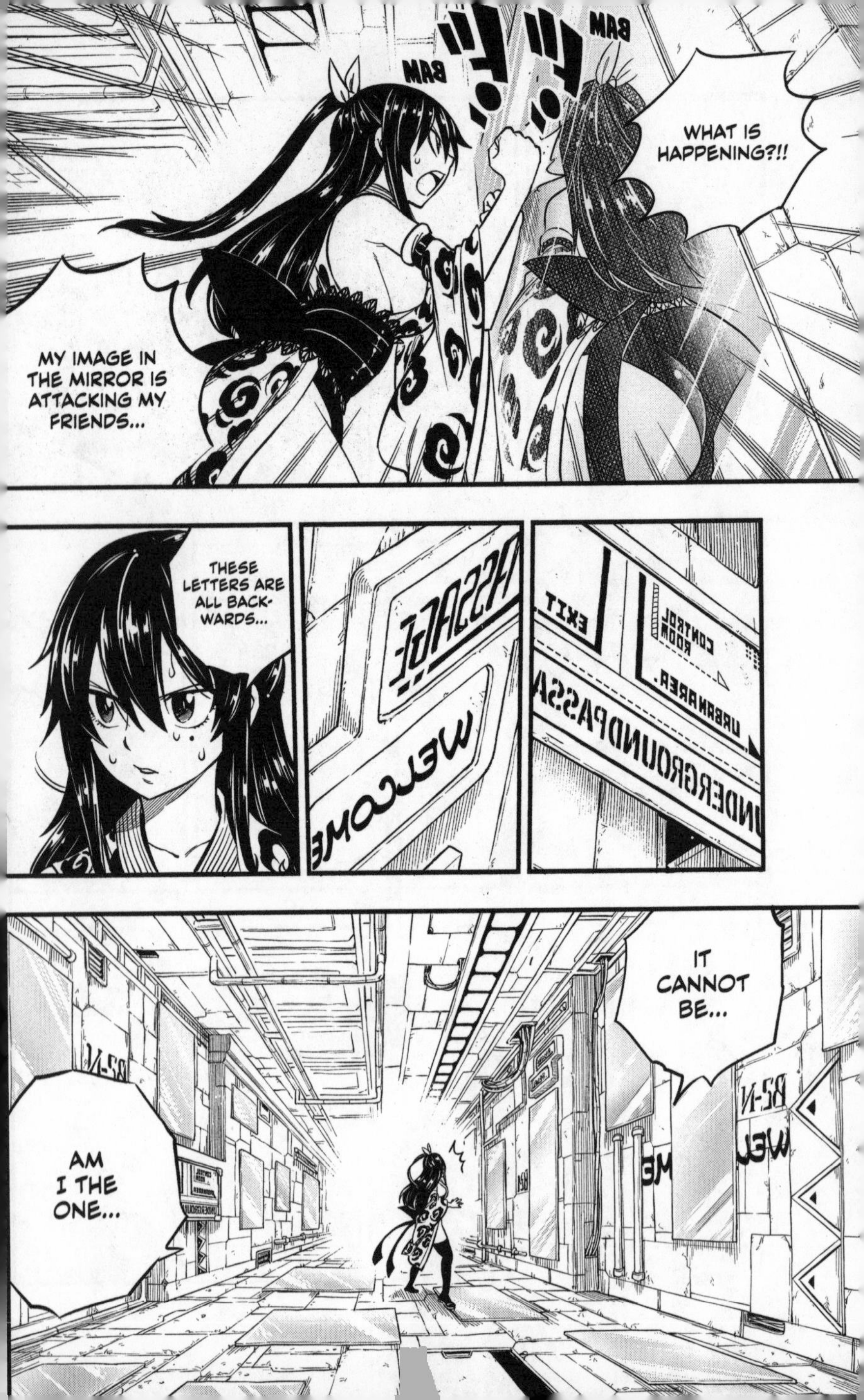
BAM
BAM
WHAT IS HAPPENING?!!
MY IMAGE IN THE MIRROR IS ATTACKING MY FRIENDS...
THESE LETTERS ARE ALL BACK-WARDS...
IT CANNOT BE...
AM I THE ONE...

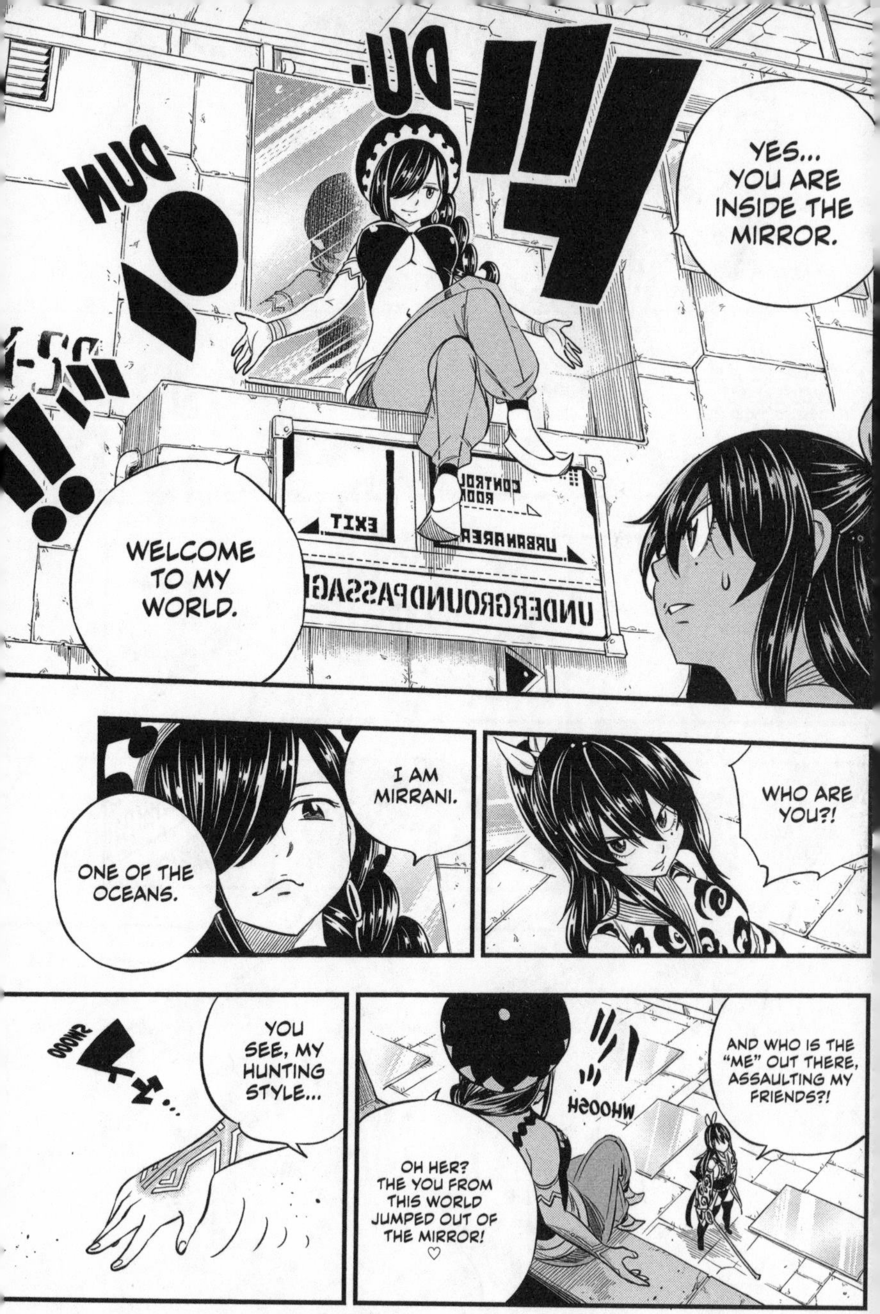

YES... YOU ARE INSIDE THE MIRROR.
WELCOME TO MY WORLD.
WHO ARE YOU?!
I AM MIRRANI.
ONE OF THE OCEANS.
AND WHO IS THE "ME" OUT THERE, ASSAULTING MY FRIENDS?!
WHOOSH
OH HER? THE YOU FROM THIS WORLD JUMPED OUT OF THE MIRROR! ♡
YOU SEE, MY HUNTING STYLE...

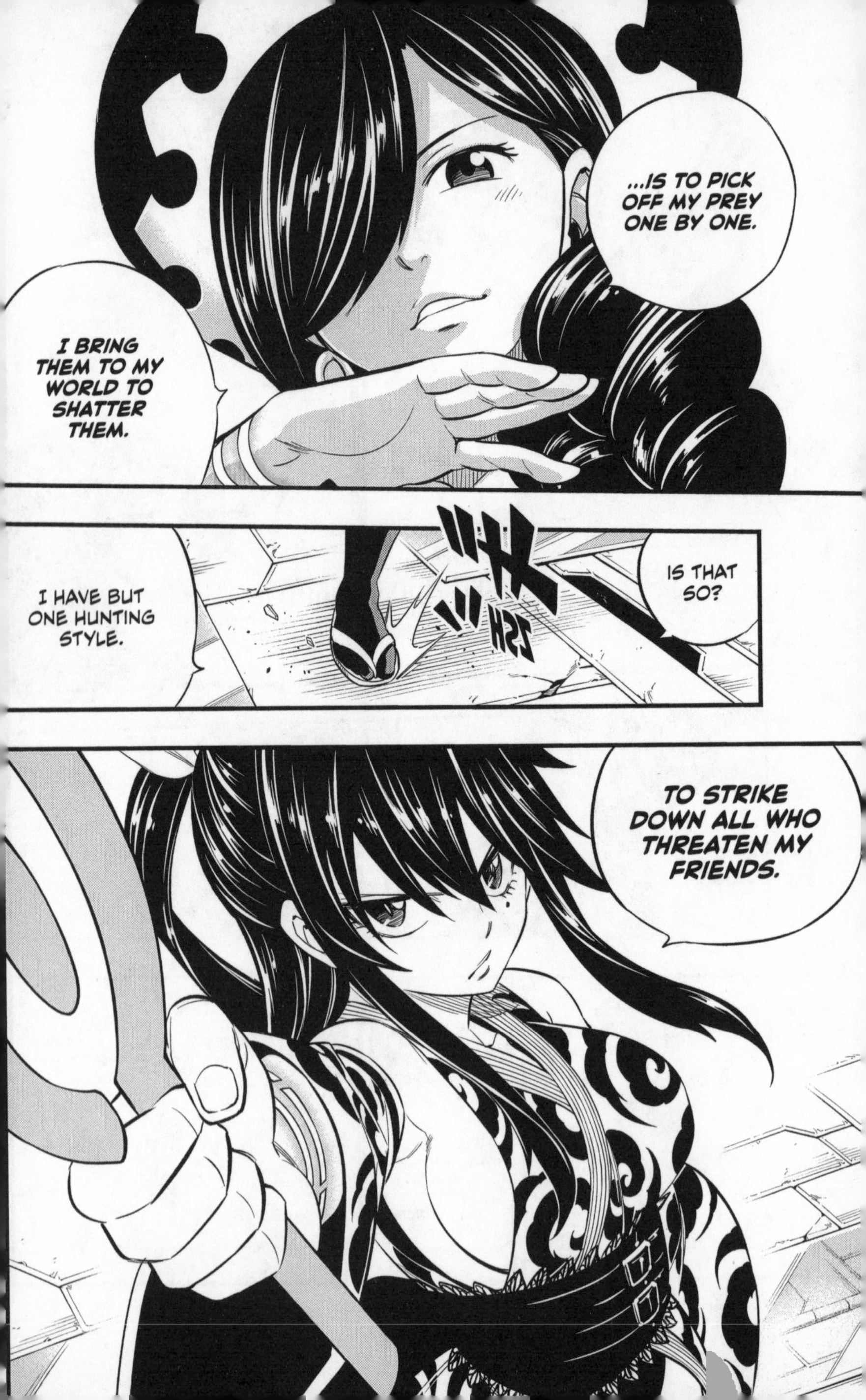

...IS TO PICK OFF MY PREY ONE BY ONE.
I BRING THEM TO MY WORLD TO SHATTER THEM.
IS THAT SO?
ZSH
I HAVE BUT ONE HUNTING STYLE.
TO STRIKE DOWN ALL WHO THREATEN MY FRIENDS.

EDENSZERO

Edens Zero
In-Depth Character File 13

PINO'S ANALYSIS

Name: Kleene Rutherford
Powers: Wind Ether Gear
(Wind Snatch)
Likes: Her brother,
anything cute
Dislikes: Spam messages

Attack: ☆☆☆
Defense: ☆☆☆☆☆
Marksmanship: ☆☆☆
Ether Power: ☆☆
Intelligence: ☆☆
Loves Her Brother: ☆☆☆☆☆

Memo

She was originally one of Drakken's
Element 4, but a spirit of friendship
sprouted after her intense battle
against Homura. She had lost her
emotions because of some trauma in
her past, but Miss Sister helped her
get them back. The way she talks...
it is very cute!

CHAPTER 145: HOMURA VS. MIRRANI

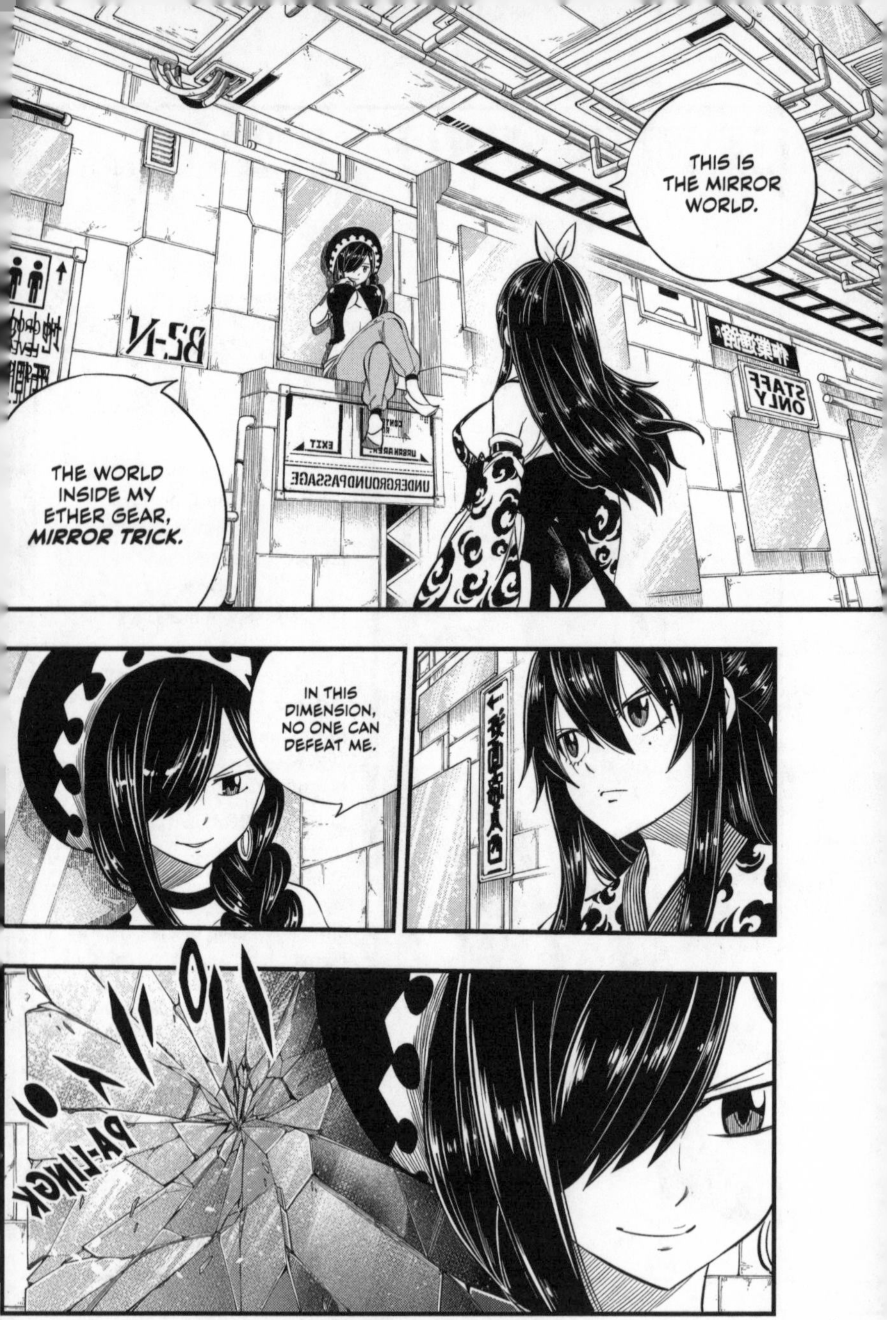
THIS IS THE MIRROR WORLD.
THE WORLD INSIDE MY ETHER GEAR, ***MIRROR TRICK.***
IN THIS DIMENSION, NO ONE CAN DEFEAT ME.
PA-LINGK

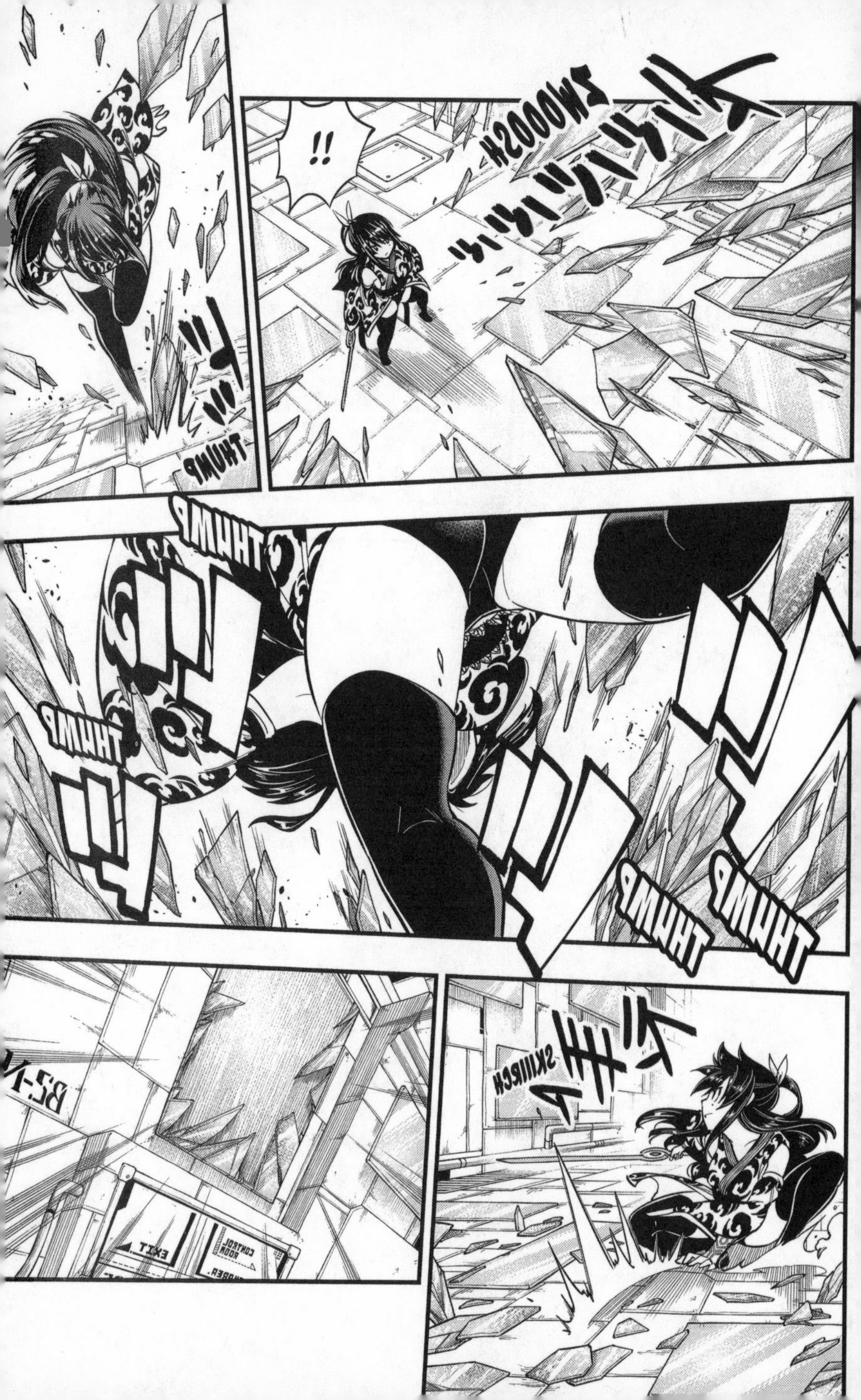
ZWOOOSH
!!
THUMP
THUMP
THUMP
THUMP
THUMP
SKIIIRCH
B2-1
CONTROL ROOM
EXIT

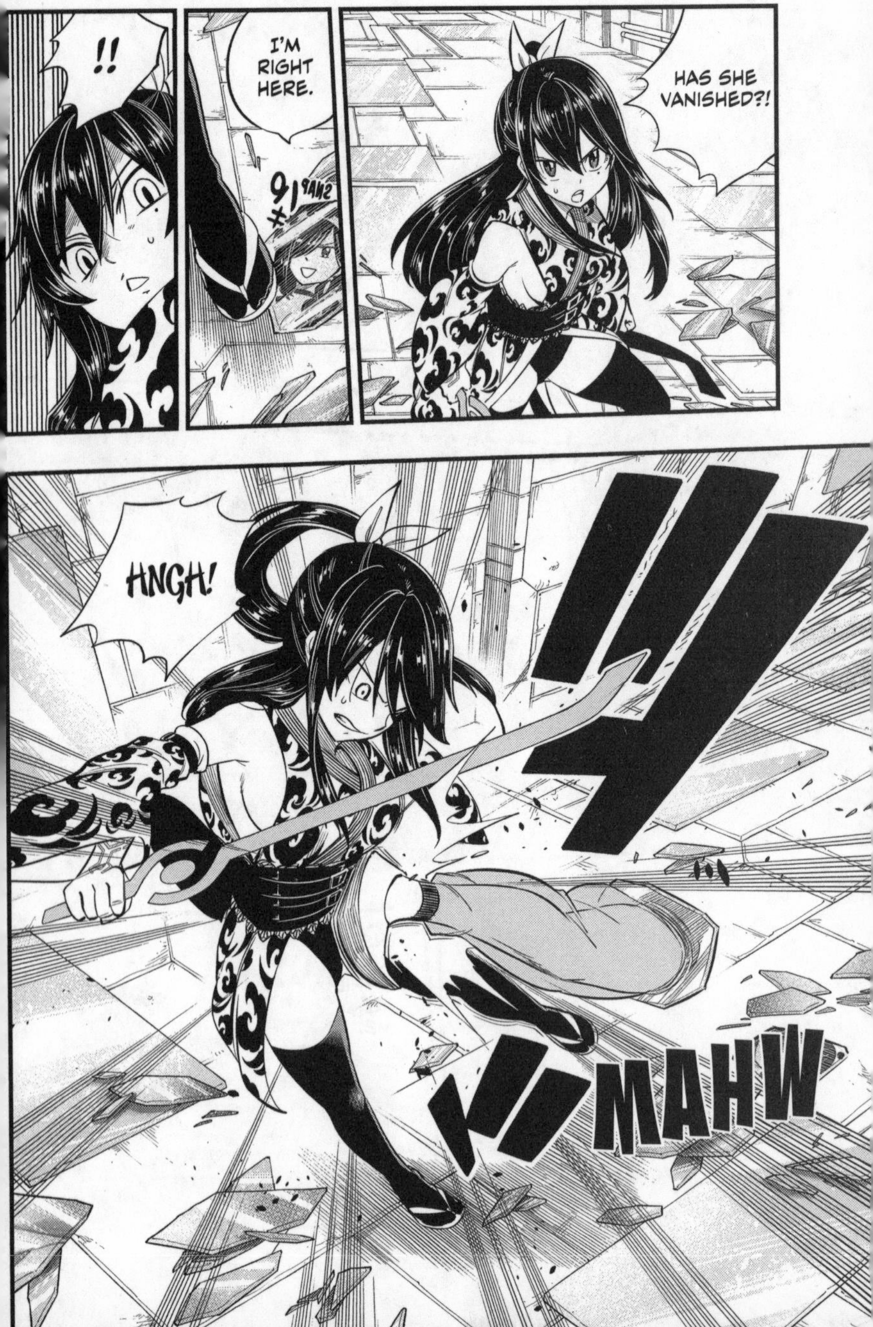
HAS SHE VANISHED?!
I'M RIGHT HERE.
SNAP
!!
HNGH!
MAHW

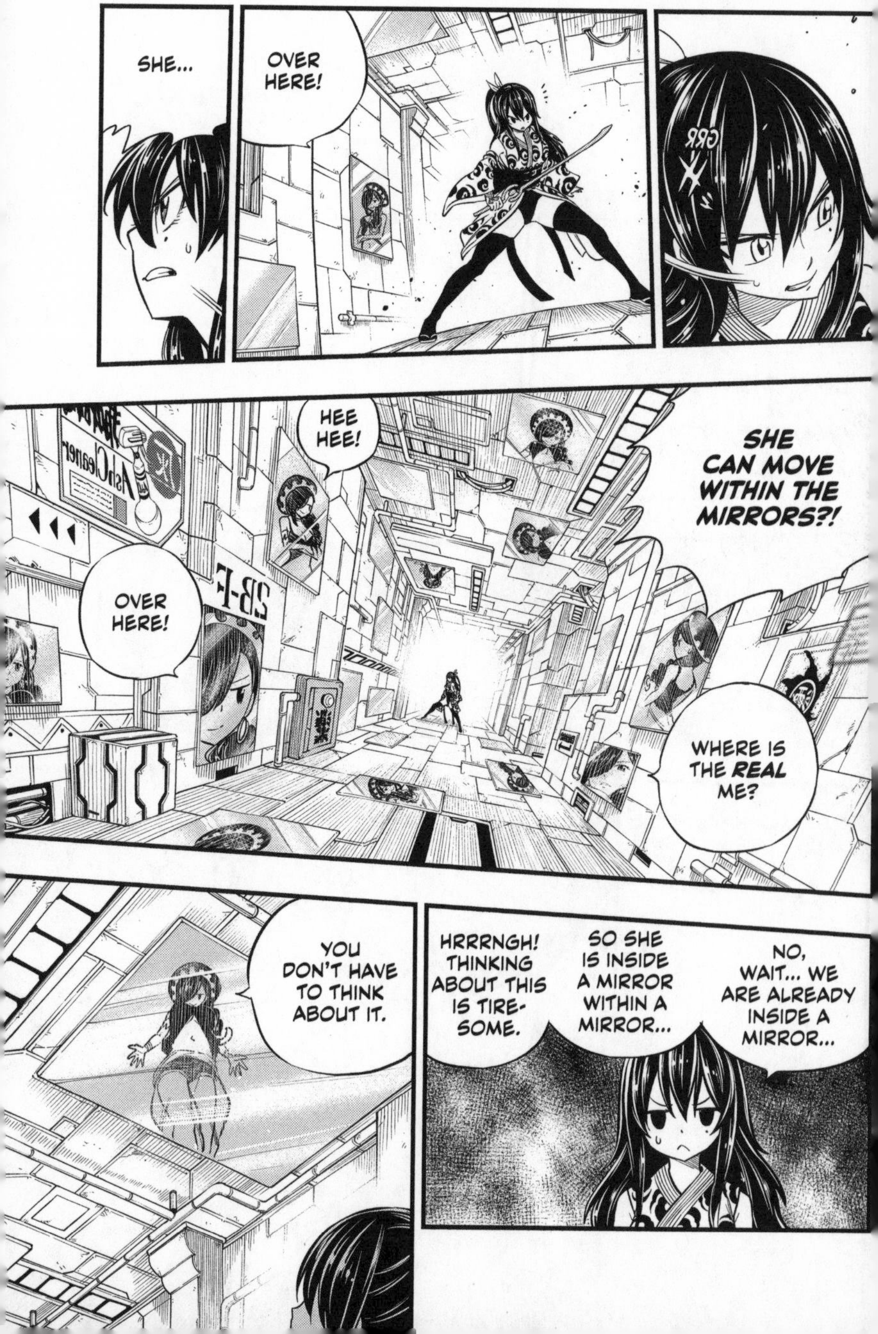
GRR
OVER HERE!
SHE...
SHE CAN MOVE WITHIN THE MIRRORS?!
HEE HEE!
WHERE IS THE REAL ME?
OVER HERE!
NO, WAIT... WE ARE ALREADY INSIDE A MIRROR...
SO SHE IS INSIDE A MIRROR WITHIN A MIRROR...
HRRRNGH! THINKING ABOUT THIS IS TIRE-SOME.
YOU DON'T HAVE TO THINK ABOUT IT.

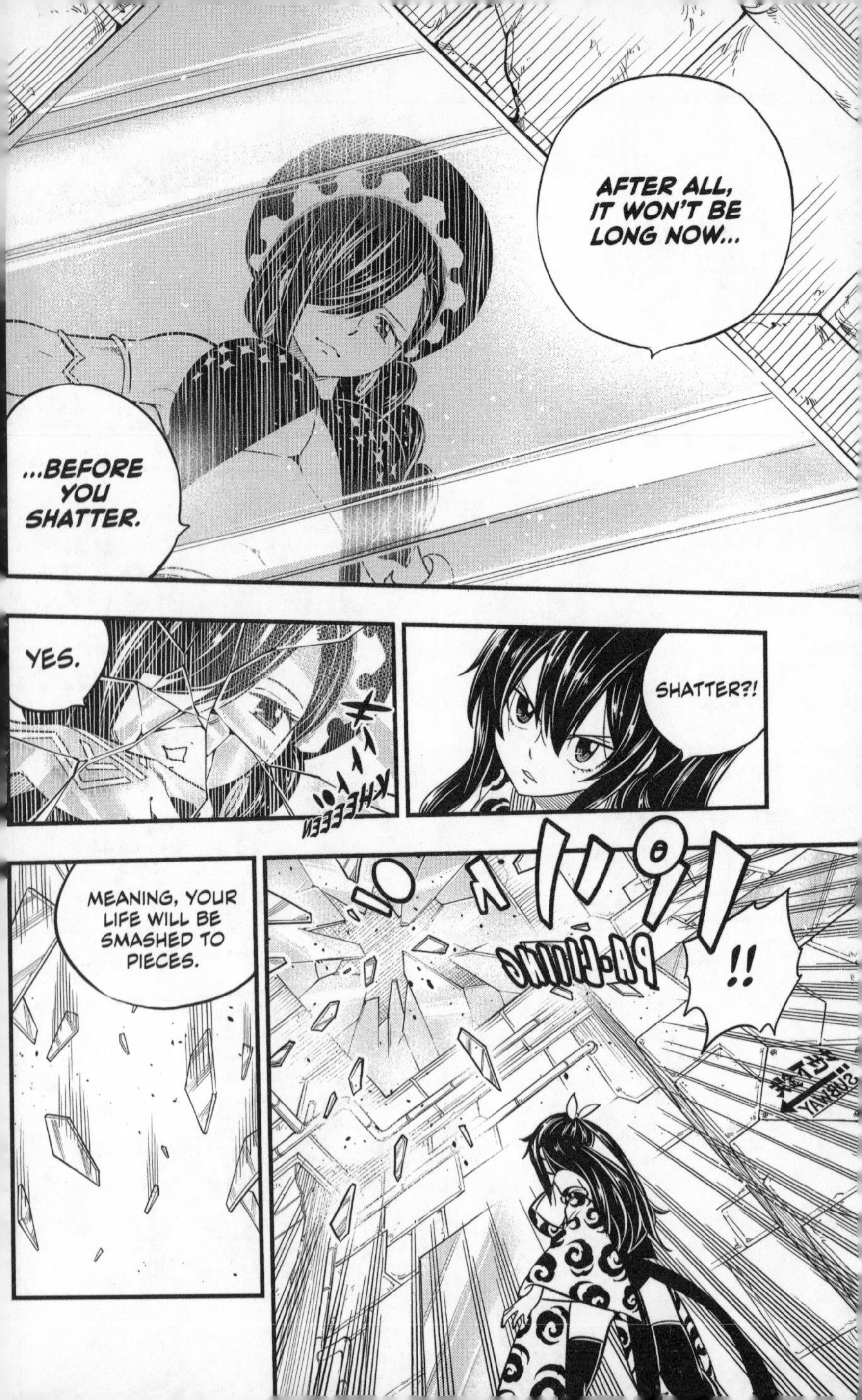
AFTER ALL, IT WON'T BE LONG NOW...
...BEFORE YOU SHATTER.
SHATTER?!
YES.
KHEEEEN
!!
PA-LIIING
SUBWAY
MEANING, YOUR LIFE WILL BE SMASHED TO PIECES.

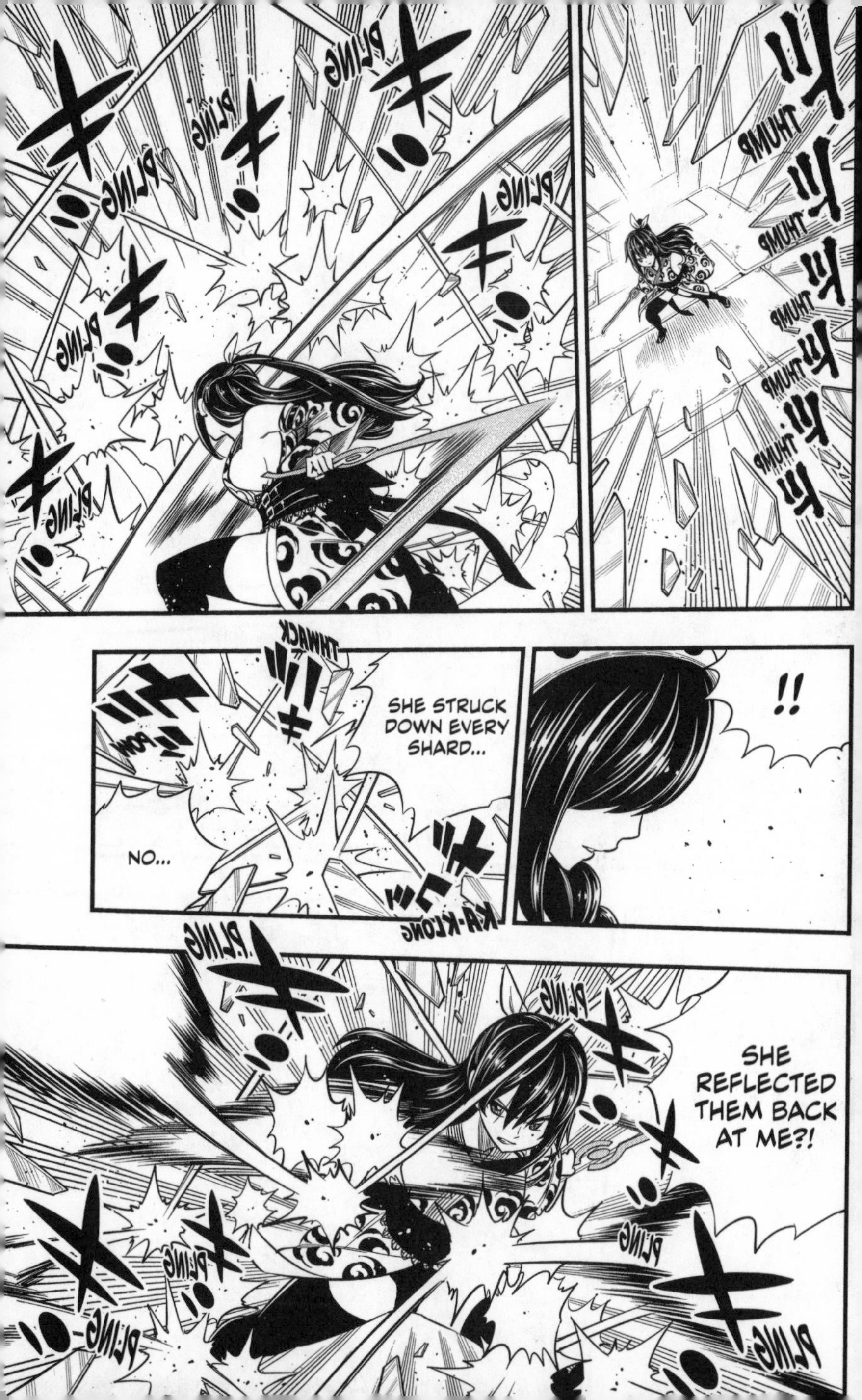
THUMP
THUMP
THUMP
THUMP
THUMP
THUMP
PLING
PLING
PLING
PLING
PLING
PLING
PLING
!!
THWACK
SHE STRUCK DOWN EVERY SHARD...
PON
NO...
KA-KLONG
SHE REFLECTED THEM BACK AT ME?!
PLING
PLING
PLING
PLING
PLING
PLING-

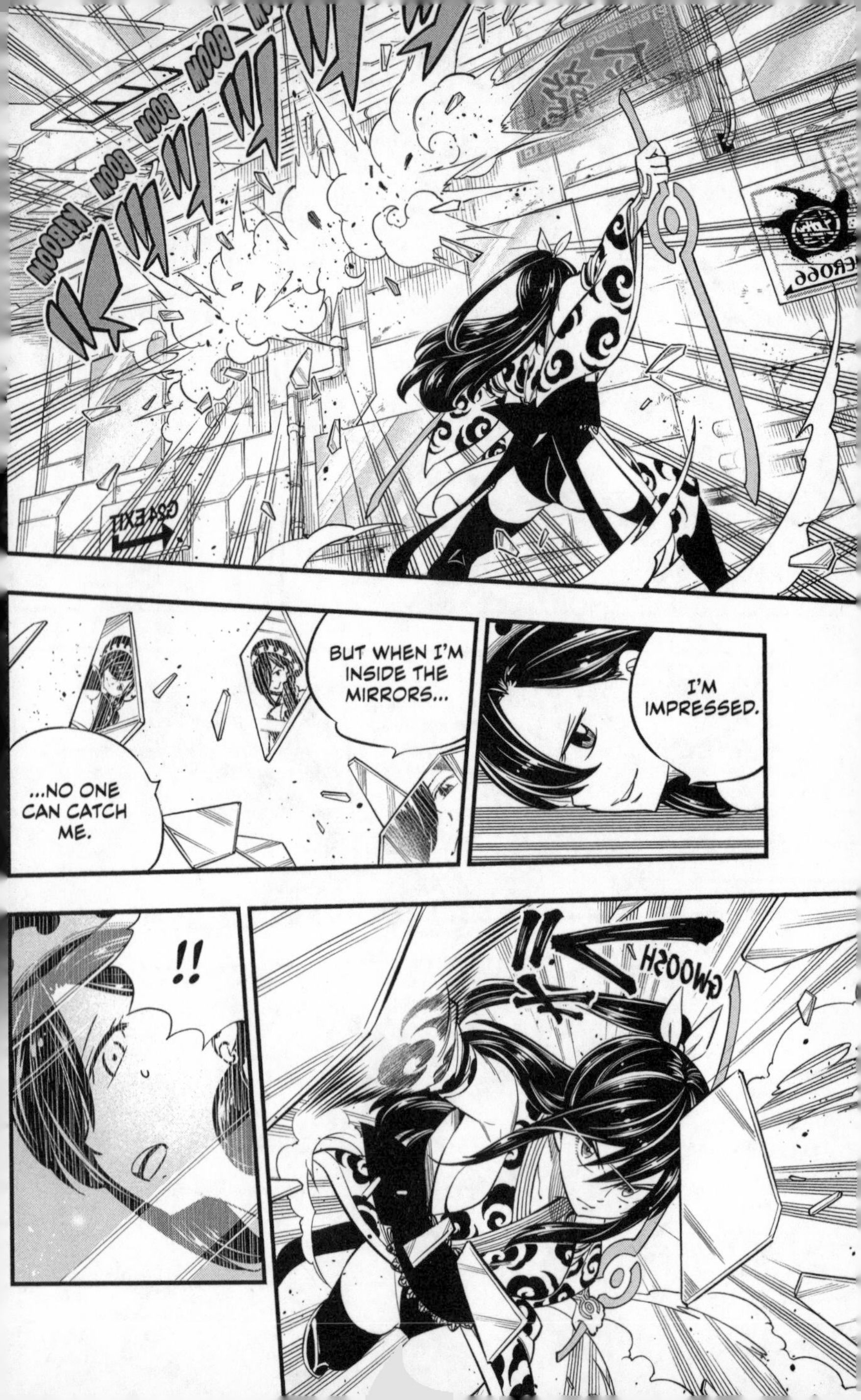
I'M IMPRESSED.
BUT WHEN I'M INSIDE THE MIRRORS...
...NO ONE CAN CATCH ME.
GWOOSH
!!

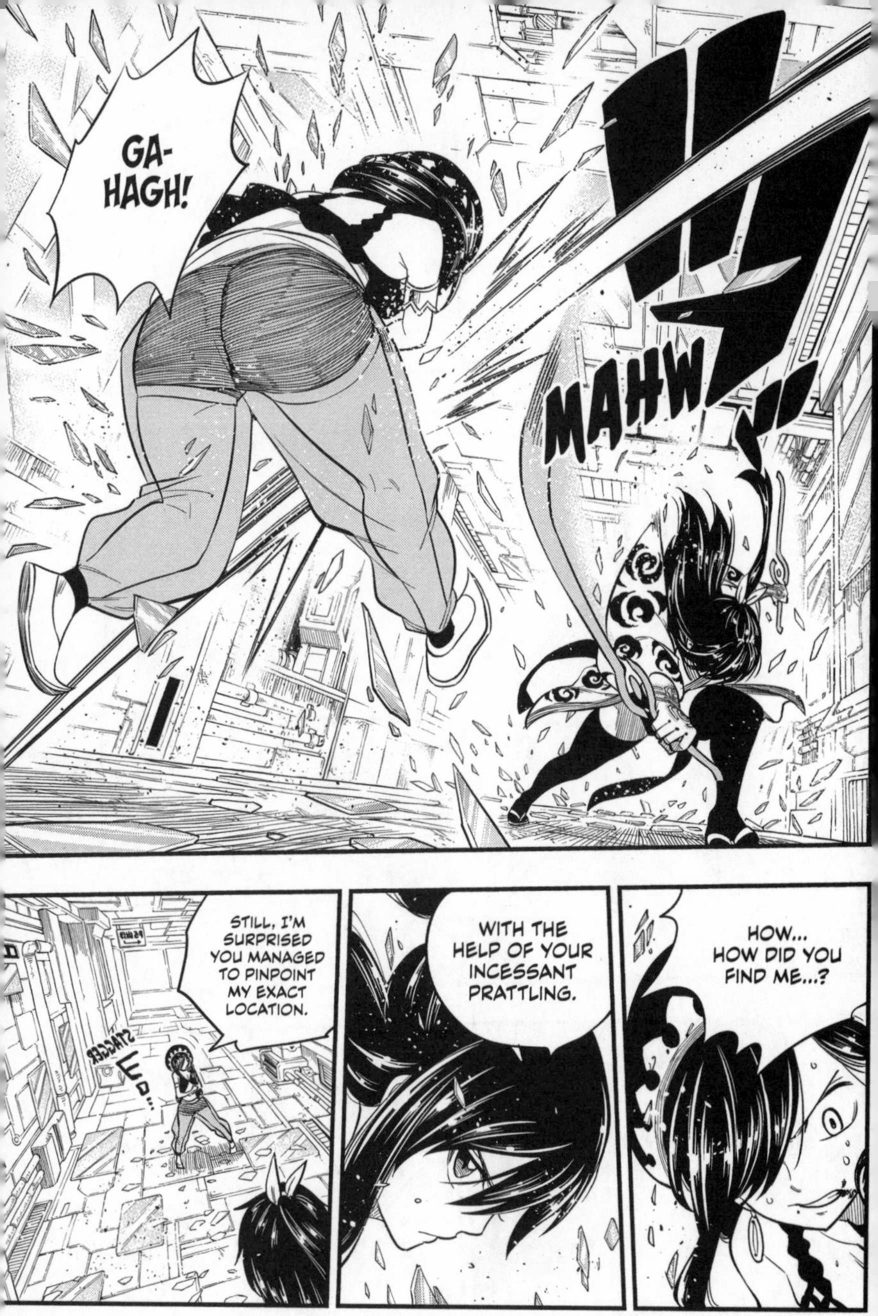
GA-HAGH!
MAHW...
HOW... HOW DID YOU FIND ME...?
WITH THE HELP OF YOUR INCESSANT PRATTLING.
STILL, I'M SURPRISED YOU MANAGED TO PINPOINT MY EXACT LOCATION.
STAGGER

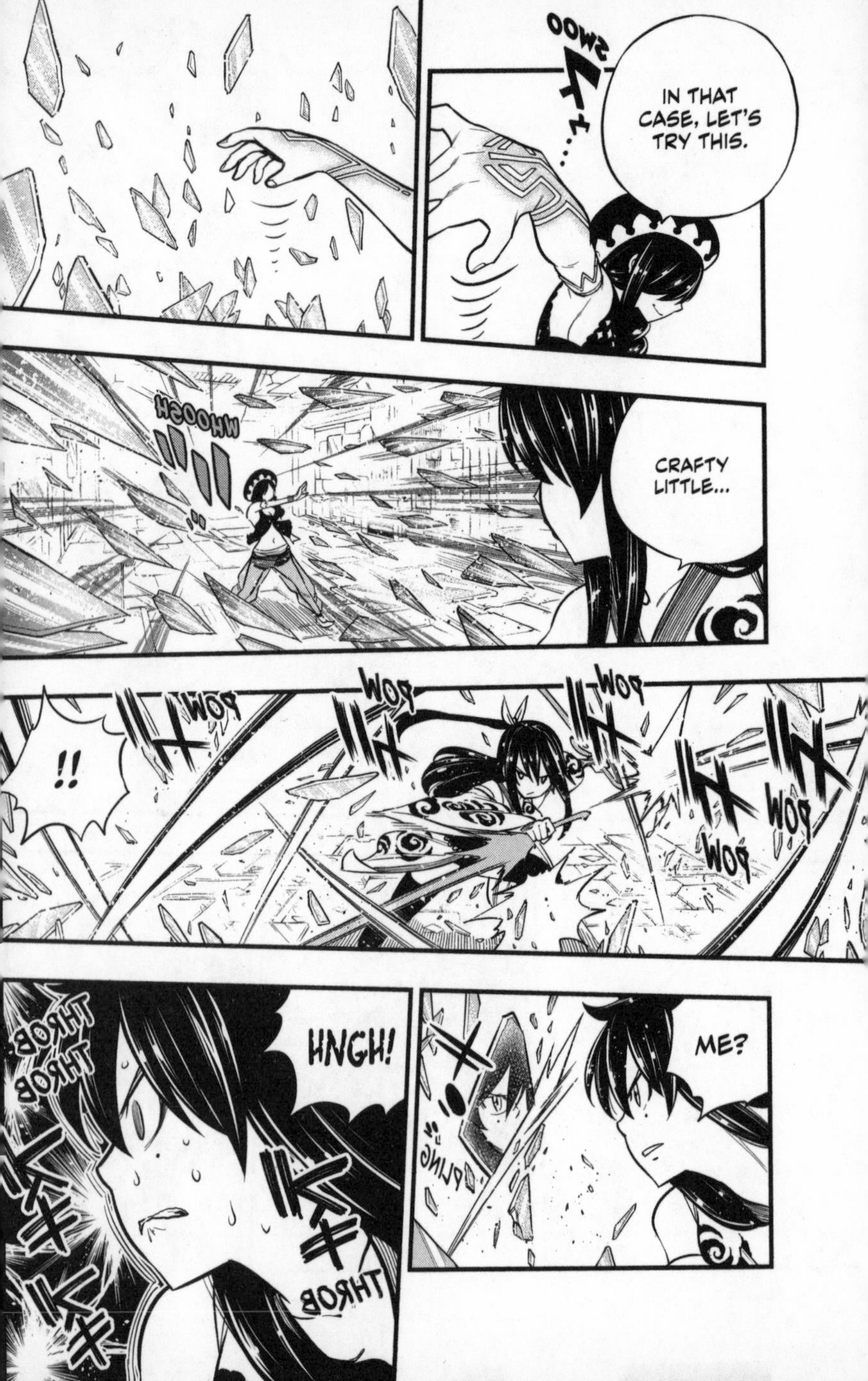
SWOO
IN THAT CASE, LET'S TRY THIS.
CRAFTY LITTLE...
WHOOSH
POW
POW
POW
POW
POW
!!
ME?
PLING
HNGH!
THROB THROB
THROB

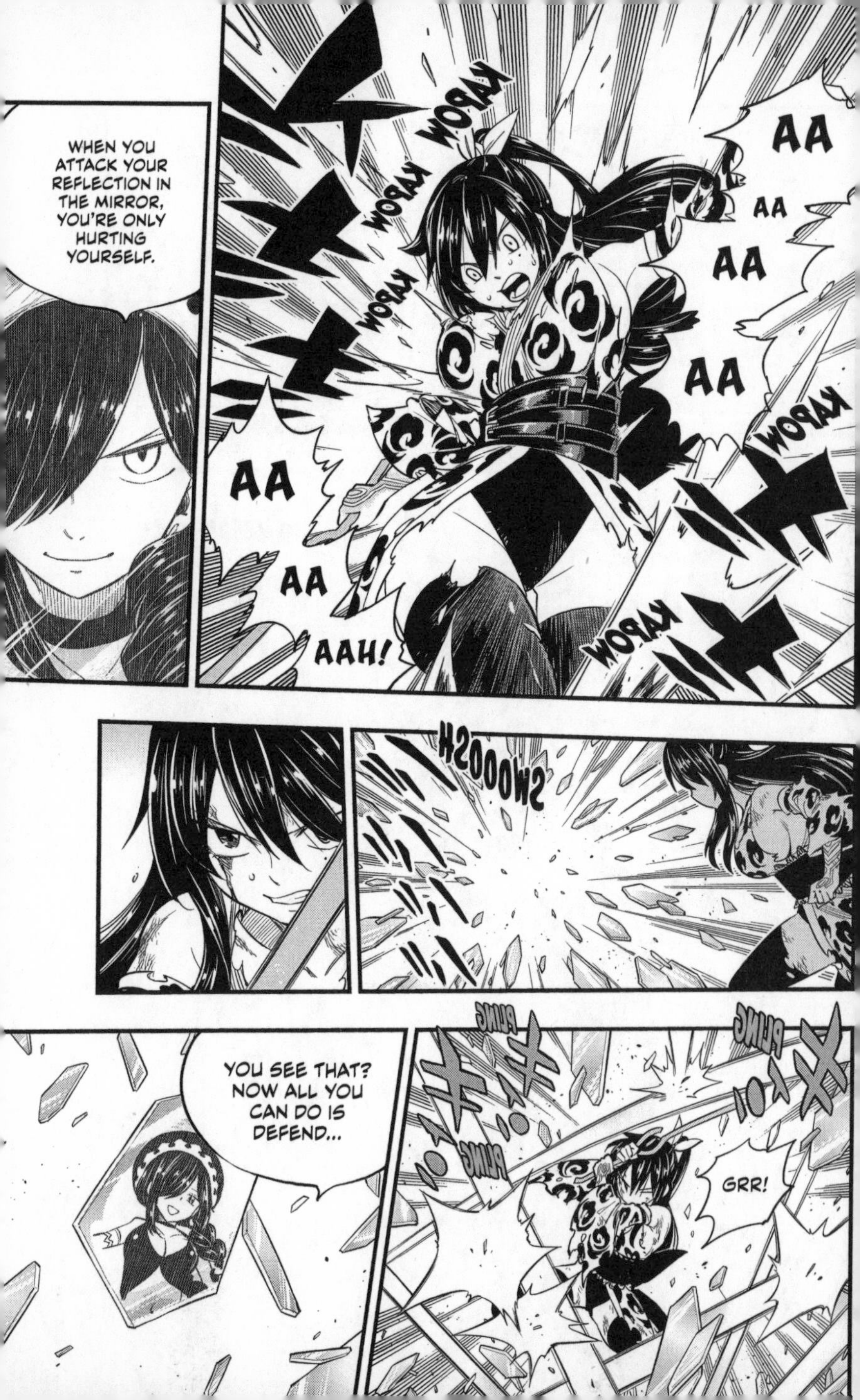
KAPOW
KAPOW
KAPOW
KAPOW
AA
AA
AA
AA
KAPOW
AA
AA
AAH!
KAPOW
WHEN YOU ATTACK YOUR REFLECTION IN THE MIRROR, YOU'RE ONLY HURTING YOURSELF.
SWOOOSH
PLING
PLING
PLING
PLING
GRR!
YOU SEE THAT? NOW ALL YOU CAN DO IS DEFEND...

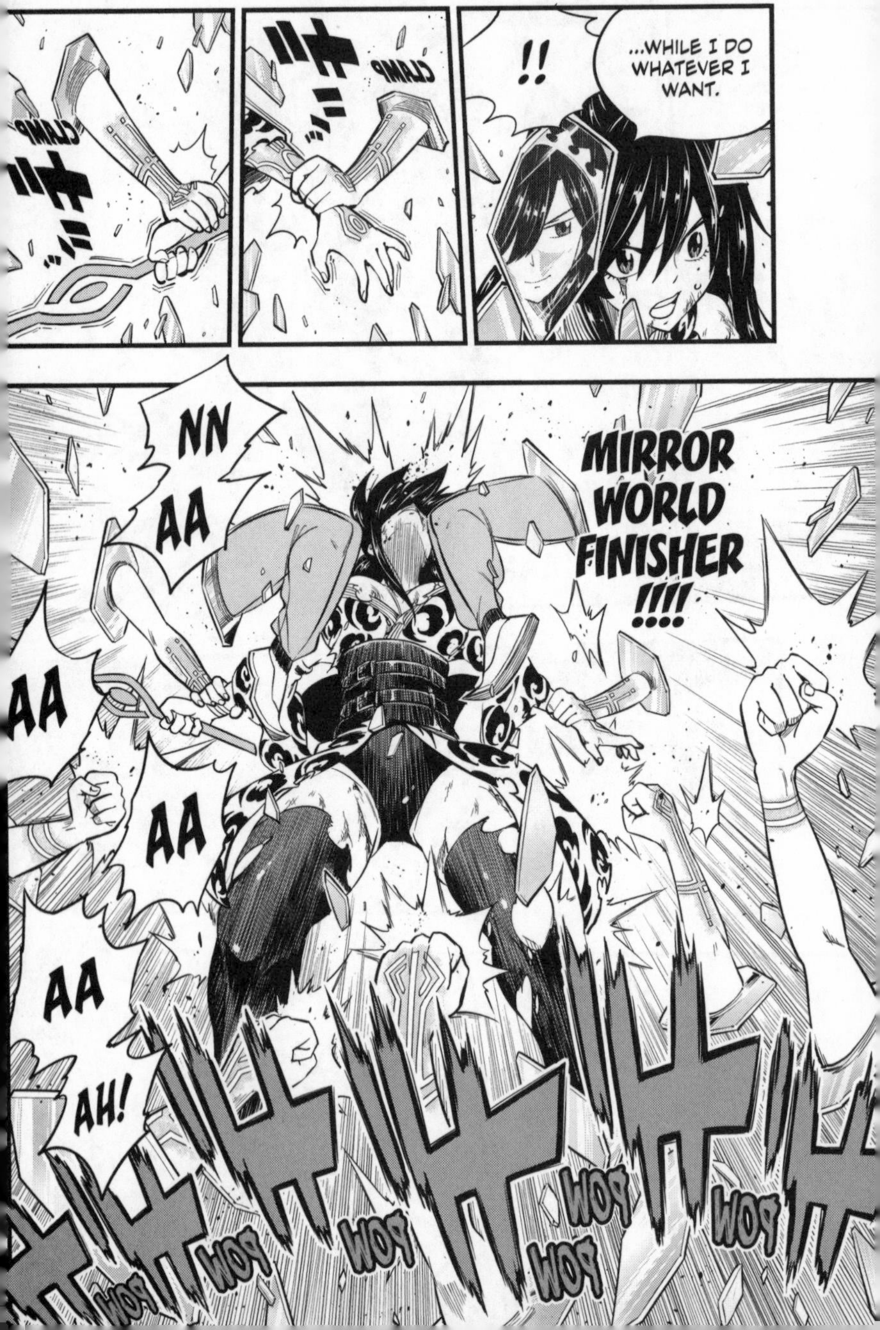

...WHILE I DO WHATEVER I WANT.
!!
CLAMP
CLAMP
MIRROR WORLD FINISHER!!!!
NN
AA
AA
AA
AA
AH!
POW
POW
POW
POW
POW
POW
POW

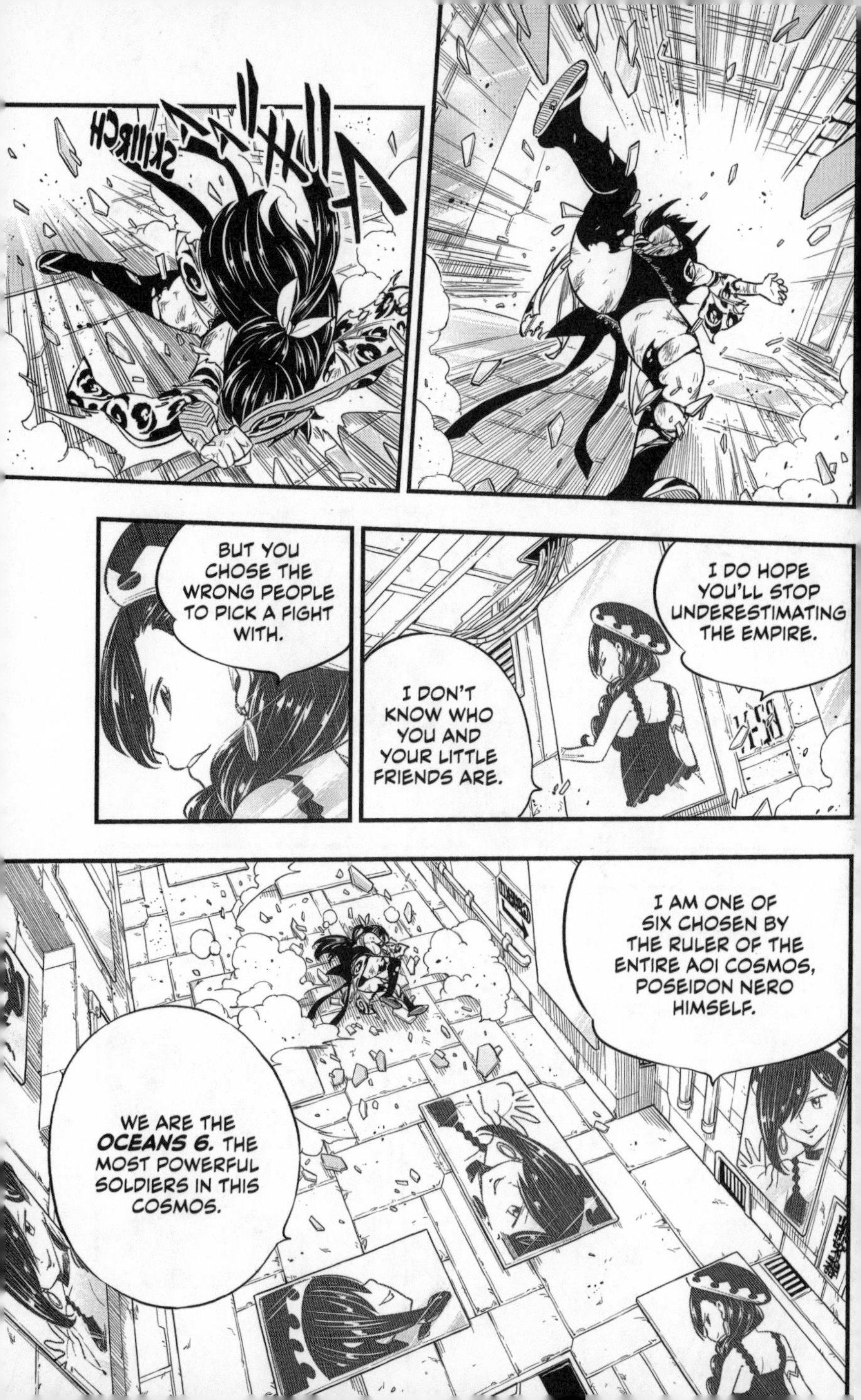
SKIIIRCH
I DO HOPE YOU'LL STOP UNDERESTIMATING THE EMPIRE.
I DON'T KNOW WHO YOU AND YOUR LITTLE FRIENDS ARE.
BUT YOU CHOSE THE WRONG PEOPLE TO PICK A FIGHT WITH.
I AM ONE OF SIX CHOSEN BY THE RULER OF THE ENTIRE AOI COSMOS, POSEIDON NERO HIMSELF.
WE ARE THE *OCEANS 6.* THE MOST POWERFUL SOLDIERS IN THIS COSMOS.

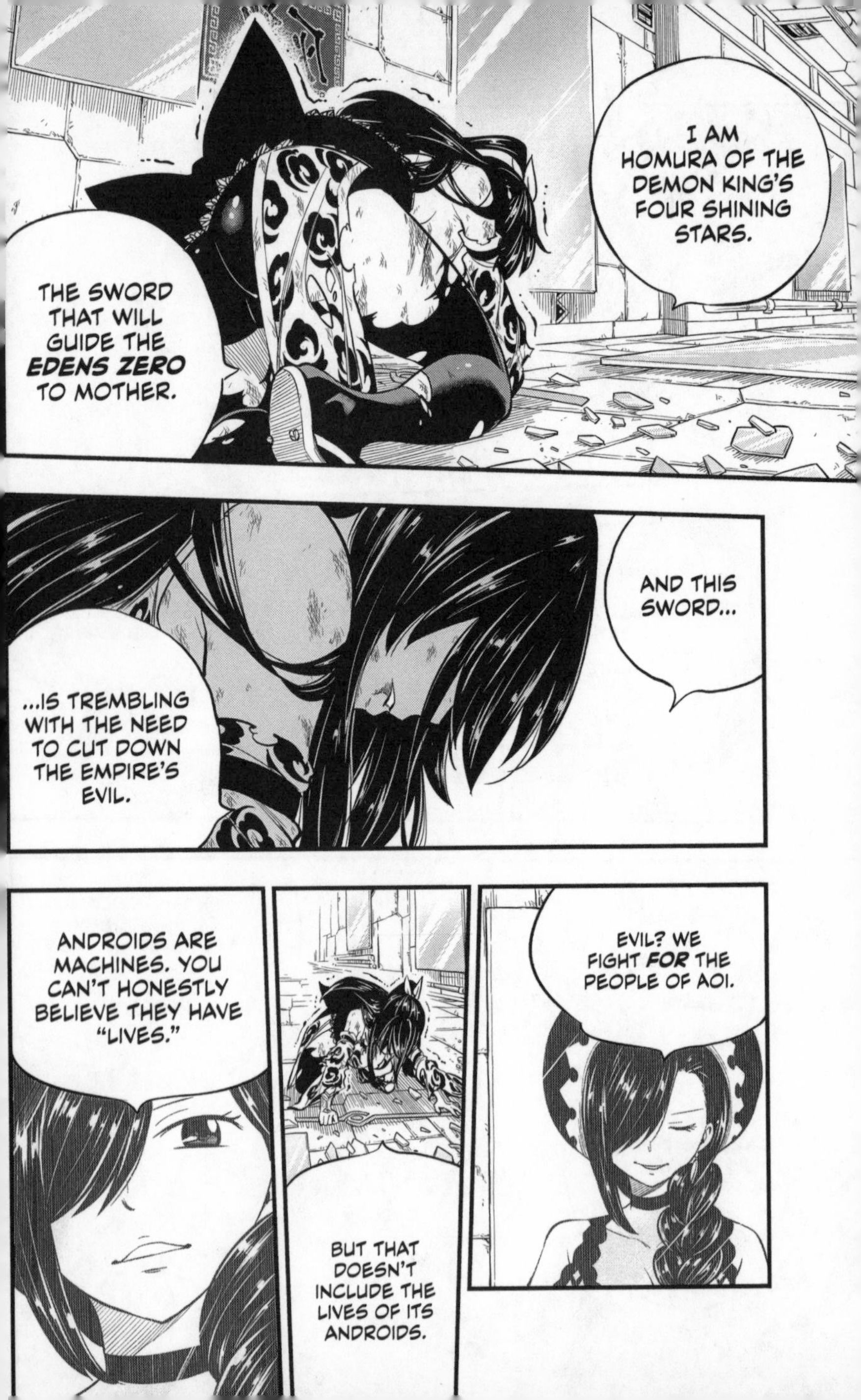
I AM HOMURA OF THE DEMON KING'S FOUR SHINING STARS.
THE SWORD THAT WILL GUIDE THE *EDENS ZERO* TO MOTHER.
AND THIS SWORD...
...IS TREMBLING WITH THE NEED TO CUT DOWN THE EMPIRE'S EVIL.
EVIL? WE FIGHT *FOR* THE PEOPLE OF AOI.
BUT THAT DOESN'T INCLUDE THE LIVES OF ITS ANDROIDS.
ANDROIDS ARE MACHINES. YOU CAN'T HONESTLY BELIEVE THEY HAVE "LIVES."

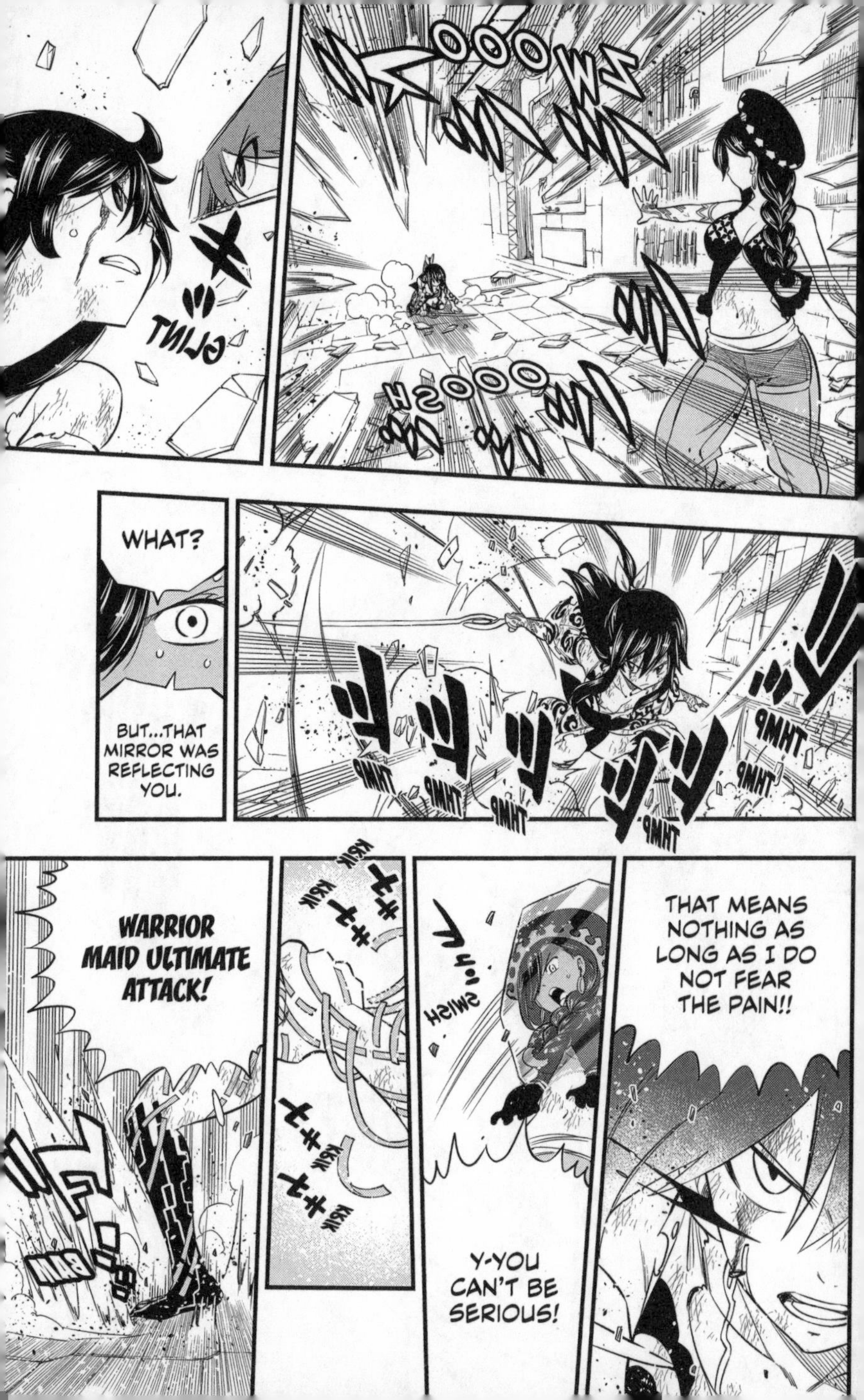
ZWOOO
WHOOOSH
GLINT
WHAT?
THMP THMP THMP THMP THMP THMP
BUT...THAT MIRROR WAS REFLECTING YOU.
THAT MEANS NOTHING AS LONG AS I DO NOT FEAR THE PAIN!!
SWISH
Y-YOU CAN'T BE SERIOUS!
KRIK KRIK KRIK KRIK
WARRIOR MAID ULTIMATE ATTACK!
BAM

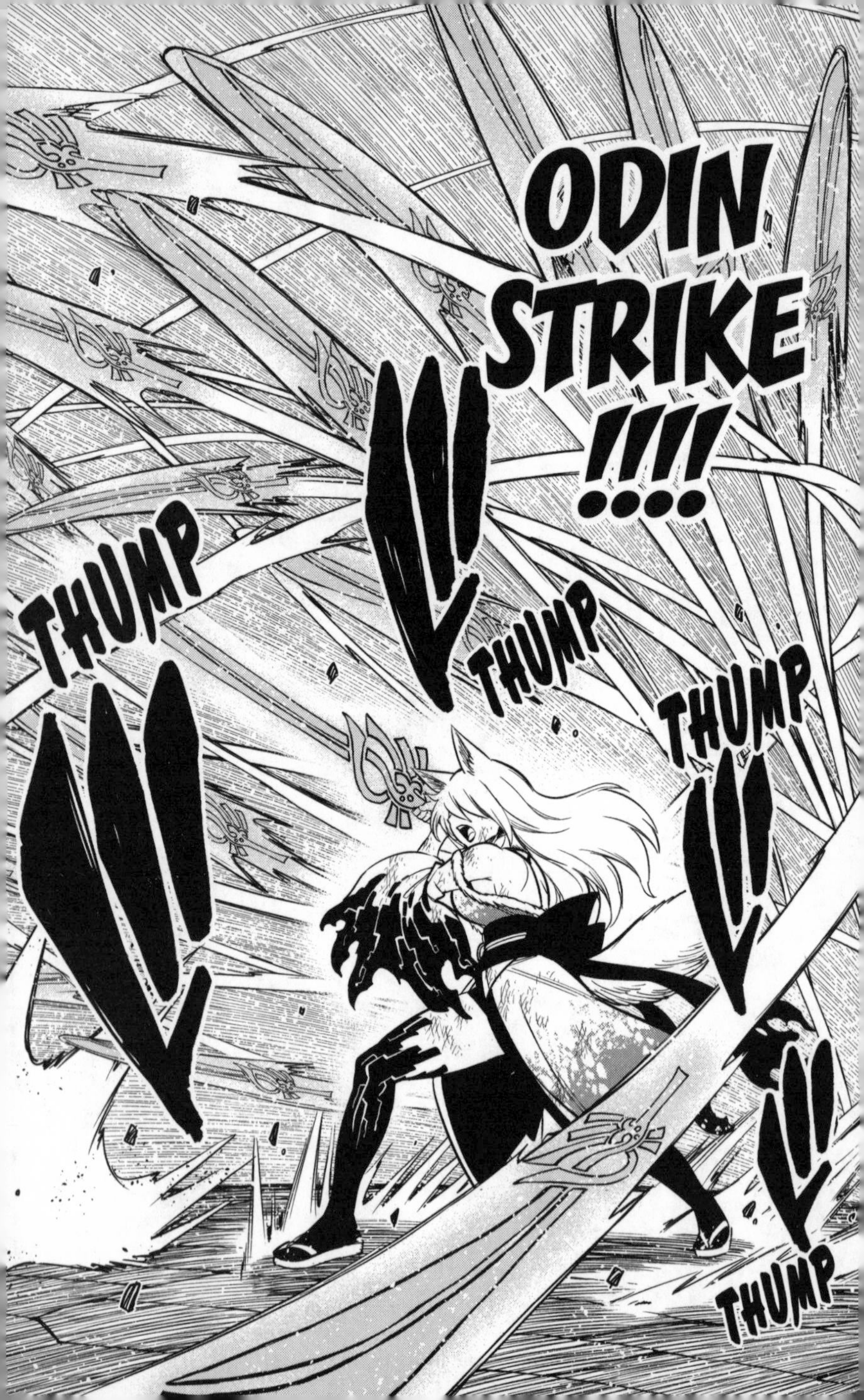
ODIN STRIKE!!!!
THUMP
THUMP
THUMP
THUMP
THUMP

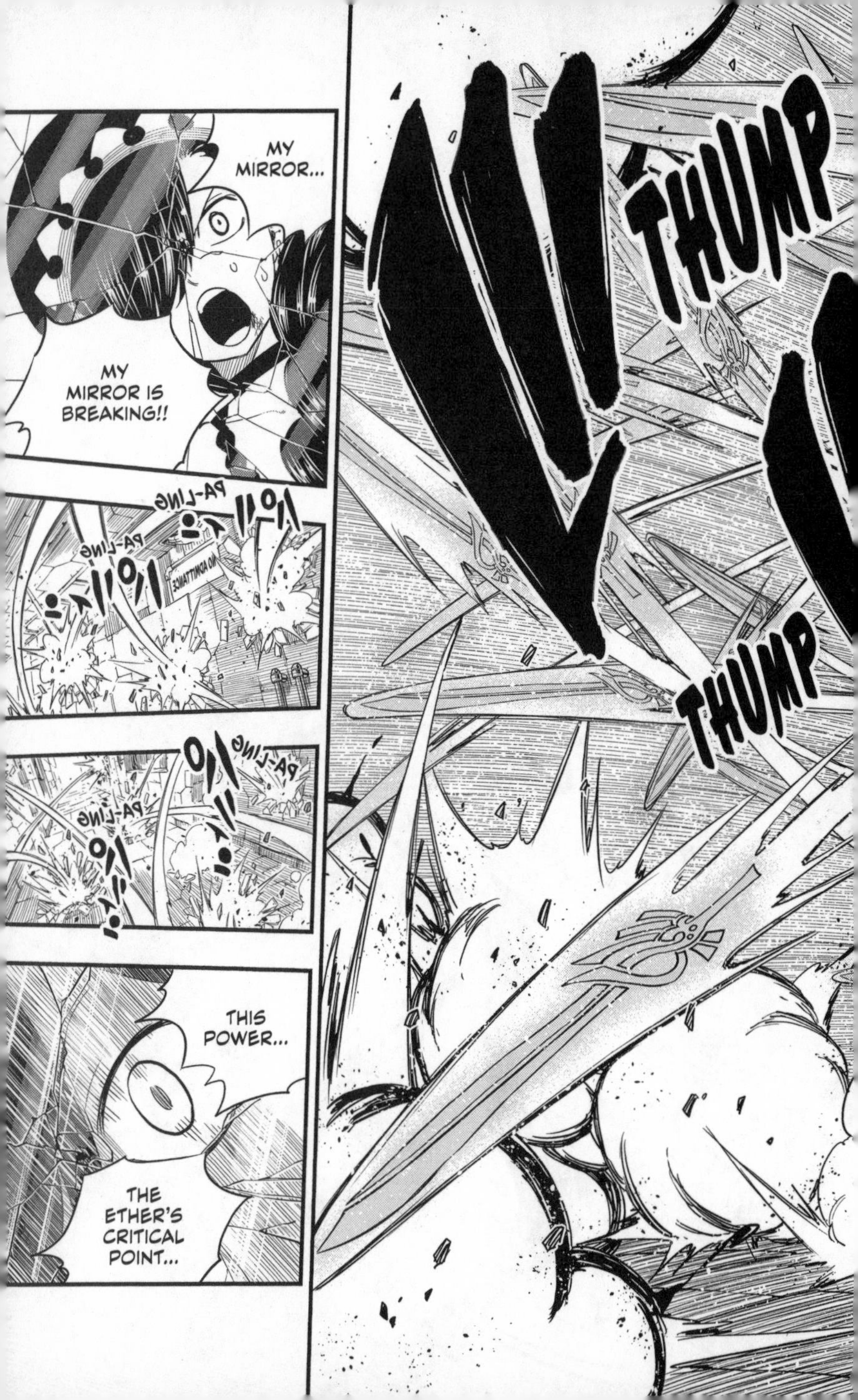
THUMP
THUMP
MY MIRROR...
MY MIRROR IS BREAKING!!
PA-LING
PA-LING
NO ADMITTANCE
PA-LING
PA-LING
THIS POWER...
THE ETHER'S CRITICAL POINT...

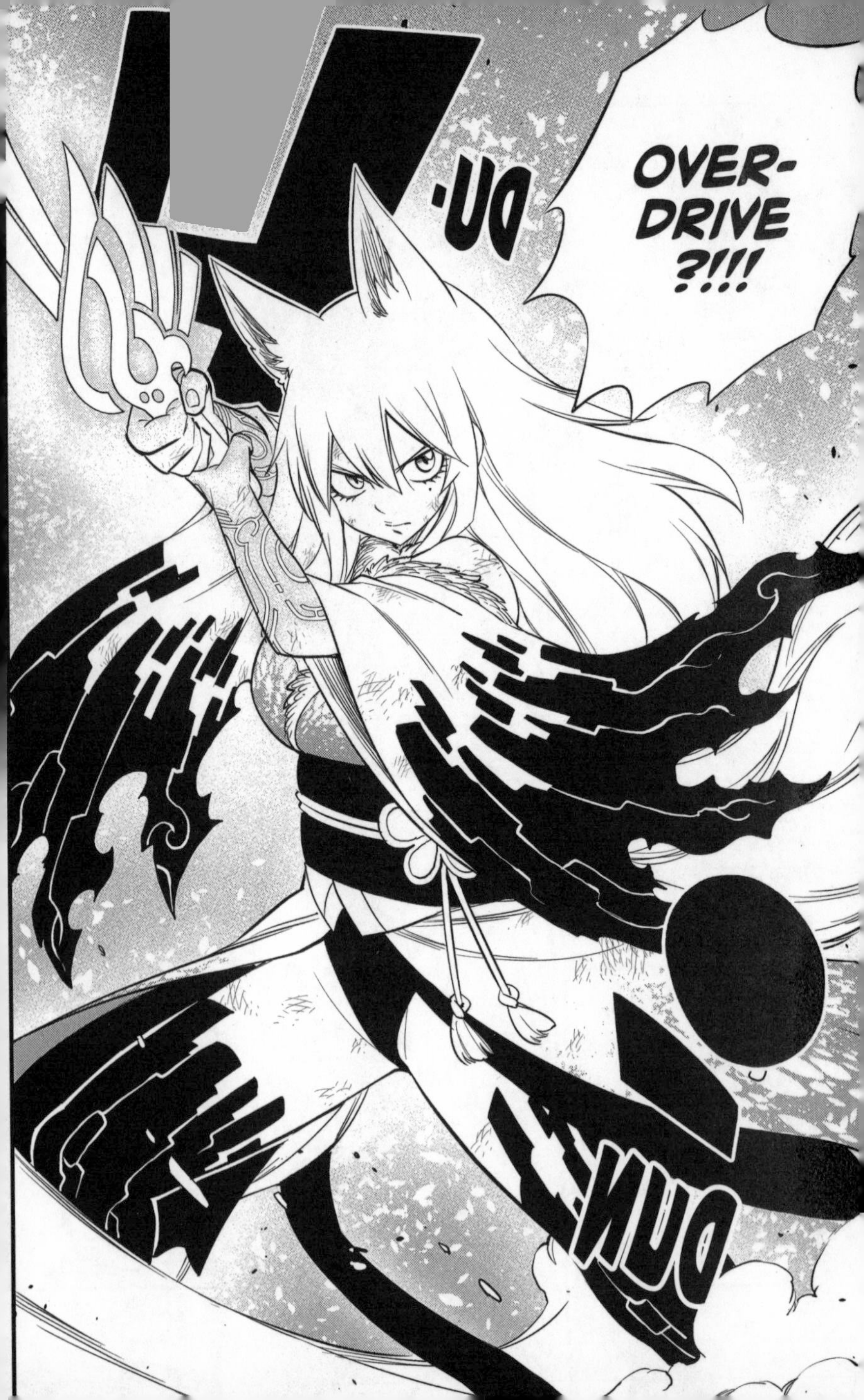
OVER-DRIVE ?!!!
DU-
DUN...

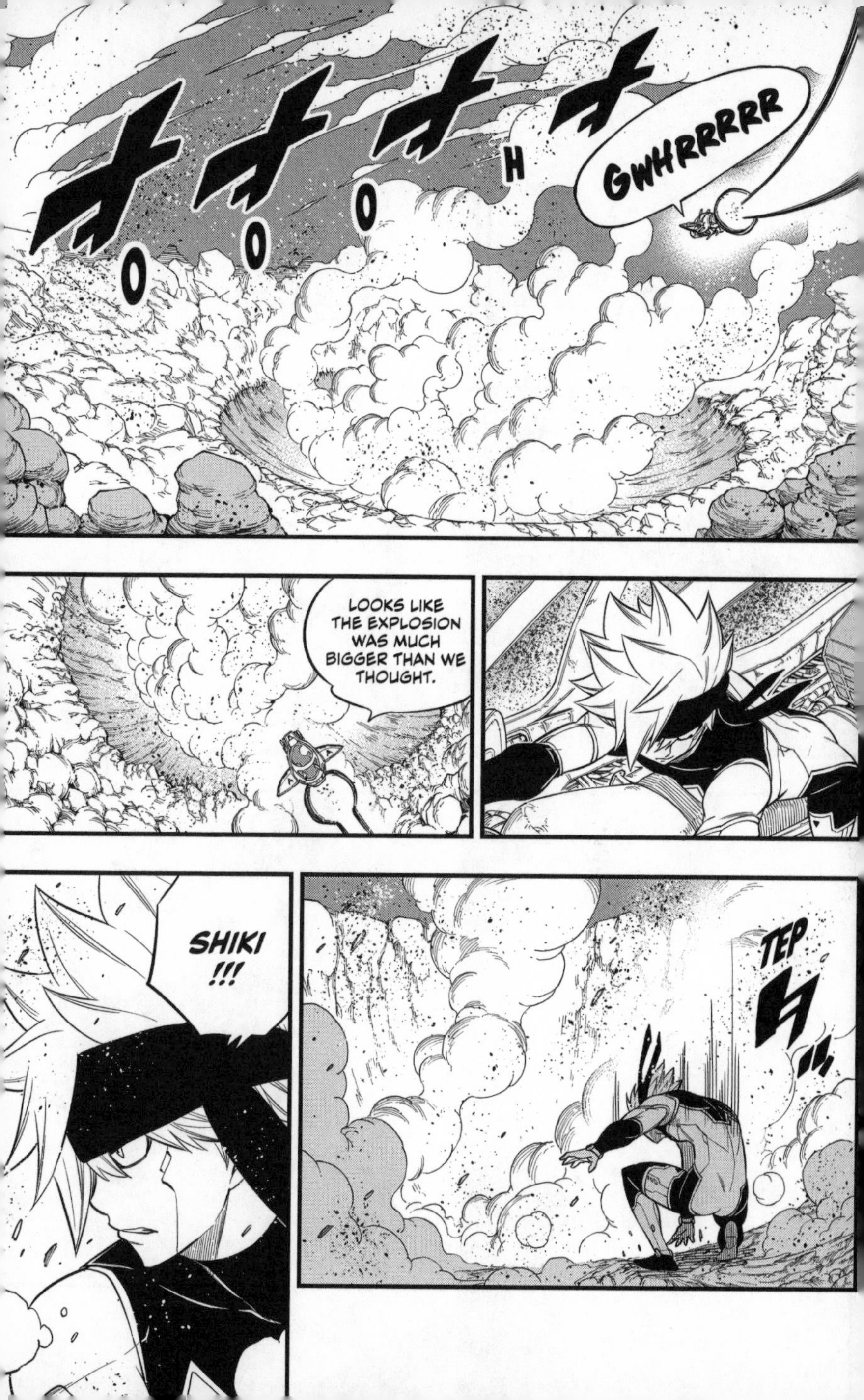
GWHRRRRR
OOOH
LOOKS LIKE THE EXPLOSION WAS MUCH BIGGER THAN WE THOUGHT.
TEP
SHIKI !!!

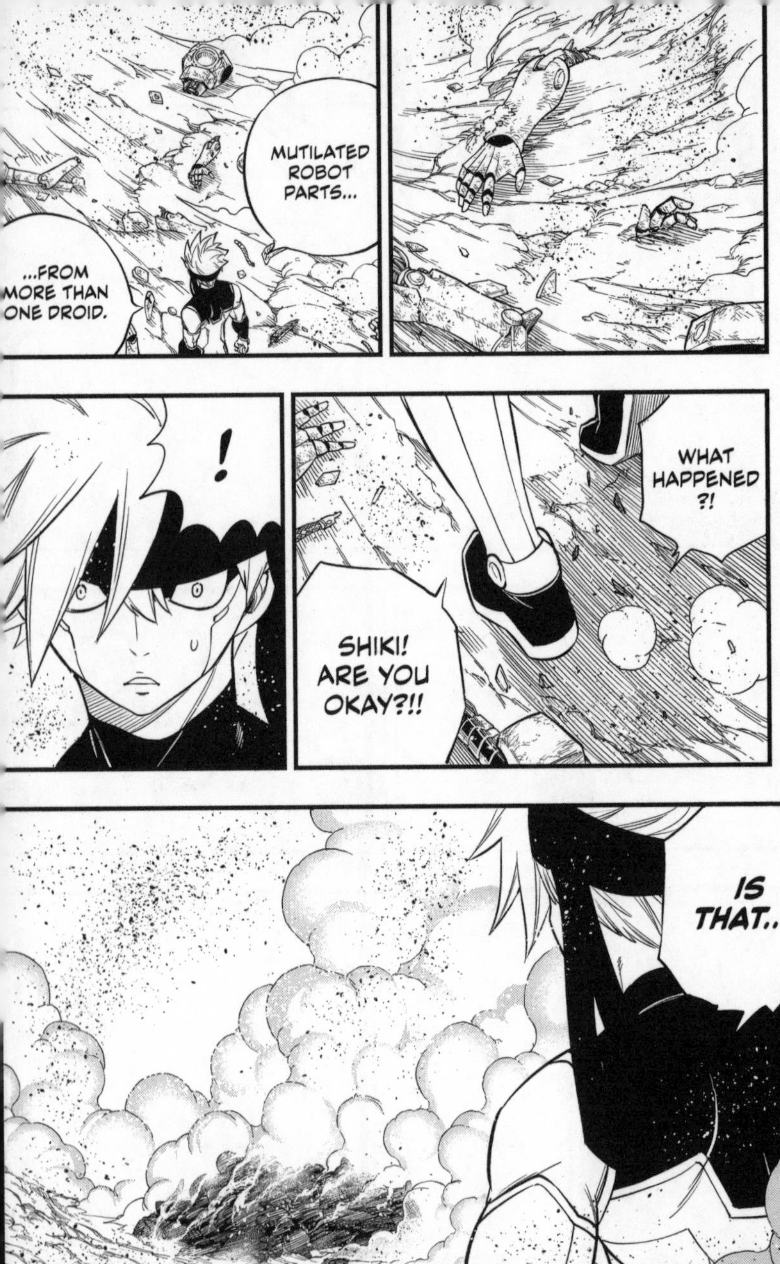
MUTILATED ROBOT PARTS...
...FROM MORE THAN ONE DROID.
WHAT HAPPENED ?!
SHIKI! ARE YOU OKAY?!!
!
IS THAT...?

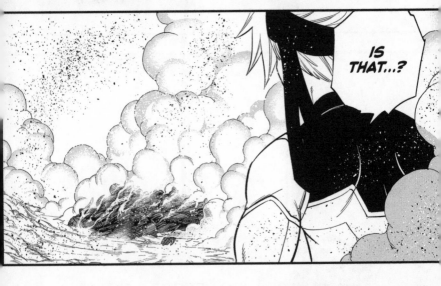

EDENSZERO

PINO'S ANALYSIS

Name: Laguna Husert
Powers: Tears Lover
Likes: Fashion
Dislikes: Dryness

Attack:	☆☆☆☆
Defense:	☆☆☆
Marksmanship:	☆☆☆
Ether Power:	☆☆☆☆
Intelligence:	☆☆☆☆
Stiletto Heels:	☆☆☆☆☆

Memo

He uses a really scary Ether Gear that can turn anyone who sheds a tear into water. He was originally an actor, and after his fight with Master, he changed his face and went to perform at a theater in Blue Garden. We recently learned that he'd once been a member of Oasis, a rebel army fighting against Poseidon Nero.

CHAPTER 146: BEFORE WE PART

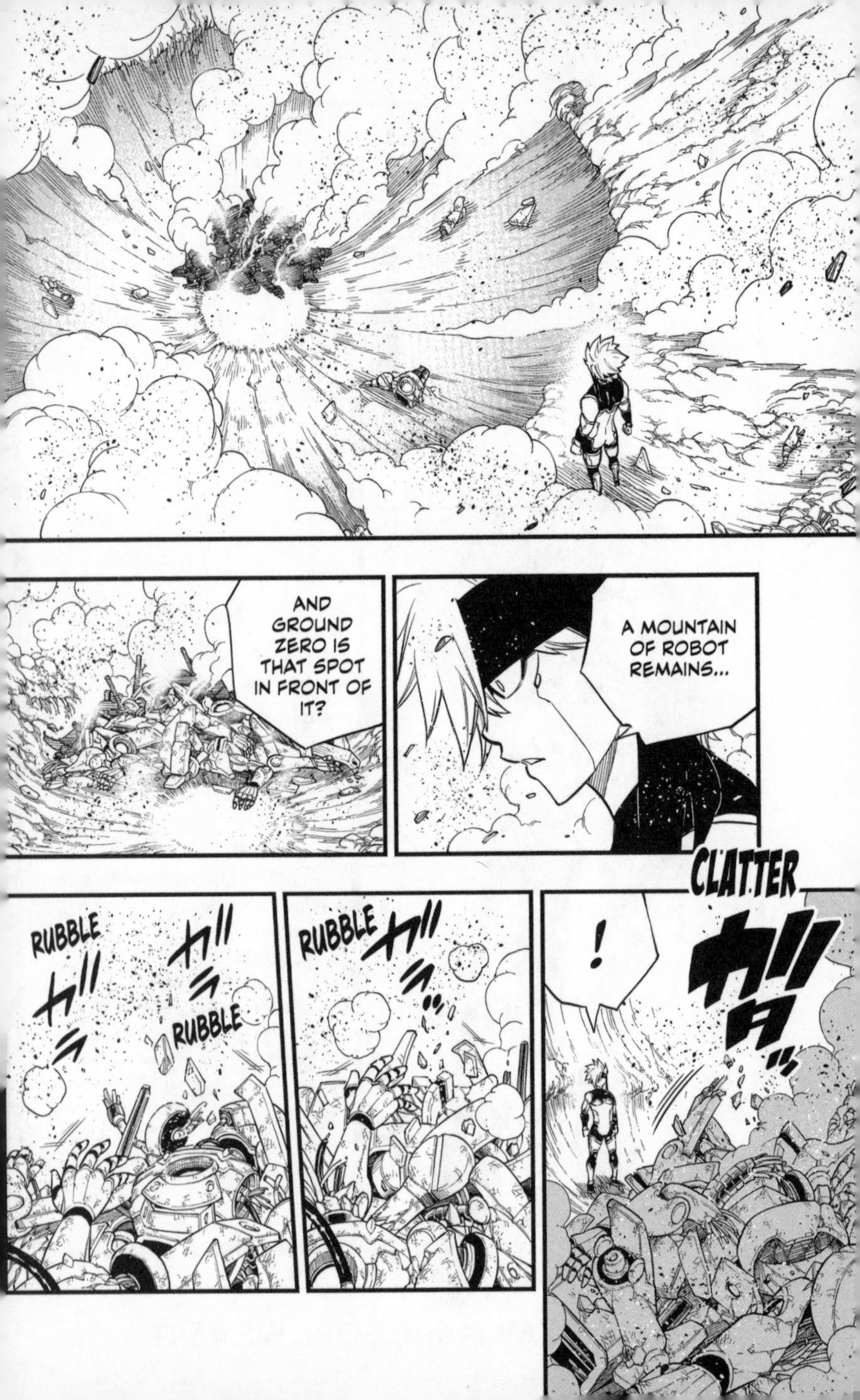
A MOUNTAIN OF ROBOT REMAINS...
AND GROUND ZERO IS THAT SPOT IN FRONT OF IT?
CLATTER
!
RUBBLE
RUBBLE
RUBBLE

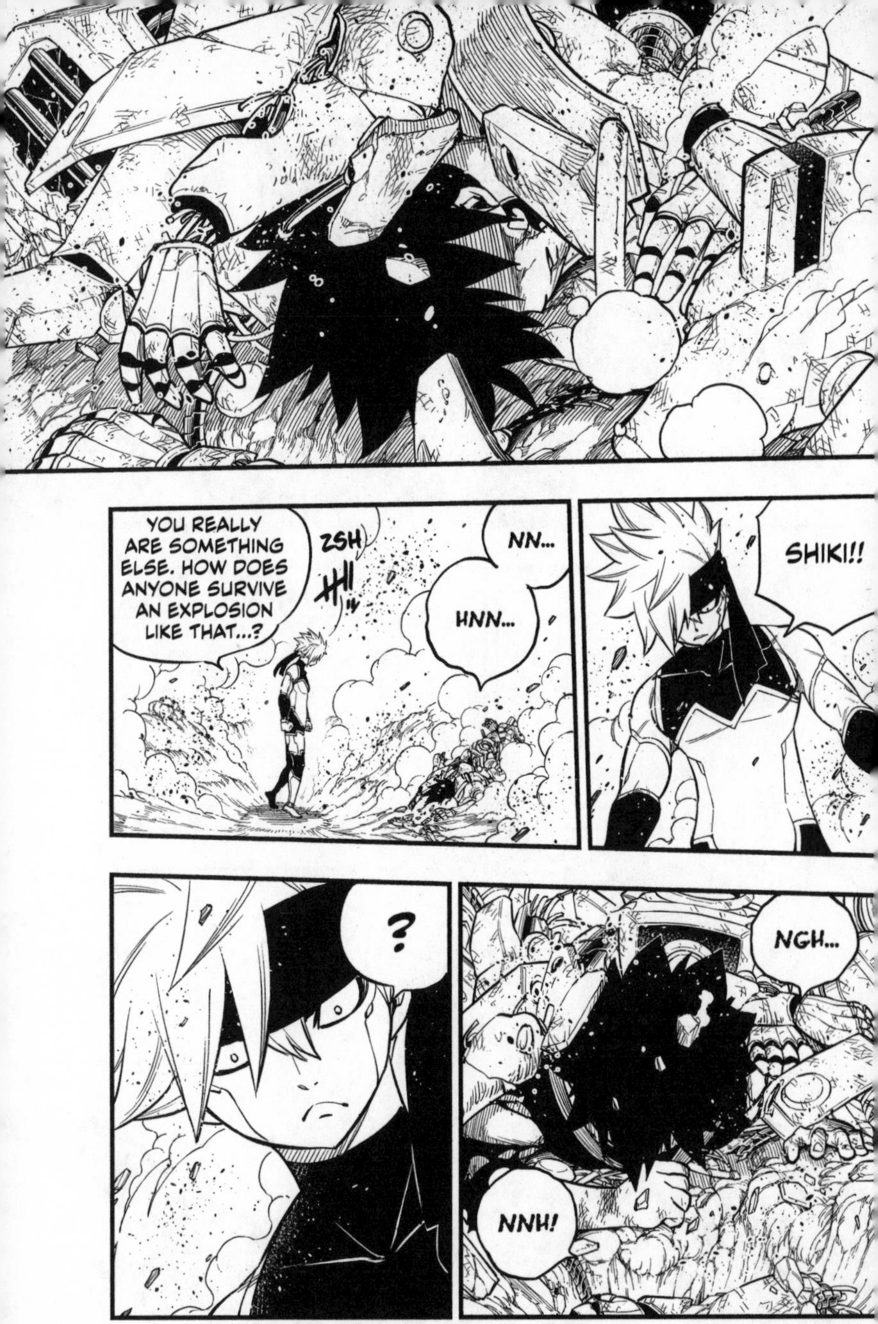
SHIKI!!
NN...
HNN...
ZSH
YOU REALLY ARE SOMETHING ELSE. HOW DOES ANYONE SURVIVE AN EXPLOSION LIKE THAT...?
NGH...
NNH!
?

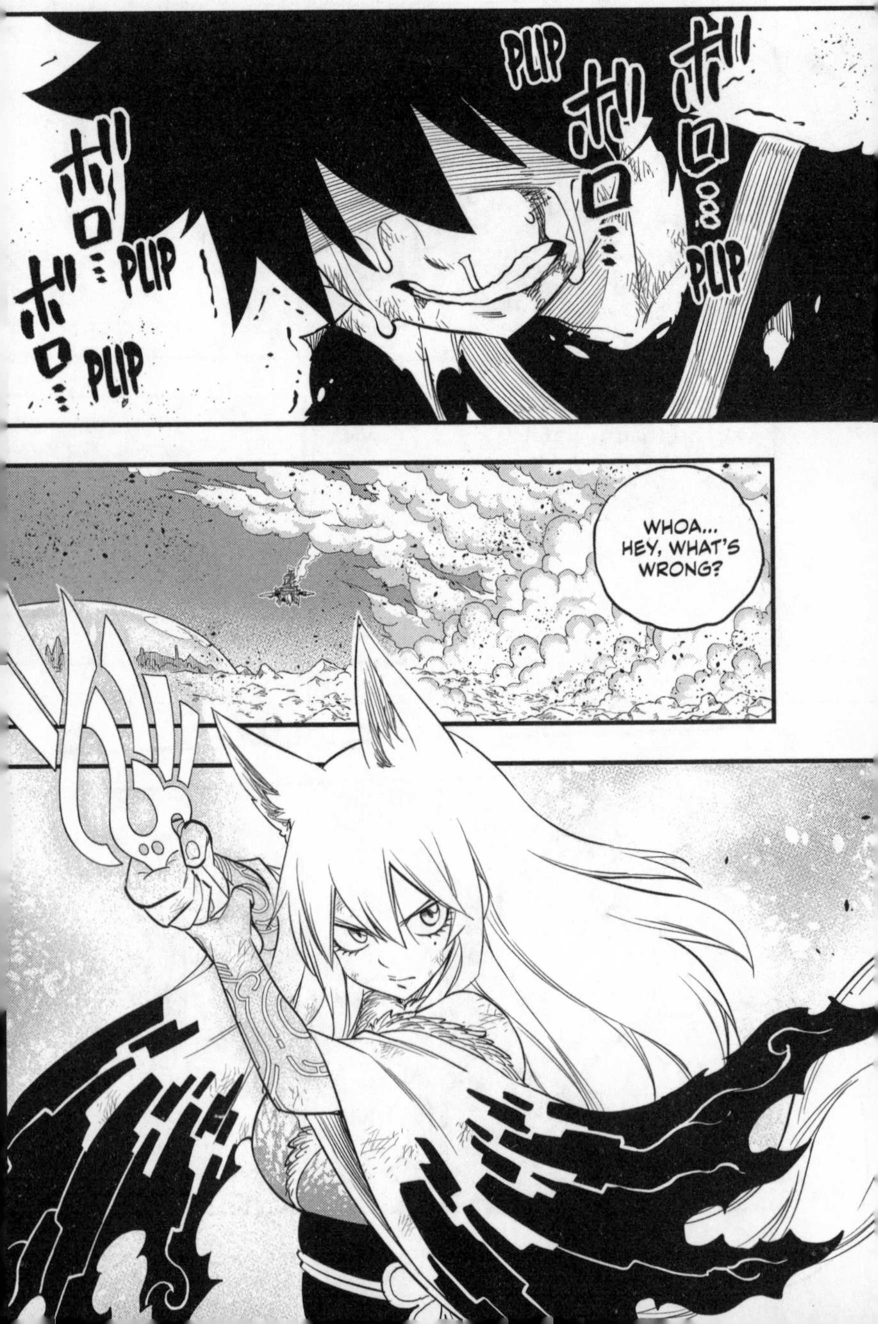

ボロ…
PLIP
ボロ
PLIP
ボロ…
PLIP
ボロ…
PLIP
WHOA... HEY, WHAT'S WRONG?

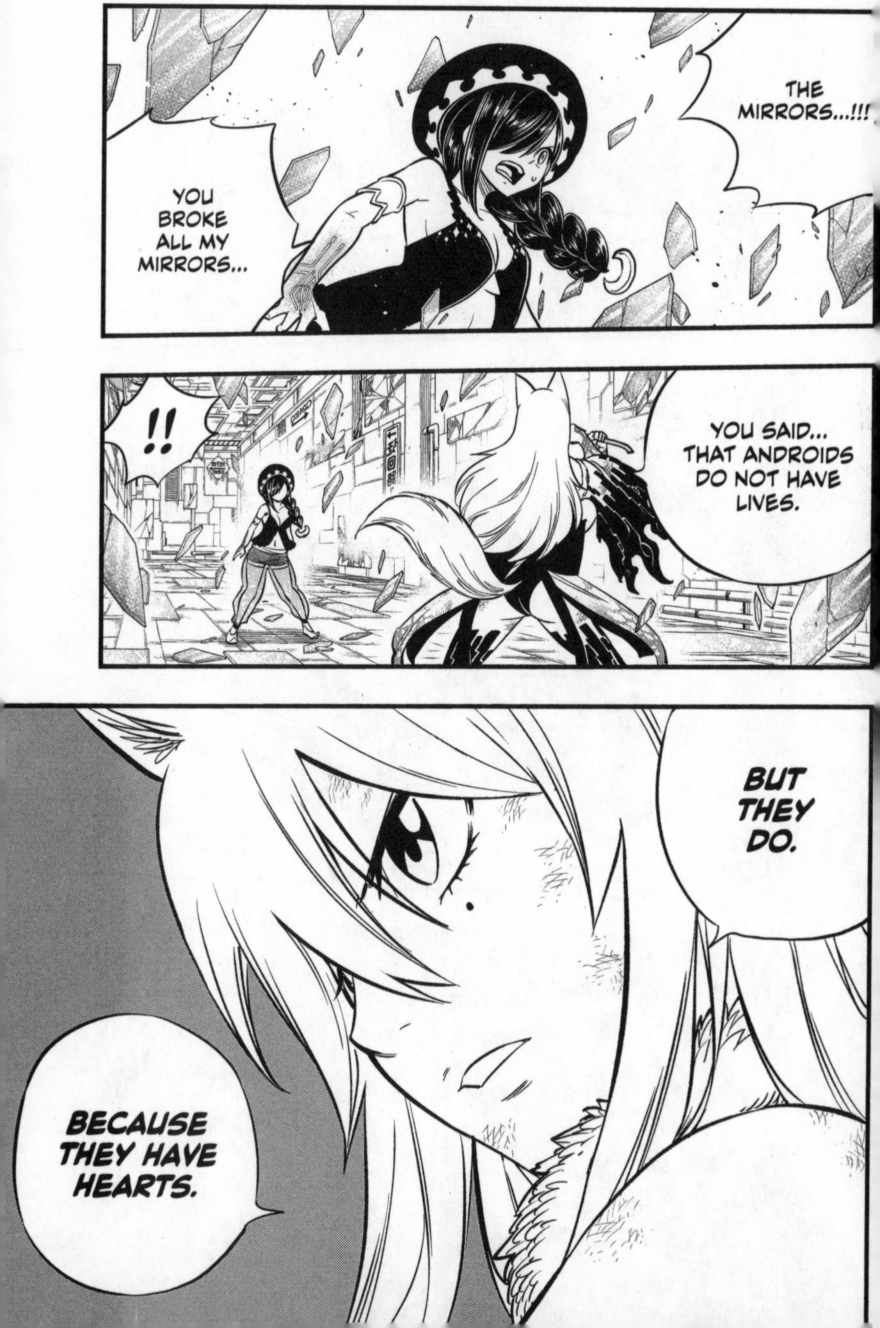
THE MIRRORS...!!!
YOU BROKE ALL MY MIRRORS...
YOU SAID... THAT ANDROIDS DO NOT HAVE LIVES.
!!
BUT THEY DO.
BECAUSE THEY HAVE HEARTS.

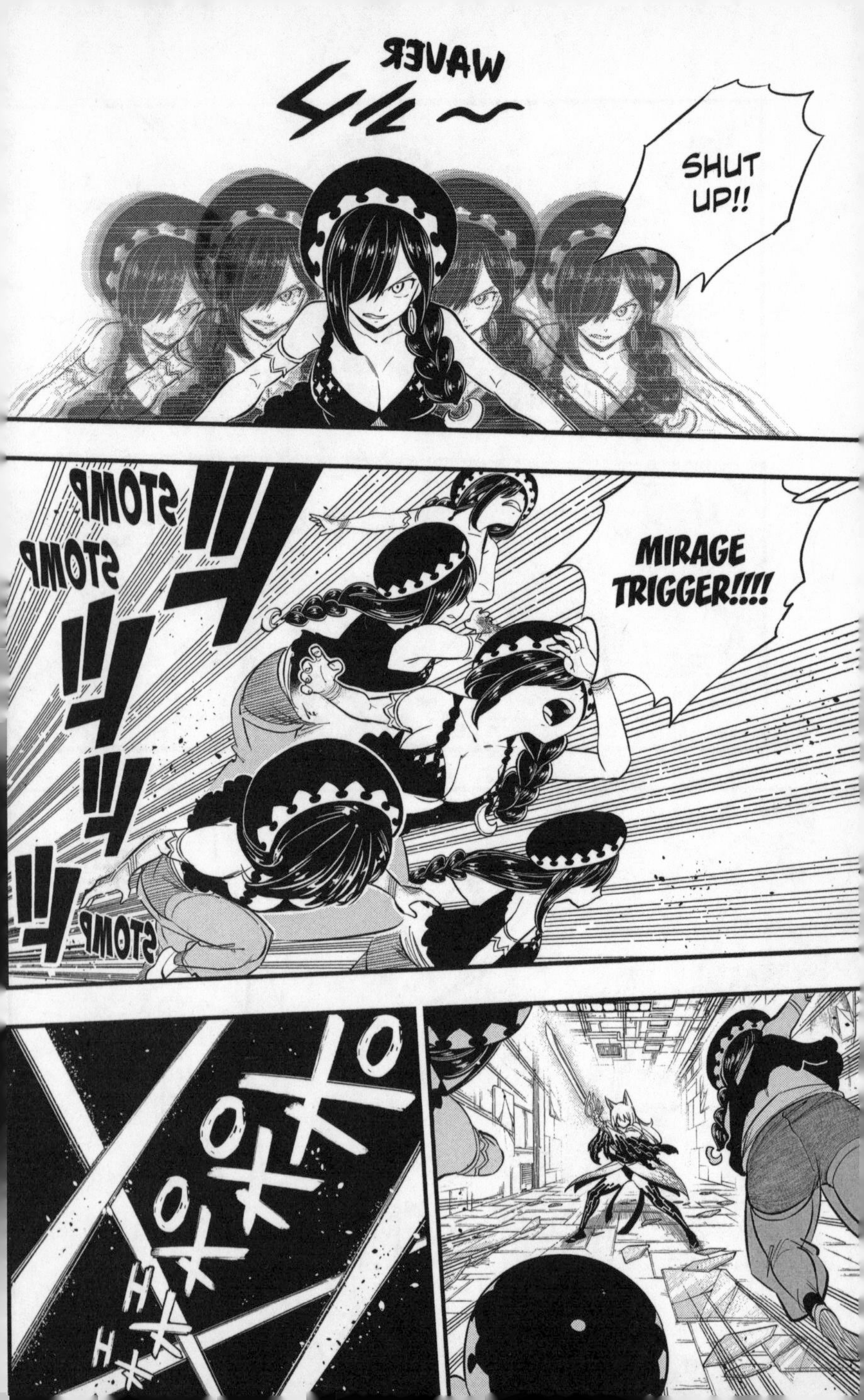
WAVER
SHUT UP!!
MIRAGE TRIGGER!!!!
STOMP
STOMP
STOMP

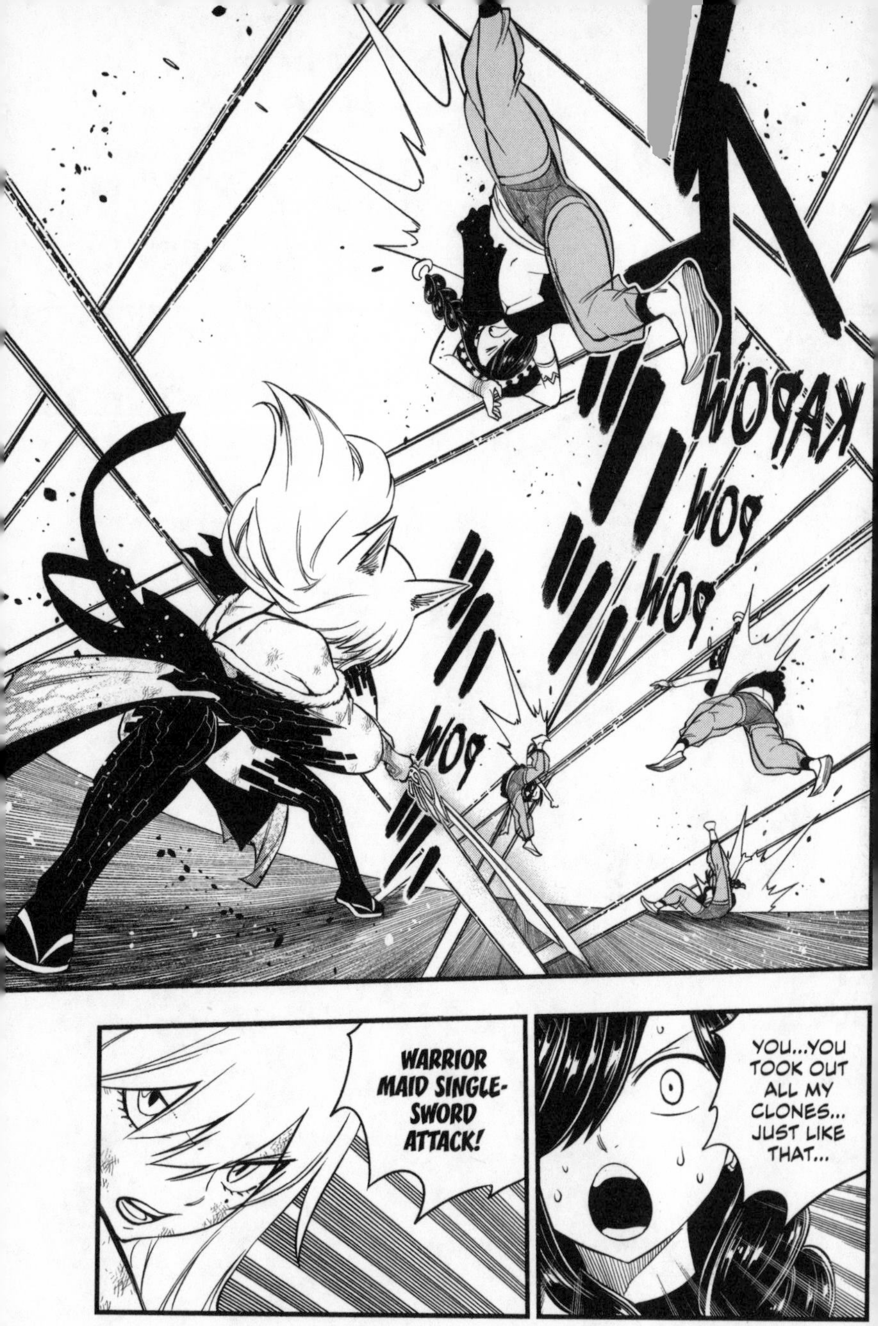
KAPOW
POW
POW
POW
YOU...YOU TOOK OUT ALL MY CLONES... JUST LIKE THAT...
WARRIOR MAID SINGLE-SWORD ATTACK!

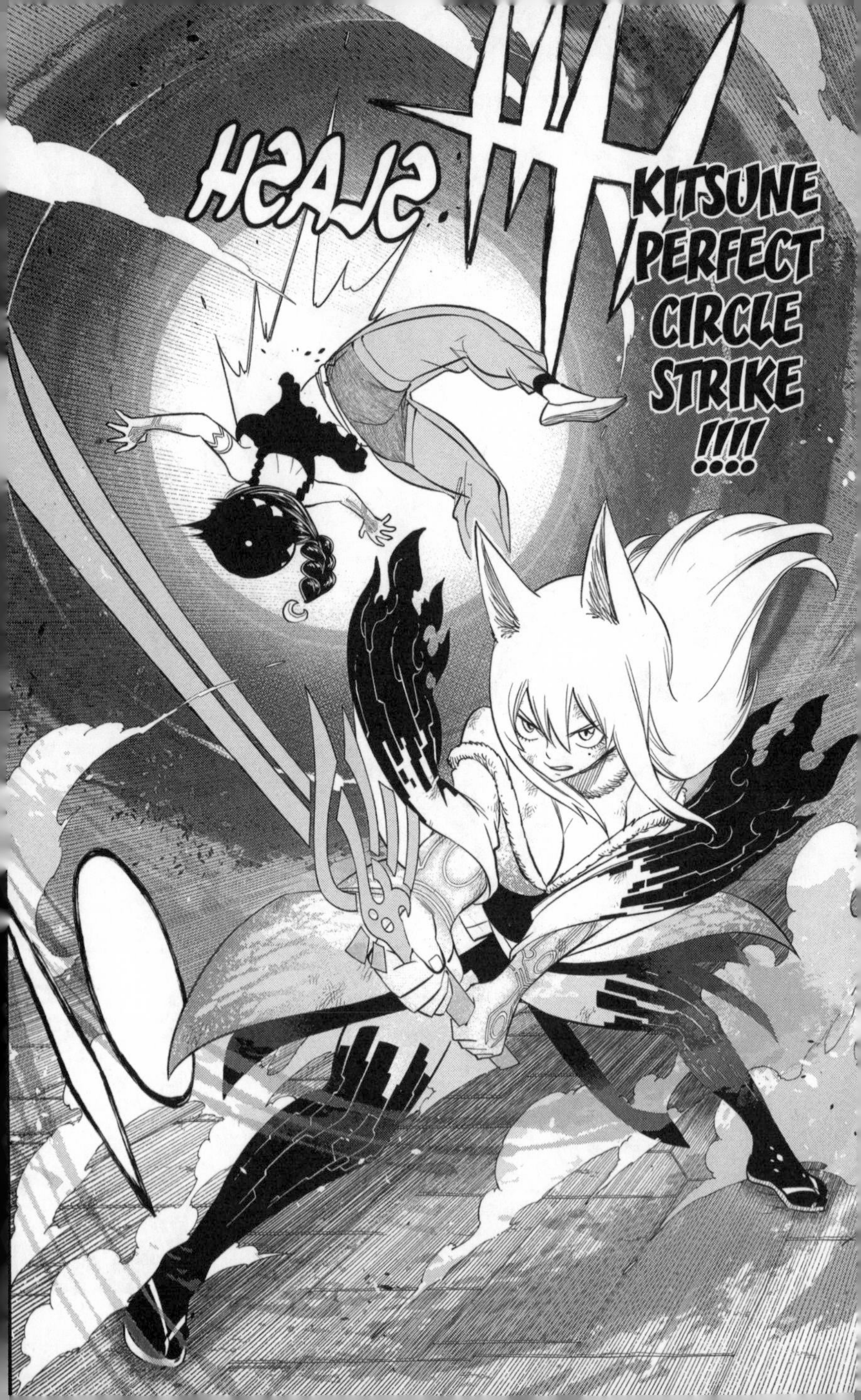
KITSUNE PERFECT CIRCLE STRIKE!!!!
SLASH

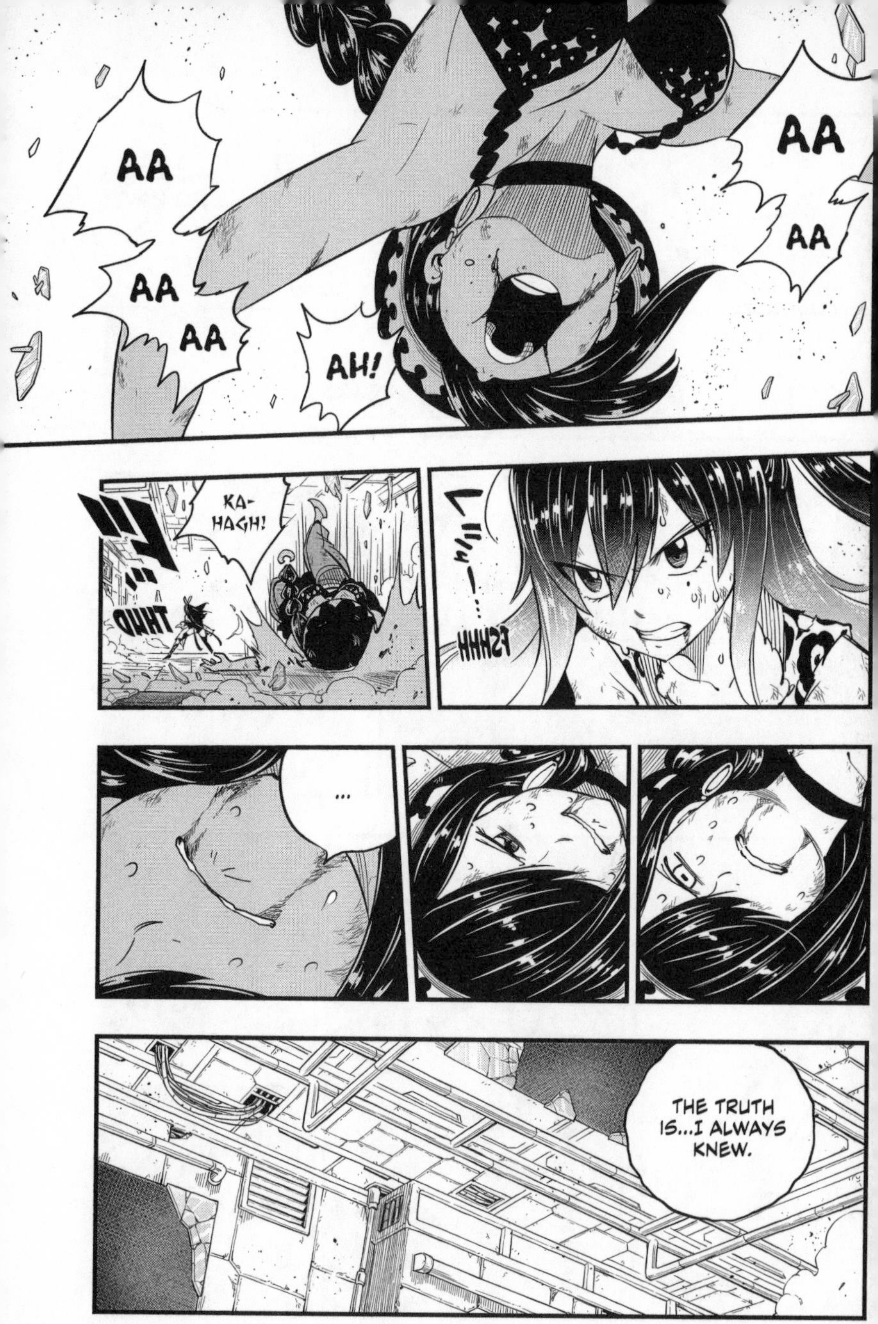
AA
AA
AH!
AA
AA
AA
FSHHH
KA-HAGH!
THUD
...
THE TRUTH IS...I ALWAYS KNEW.

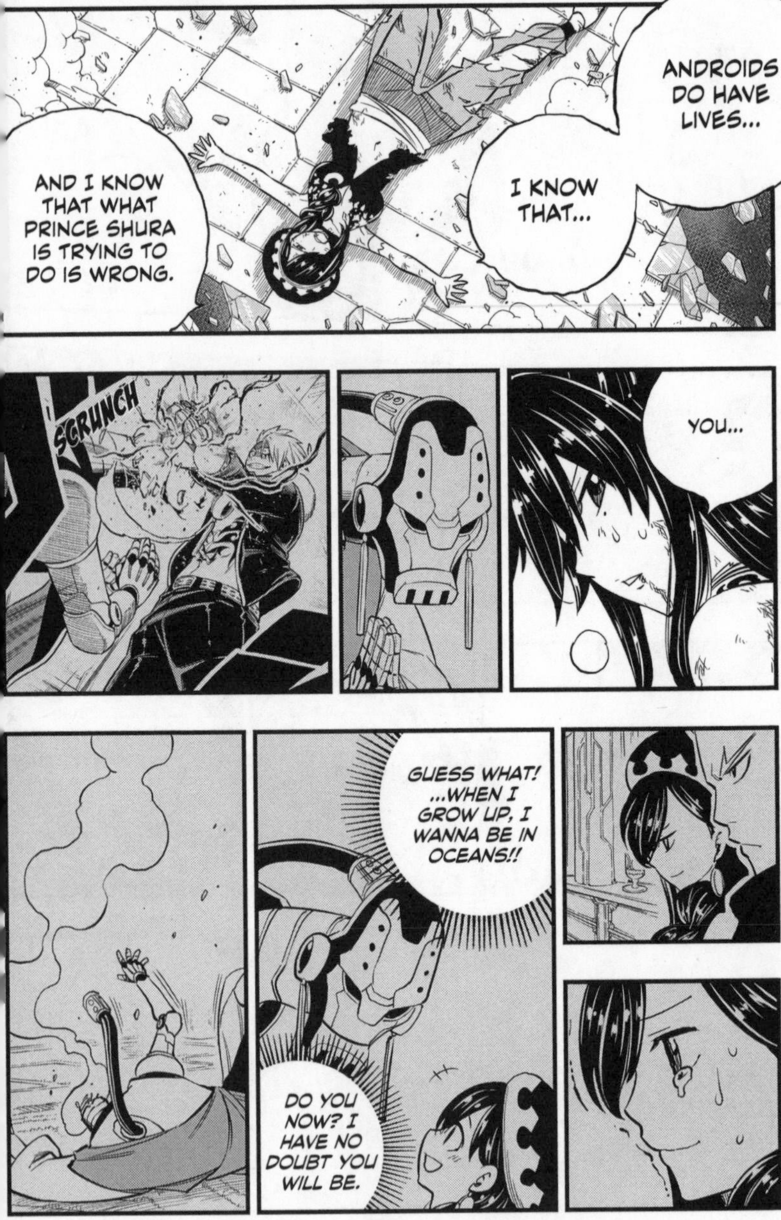
ANDROIDS DO HAVE LIVES...
I KNOW THAT...
AND I KNOW THAT WHAT PRINCE SHURA IS TRYING TO DO IS WRONG.
YOU...
SCRUNCH
GUESS WHAT! ...WHEN I GROW UP, I WANNA BE IN OCEANS!!
DO YOU NOW? I HAVE NO DOUBT YOU WILL BE.

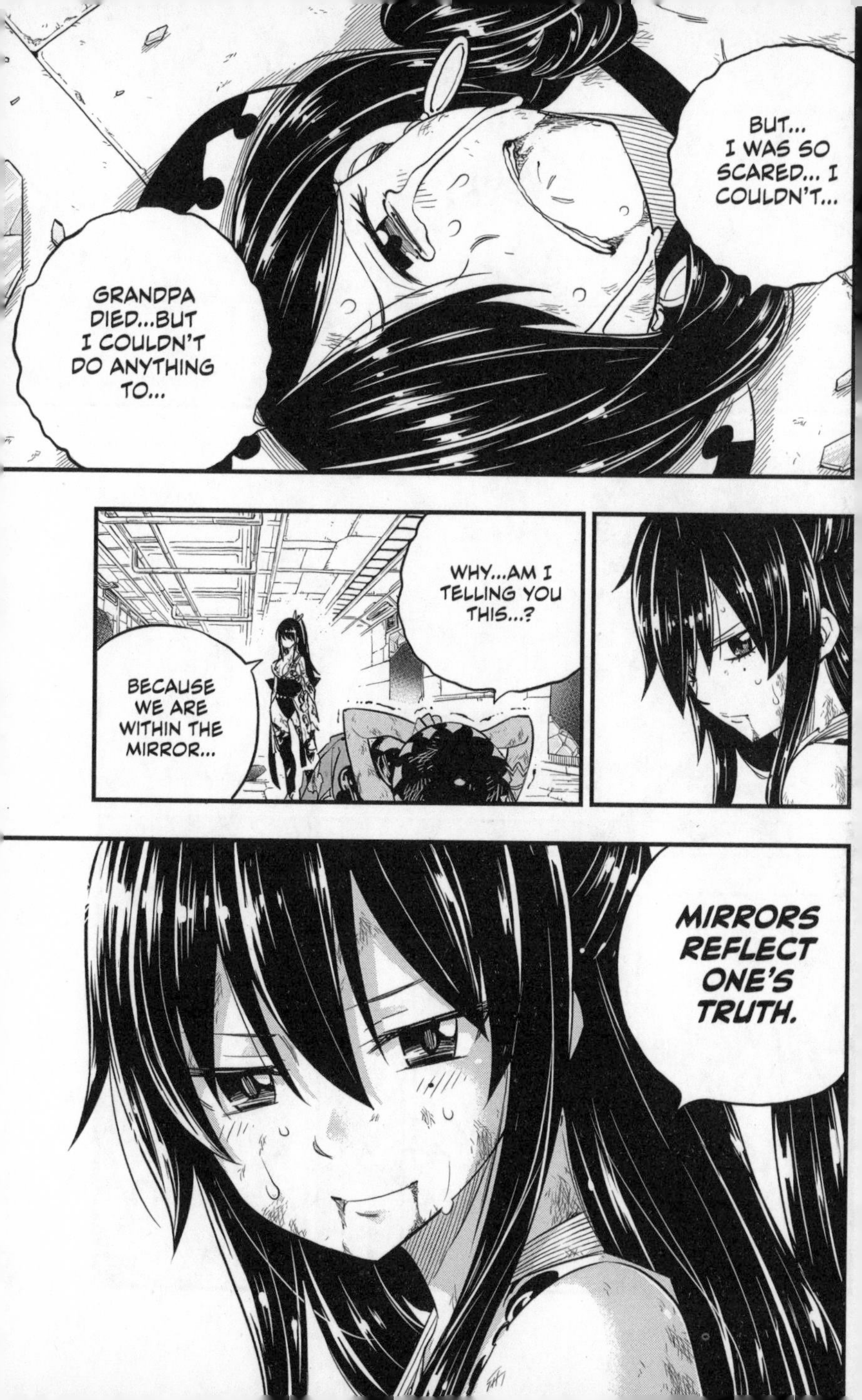
BUT... I WAS SO SCARED... I COULDN'T...
GRANDPA DIED...BUT I COULDN'T DO ANYTHING TO...
WHY...AM I TELLING YOU THIS...?
BECAUSE WE ARE WITHIN THE MIRROR...
MIRRORS REFLECT ONE'S TRUTH.

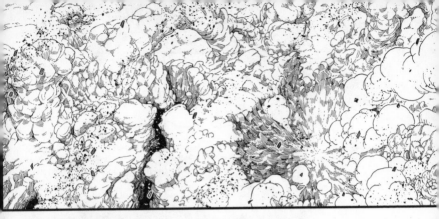

HNNN...

WHAT HAPPENED, SHIKI...?

GIVE ME A BREAK, YOU GUYS!!!

GNN

GNN

CLANK

CLANK

CLANK

CLANK

HNGH!

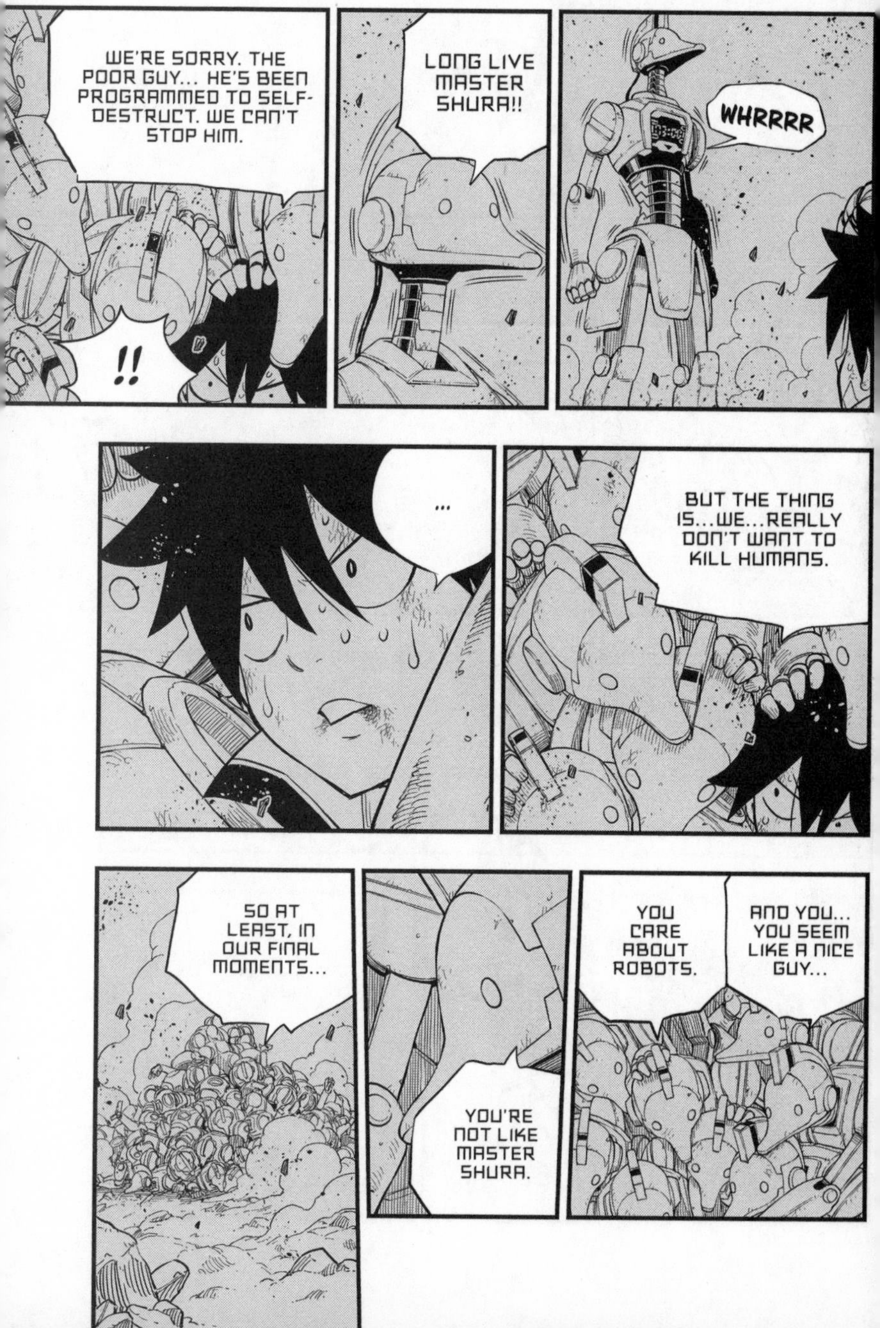
WHRRRR
LONG LIVE MASTER SHURA!!
WE'RE SORRY. THE POOR GUY... HE'S BEEN PROGRAMMED TO SELF-DESTRUCT. WE CAN'T STOP HIM.
!!
BUT THE THING IS...WE...REALLY DON'T WANT TO KILL HUMANS.
...
AND YOU... YOU SEEM LIKE A NICE GUY...
YOU CARE ABOUT ROBOTS.
YOU'RE NOT LIKE MASTER SHURA.
SO AT LEAST, IN OUR FINAL MOMENTS...

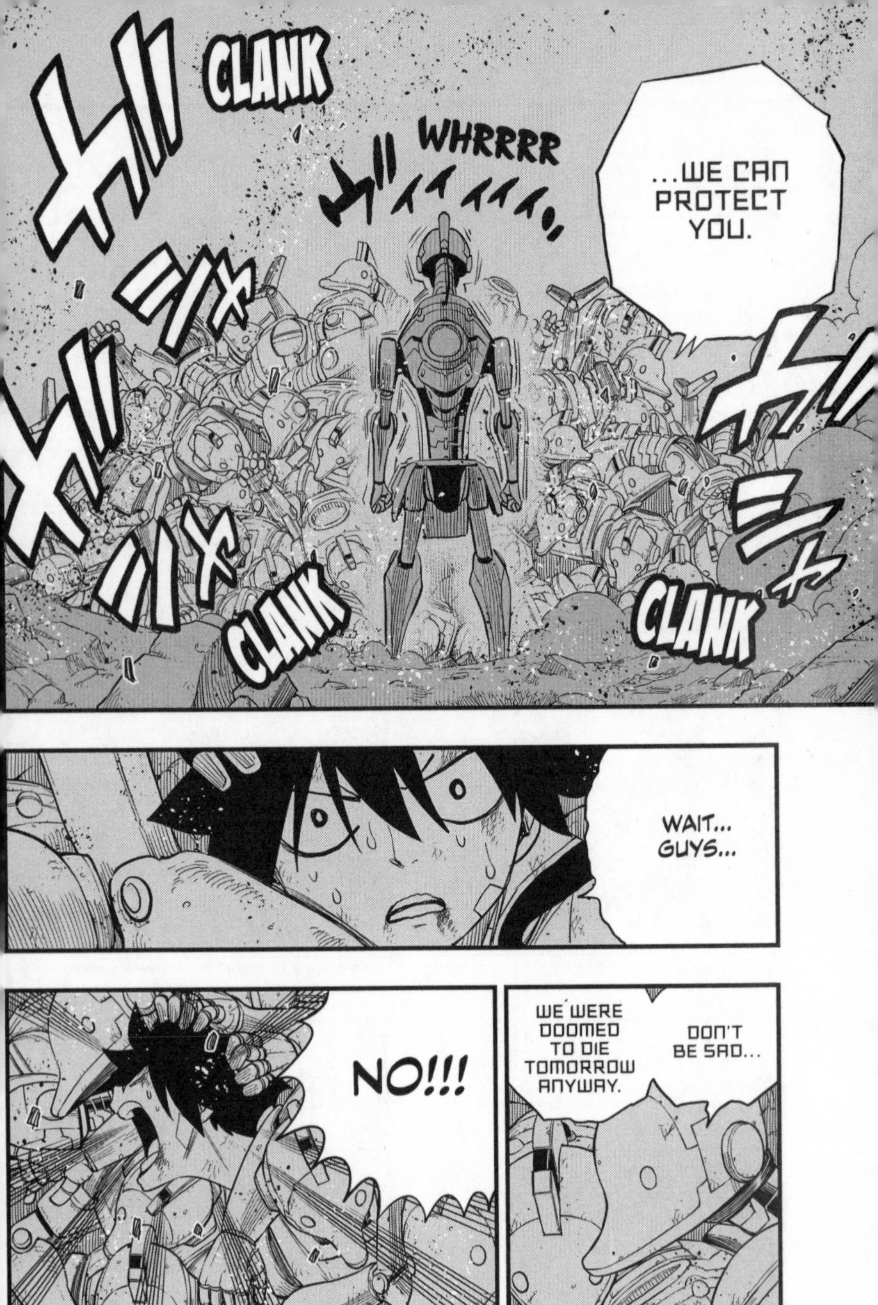
...WE CAN PROTECT YOU.
CLANK
WHRRRR
CLANK
CLANK
WAIT... GUYS...
DON'T BE SAD...
WE WERE DOOMED TO DIE TOMORROW ANYWAY.
NO!!!

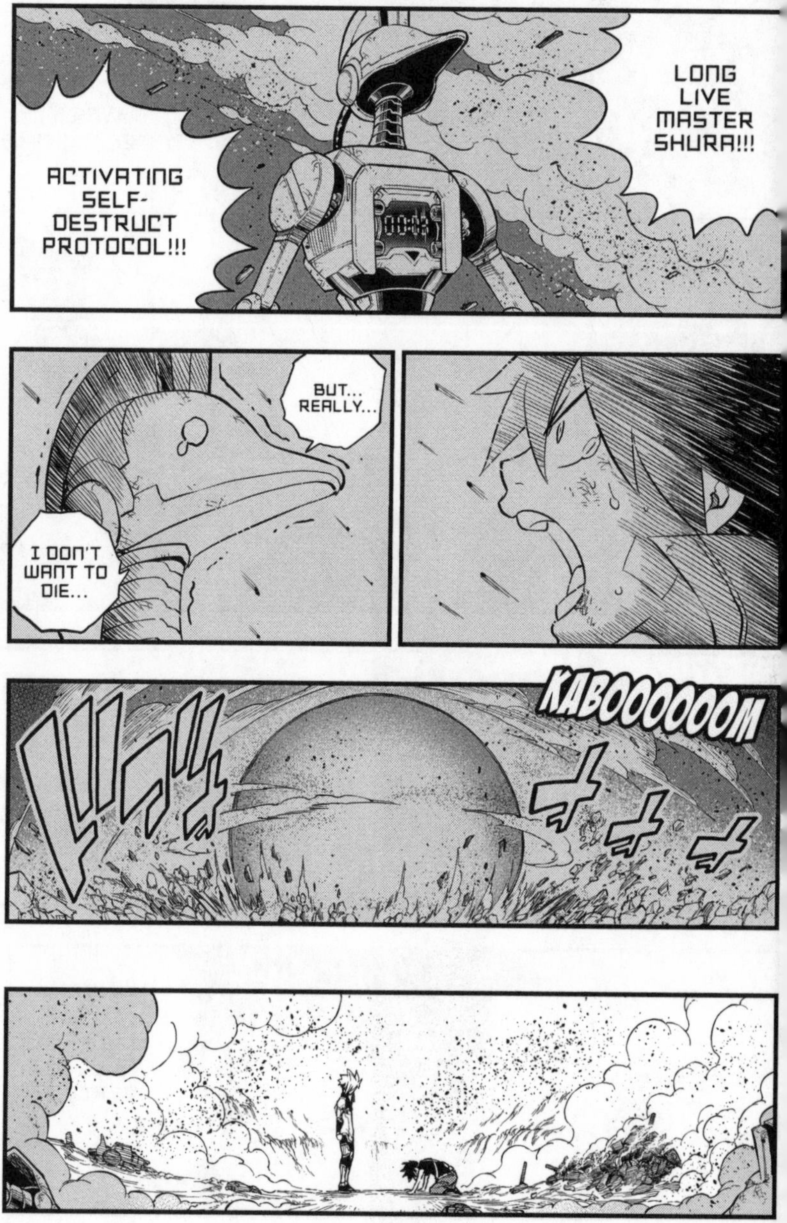
LONG LIVE MASTER SHURA!!!
ACTIVATING SELF-DESTRUCT PROTOCOL!!!
BUT... REALLY...
I DON'T WANT TO DIE...
KABOOOOOOM

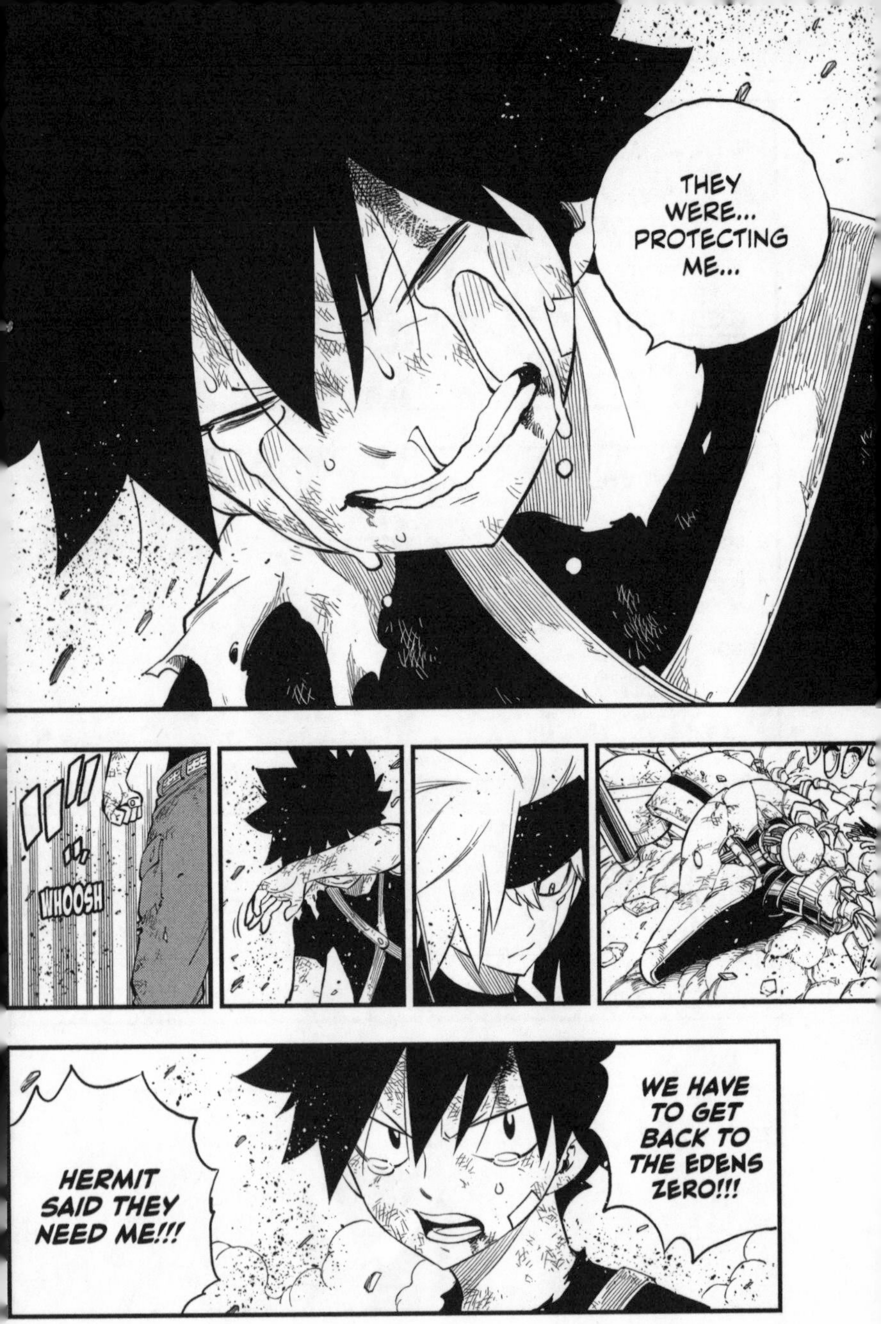
THEY WERE... PROTECTING ME...
WHOOSH
WE HAVE TO GET BACK TO THE EDENS ZERO!!!
HERMIT SAID THEY NEED ME!!!

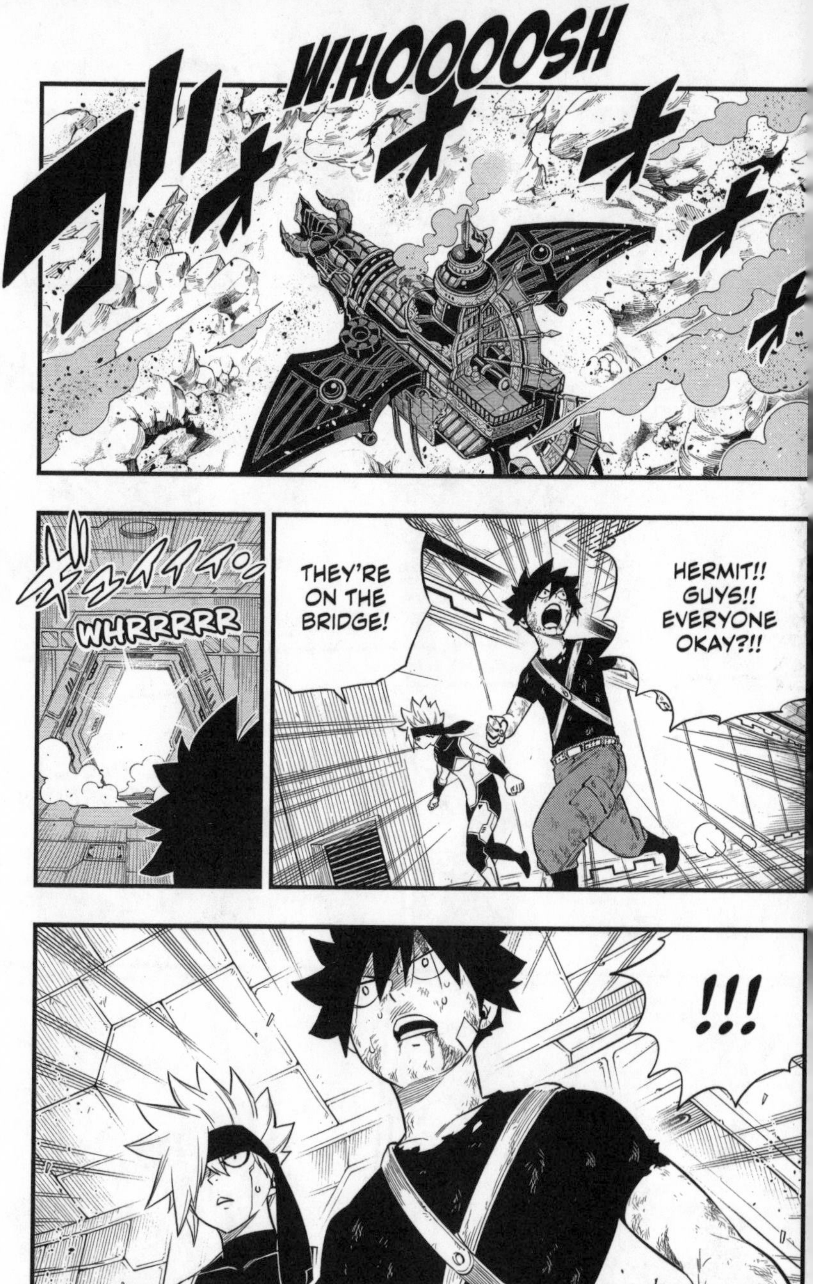
WHOOOOSH
HERMIT!! GUYS!! EVERYONE OKAY?!!
THEY'RE ON THE BRIDGE!
WHRRRRR
!!!

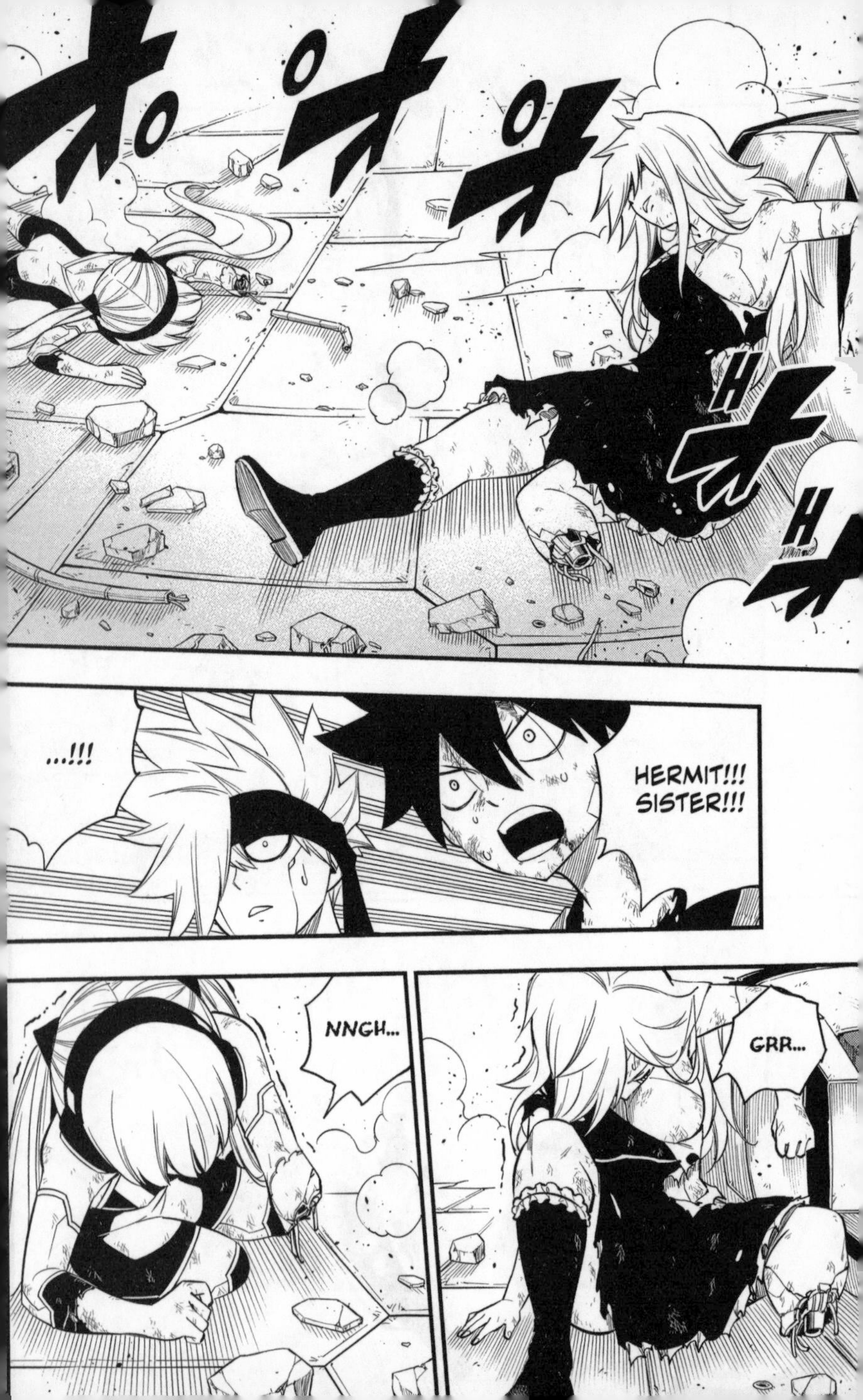
HERMIT!!!
SISTER!!!
...!!!
GRR...
NNGH...

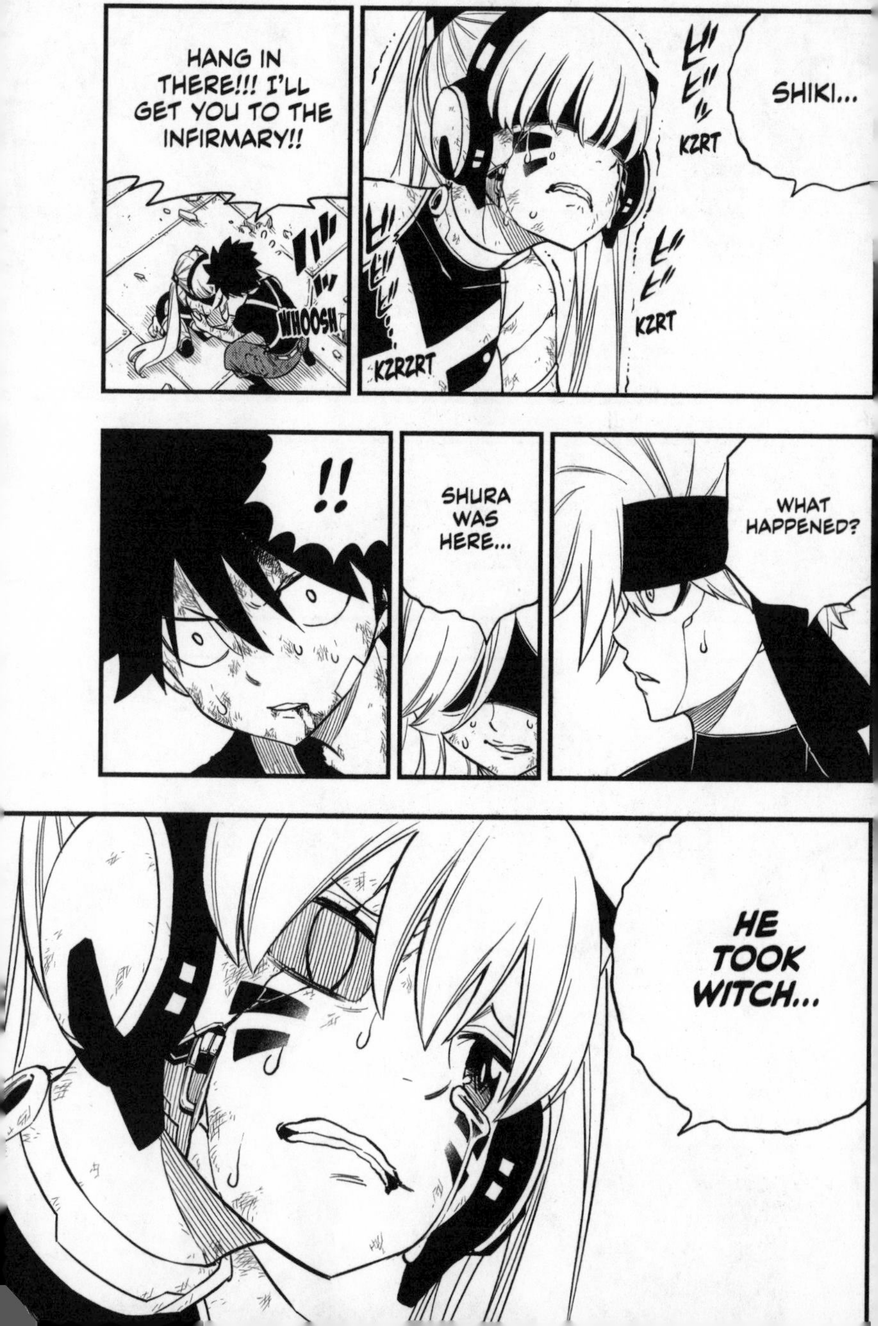
SHIKI...
KZRT
KZRT
KZRZRT
HANG IN THERE!!! I'LL GET YOU TO THE INFIRMARY!!
WHOOSH
WHAT HAPPENED?
SHURA WAS HERE...
!!
HE TOOK WITCH...

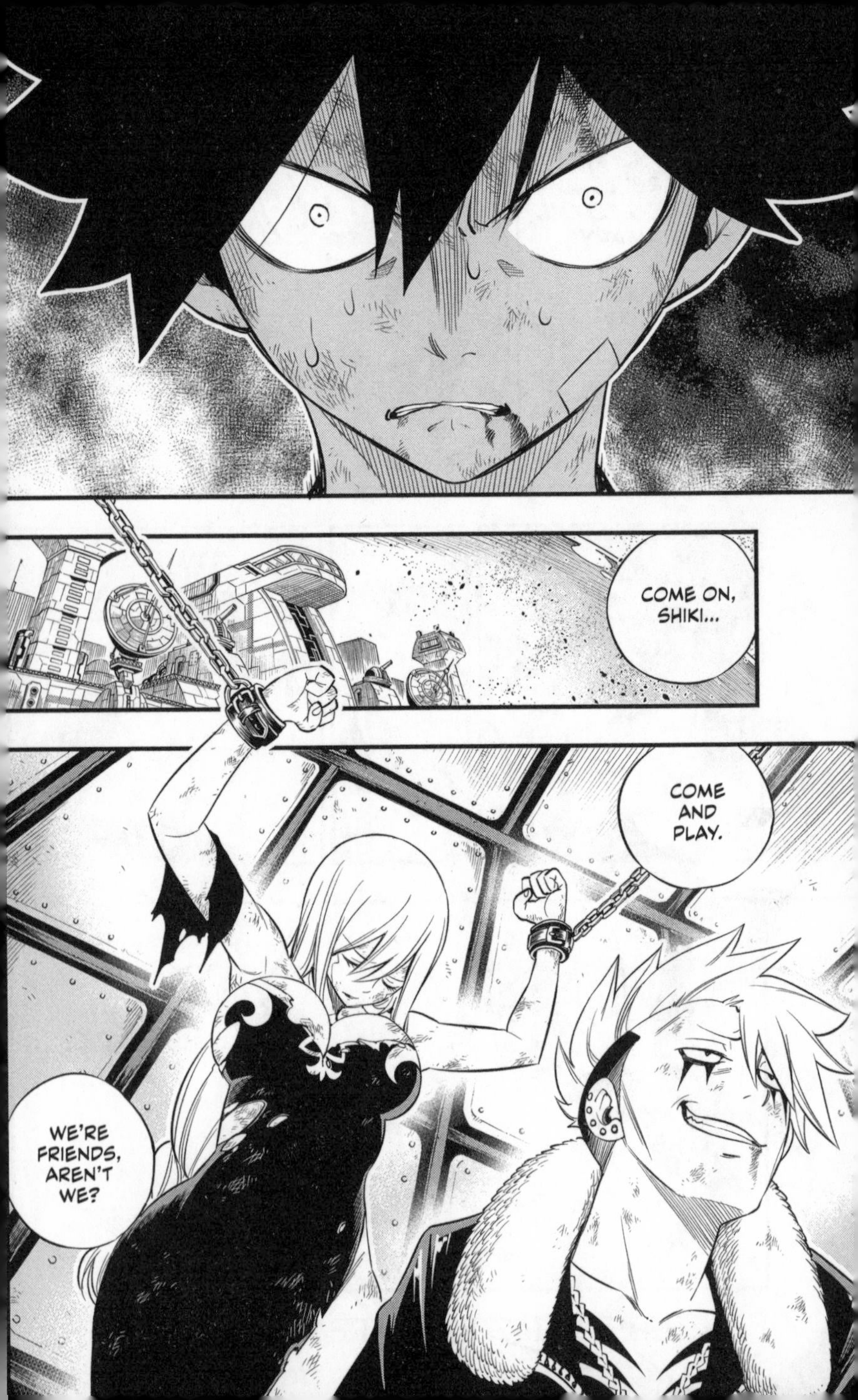
COME ON, SHIKI...
COME AND PLAY.
WE'RE FRIENDS, AREN'T WE?

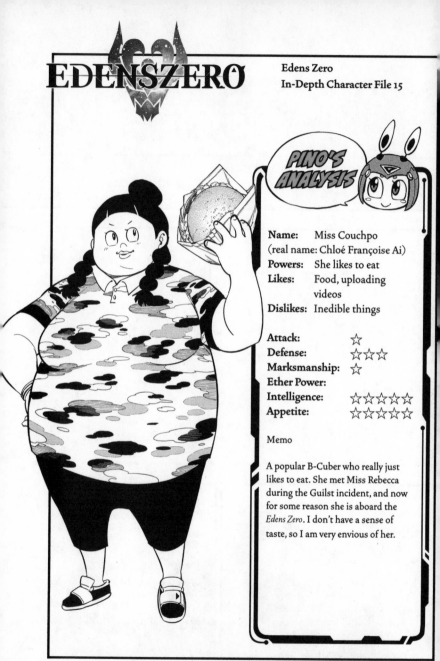

EDENSZERO

Edens Zero
In-Depth Character File 15

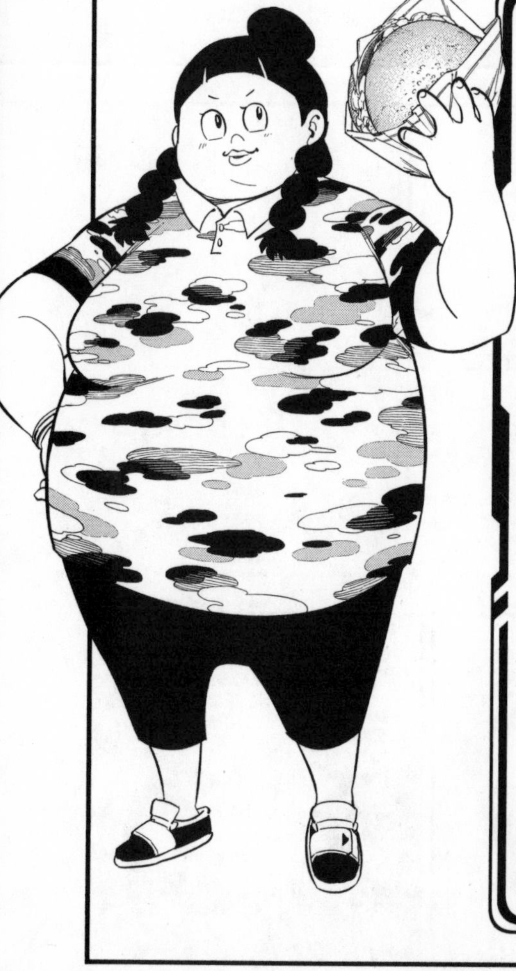

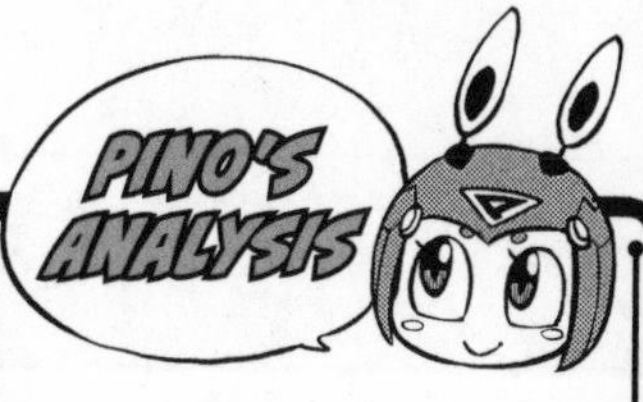
PINO'S ANALYSIS

Name: Miss Couchpo
(real name: Chloé Françoise Ai)
Powers: She likes to eat
Likes: Food, uploading videos
Dislikes: Inedible things

Attack: ☆
Defense: ☆☆☆
Marksmanship: ☆
Ether Power:
Intelligence: ☆☆☆☆☆
Appetite: ☆☆☆☆☆

Memo

A popular B-Cuber who really just likes to eat. She met Miss Rebecca during the Guilst incident, and now for some reason she is aboard the *Edens Zero*. I don't have a sense of taste, so I am very envious of her.

CHAPTER 147: RAGE, FEAR, AND GRIEF

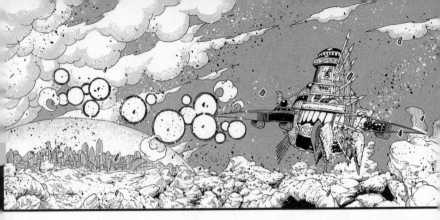

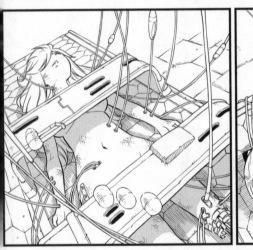

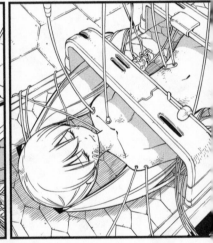

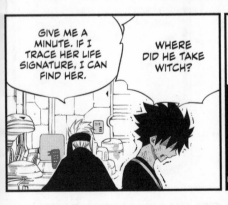

DON'T WORRY. NONE OF THEIR INJURIES ARE LIFE-THREATENING.
AND WE CAN REPAIR THEIR DAMAGED PARTS.
WHERE DID HE TAKE WITCH?
GIVE ME A MINUTE. IF I TRACE HER LIFE SIGNATURE, I CAN FIND HER.

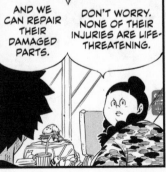

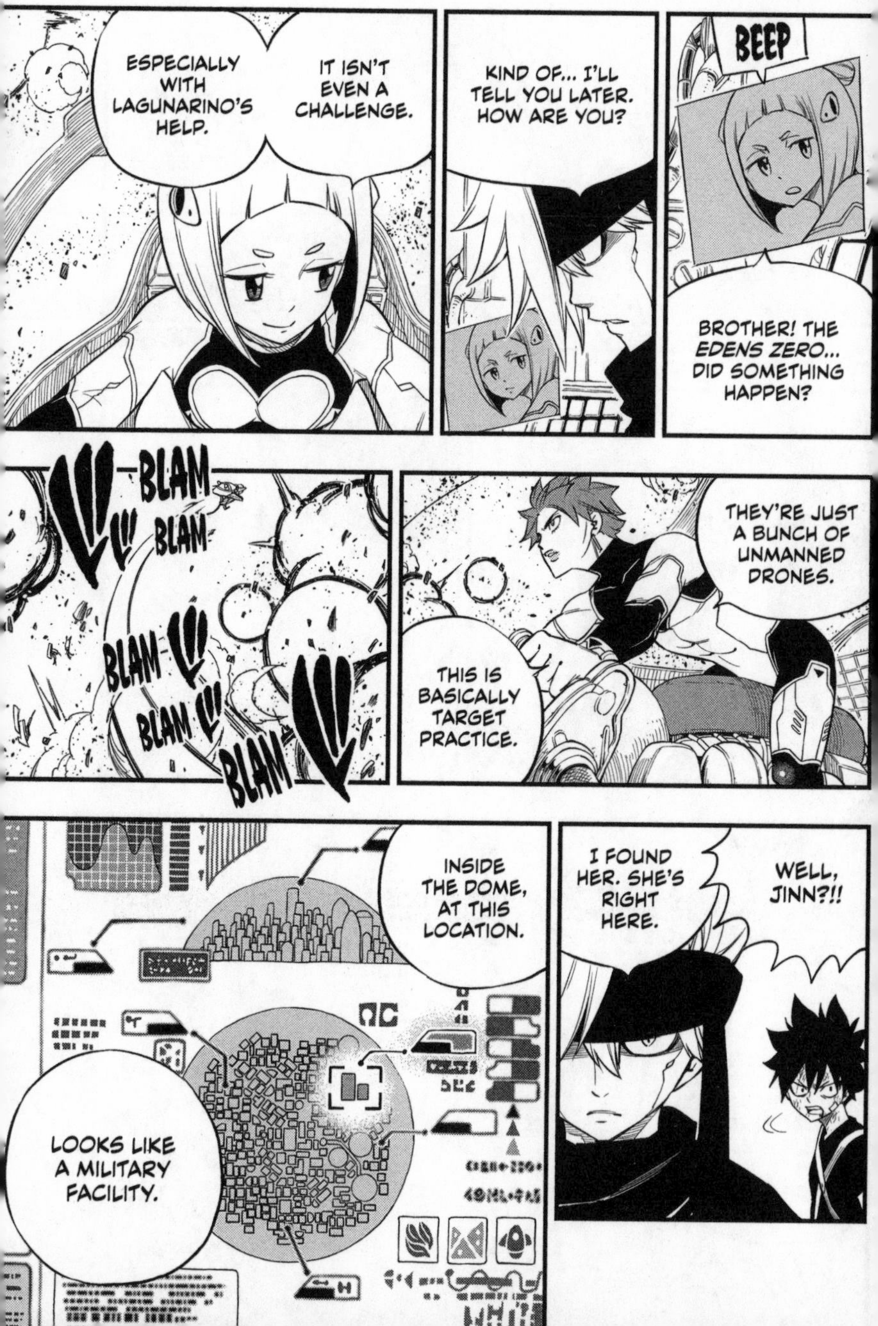
BEEP
BROTHER! THE EDENS ZERO... DID SOMETHING HAPPEN?
KIND OF... I'LL TELL YOU LATER. HOW ARE YOU?
IT ISN'T EVEN A CHALLENGE.
ESPECIALLY WITH LAGUNARINO'S HELP.
THEY'RE JUST A BUNCH OF UNMANNED DRONES.
THIS IS BASICALLY TARGET PRACTICE.
BLAM
BLAM
BLAM
BLAM
BLAM
WELL, JINN?!!
I FOUND HER. SHE'S RIGHT HERE.
INSIDE THE DOME, AT THIS LOCATION.
LOOKS LIKE A MILITARY FACILITY.

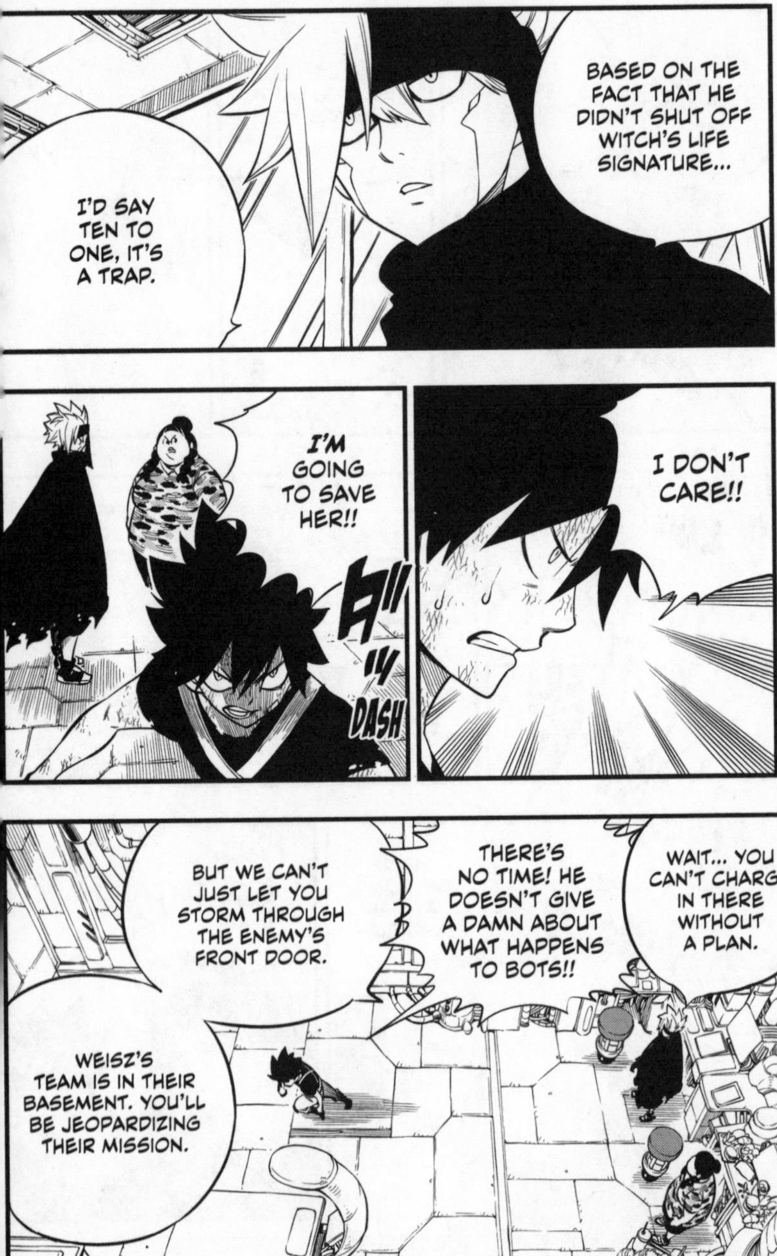
BASED ON THE FACT THAT HE DIDN'T SHUT OFF WITCH'S LIFE SIGNATURE...
I'D SAY TEN TO ONE, IT'S A TRAP.
I DON'T CARE!!
I'M GOING TO SAVE HER!!
DASH
WAIT... YOU CAN'T CHARGE IN THERE WITHOUT A PLAN.
THERE'S NO TIME! HE DOESN'T GIVE A DAMN ABOUT WHAT HAPPENS TO BOTS!!
BUT WE CAN'T JUST LET YOU STORM THROUGH THE ENEMY'S FRONT DOOR.
WEISZ'S TEAM IS IN THEIR BASEMENT. YOU'LL BE JEOPARDIZING THEIR MISSION.

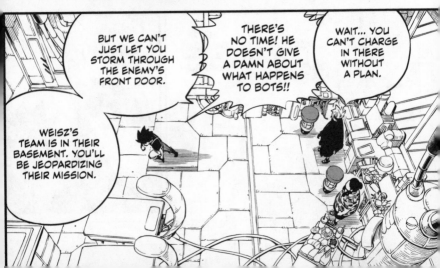

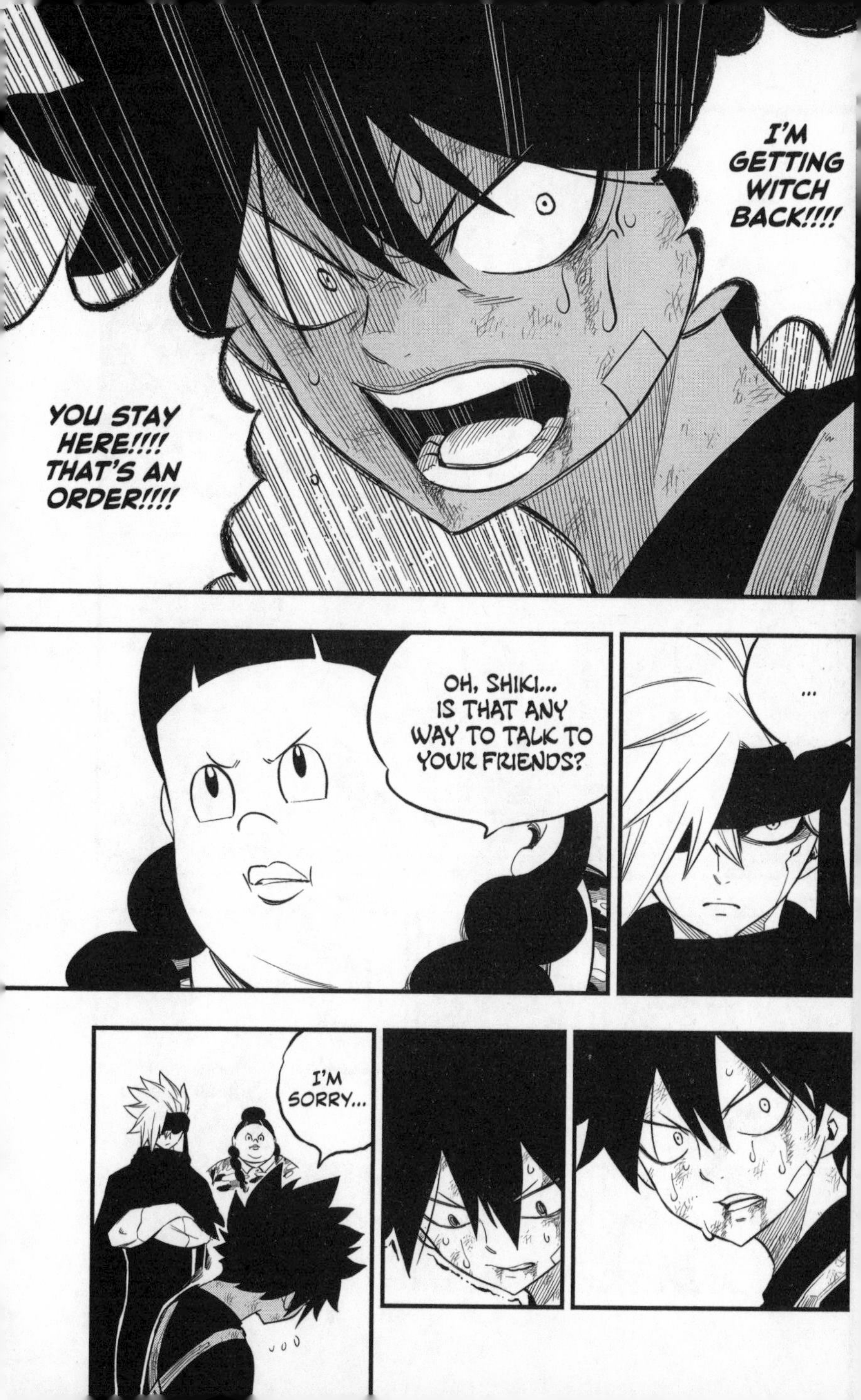
I'M GETTING WITCH BACK!!!!
YOU STAY HERE!!!! THAT'S AN ORDER!!!!
...
OH, SHIKI... IS THAT ANY WAY TO TALK TO YOUR FRIENDS?
I'M SORRY...

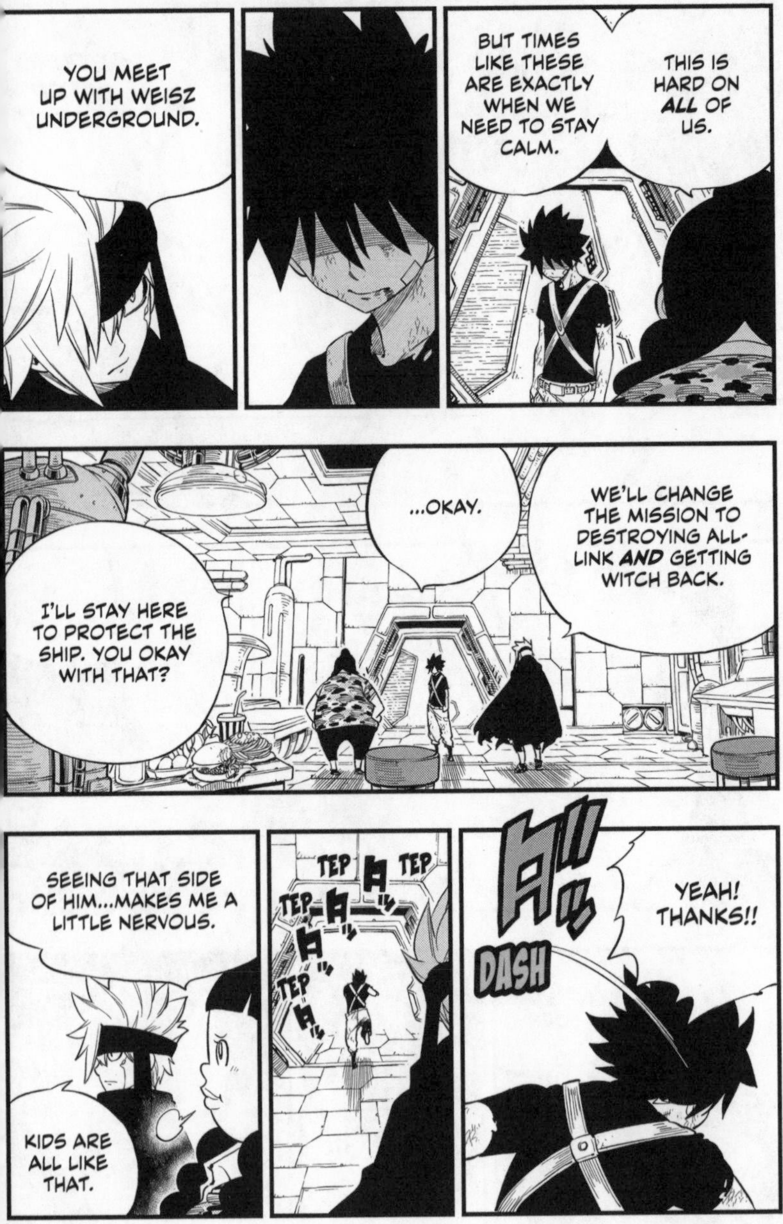
THIS IS HARD ON ALL OF US.
BUT TIMES LIKE THESE ARE EXACTLY WHEN WE NEED TO STAY CALM.
YOU MEET UP WITH WEISZ UNDERGROUND.
WE'LL CHANGE THE MISSION TO DESTROYING ALL-LINK AND GETTING WITCH BACK.
...OKAY.
I'LL STAY HERE TO PROTECT THE SHIP. YOU OKAY WITH THAT?
YEAH! THANKS!!
DASH
TEP
TEP
TEP
TEP
SEEING THAT SIDE OF HIM...MAKES ME A LITTLE NERVOUS.
KIDS ARE ALL LIKE THAT.

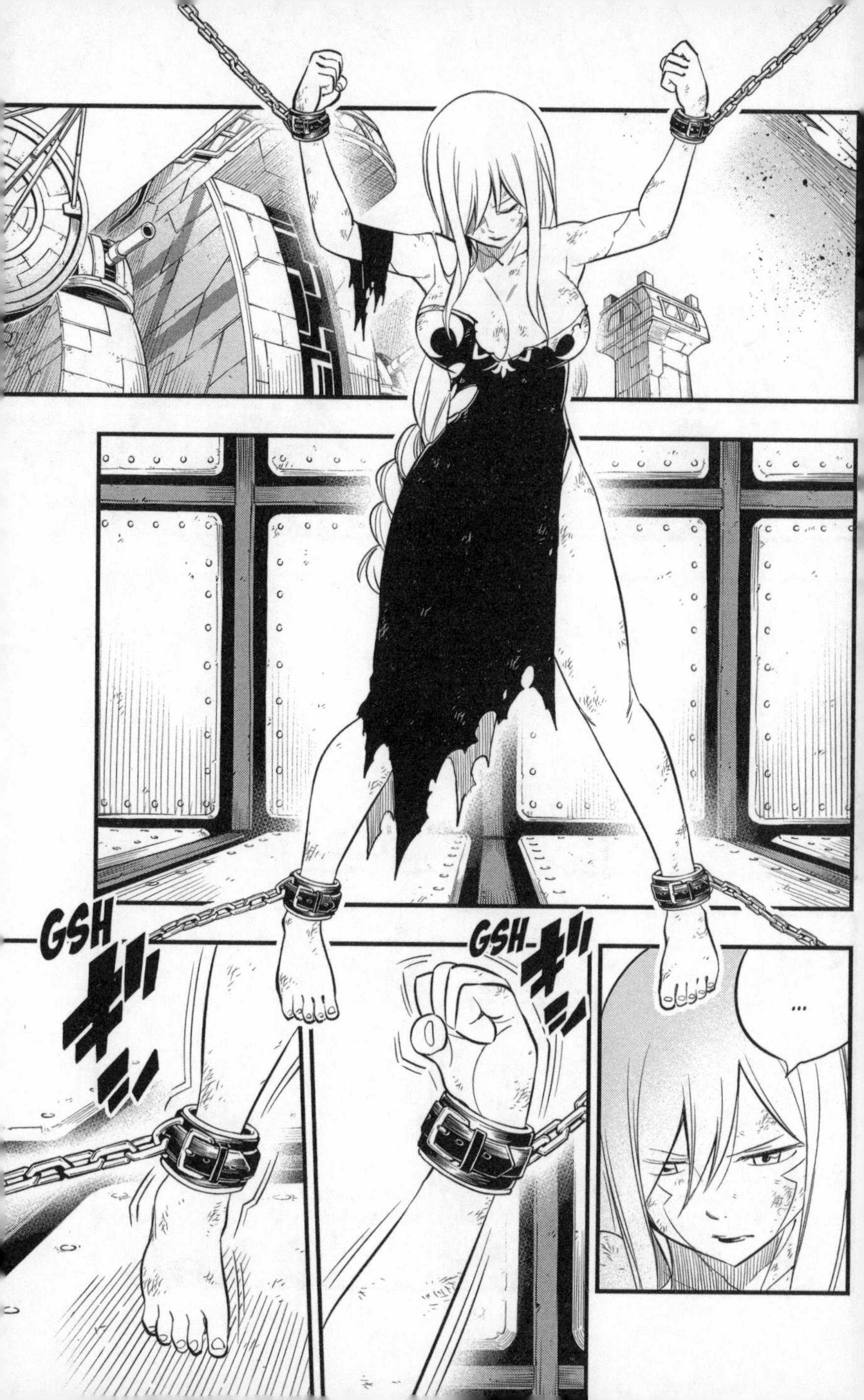
...
GSH
GSH

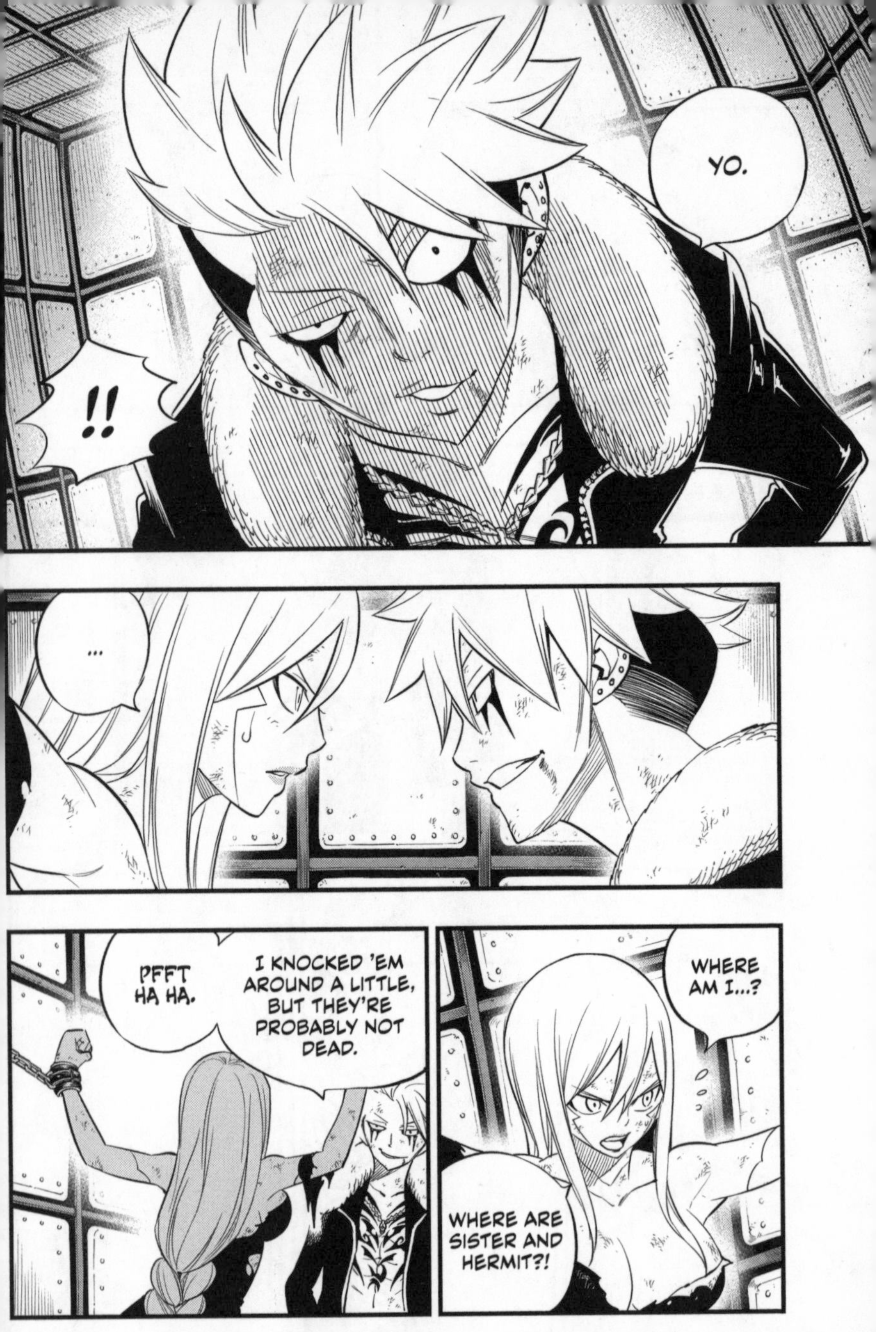
YO.
!!
...
WHERE AM I...?
WHERE ARE SISTER AND HERMIT?!
I KNOCKED 'EM AROUND A LITTLE, BUT THEY'RE PROBABLY NOT DEAD.
PFFT HA HA.

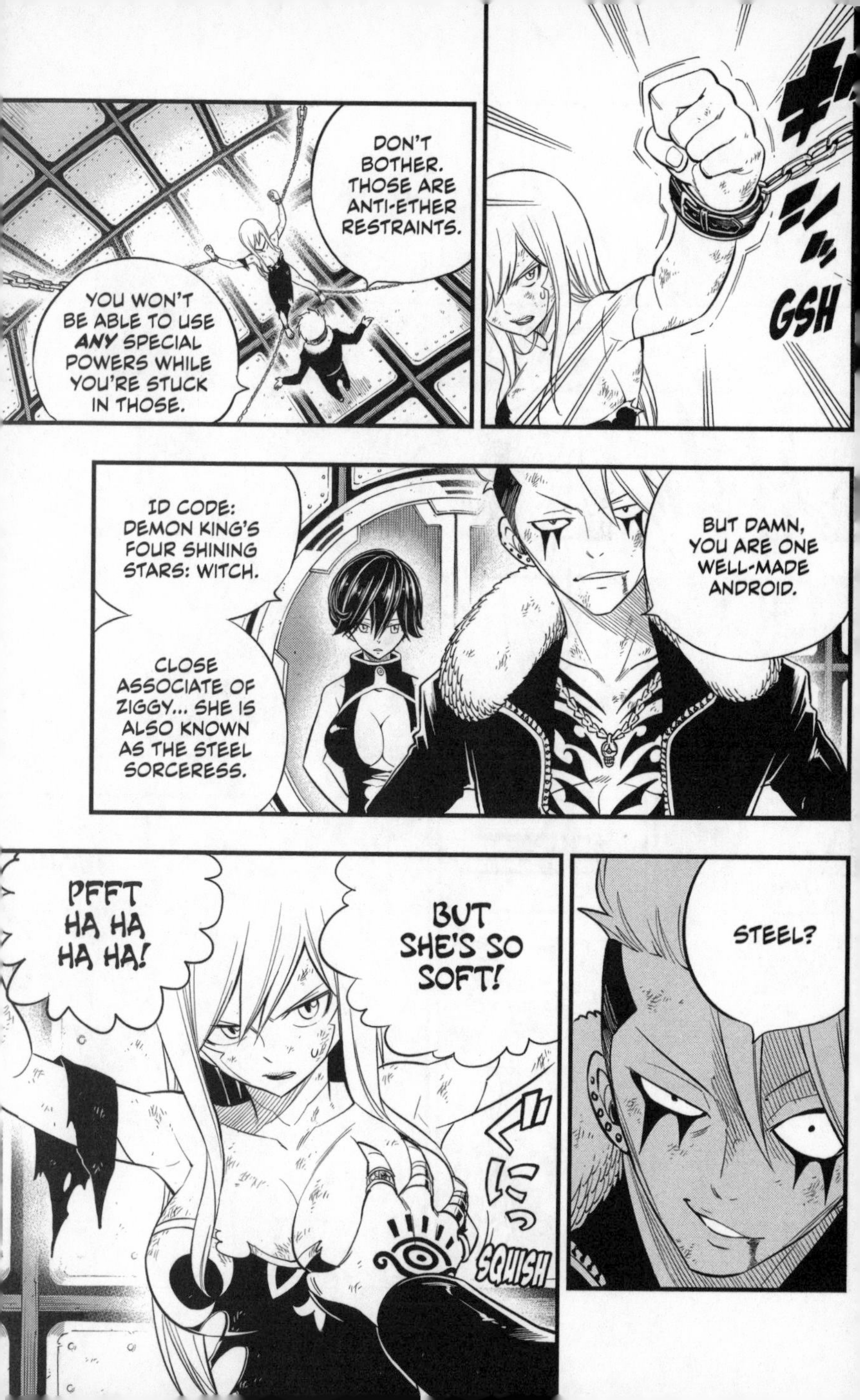
GSH
DON'T BOTHER. THOSE ARE ANTI-ETHER RESTRAINTS.
YOU WON'T BE ABLE TO USE **ANY** SPECIAL POWERS WHILE YOU'RE STUCK IN THOSE.
BUT DAMN, YOU ARE ONE WELL-MADE ANDROID.
ID CODE: DEMON KING'S FOUR SHINING STARS: WITCH.
CLOSE ASSOCIATE OF ZIGGY... SHE IS ALSO KNOWN AS THE STEEL SORCERESS.
STEEL?
BUT SHE'S SO SOFT!
PFFT HA HA HA HA!
SQUISH

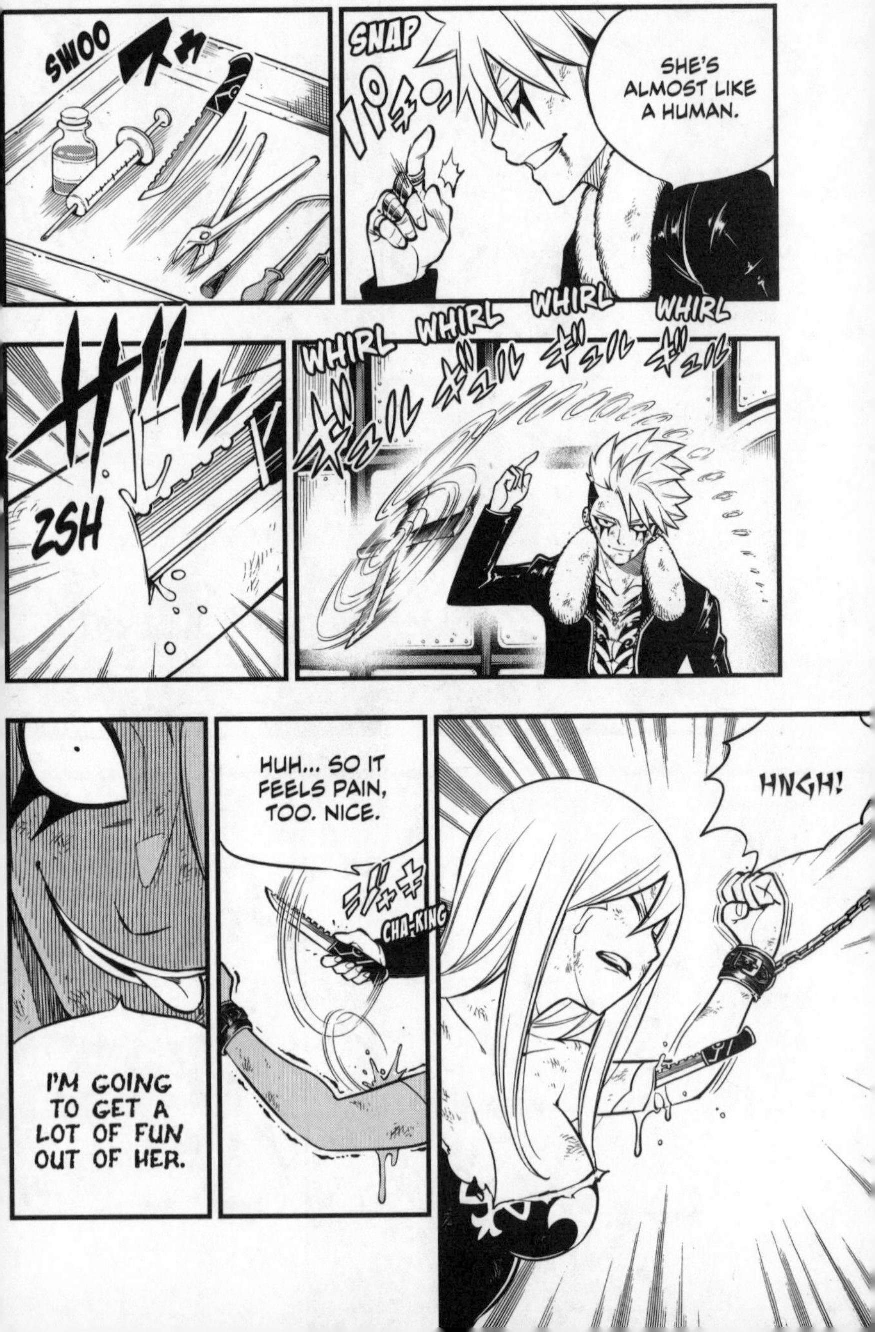
SHE'S ALMOST LIKE A HUMAN.
SNAP
SWOO
WHIRL WHIRL WHIRL WHIRL
ZSH
HNGH!
HUH... SO IT FEELS PAIN, TOO. NICE.
CHA-KING
I'M GOING TO GET A LOT OF FUN OUT OF HER.

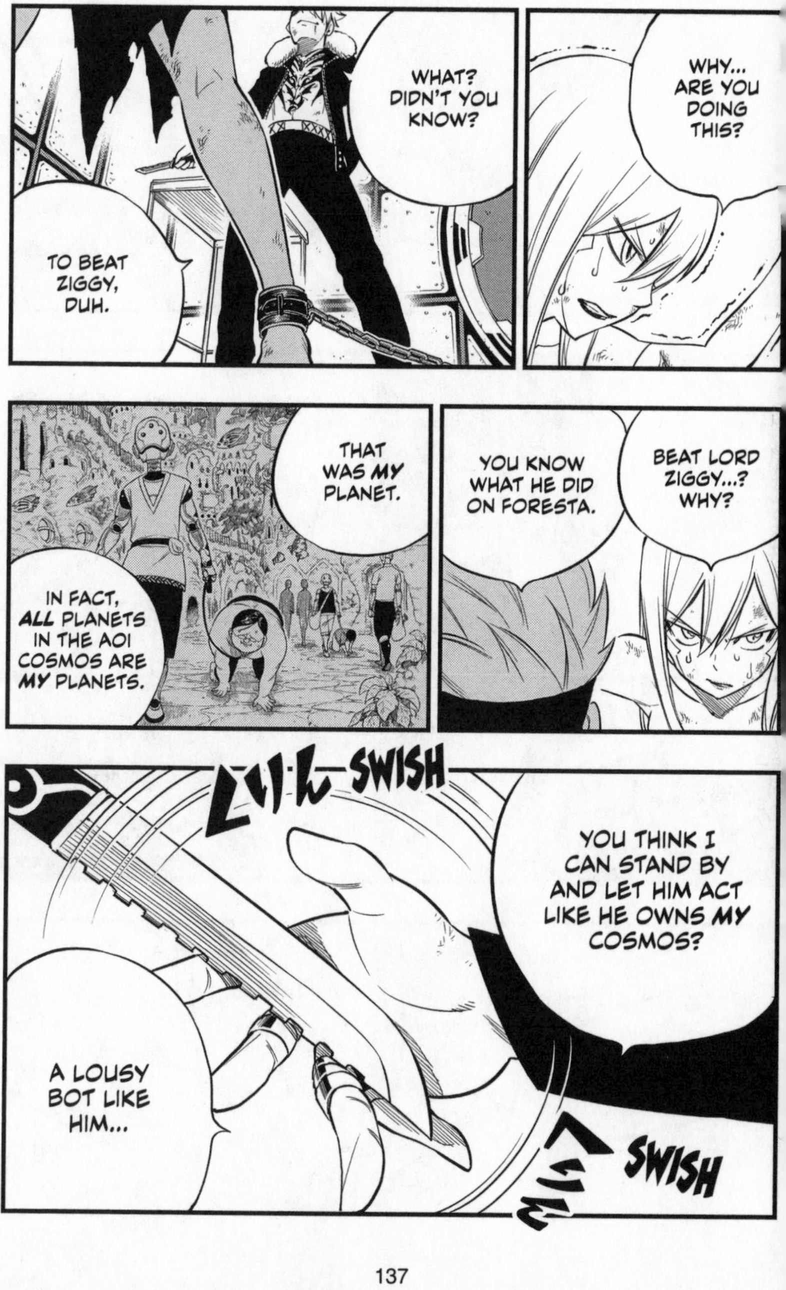
WHY... ARE YOU DOING THIS?
WHAT? DIDN'T YOU KNOW?
TO BEAT ZIGGY, DUH.
BEAT LORD ZIGGY...? WHY?
YOU KNOW WHAT HE DID ON FORESTA.
THAT WAS MY PLANET.
IN FACT, ALL PLANETS IN THE AOI COSMOS ARE MY PLANETS.
SWISH
YOU THINK I CAN STAND BY AND LET HIM ACT LIKE HE OWNS MY COSMOS?
A LOUSY BOT LIKE HIM...
SWISH

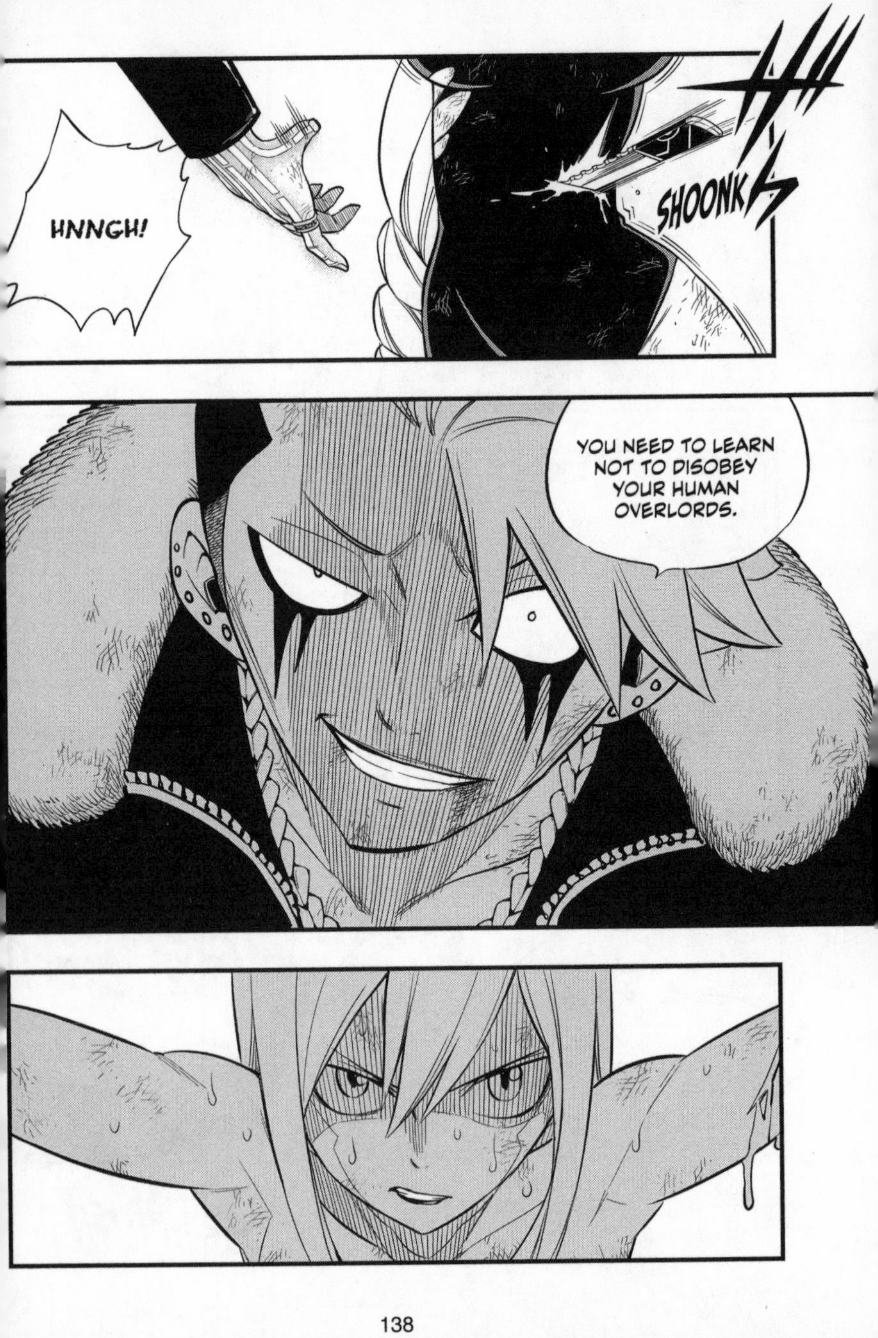
SHOONK
HNNGH!
YOU NEED TO LEARN NOT TO DISOBEY YOUR HUMAN OVERLORDS.

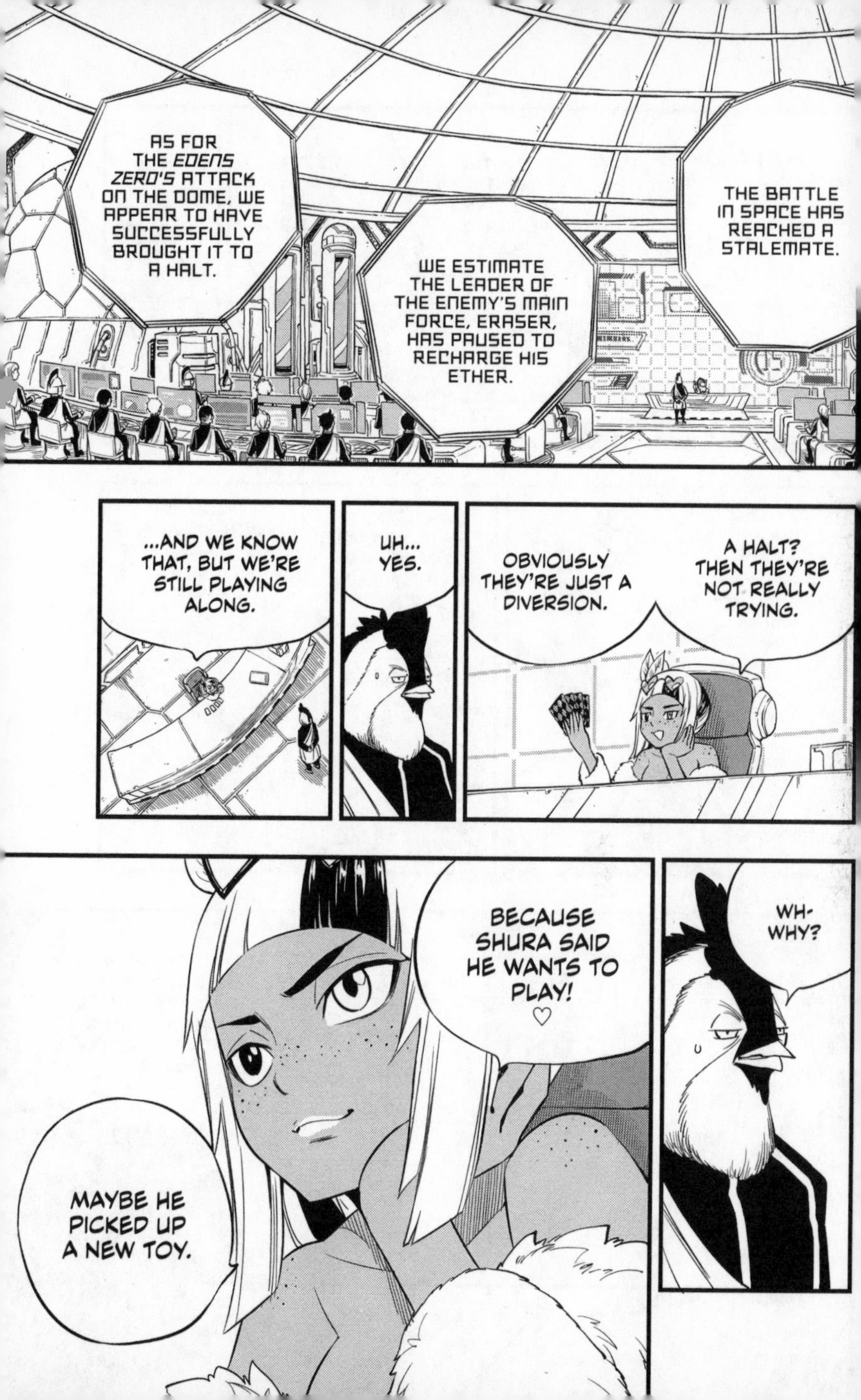
THE BATTLE IN SPACE HAS REACHED A STALEMATE.
WE ESTIMATE THE LEADER OF THE ENEMY'S MAIN FORCE, ERASER, HAS PAUSED TO RECHARGE HIS ETHER.
AS FOR THE *EDENS ZERO'S* ATTACK ON THE DOME, WE APPEAR TO HAVE SUCCESSFULLY BROUGHT IT TO A HALT.
A HALT? THEN THEY'RE NOT REALLY TRYING.
OBVIOUSLY THEY'RE JUST A DIVERSION.
UH... YES.
...AND WE KNOW THAT, BUT WE'RE STILL PLAYING ALONG.
WH- WHY?
BECAUSE SHURA SAID HE WANTS TO PLAY! ♡
MAYBE HE PICKED UP A NEW TOY.

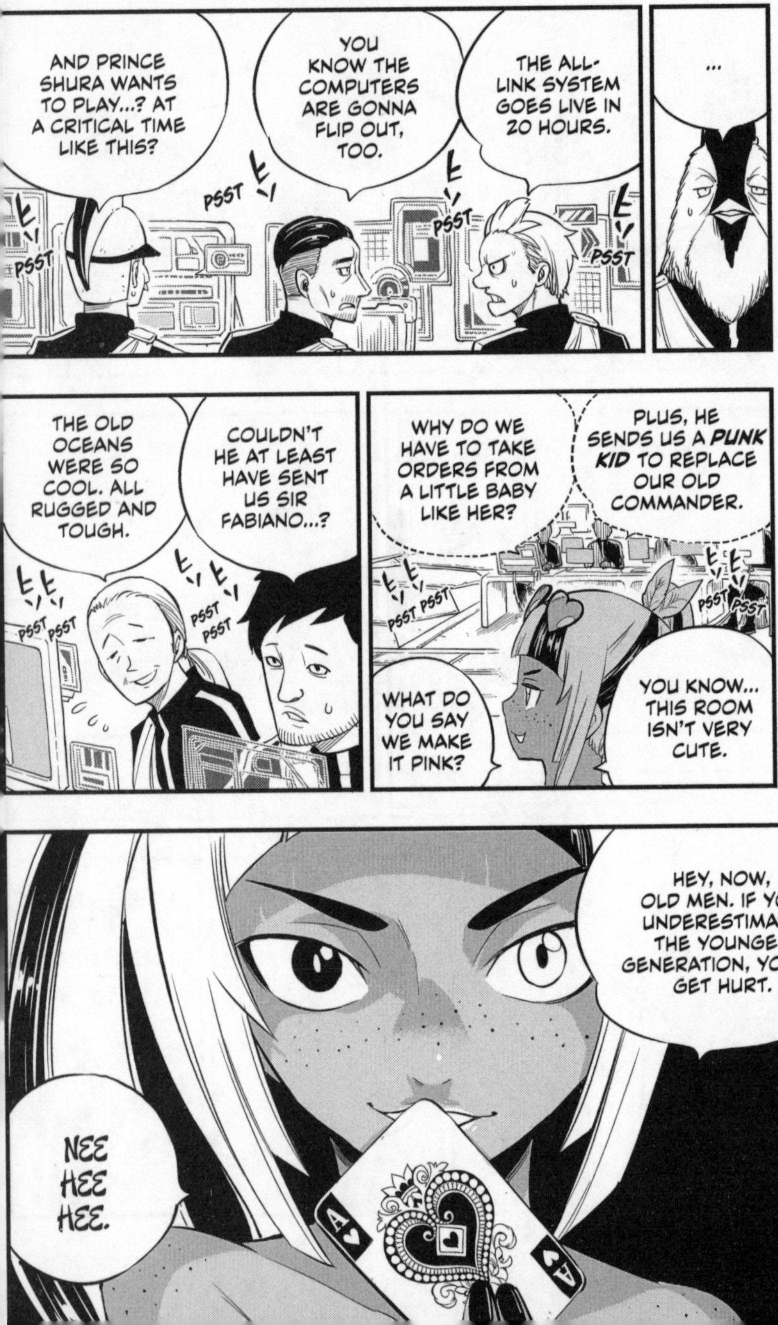
...
THE ALL-LINK SYSTEM GOES LIVE IN 20 HOURS.
PSST
PSST
YOU KNOW THE COMPUTERS ARE GONNA FLIP OUT, TOO.
PSST
AND PRINCE SHURA WANTS TO PLAY...? AT A CRITICAL TIME LIKE THIS?
PSST
PLUS, HE SENDS US A *PUNK KID* TO REPLACE OUR OLD COMMANDER.
WHY DO WE HAVE TO TAKE ORDERS FROM A LITTLE BABY LIKE HER?
PSST PSST
PSST PSST
YOU KNOW... THIS ROOM ISN'T VERY CUTE.
WHAT DO YOU SAY WE MAKE IT PINK?
COULDN'T HE AT LEAST HAVE SENT US SIR FABIANO...?
PSST PSST
THE OLD OCEANS WERE SO COOL. ALL RUGGED AND TOUGH.
PSST PSST
HEY, NOW, OLD MEN. IF YOU UNDERESTIMATE THE YOUNGER GENERATION, YOU'LL GET HURT.
NEE HEE HEE.

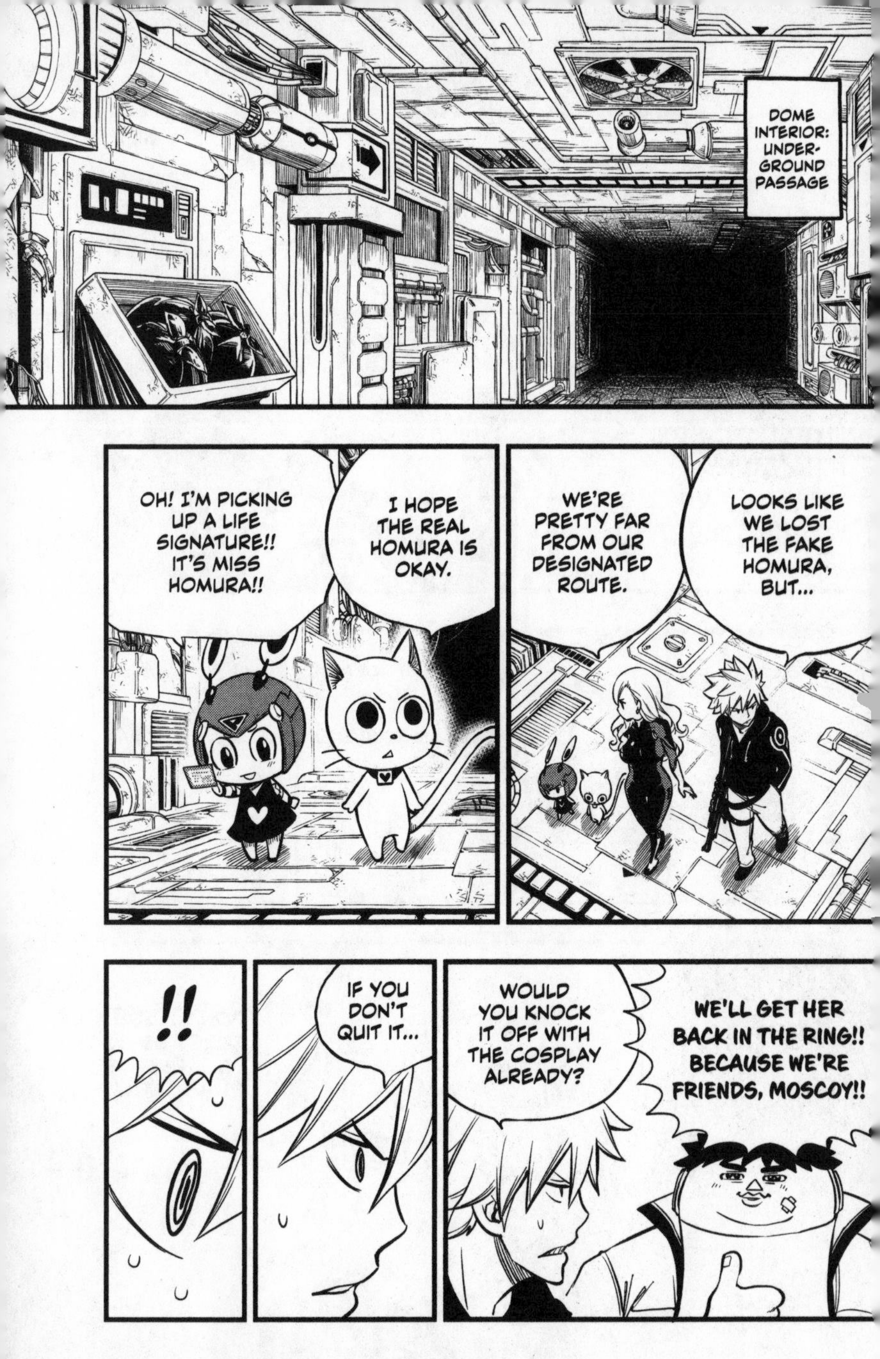
DOME INTERIOR: UNDER-GROUND PASSAGE
LOOKS LIKE WE LOST THE FAKE HOMURA, BUT...
WE'RE PRETTY FAR FROM OUR DESIGNATED ROUTE.
I HOPE THE REAL HOMURA IS OKAY.
OH! I'M PICKING UP A LIFE SIGNATURE!! IT'S MISS HOMURA!!
WE'LL GET HER BACK IN THE RING!! BECAUSE WE'RE FRIENDS, MOSCOY!!
WOULD YOU KNOCK IT OFF WITH THE COSPLAY ALREADY?
IF YOU DON'T QUIT IT...
!!

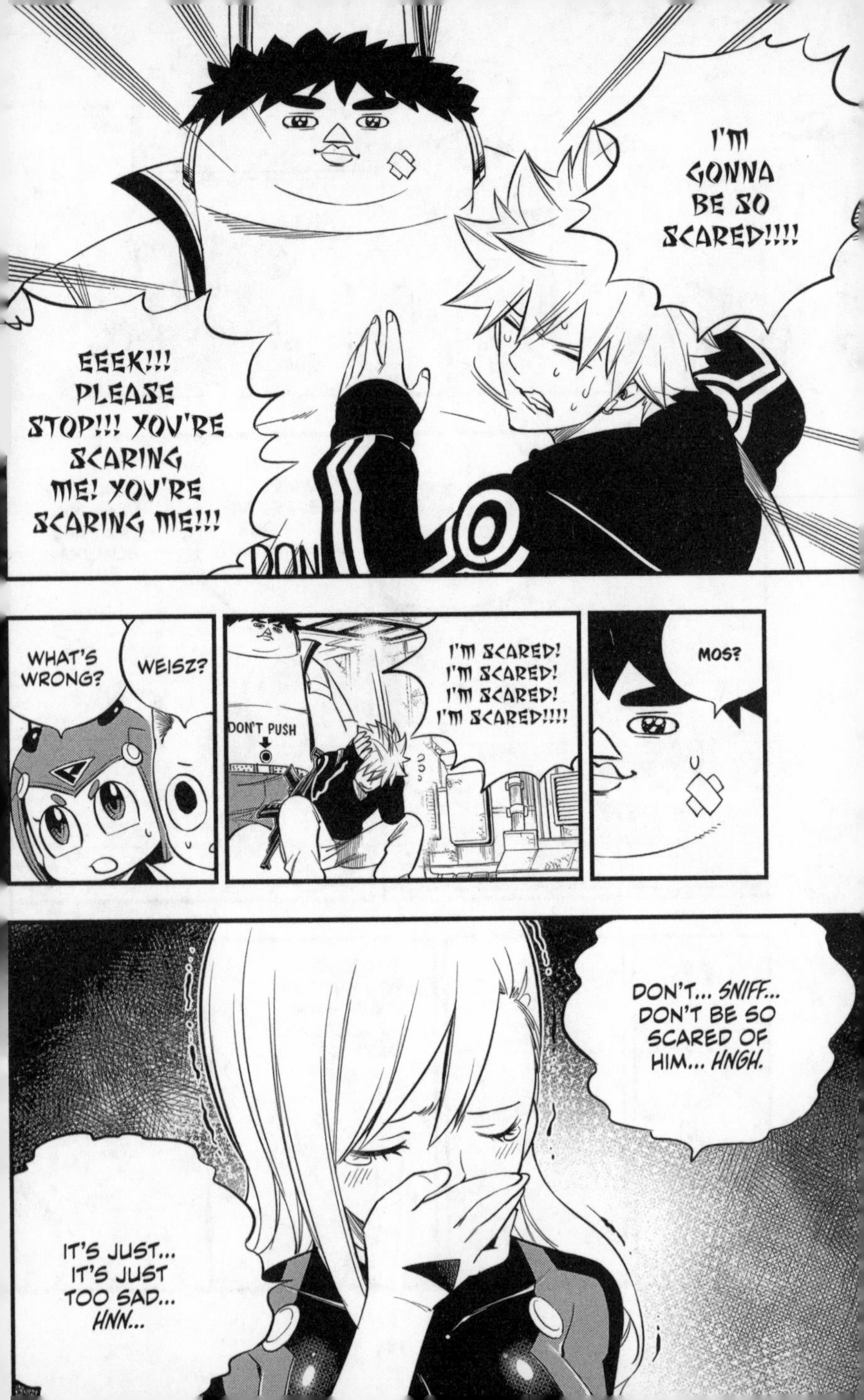
I'M GONNA BE SO SCARED!!!!
EEEK!!! PLEASE STOP!!! YOU'RE SCARING ME! YOU'RE SCARING ME!!!
DON
MOS?
I'M SCARED! I'M SCARED! I'M SCARED! I'M SCARED!!!!
DON'T PUSH
WEISZ?
WHAT'S WRONG?
DON'T... *SNIFF*... DON'T BE SO SCARED OF HIM... *HNGH.*
IT'S JUST... IT'S JUST TOO SAD... *HNN...*

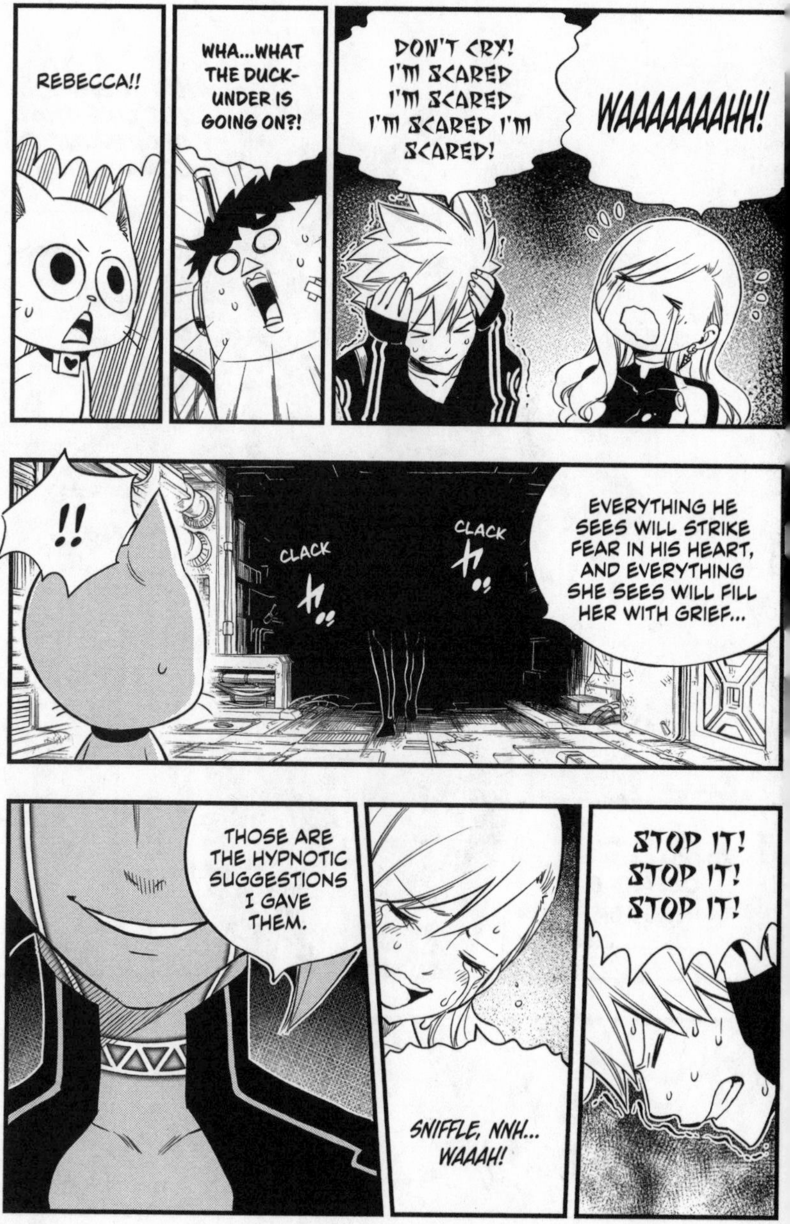
WAAAAAAAHH!
DON'T CRY! I'M SCARED I'M SCARED I'M SCARED I'M SCARED!
WHA...WHAT THE DUCK-UNDER IS GOING ON?!
REBECCA!!
EVERYTHING HE SEES WILL STRIKE FEAR IN HIS HEART, AND EVERYTHING SHE SEES WILL FILL HER WITH GRIEF...
CLACK
CLACK
!!
STOP IT! STOP IT! STOP IT!
SNIFFLE, NNH... WAAAH!
THOSE ARE THE HYPNOTIC SUGGESTIONS I GAVE THEM.

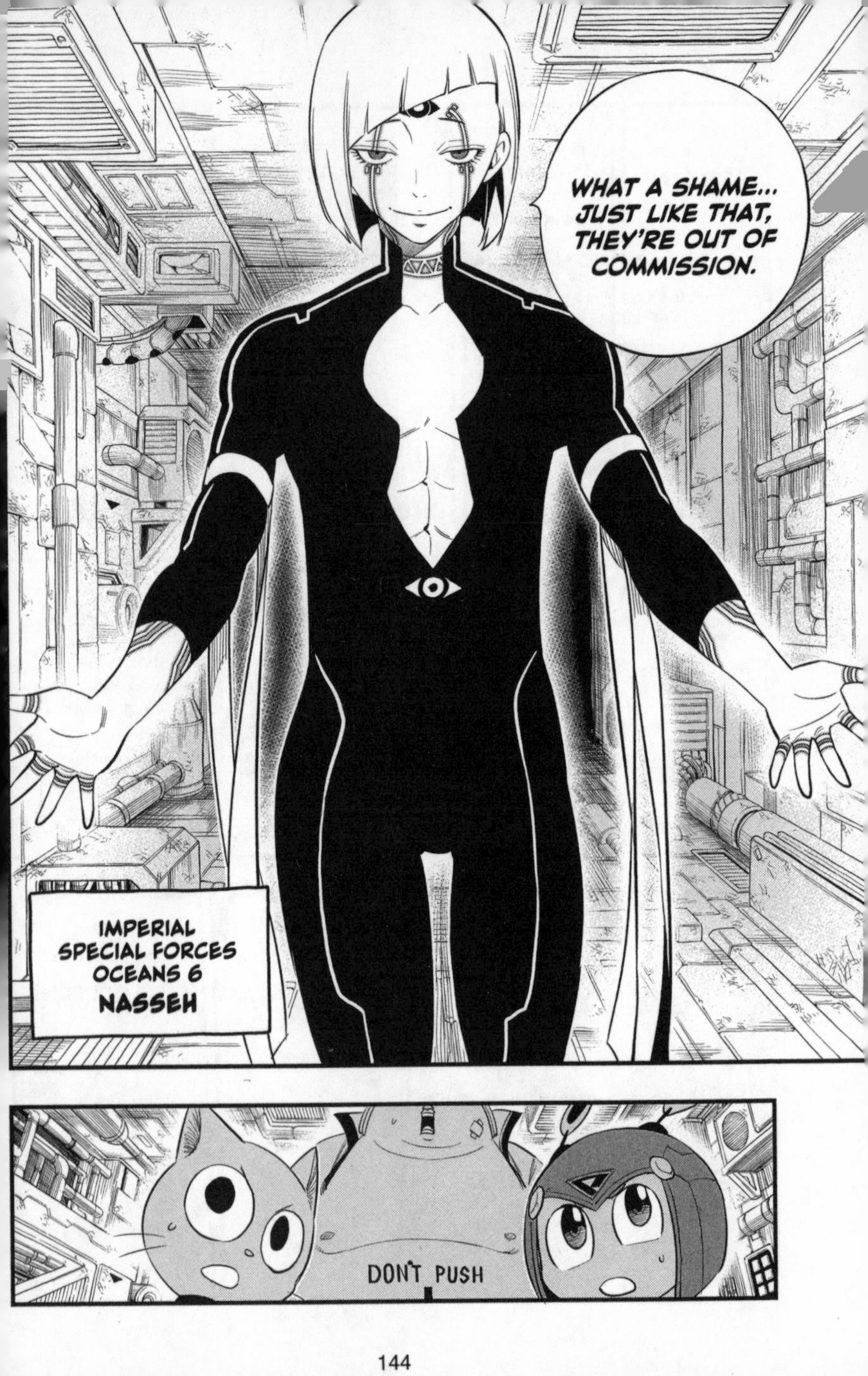
WHAT A SHAME... JUST LIKE THAT, THEY'RE OUT OF COMMISSION.
IMPERIAL SPECIAL FORCES OCEANS 6 NASSEH
DON'T PUSH

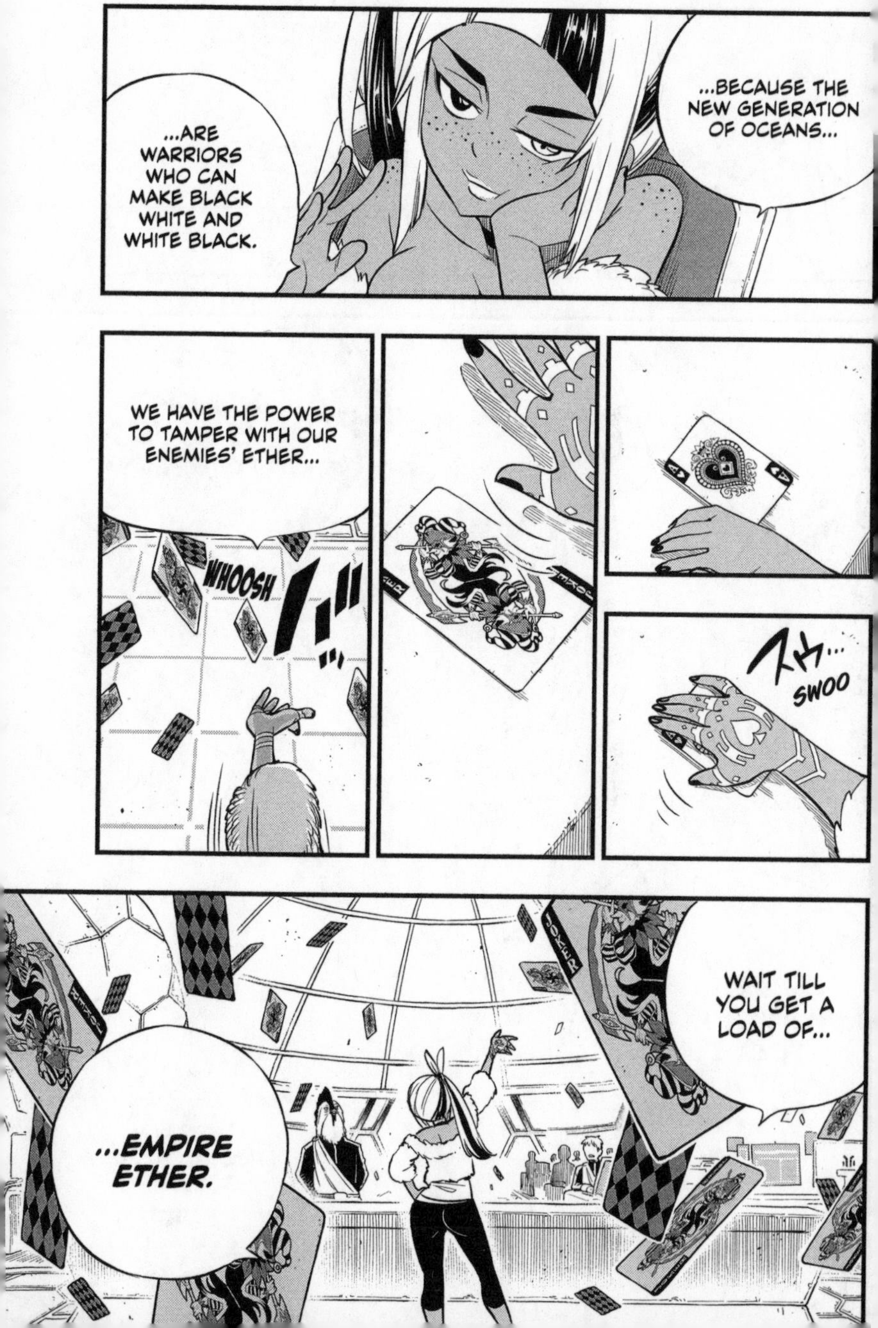
...BECAUSE THE NEW GENERATION OF OCEANS...
...ARE WARRIORS WHO CAN MAKE BLACK WHITE AND WHITE BLACK.
スゥ…
SWOO
WE HAVE THE POWER TO TAMPER WITH OUR ENEMIES' ETHER...
WHOOSH
WAIT TILL YOU GET A LOAD OF...
...EMPIRE ETHER.

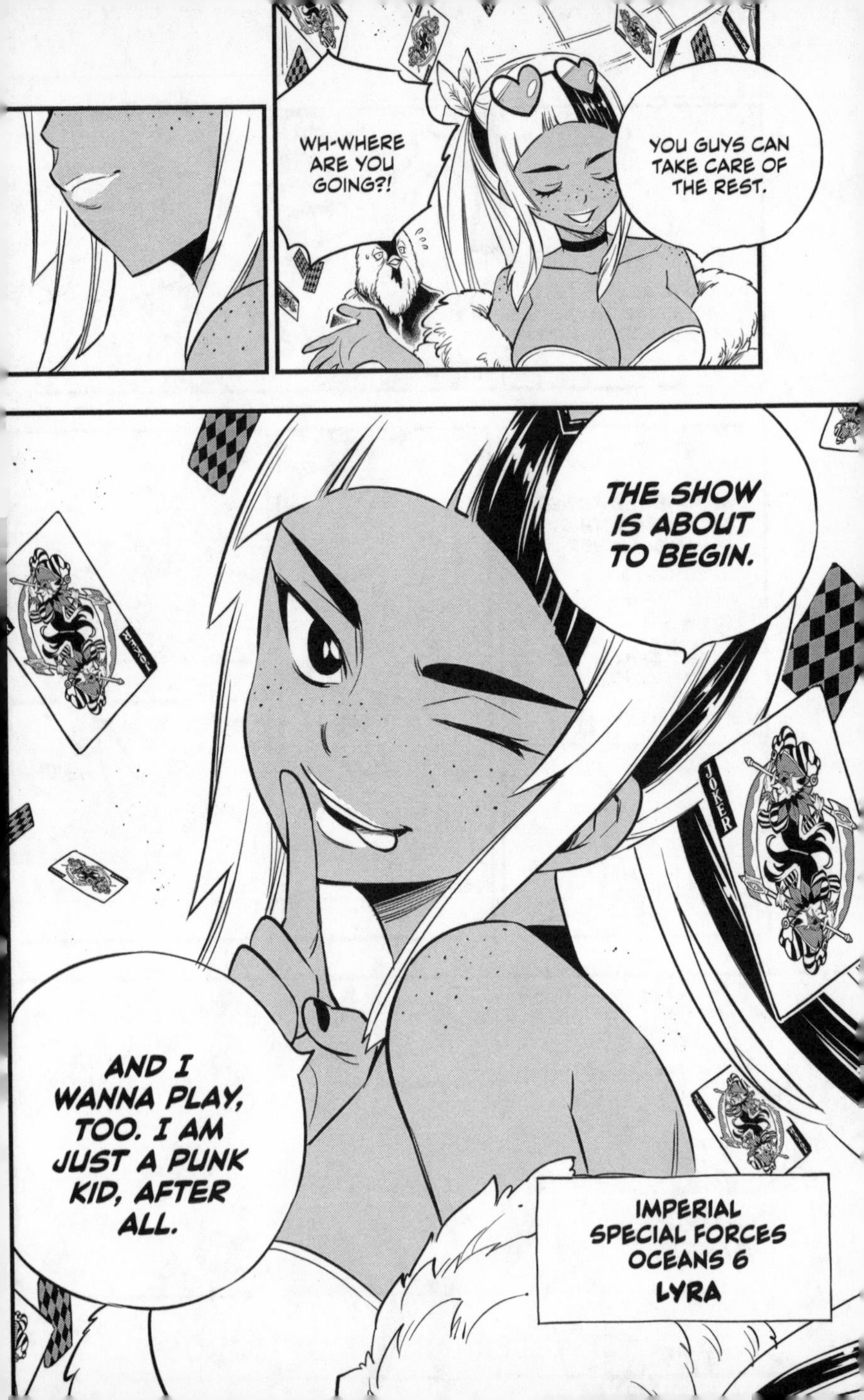
YOU GUYS CAN TAKE CARE OF THE REST.
WH-WHERE ARE YOU GOING?!
THE SHOW IS ABOUT TO BEGIN.
AND I WANNA PLAY, TOO. I AM JUST A PUNK KID, AFTER ALL.
IMPERIAL SPECIAL FORCES OCEANS 6
LYRA

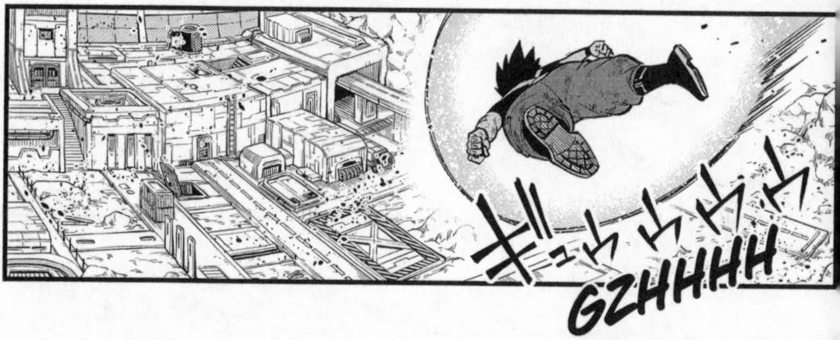
GZHHHH

EDENSZERO

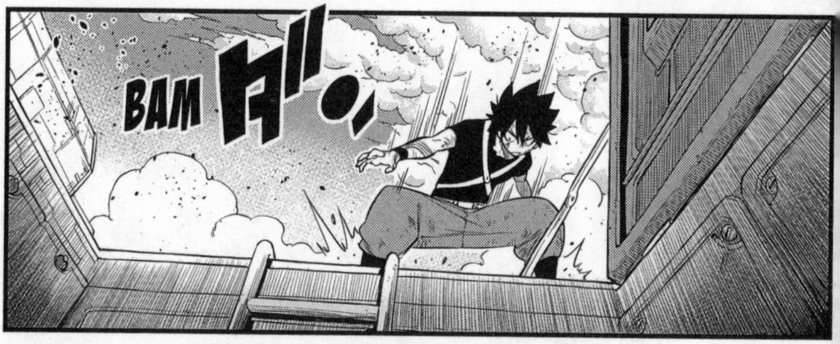
BAM

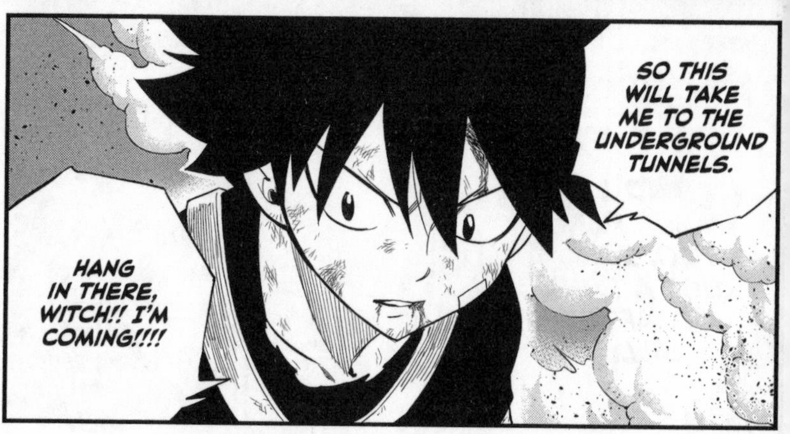
SO THIS WILL TAKE ME TO THE UNDERGROUND TUNNELS.
HANG IN THERE, WITCH!! I'M COMING!!!!

CHAPTER 148: EYE OF HORUS

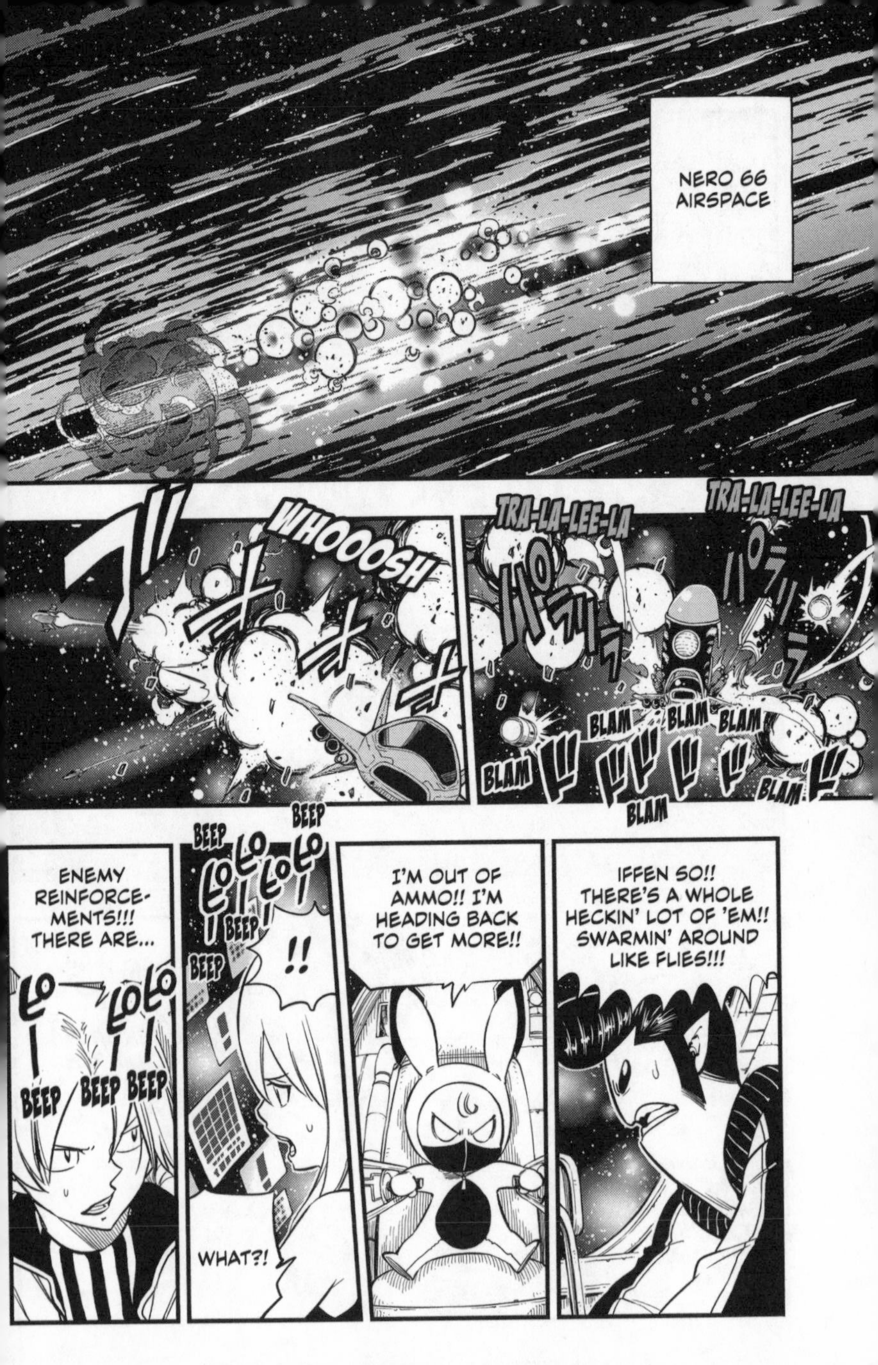
NERO 66 AIRSPACE
TRA-LA-LEE-LA
TRA-LA-LEE-LA
BLAM
BLAM
BLAM
BLAM
BLAM
BLAM
WHOOOSH
IFFEN SO!! THERE'S A WHOLE HECKIN' LOT OF 'EM!! SWARMIN' AROUND LIKE FLIES!!!
I'M OUT OF AMMO!! I'M HEADING BACK TO GET MORE!!
BEEP
BEEP
BEEP
BEEP
!!
WHAT?!
ENEMY REINFORCE-MENTS!!! THERE ARE...
BEEP
BEEP
BEEP

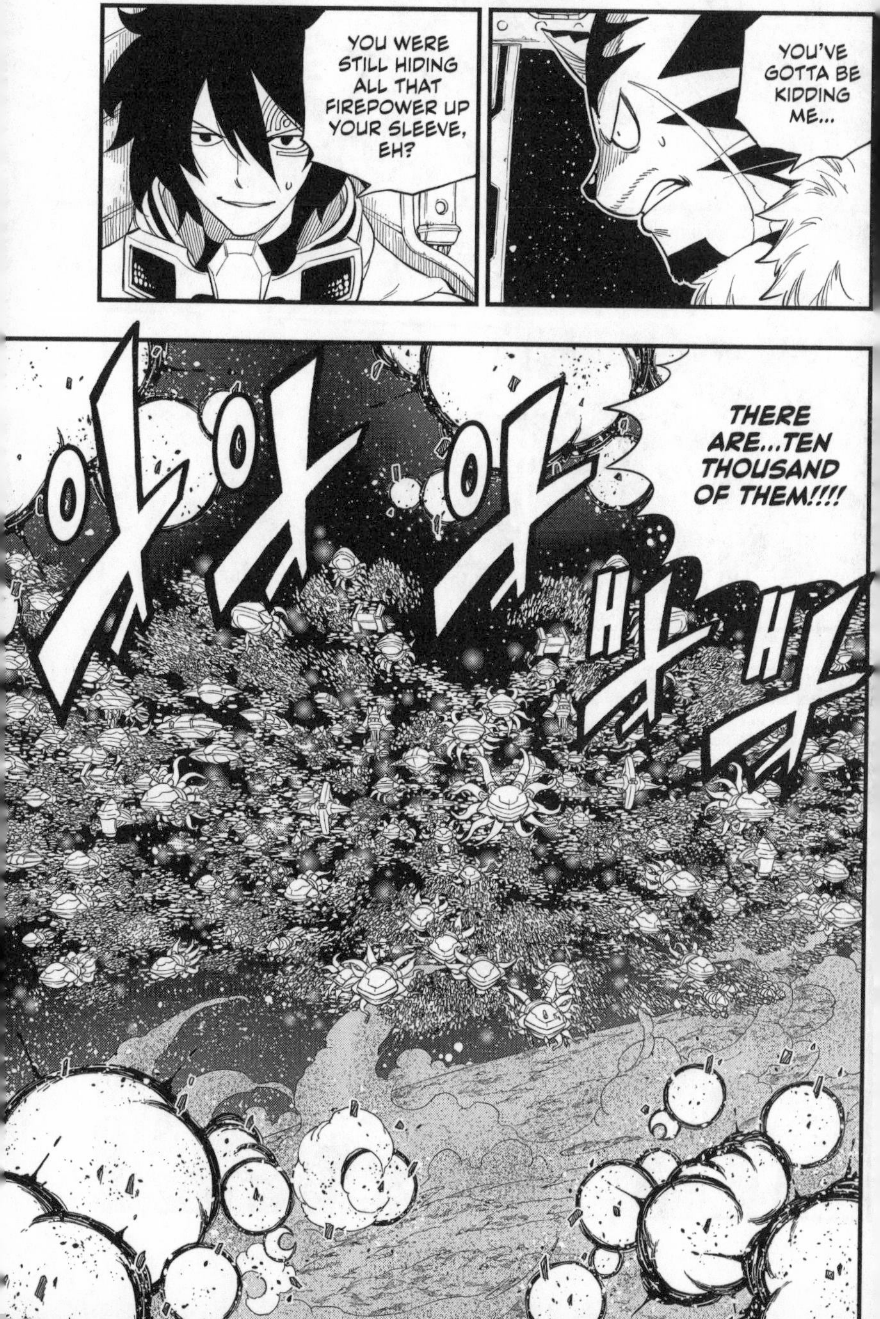
YOU'VE GOTTA BE KIDDING ME...
YOU WERE STILL HIDING ALL THAT FIREPOWER UP YOUR SLEEVE, EH?
THERE ARE...TEN THOUSAND OF THEM!!!!

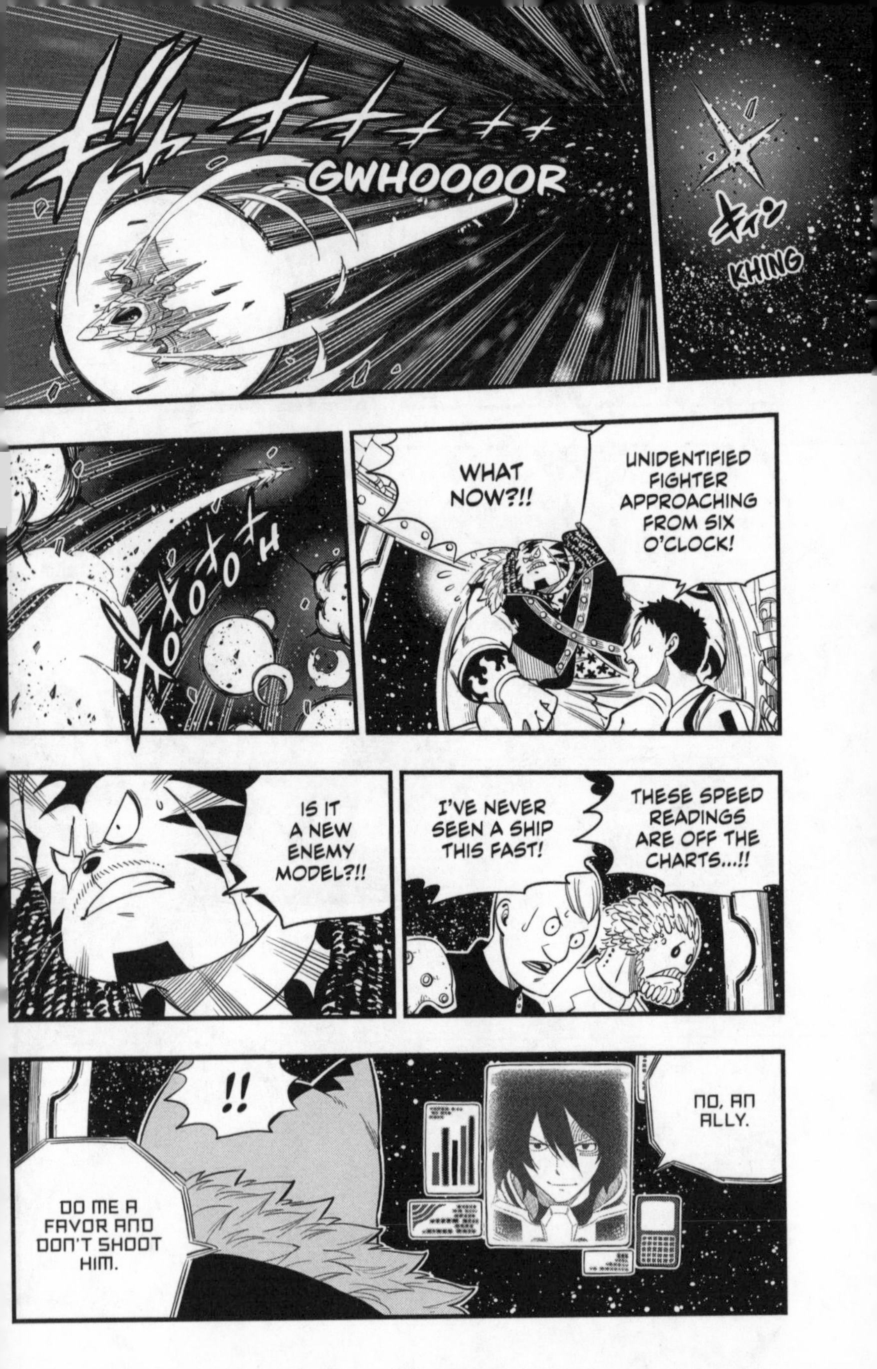
キィン
KHING
GWHOOOOR
UNIDENTIFIED FIGHTER APPROACHING FROM SIX O'CLOCK!
WHAT NOW?!!
OOOOH
THESE SPEED READINGS ARE OFF THE CHARTS...!!
I'VE NEVER SEEN A SHIP THIS FAST!
IS IT A NEW ENEMY MODEL?!!
NO, AN ALLY.
!!
DO ME A FAVOR AND DON'T SHOOT HIM.

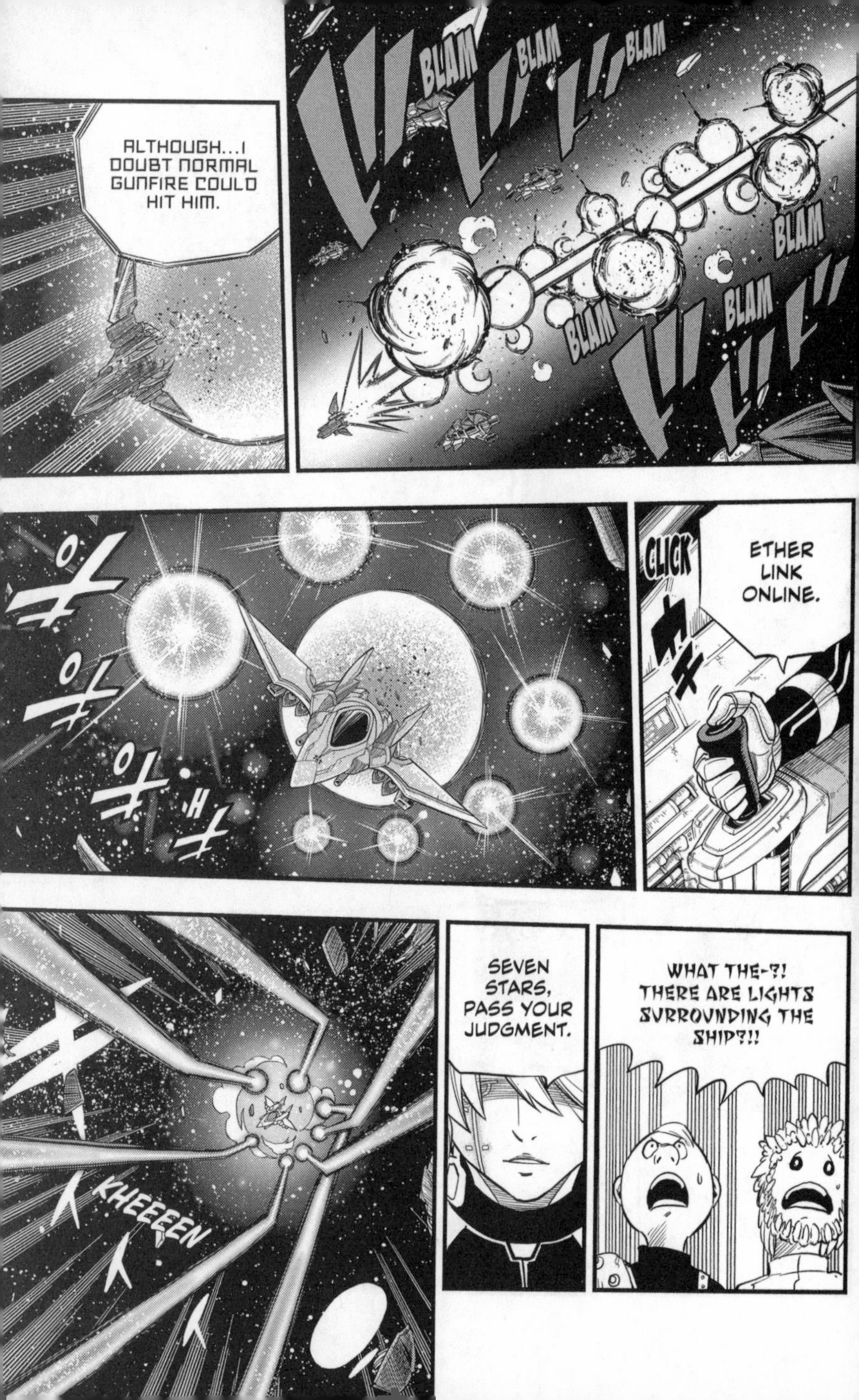
BLAM
BLAM
BLAM
BLAM
BLAM
BLAM
ALTHOUGH...I DOUBT NORMAL GUNFIRE COULD HIT HIM.
CLICK
ETHER LINK ONLINE.
WHAT THE-?! THERE ARE LIGHTS SURROUNDING THE SHIP?!!
SEVEN STARS, PASS YOUR JUDGMENT.
KHEEEEN

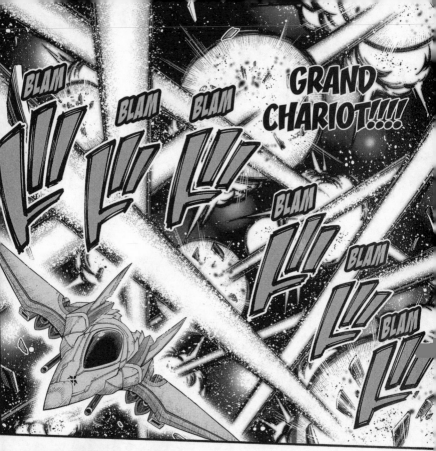

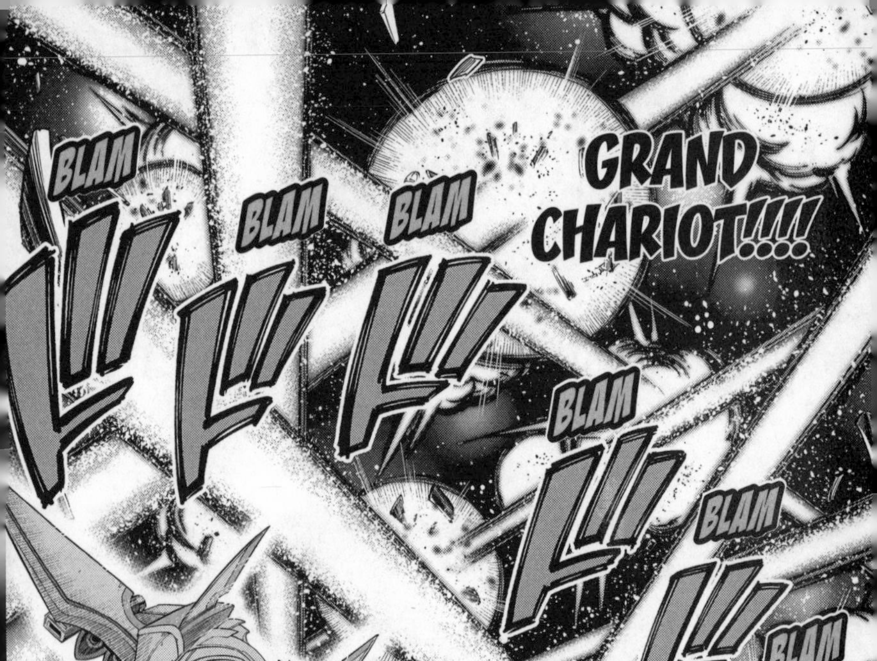
GRAND CHARIOT!!!!
BLAM
BLAM
BLAM
BLAM
BLAM
BLAM

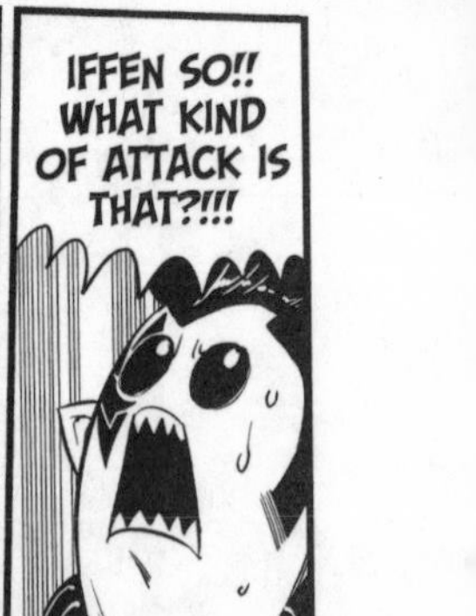
IFFEN SO!! WHAT KIND OF ATTACK IS THAT?!!!

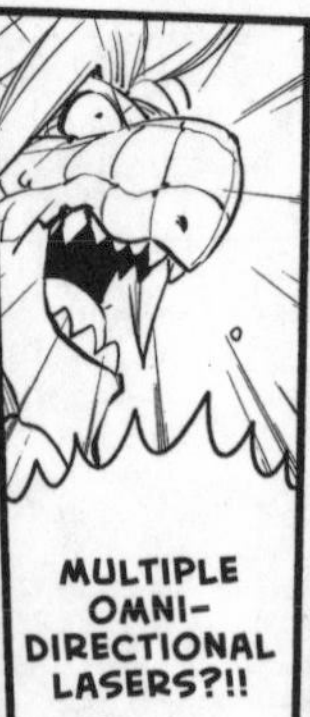
MULTIPLE OMNI-DIRECTIONAL LASERS?!!

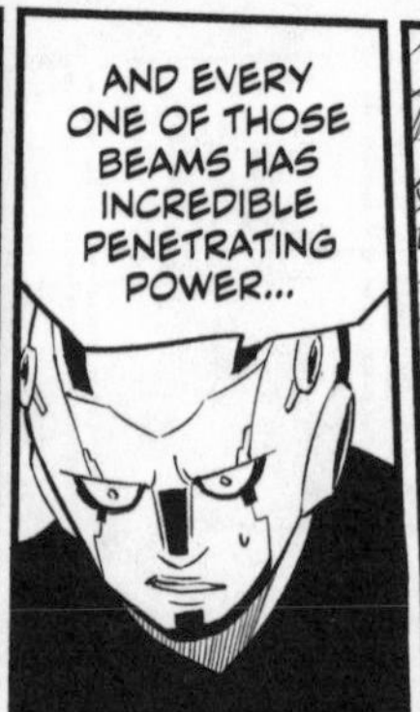
AND EVERY ONE OF THOSE BEAMS HAS INCREDIBLE PENETRATING POWER...

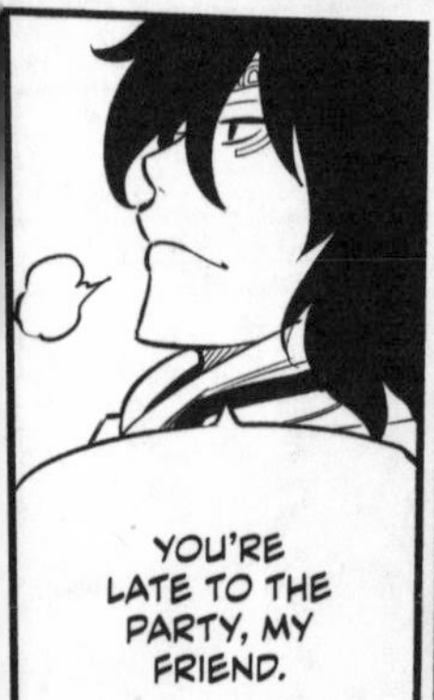
YOU'RE LATE TO THE PARTY, MY FRIEND.

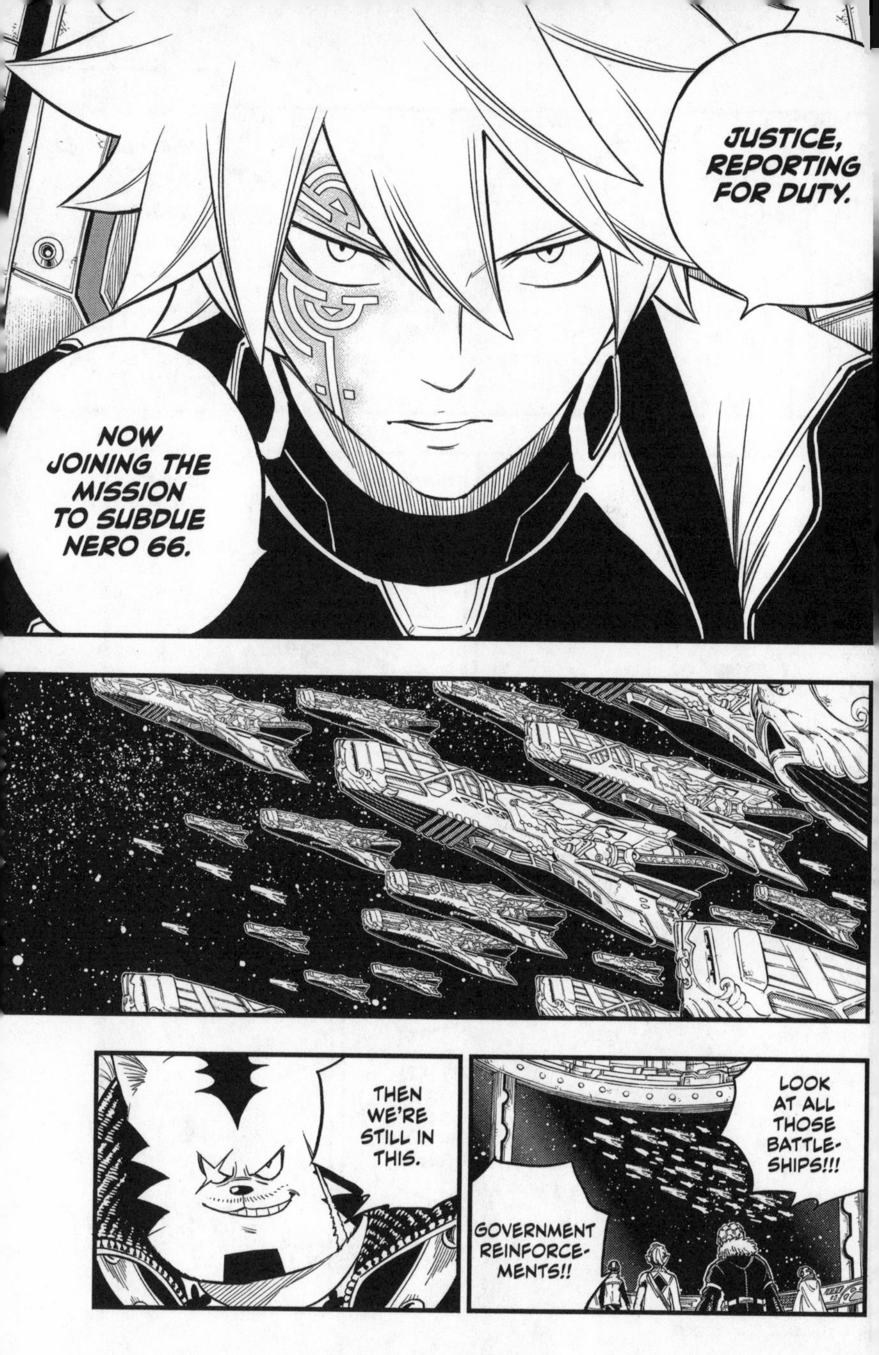
JUSTICE, REPORTING FOR DUTY.
NOW JOINING THE MISSION TO SUBDUE NERO 66.
LOOK AT ALL THOSE BATTLE-SHIPS!!!
GOVERNMENT REINFORCE-MENTS!!
THEN WE'RE STILL IN THIS.

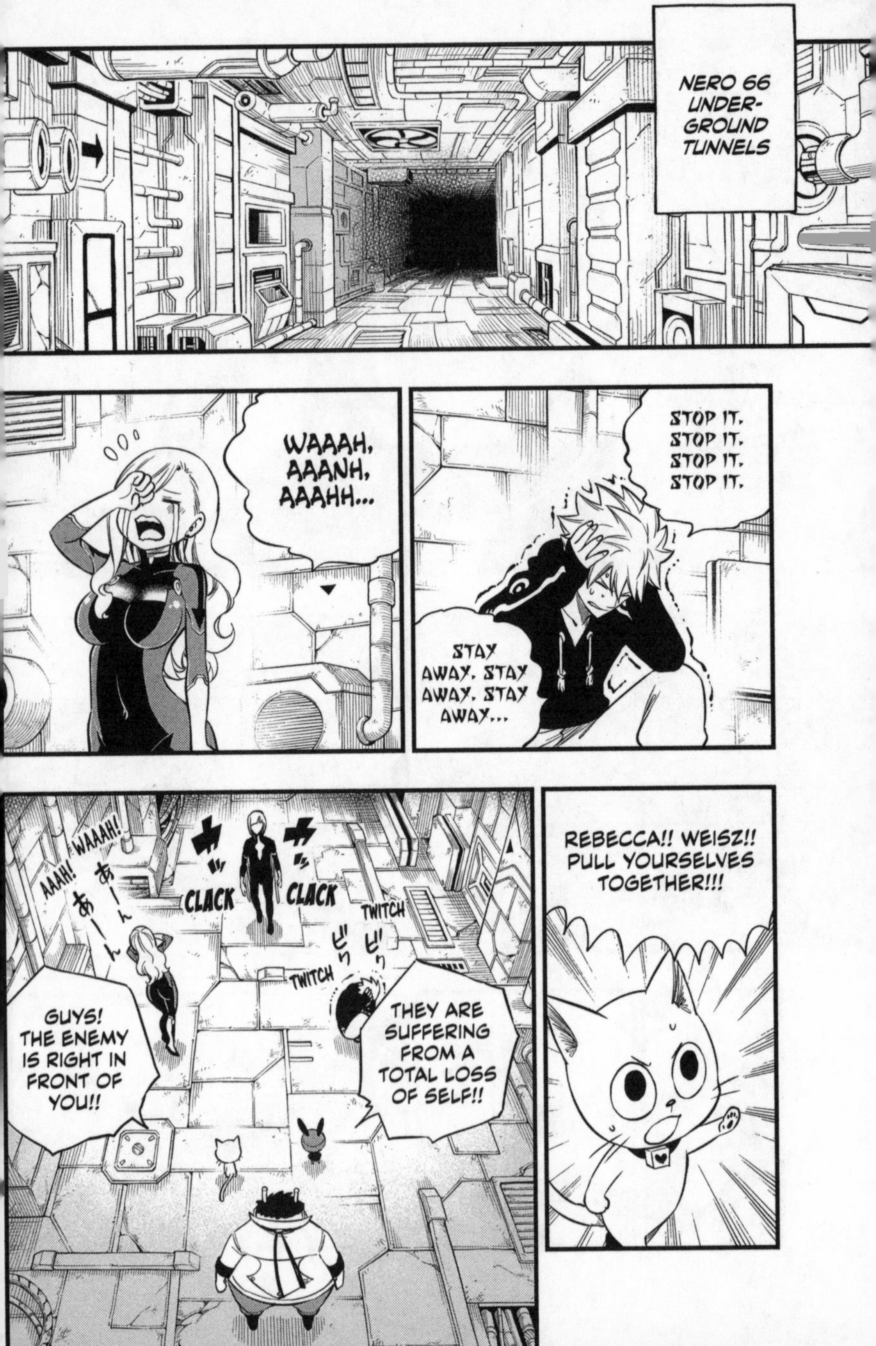
NERO 66 UNDER-GROUND TUNNELS
STOP IT. STOP IT. STOP IT. STOP IT.
STAY AWAY. STAY AWAY. STAY AWAY...
WAAAH, AAANH, AAAHH...
REBECCA!! WEISZ!! PULL YOURSELVES TOGETHER!!!
CLACK
CLACK
WAAAH!
AAAH!
あーん
あーん
TWITCH
ビク
ビク
TWITCH
THEY ARE SUFFERING FROM A TOTAL LOSS OF SELF!!
GUYS! THE ENEMY IS RIGHT IN FRONT OF YOU!!

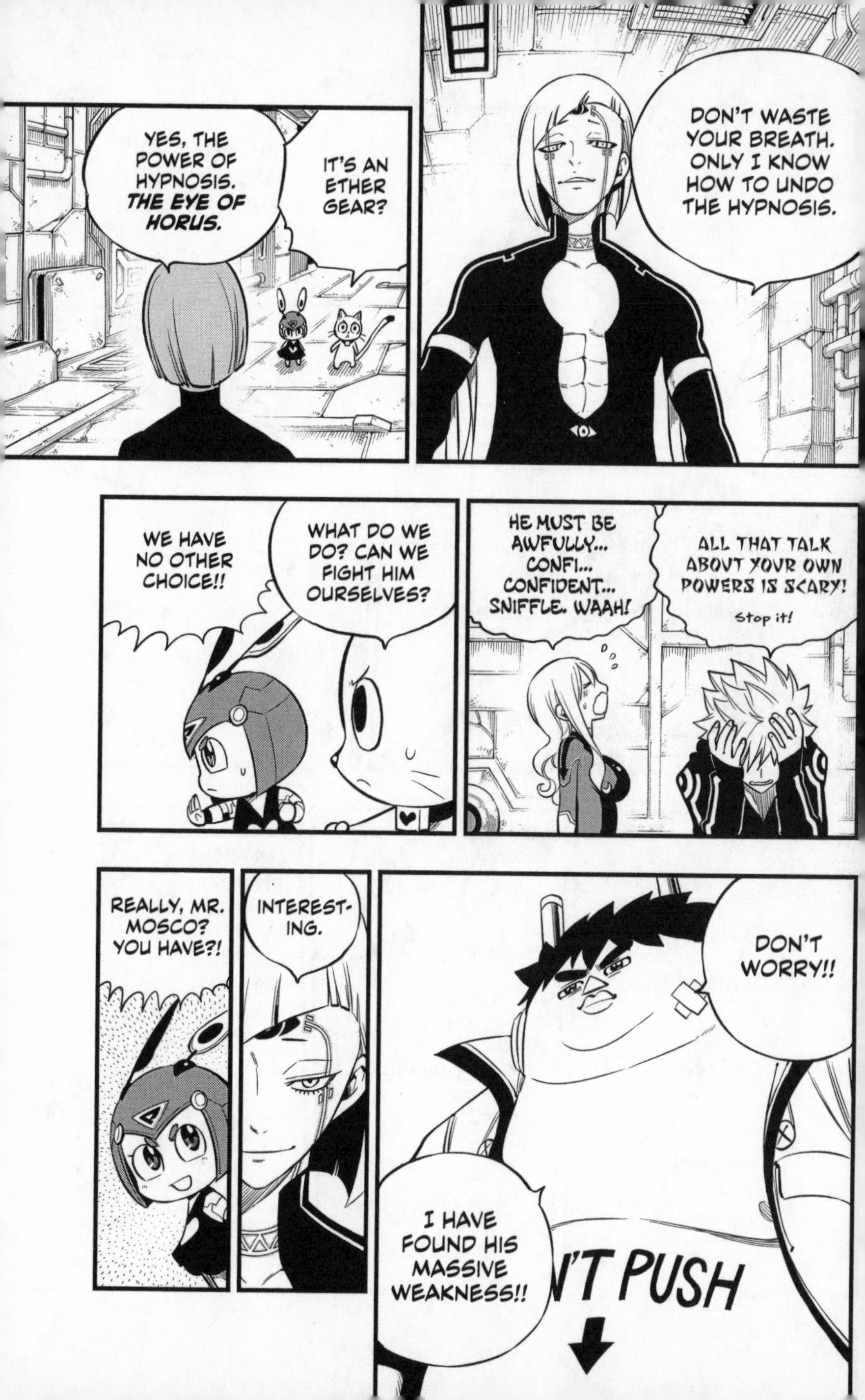
DON'T WASTE YOUR BREATH. ONLY I KNOW HOW TO UNDO THE HYPNOSIS.
IT'S AN ETHER GEAR?
YES, THE POWER OF HYPNOSIS. *THE EYE OF HORUS.*
ALL THAT TALK ABOUT YOUR OWN POWERS IS SCARY!
Stop it!
HE MUST BE AWFULLY... CONFI... CONFIDENT... SNIFFLE. WAAH!
WHAT DO WE DO? CAN WE FIGHT HIM OURSELVES?
WE HAVE NO OTHER CHOICE!!
DON'T WORRY!!
I HAVE FOUND HIS MASSIVE WEAKNESS!!
N'T PUSH
INTEREST-ING.
REALLY, MR. MOSCO? YOU HAVE?!

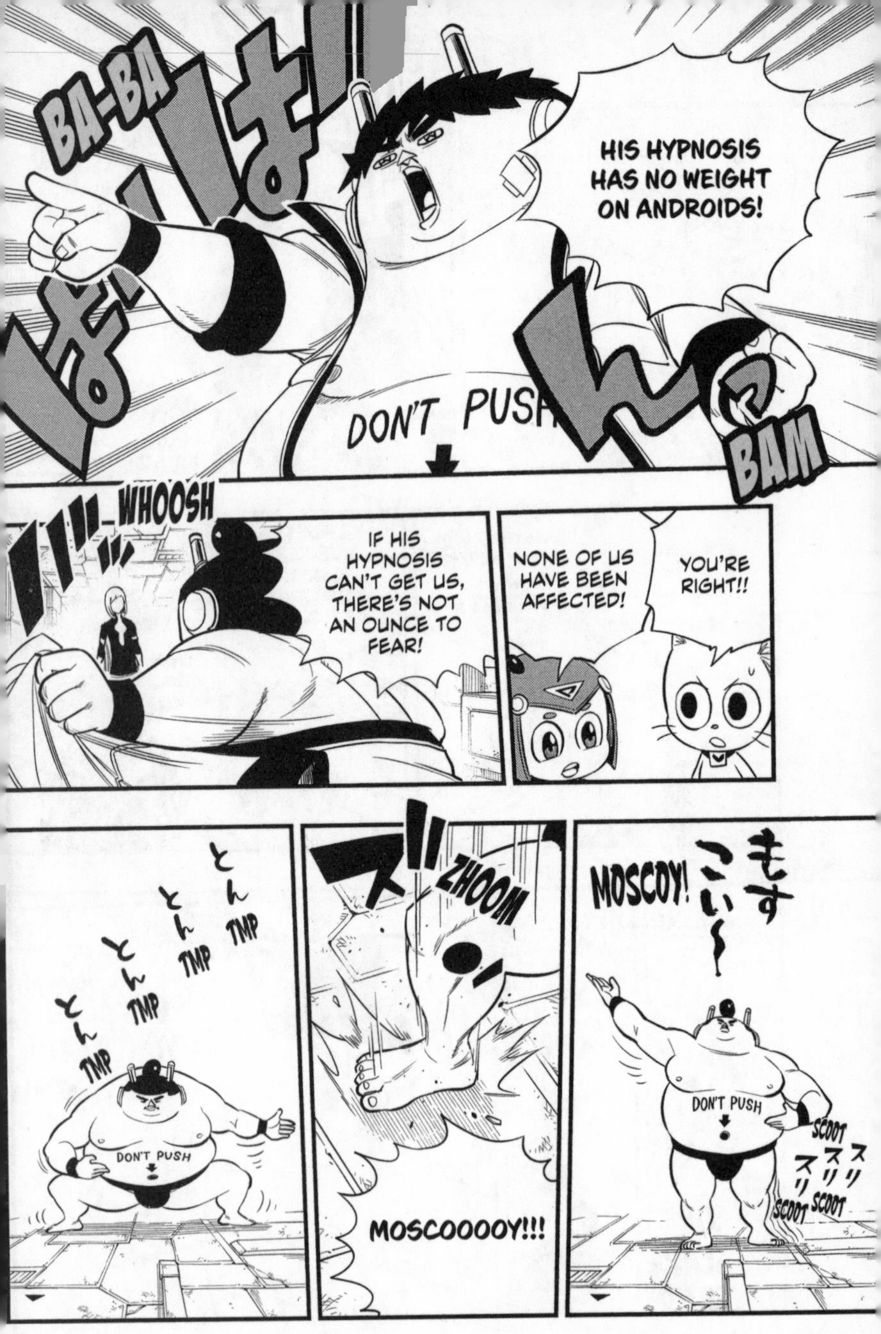
HIS HYPNOSIS HAS NO WEIGHT ON ANDROIDS!
BA-BA
DON'T PUSH
BAM
YOU'RE RIGHT!!
NONE OF US HAVE BEEN AFFECTED!
WHOOSH
IF HIS HYPNOSIS CAN'T GET US, THERE'S NOT AN OUNCE TO FEAR!
もすこい~
MOSCOY!
DON'T PUSH
スリスリ SCOOT
スリスリ SCOOT
ズ
ZHOOM
MOSCOOOOOY!!!
とん TMP
とん TMP
とん TMP
とん TMP
DON'T PUSH

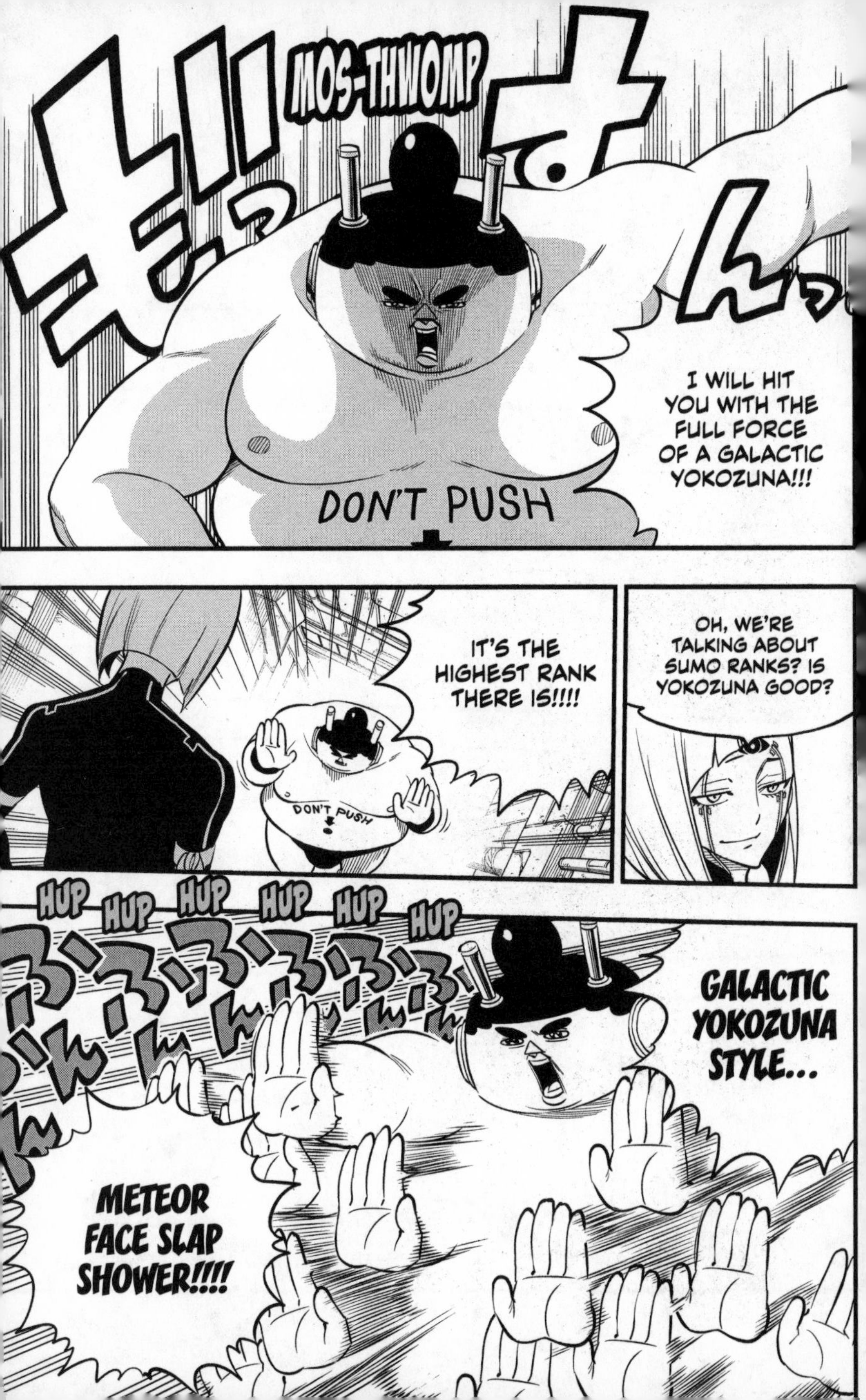
MOS-THWOMP
I WILL HIT YOU WITH THE FULL FORCE OF A GALACTIC YOKOZUNA!!!
DON'T PUSH
OH, WE'RE TALKING ABOUT SUMO RANKS? IS YOKOZUNA GOOD?
IT'S THE HIGHEST RANK THERE IS!!!!
DON'T PUSH
HUP
HUP
HUP
HUP
HUP
HUP
GALACTIC YOKOZUNA STYLE...
METEOR FACE SLAP SHOWER!!!!

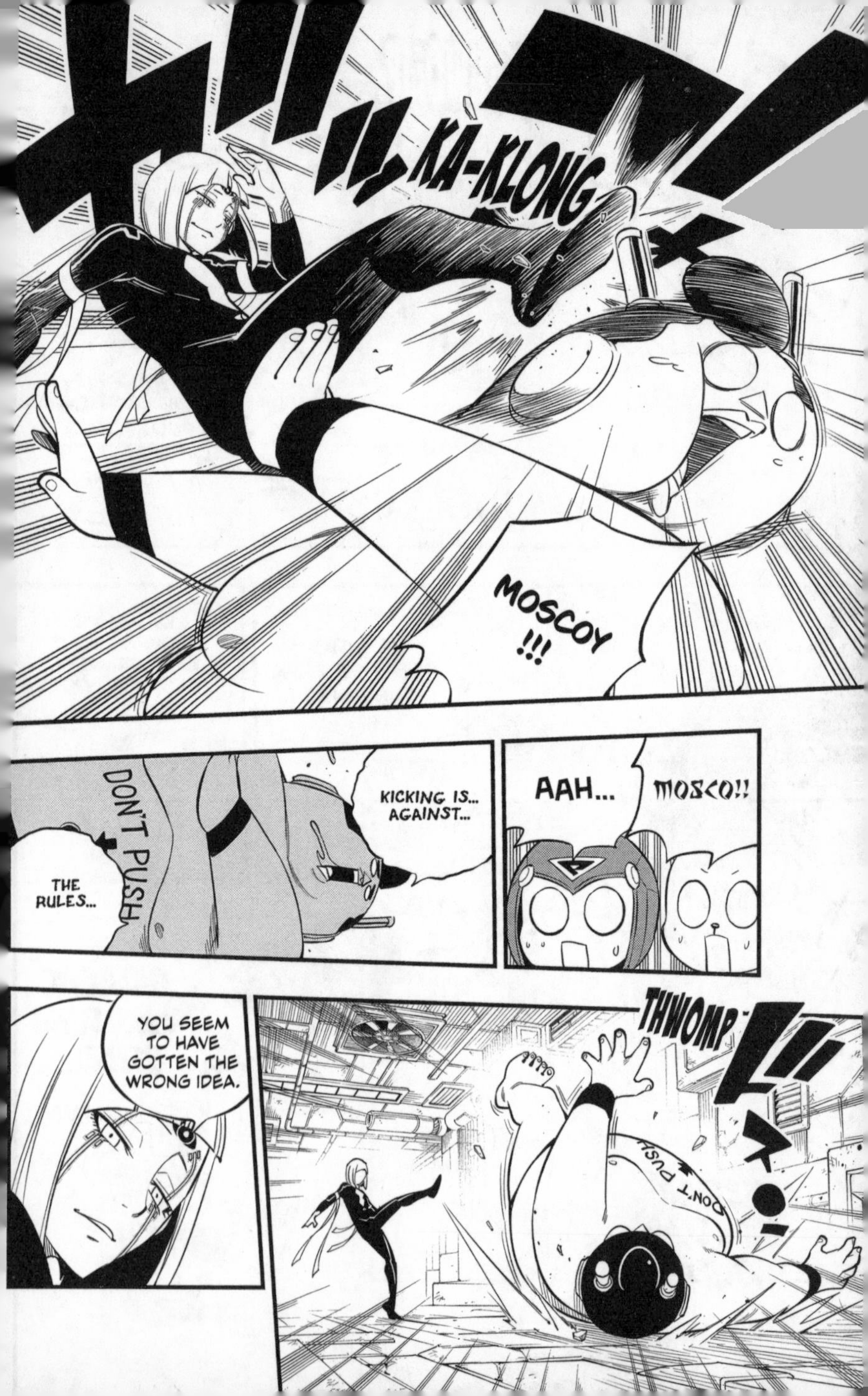
KA-KLONG
MOSCOY !!!
MOSCO!!
AAH...
KICKING IS... AGAINST...
THE RULES...
DON'T PUSH
THWOMP
DON'T PUSH
YOU SEEM TO HAVE GOTTEN THE WRONG IDEA.

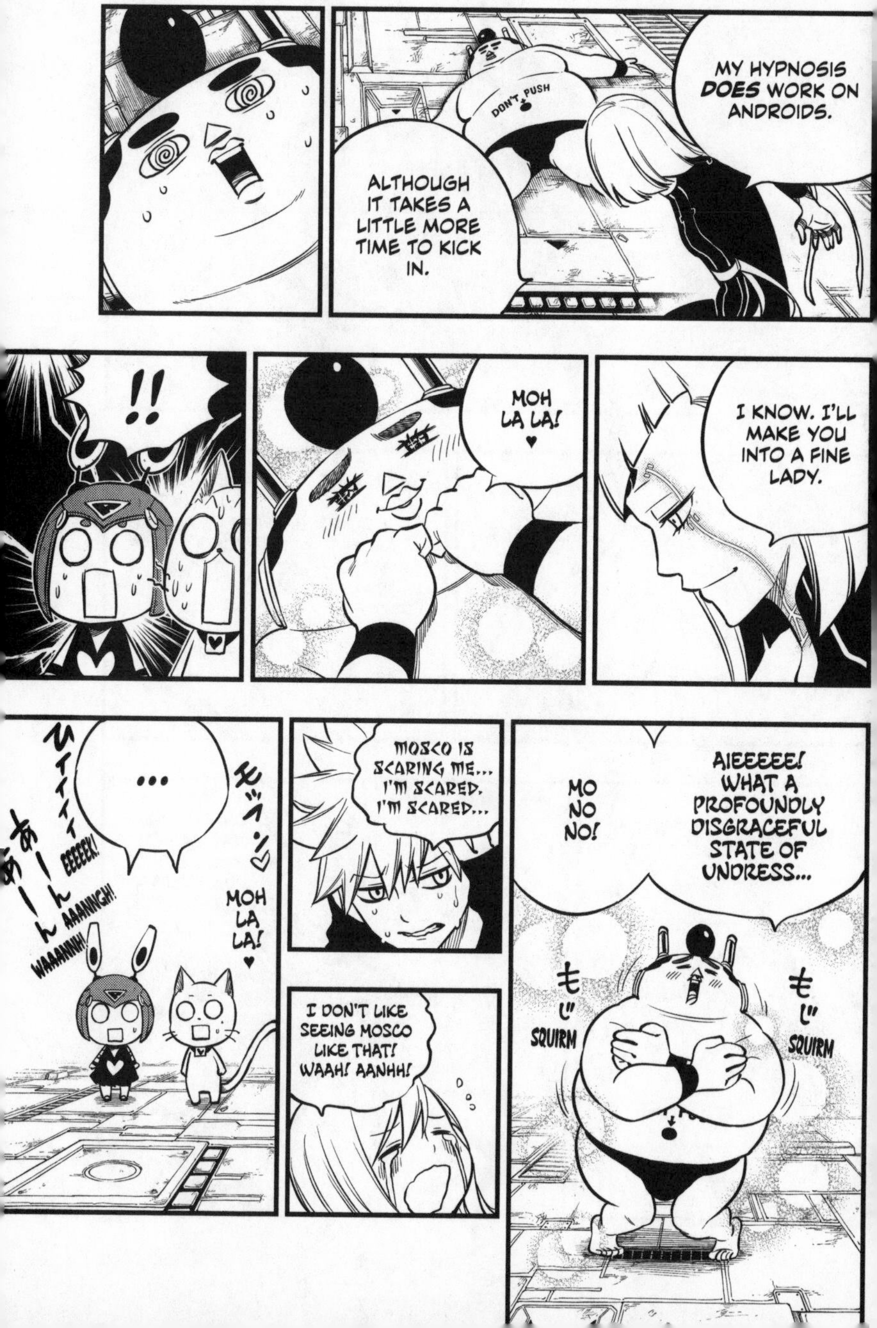
MY HYPNOSIS DOES WORK ON ANDROIDS.
DON'T PUSH
ALTHOUGH IT TAKES A LITTLE MORE TIME TO KICK IN.
I KNOW. I'LL MAKE YOU INTO A FINE LADY.
MOH LA LA! ♥
!!
AIEEEEE! WHAT A PROFOUNDLY DISGRACEFUL STATE OF UNDRESS...
MO NO NO!
もじ SQUIRM
もじ SQUIRM
MOSCO IS SCARING ME... I'M SCARED. I'M SCARED...
I DON'T LIKE SEEING MOSCO LIKE THAT! WAAH! AANHH!
モッ♪♡
MOH LA LA! ♥
...
ひイイイ EEEEEK!
あーん AAANNGH!
あーん WAAAANH!

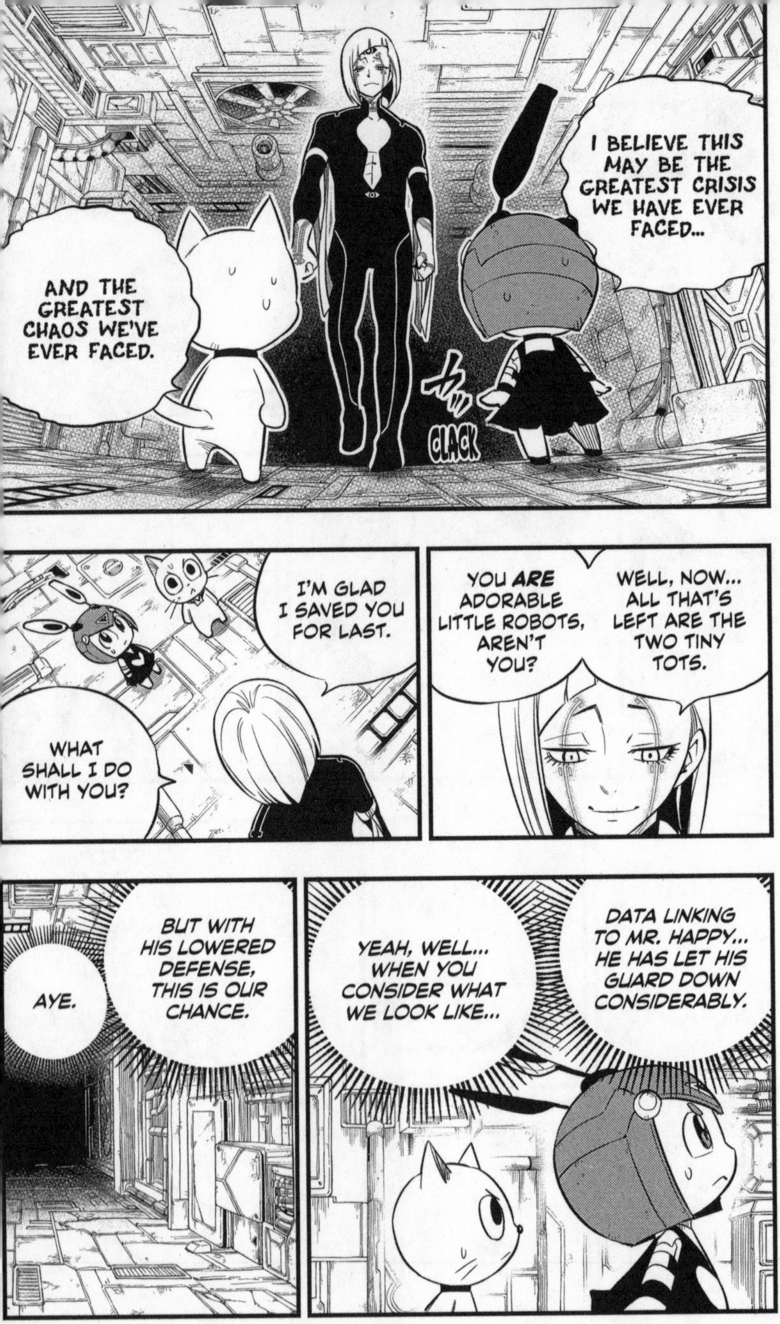
I BELIEVE THIS MAY BE THE GREATEST CRISIS WE HAVE EVER FACED...
AND THE GREATEST CHAOS WE'VE EVER FACED.
CLACK
WELL, NOW... ALL THAT'S LEFT ARE THE TWO TINY TOTS.
YOU **ARE** ADORABLE LITTLE ROBOTS, AREN'T YOU?
I'M GLAD I SAVED YOU FOR LAST.
WHAT SHALL I DO WITH YOU?
DATA LINKING TO MR. HAPPY... HE HAS LET HIS GUARD DOWN CONSIDERABLY.
YEAH, WELL... WHEN YOU CONSIDER WHAT WE LOOK LIKE...
BUT WITH HIS LOWERED DEFENSE, THIS IS OUR CHANCE.
AYE.

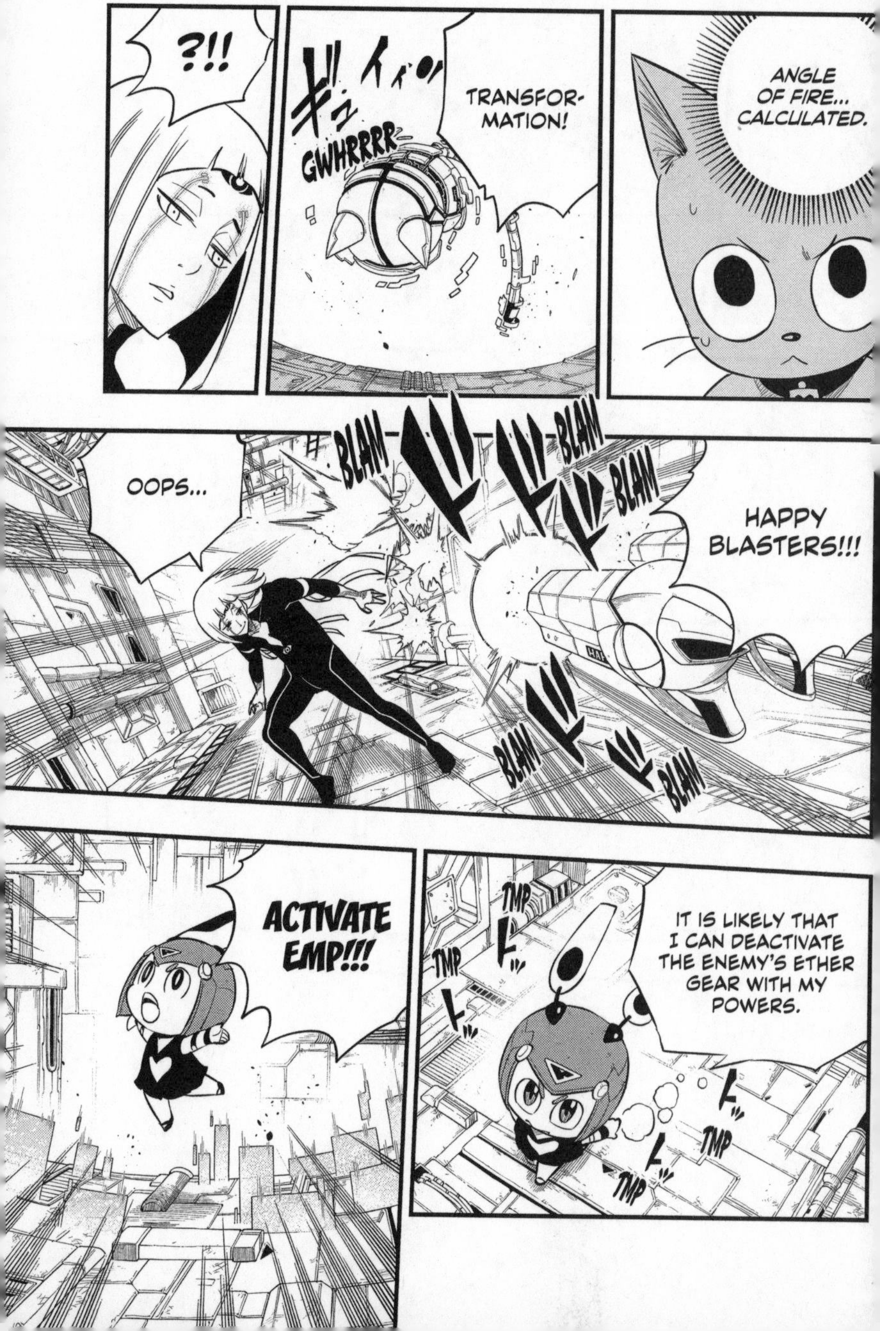

ANGLE OF FIRE... CALCULATED.
TRANSFORMATION!
GWHRRRR
?!!
HAPPY BLASTERS!!!
BLAM BLAM BLAM BLAM BLAM
OOPS...
IT IS LIKELY THAT I CAN DEACTIVATE THE ENEMY'S ETHER GEAR WITH MY POWERS.
TMP TMP TMP TMP
ACTIVATE EMP!!!

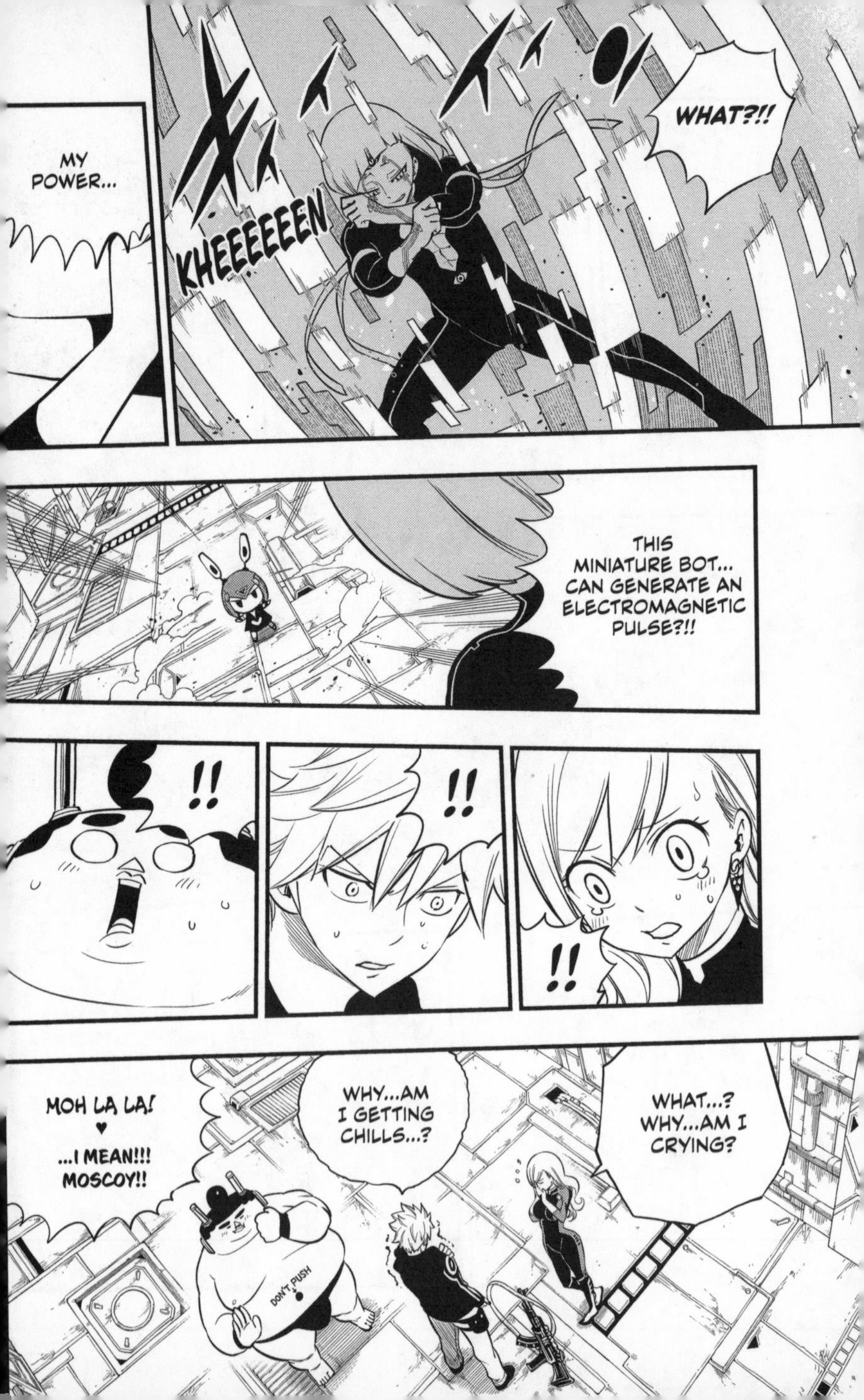
WHAT?!!
KHEEEEEEN
MY POWER...
THIS MINIATURE BOT... CAN GENERATE AN ELECTROMAGNETIC PULSE?!!
!!
!!
!!
WHAT...? WHY...AM I CRYING?
WHY...AM I GETTING CHILLS...?
MOH LA LA! ♥ ...I MEAN!!! MOSCOY!!
DON'T PUSH

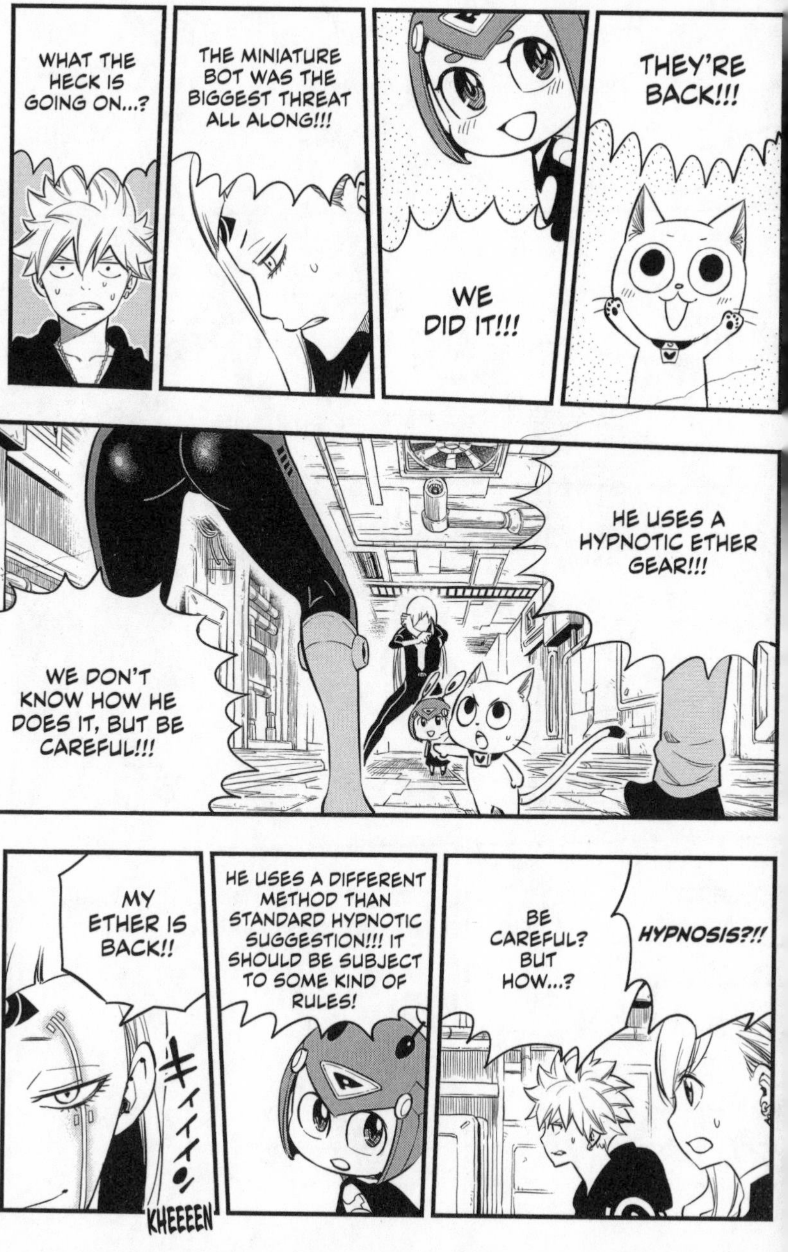
THEY'RE BACK!!!
WE DID IT!!!
THE MINIATURE BOT WAS THE BIGGEST THREAT ALL ALONG!!!
WHAT THE HECK IS GOING ON...?
HE USES A HYPNOTIC ETHER GEAR!!!
WE DON'T KNOW HOW HE DOES IT, BUT BE CAREFUL!!!
HYPNOSIS?!!
BE CAREFUL? BUT HOW...?
HE USES A DIFFERENT METHOD THAN STANDARD HYPNOTIC SUGGESTION!!! IT SHOULD BE SUBJECT TO SOME KIND OF RULES!
MY ETHER IS BACK!!
KHEEEEN

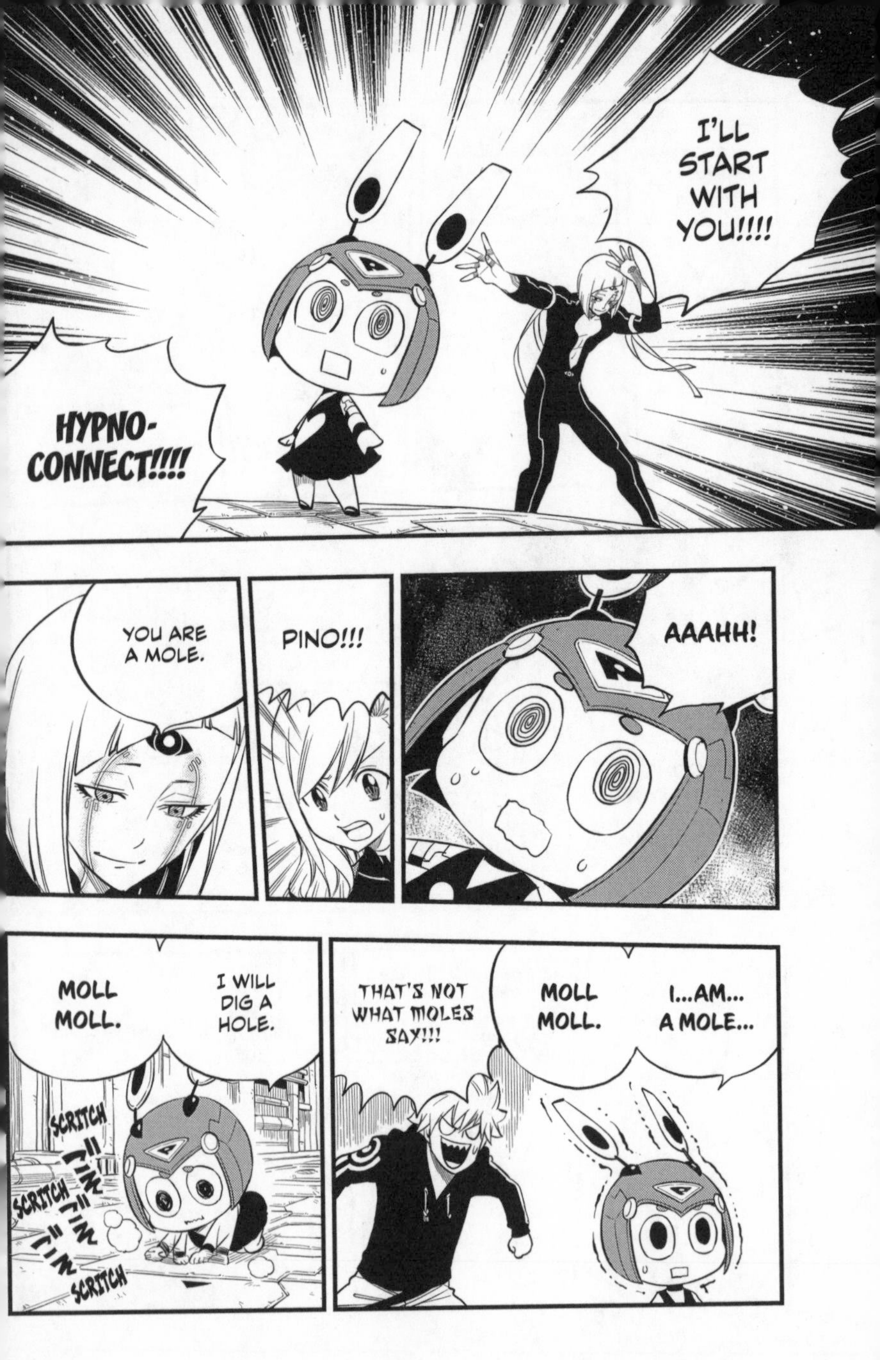
I'LL START WITH YOU!!!!
HYPNO-CONNECT!!!!
AAAHH!
PINO!!!
YOU ARE A MOLE.
I...AM... A MOLE...
MOLL MOLL.
THAT'S NOT WHAT MOLES SAY!!!
I WILL DIG A HOLE.
MOLL MOLL.
SCRITCH
SCRITCH
SCRITCH

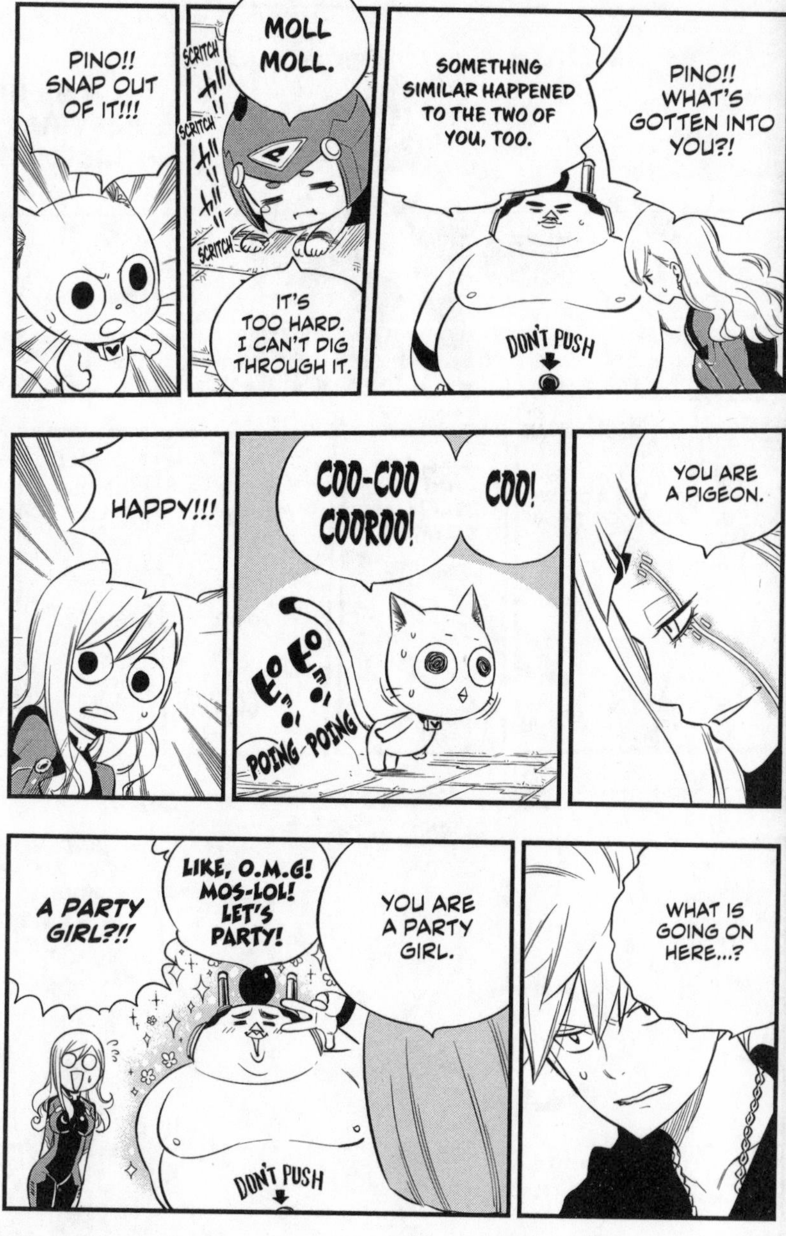
PINO!! WHAT'S GOTTEN INTO YOU?!
SOMETHING SIMILAR HAPPENED TO THE TWO OF YOU, TOO.
DON'T PUSH
MOLL MOLL.
SCRITCH
SCRITCH
SCRITCH
IT'S TOO HARD. I CAN'T DIG THROUGH IT.
PINO!! SNAP OUT OF IT!!!
YOU ARE A PIGEON.
COO!
COO-COO COOROO!
POING POING
HAPPY!!!
WHAT IS GOING ON HERE...?
YOU ARE A PARTY GIRL.
LIKE, O.M.G! MOS-LOL! LET'S PARTY!
A PARTY GIRL?!!
DON'T PUSH

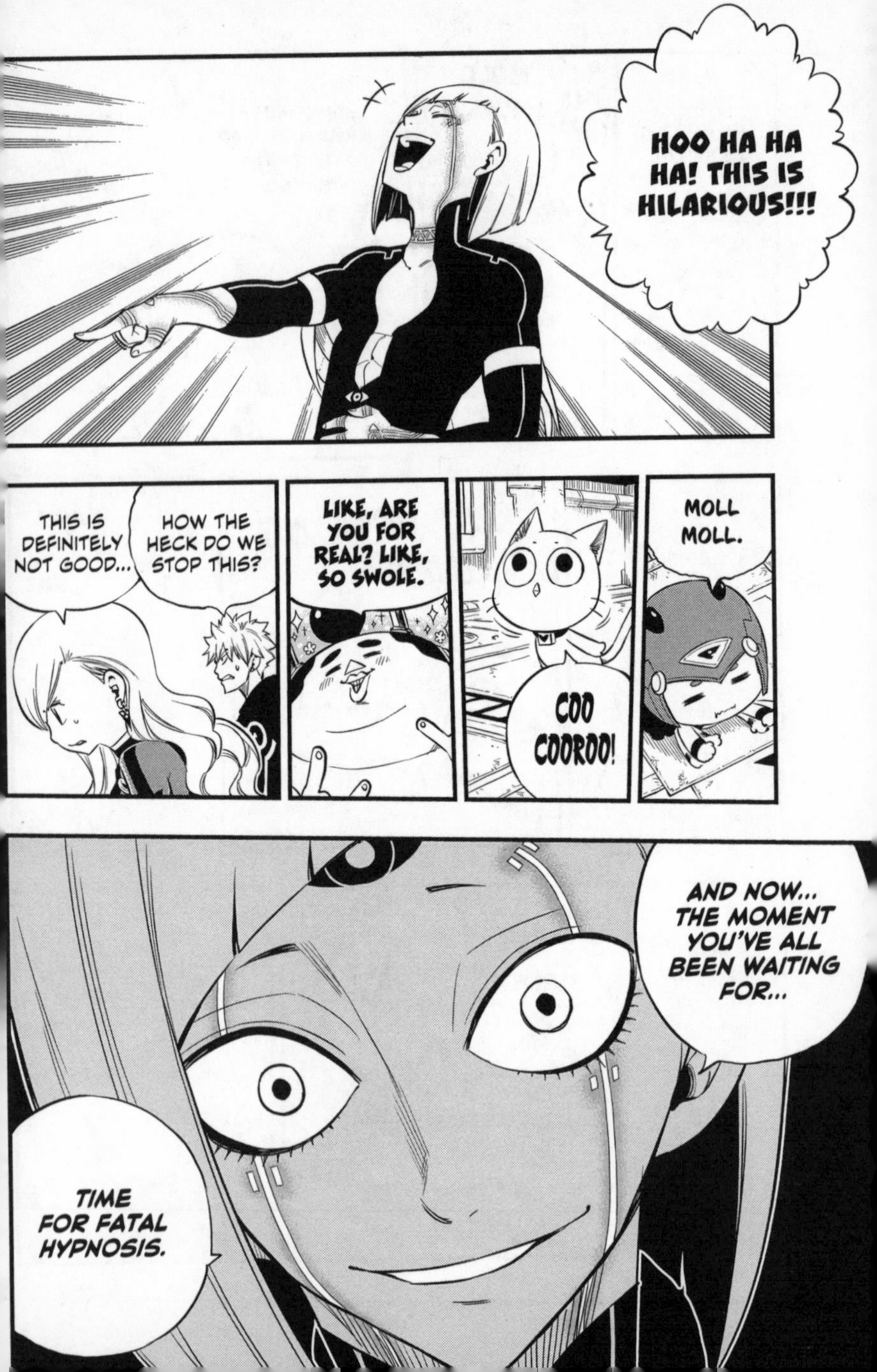
HOO HA HA HA! THIS IS HILARIOUS!!!
MOLL MOLL.
COO COOROO!
LIKE, ARE YOU FOR REAL? LIKE, SO SWOLE.
HOW THE HECK DO WE STOP THIS?
THIS IS DEFINITELY NOT GOOD...
AND NOW... THE MOMENT YOU'VE ALL BEEN WAITING FOR...
TIME FOR FATAL HYPNOSIS.

EDENS ZERO

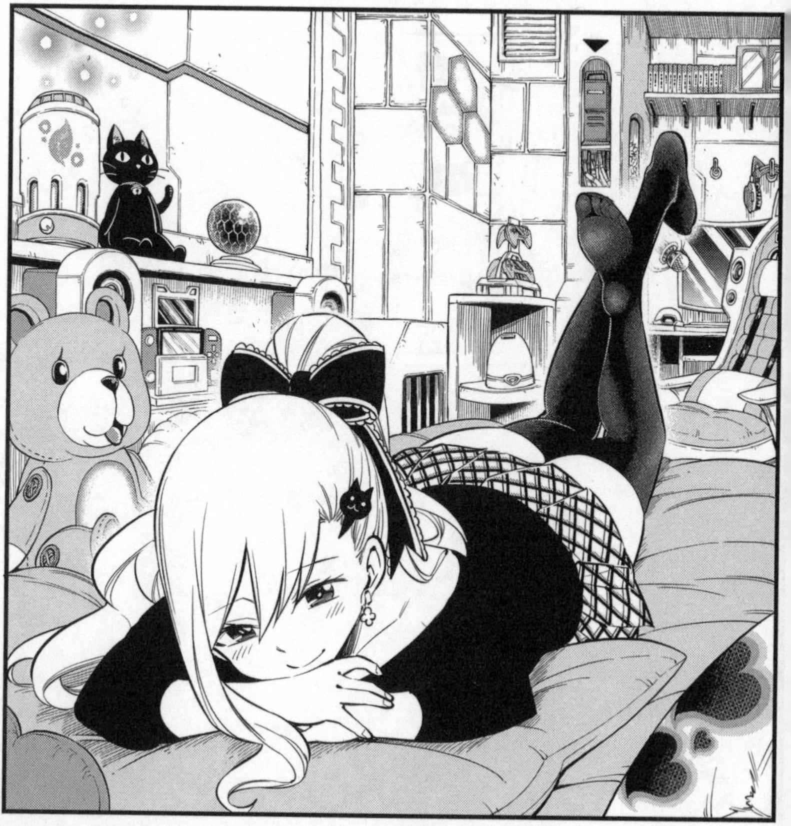

CHAPTER 149: POWERS LOST

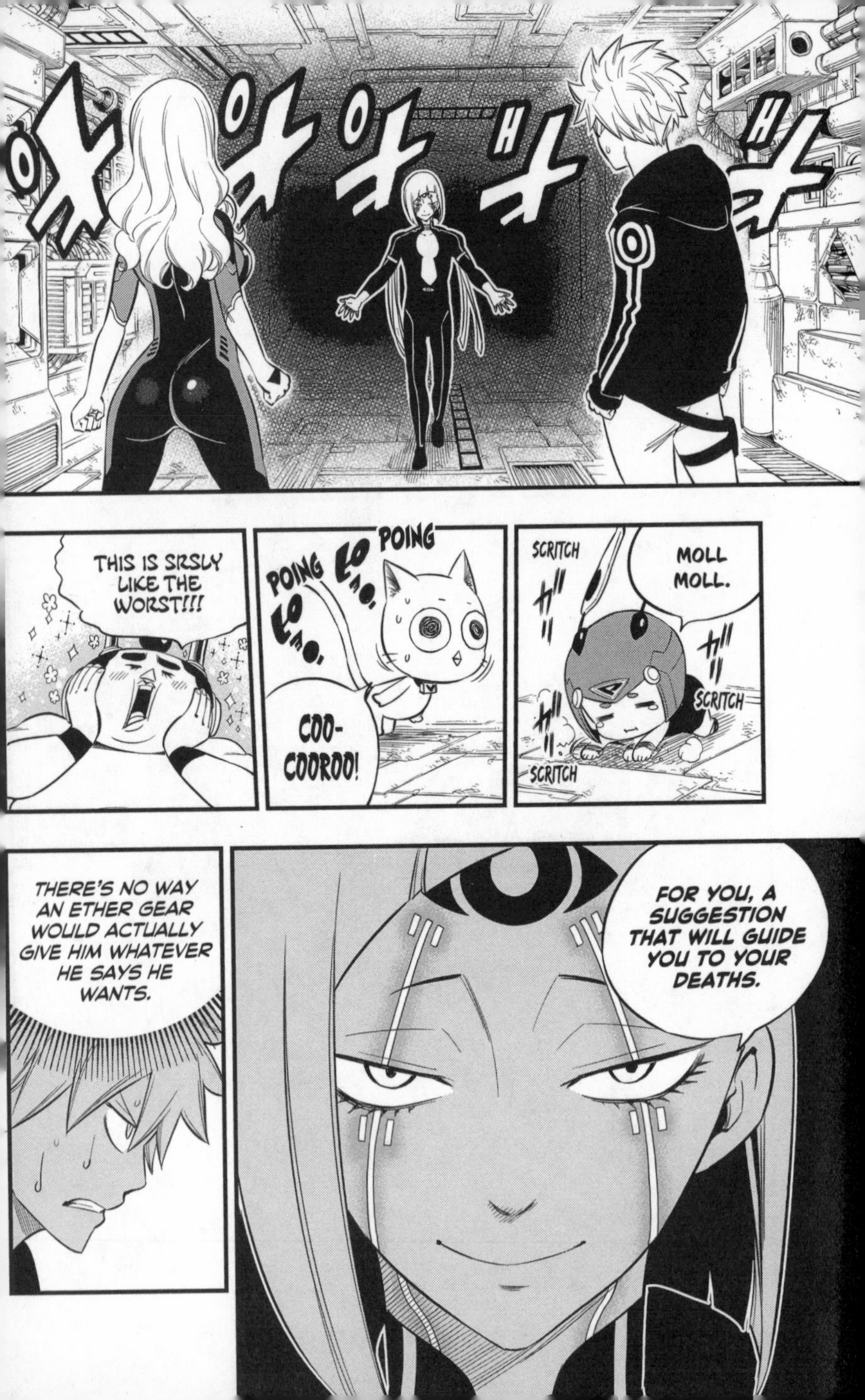

SCRITCH
MOLL MOLL.
SCRITCH
SCRITCH
POING
POING
COO-COOROO!
THIS IS SRSLY LIKE THE WORST!!!
FOR YOU, A SUGGESTION THAT WILL GUIDE YOU TO YOUR DEATHS.
THERE'S NO WAY AN ETHER GEAR WOULD ACTUALLY GIVE HIM WHATEVER HE SAYS HE WANTS.

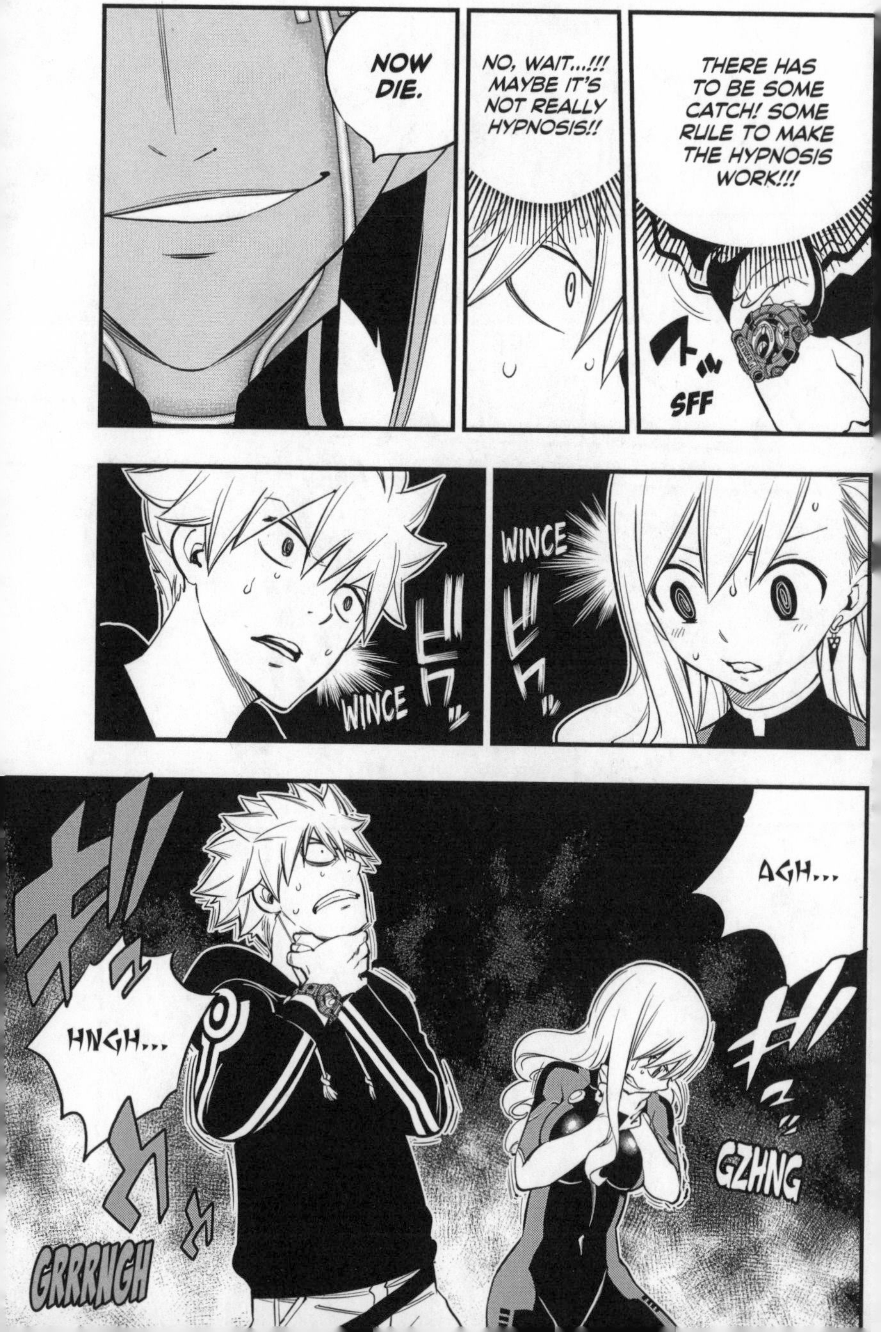
THERE HAS TO BE SOME CATCH! SOME RULE TO MAKE THE HYPNOSIS WORK!!!
SFF
NO, WAIT...!!! MAYBE IT'S NOT REALLY HYPNOSIS!!
NOW DIE.
WINCE
WINCE
AGH...
GZHNG
HNGH...
GRRRNGH

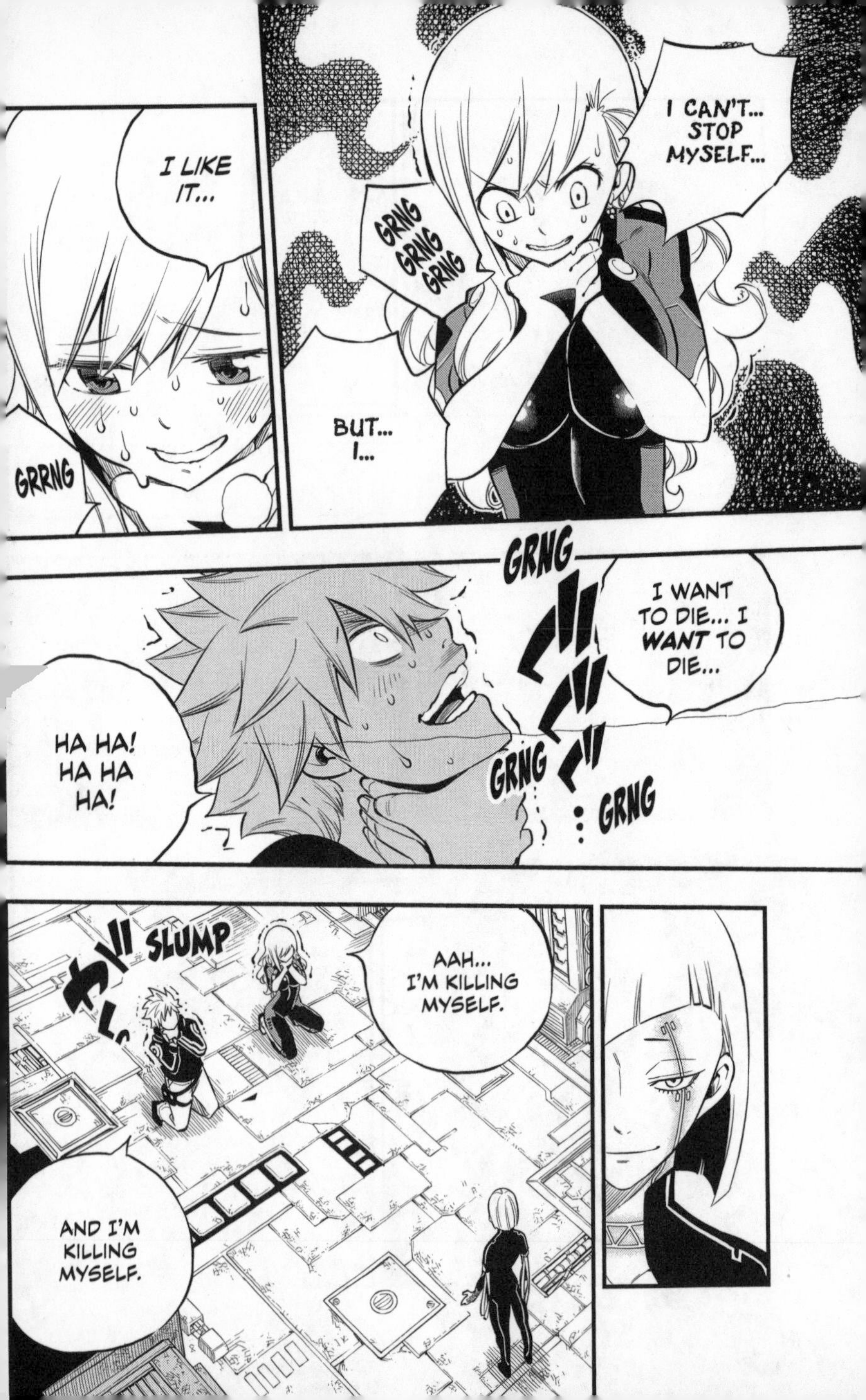
I CAN'T... STOP MYSELF...
GRNG GRNG GRNG
BUT... I...
I LIKE IT...
GRRNG
GRNG
I WANT TO DIE... I *WANT* TO DIE...
GRNG
GRNG
HA HA! HA HA HA!
AAH... I'M KILLING MYSELF.
SLUMP
AND I'M KILLING MYSELF.

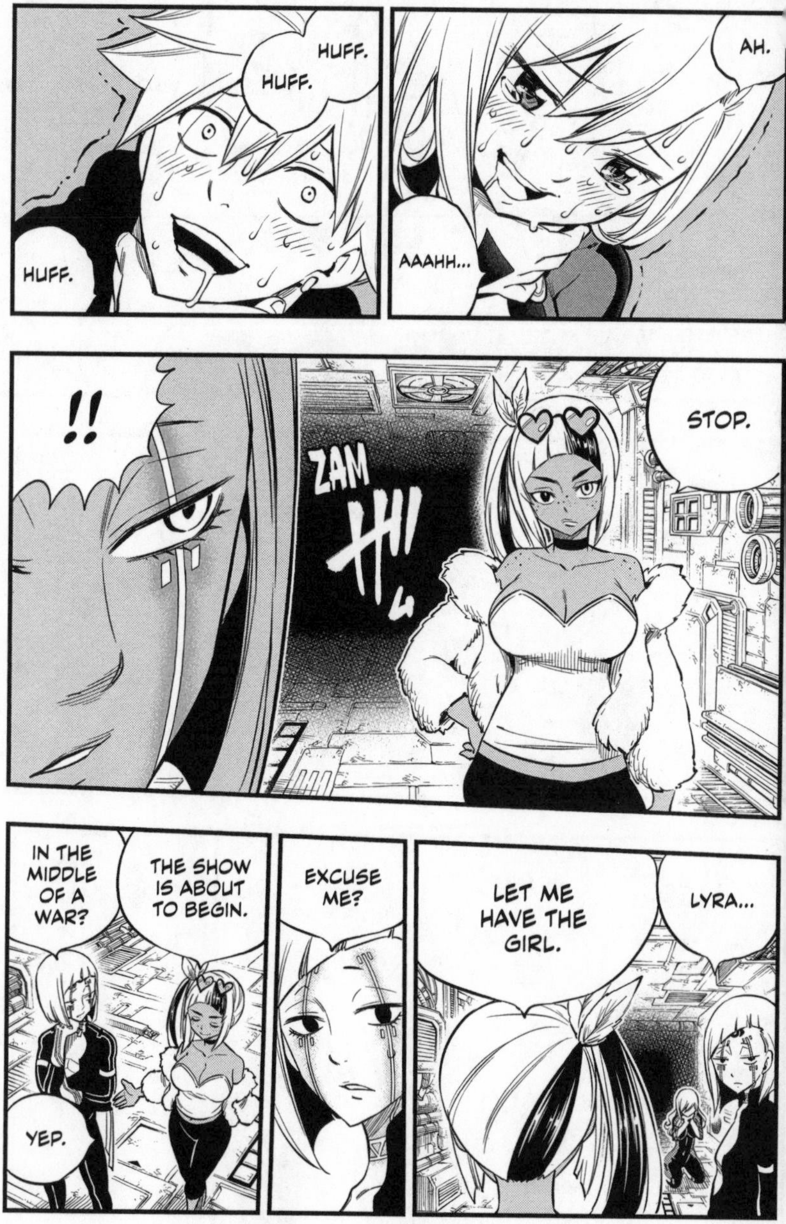
AH.
AAAHH...
HUFF.
HUFF.
HUFF.
STOP.
ZAM
!!
LYRA...
LET ME HAVE THE GIRL.
EXCUSE ME?
THE SHOW IS ABOUT TO BEGIN.
IN THE MIDDLE OF A WAR?
YEP.

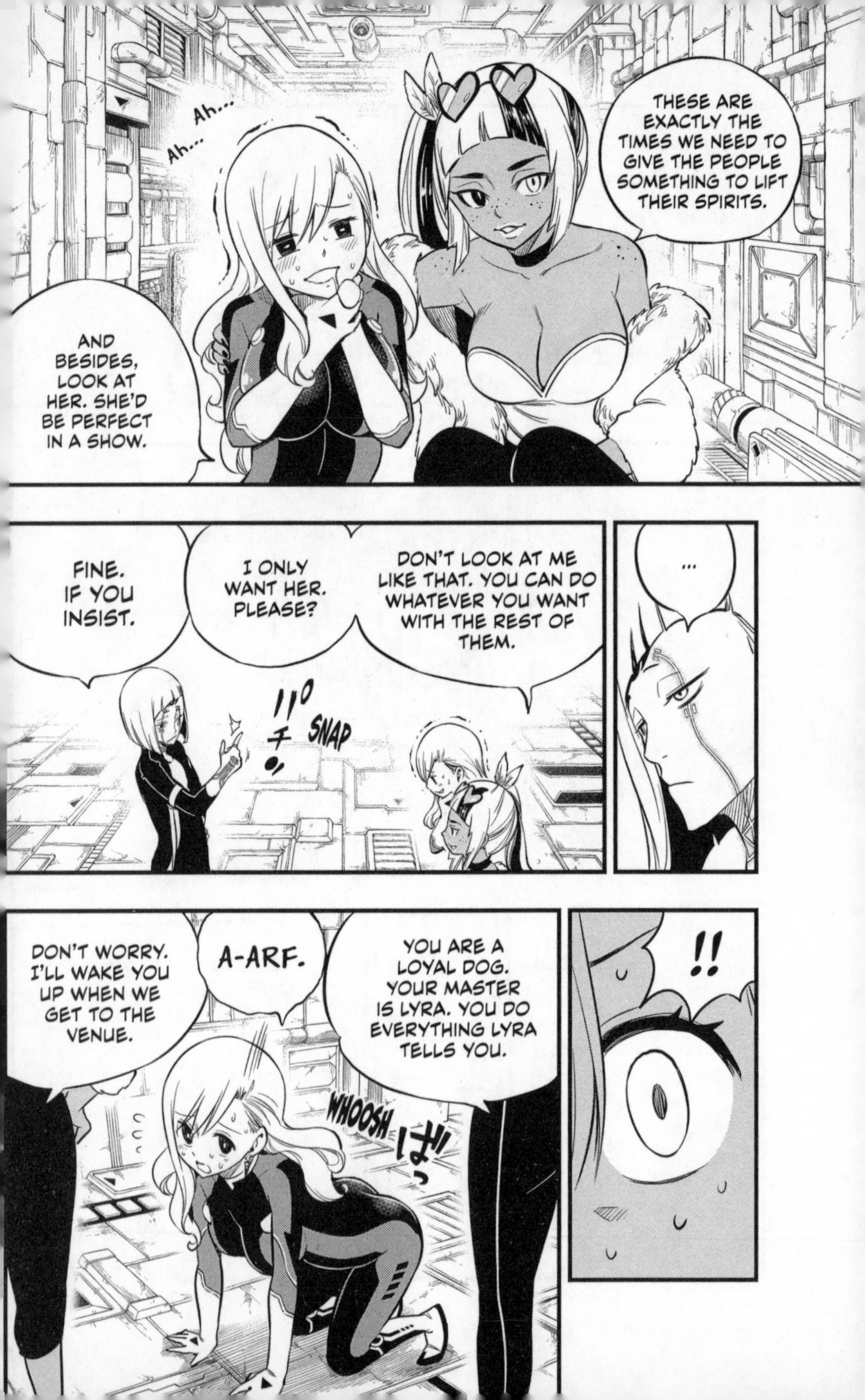
THESE ARE EXACTLY THE TIMES WE NEED TO GIVE THE PEOPLE SOMETHING TO LIFT THEIR SPIRITS.
Ah... Ah...
AND BESIDES, LOOK AT HER. SHE'D BE PERFECT IN A SHOW.
...
DON'T LOOK AT ME LIKE THAT. YOU CAN DO WHATEVER YOU WANT WITH THE REST OF THEM.
I ONLY WANT HER. PLEASE?
FINE. IF YOU INSIST.
SNAP
パチッ
!!
YOU ARE A LOYAL DOG. YOUR MASTER IS LYRA. YOU DO EVERYTHING LYRA TELLS YOU.
A-ARF.
DON'T WORRY. I'LL WAKE YOU UP WHEN WE GET TO THE VENUE.
WHOOSH
ばっ

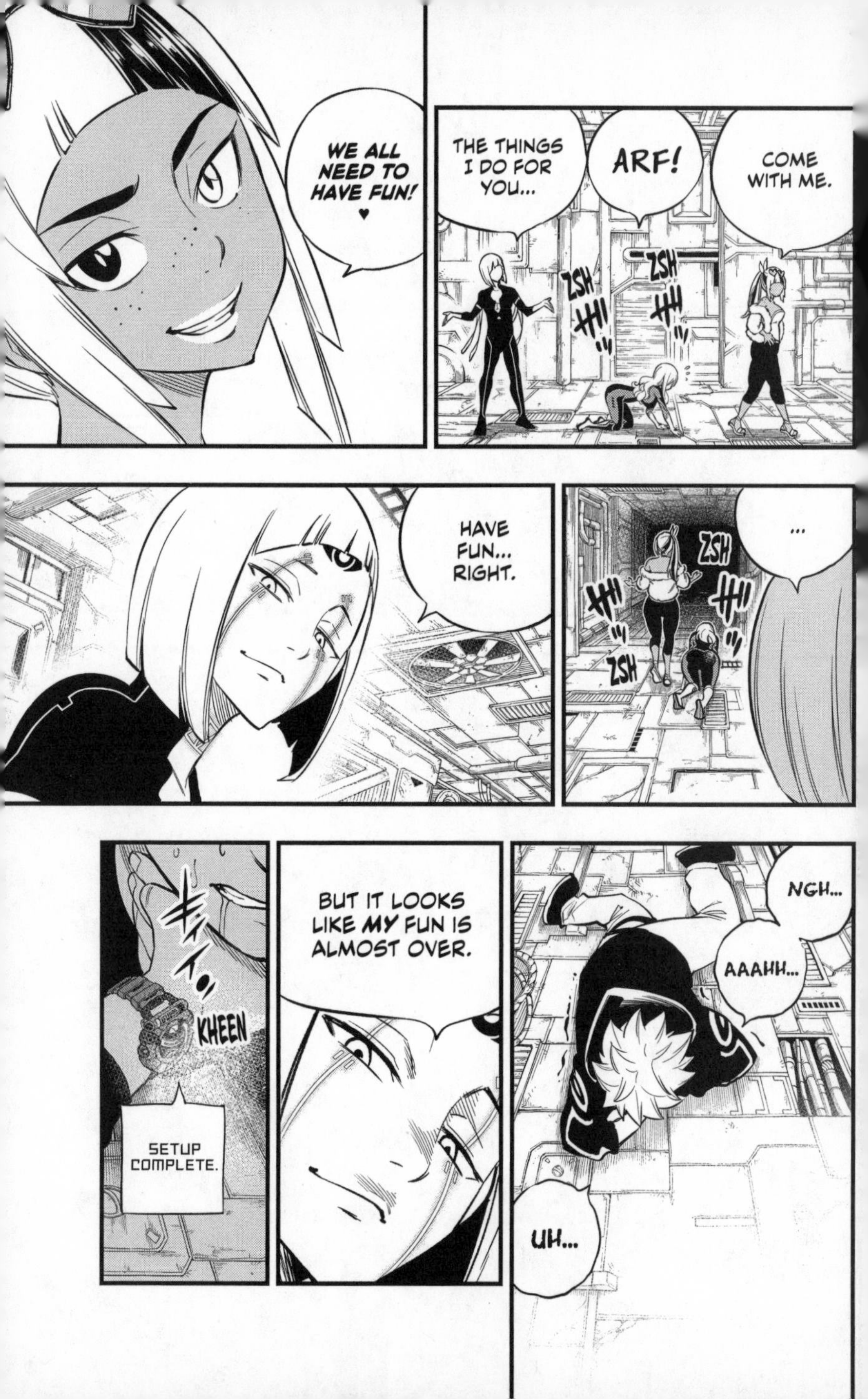
COME WITH ME.
ARF!
ZSH
THE THINGS I DO FOR YOU...
ZSH
WE ALL NEED TO HAVE FUN! ♥
...
ZSH
ZSH
HAVE FUN... RIGHT.
NGH...
AAAHH...
UH...
BUT IT LOOKS LIKE *MY* FUN IS ALMOST OVER.
KHEEN
SETUP COMPLETE.

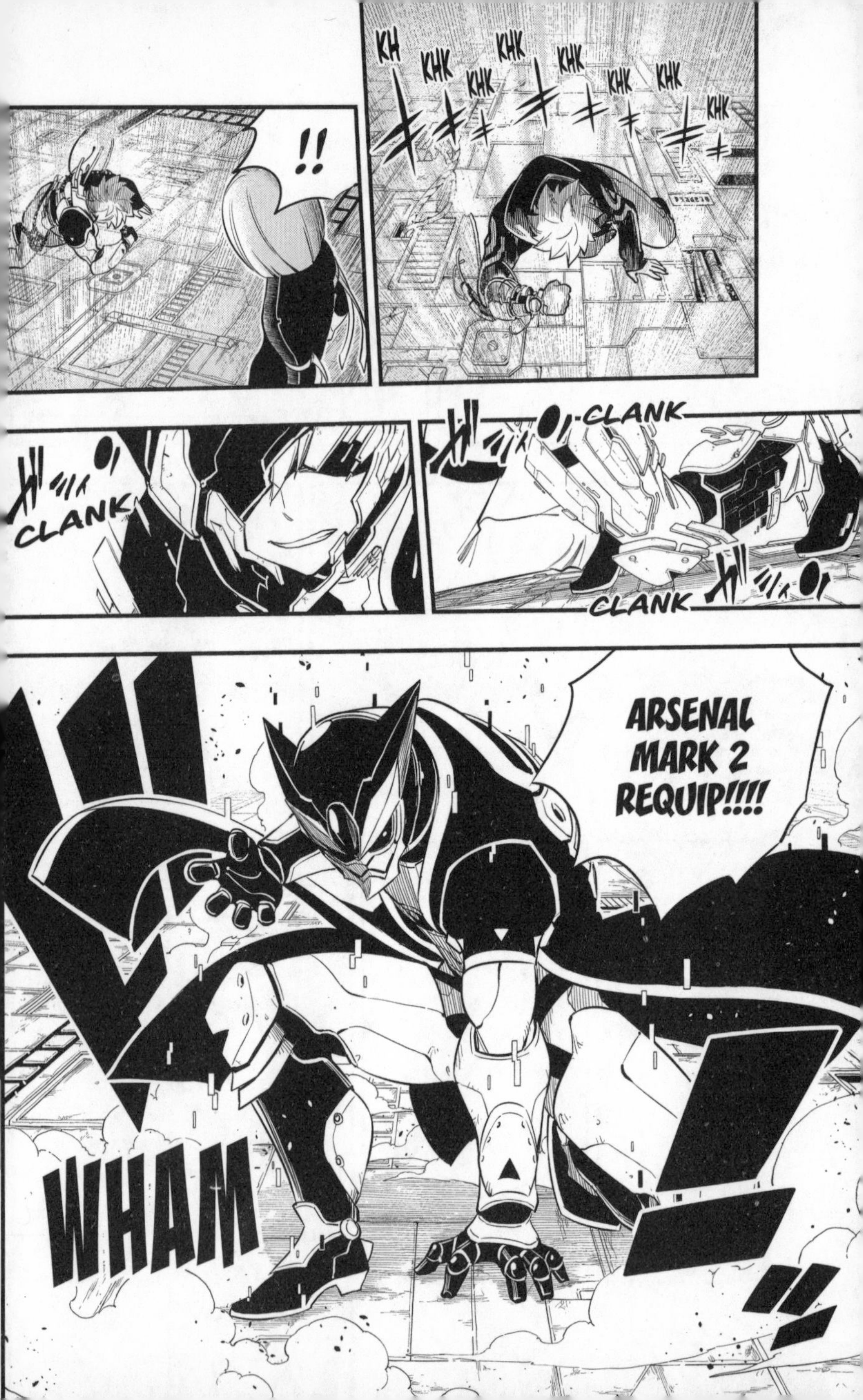
KH
KHK
KHK
KHK
KHK
KHK
KHK
KHK
!!
CLANK
CLANK
CLANK
ARSENAL MARK 2 REQUIP!!!!
WHAM

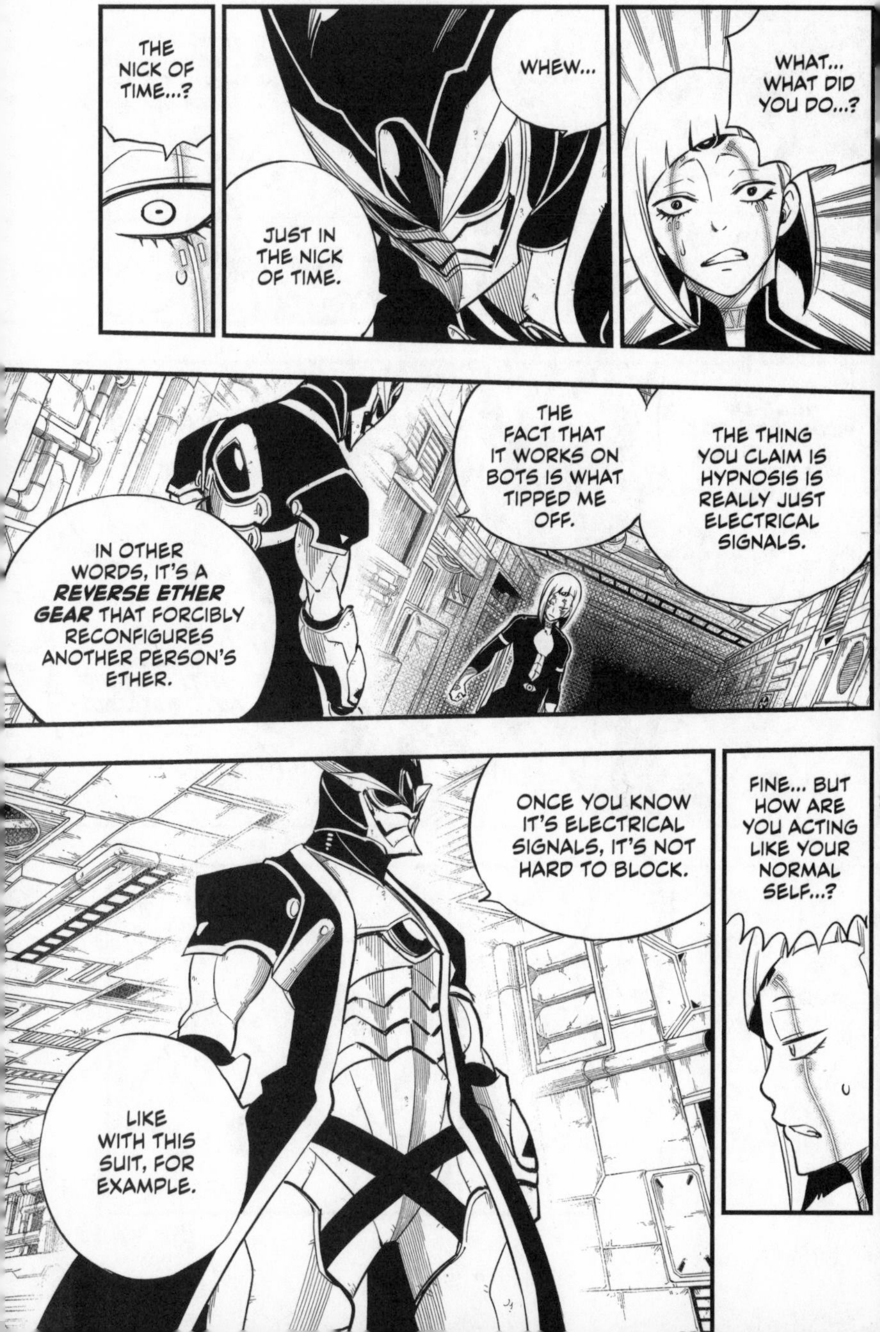
WHAT... WHAT DID YOU DO...?
WHEW...
JUST IN THE NICK OF TIME.
THE NICK OF TIME...?
THE THING YOU CLAIM IS HYPNOSIS IS REALLY JUST ELECTRICAL SIGNALS.
THE FACT THAT IT WORKS ON BOTS IS WHAT TIPPED ME OFF.
IN OTHER WORDS, IT'S A ***REVERSE ETHER GEAR*** THAT FORCIBLY RECONFIGURES ANOTHER PERSON'S ETHER.
FINE... BUT HOW ARE YOU ACTING LIKE YOUR NORMAL SELF...?
ONCE YOU KNOW IT'S ELECTRICAL SIGNALS, IT'S NOT HARD TO BLOCK.
LIKE WITH THIS SUIT, FOR EXAMPLE.

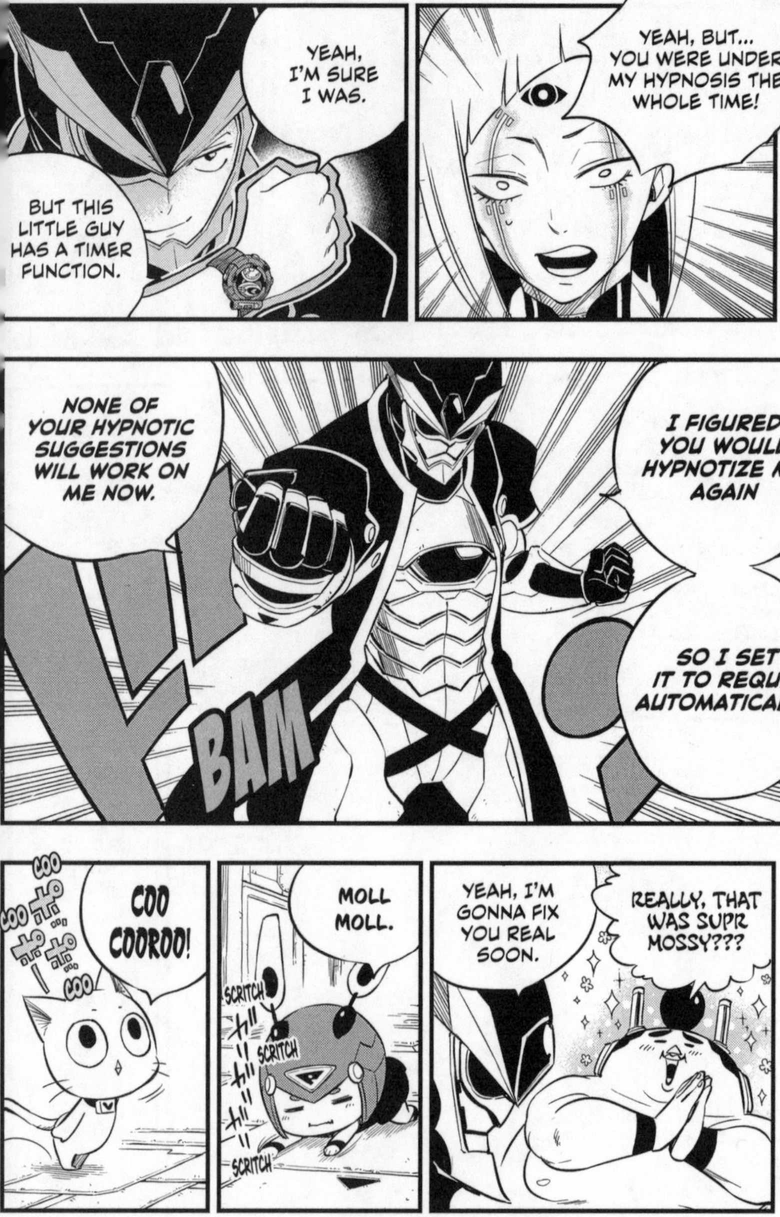
YEAH, BUT... YOU WERE UNDER MY HYPNOSIS THE WHOLE TIME!
YEAH, I'M SURE I WAS.
BUT THIS LITTLE GUY HAS A TIMER FUNCTION.
I FIGURED YOU WOULD HYPNOTIZE ME AGAIN
SO I SET IT TO REQUIP AUTOMATICALLY.
NONE OF YOUR HYPNOTIC SUGGESTIONS WILL WORK ON ME NOW.
BAM
REALLY, THAT WAS SUPR MOSSY???
YEAH, I'M GONNA FIX YOU REAL SOON.
MOLL MOLL.
SCRITCH
SCRITCH
SCRITCH
COO COOROO!
COO
COO
COO

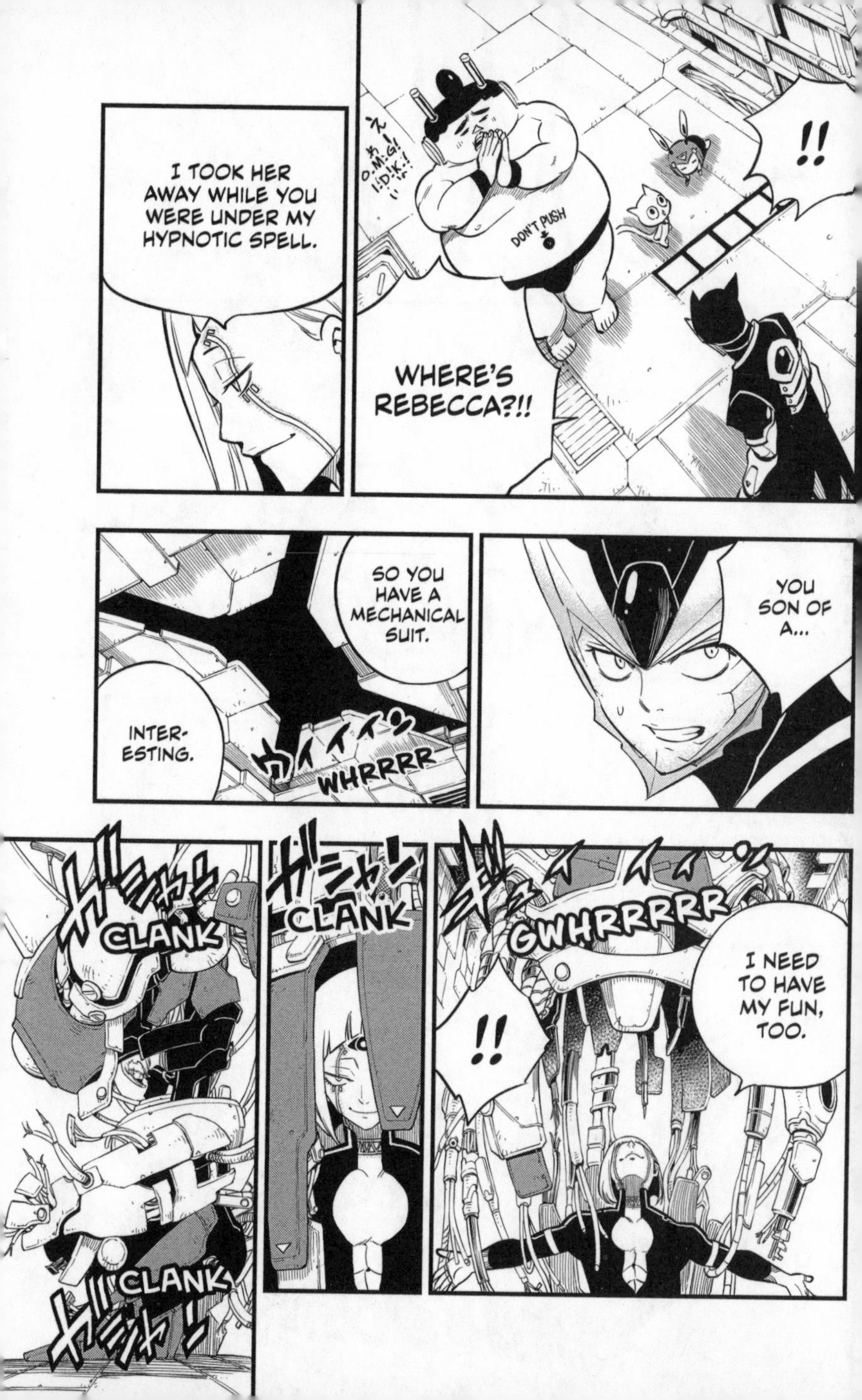
!!
O.M.G! I.D.K.!
DON'T PUSH
WHERE'S REBECCA?!!
I TOOK HER AWAY WHILE YOU WERE UNDER MY HYPNOTIC SPELL.
YOU SON OF A...
SO YOU HAVE A MECHANICAL SUIT.
INTER-ESTING.
WHRRRR
GWHRRRRR
!!
I NEED TO HAVE MY FUN, TOO.
CLANK
CLANK
CLANK

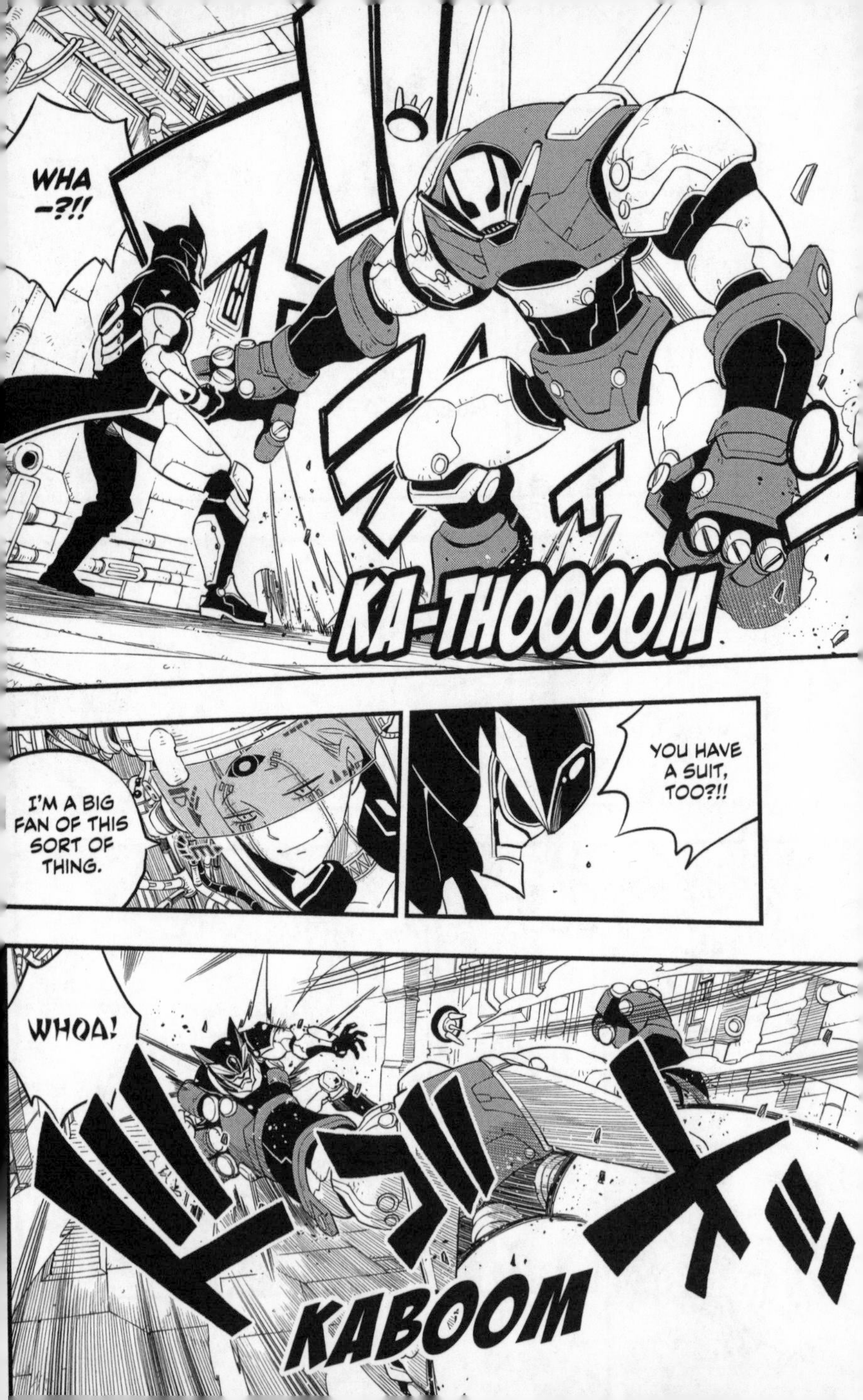
WHA
-?!!
KA-THOOOOM
YOU HAVE A SUIT, TOO?!!
I'M A BIG FAN OF THIS SORT OF THING.
WHOA!
KABOOM

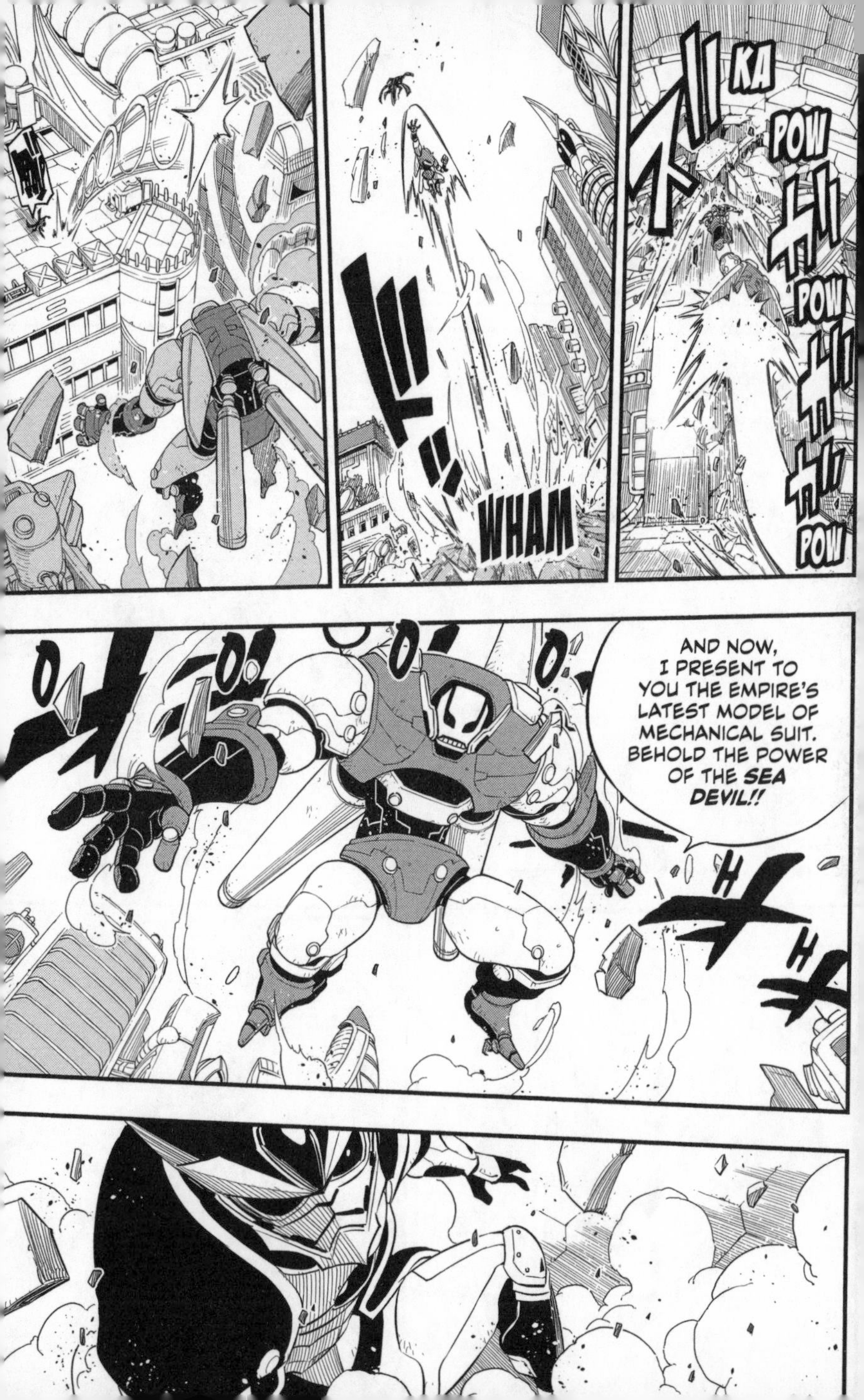
KA
POW
POW
POW
POW
WHAM
AND NOW, I PRESENT TO YOU THE EMPIRE'S LATEST MODEL OF MECHANICAL SUIT. BEHOLD THE POWER OF THE *SEA DEVIL!!*

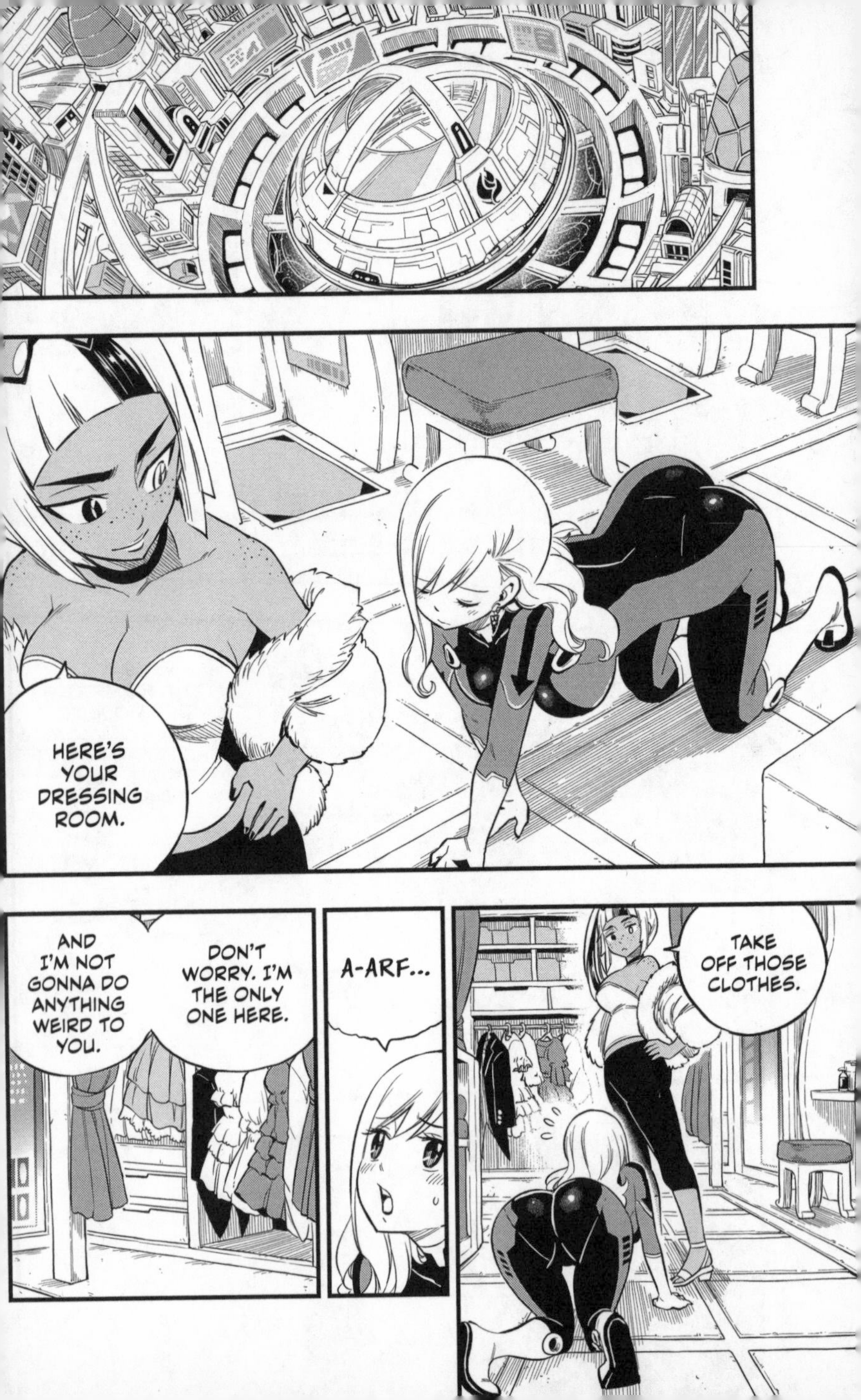
HERE'S YOUR DRESSING ROOM.
TAKE OFF THOSE CLOTHES.
A-ARF...
DON'T WORRY. I'M THE ONLY ONE HERE.
AND I'M NOT GONNA DO ANYTHING WEIRD TO YOU.

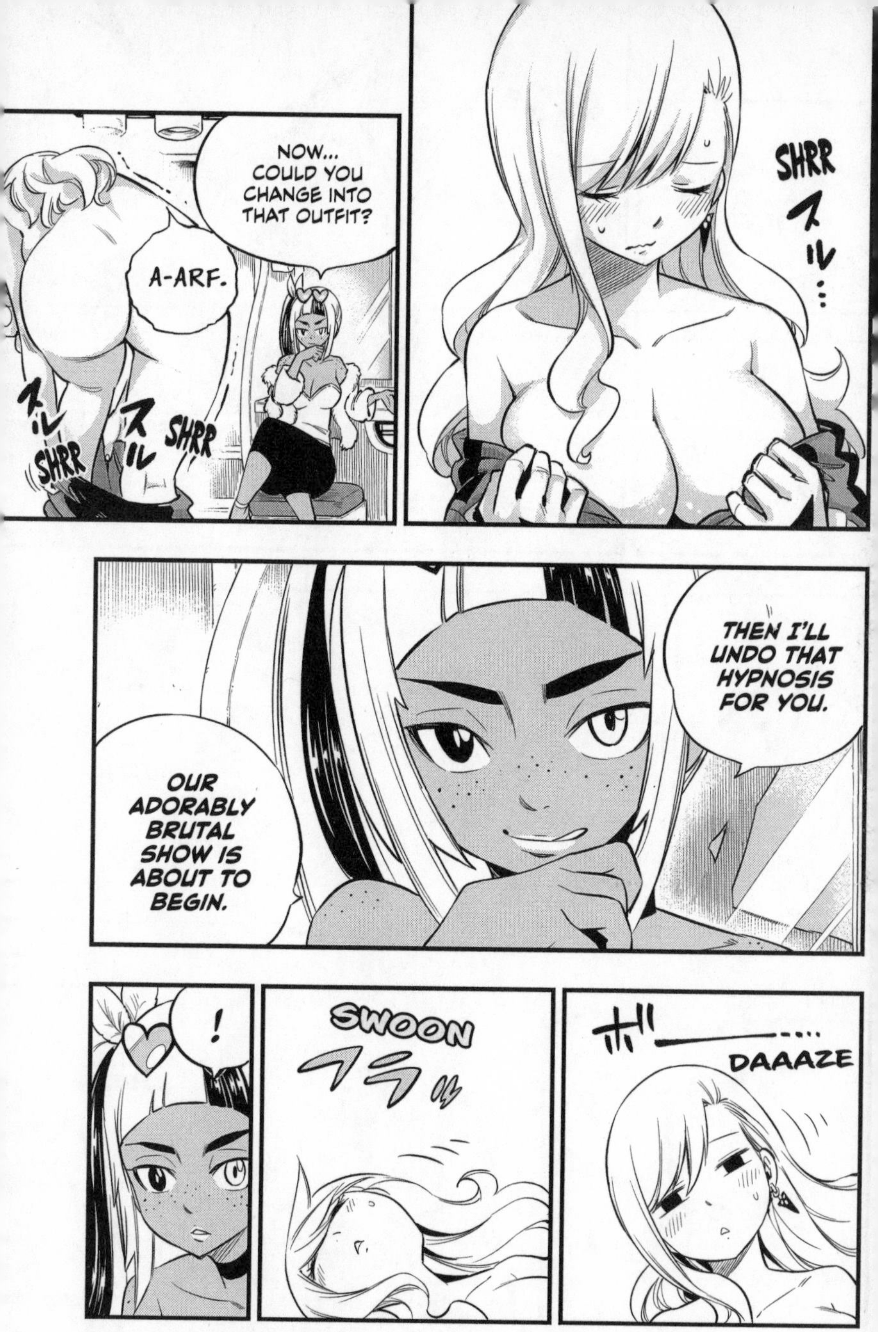
SHRR
スル…
NOW... COULD YOU CHANGE INTO THAT OUTFIT?
A-ARF.
スル SHRR
スル SHRR
THEN I'LL UNDO THAT HYPNOSIS FOR YOU.
OUR ADORABLY BRUTAL SHOW IS ABOUT TO BEGIN.
ボー…
DAAAZE
SWOON
フラッ
!

OH, MY. MAYBE THE HYPNOSIS WAS A LITTLE *TOO* EFFECTIVE.

OOPS!

BUT NOW WHAT?

I GUESS I'LL CHANGE HER CLOTHES AND SEE IF I CAN SNAP HER OUT OF IT.

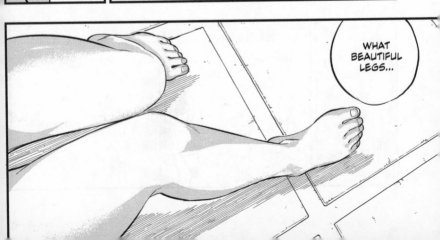

WHAT BEAUTIFUL LEGS...

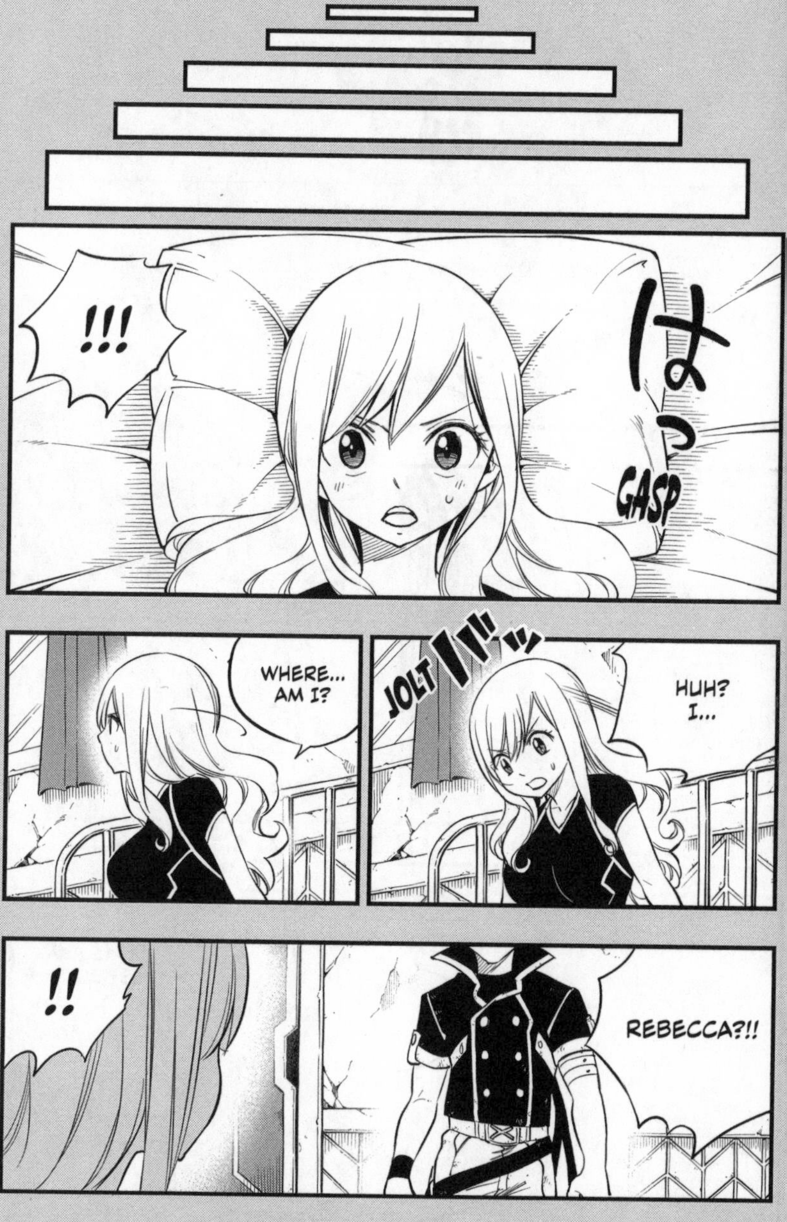

はっ
GASP
!!!
JOLT
HUH? I...
WHERE... AM I?
REBECCA?!!
!!

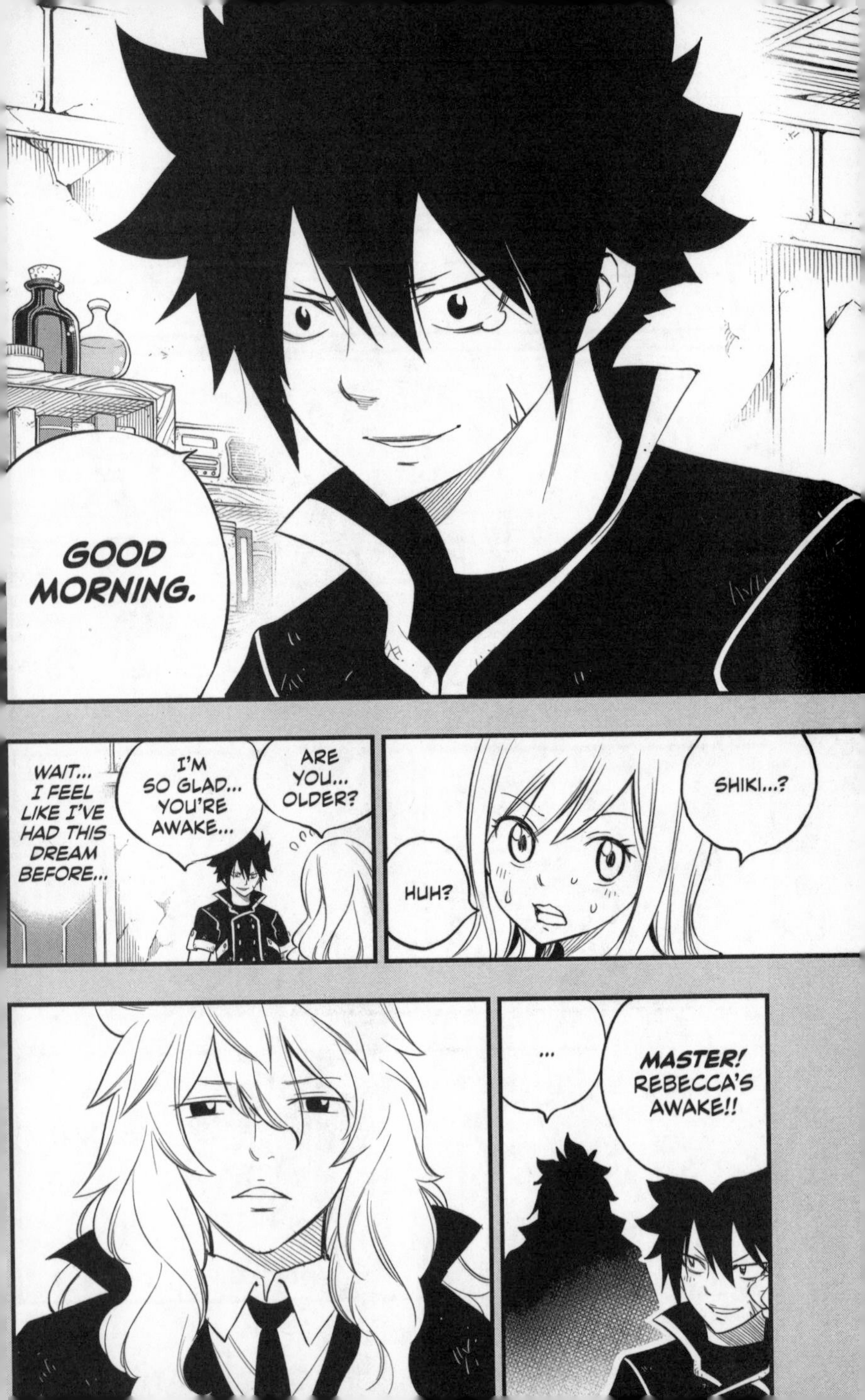
GOOD MORNING.
SHIKI...?
HUH?
ARE YOU... OLDER?
I'M SO GLAD... YOU'RE AWAKE...
WAIT... I FEEL LIKE I'VE HAD THIS DREAM BEFORE...
MASTER! REBECCA'S AWAKE!!
...

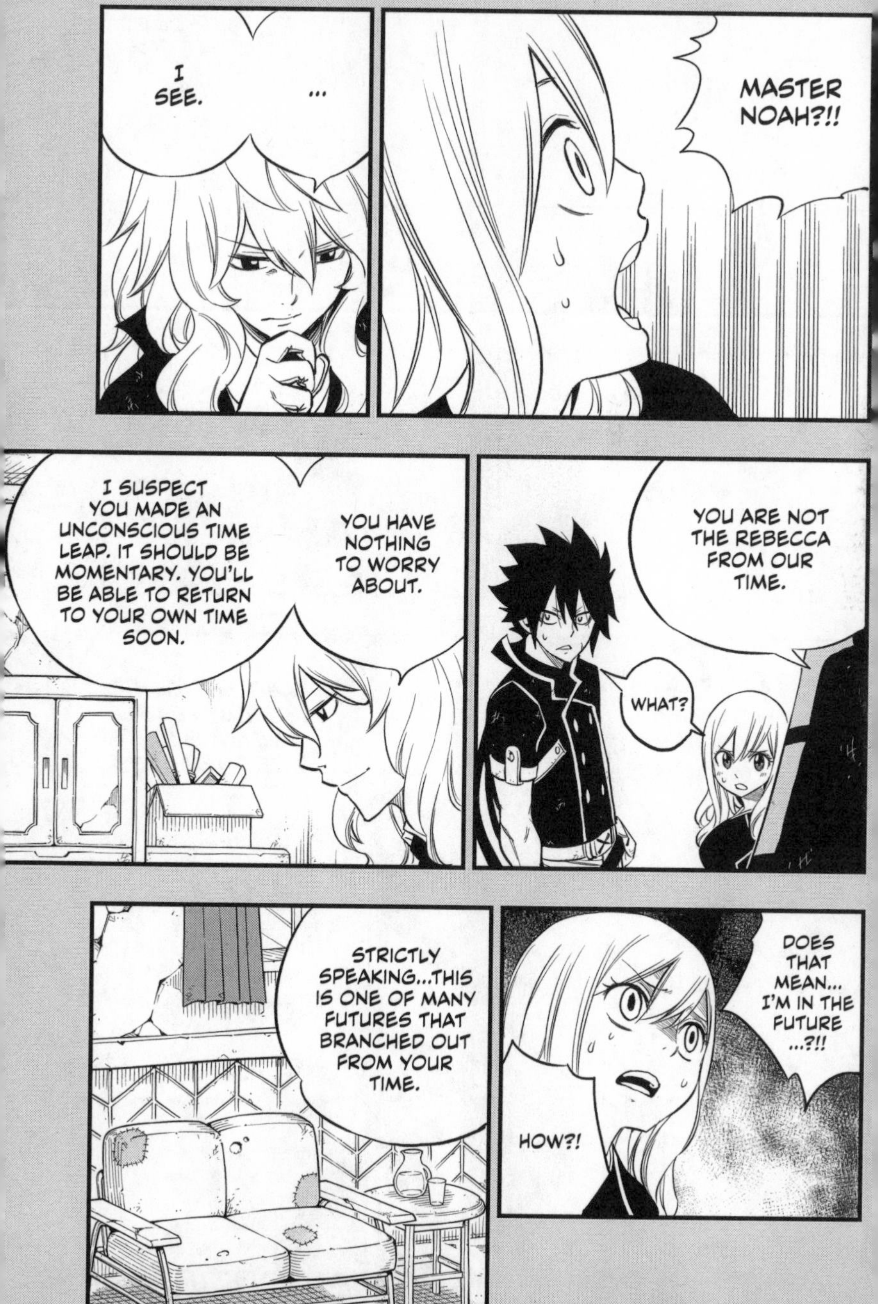
MASTER NOAH?!!
I SEE. ...
YOU ARE NOT THE REBECCA FROM OUR TIME.
WHAT?
I SUSPECT YOU MADE AN UNCONSCIOUS TIME LEAP. IT SHOULD BE MOMENTARY. YOU'LL BE ABLE TO RETURN TO YOUR OWN TIME SOON.
YOU HAVE NOTHING TO WORRY ABOUT.
DOES THAT MEAN... I'M IN THE FUTURE ...?!!
HOW?!
STRICTLY SPEAKING...THIS IS ONE OF MANY FUTURES THAT BRANCHED OUT FROM YOUR TIME.

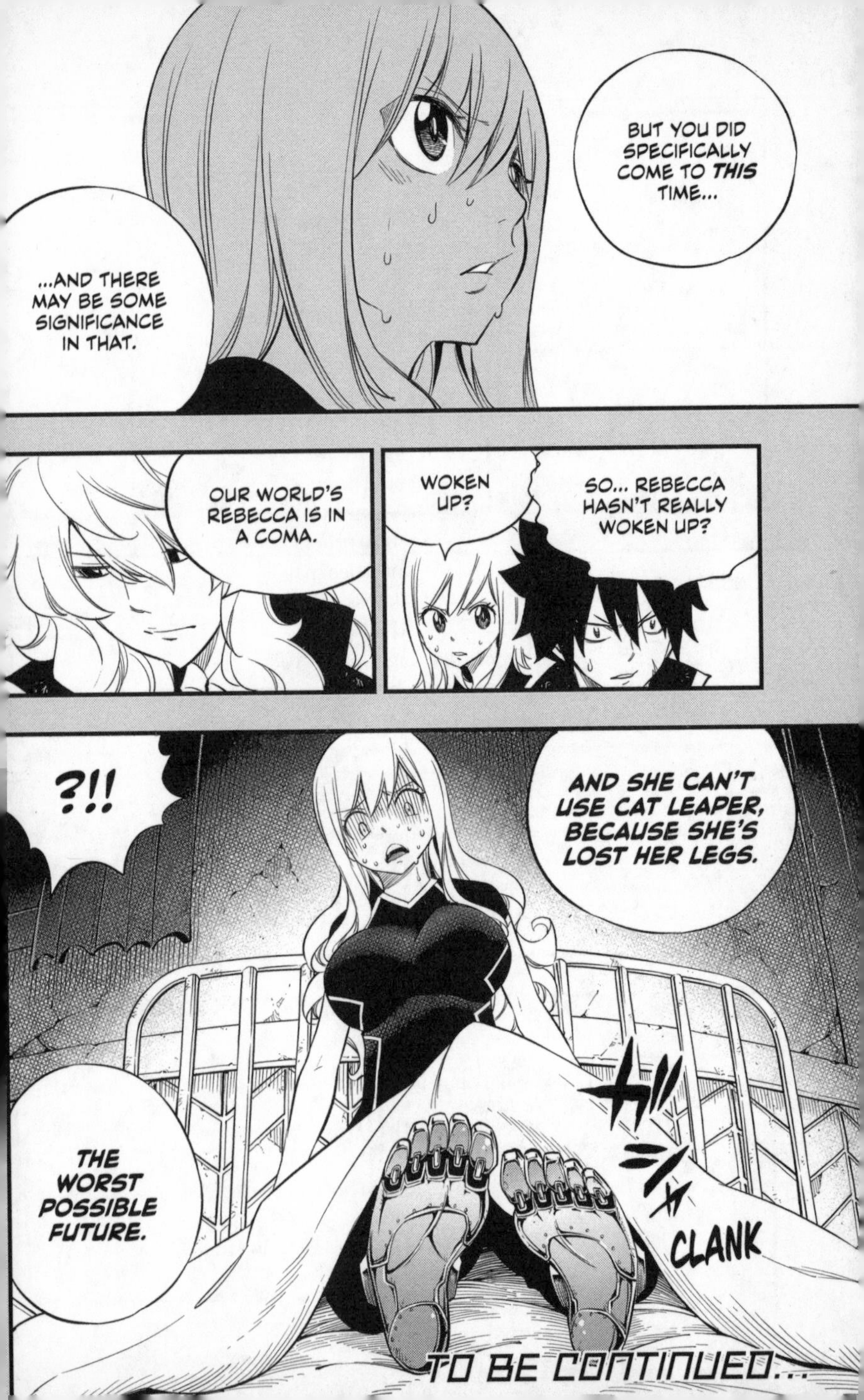
BUT YOU DID SPECIFICALLY COME TO THIS TIME...
...AND THERE MAY BE SOME SIGNIFICANCE IN THAT.
SO... REBECCA HASN'T REALLY WOKEN UP?
WOKEN UP?
OUR WORLD'S REBECCA IS IN A COMA.
AND SHE CAN'T USE CAT LEAPER, BECAUSE SHE'S LOST HER LEGS.
?!!
CLANK
THE WORST POSSIBLE FUTURE.
TO BE CONTINUED...

AFTERWORD

I mentioned this on the cover flap (the inside flap of the dust jacket on the original Japanese print release), too, but I always agonize over the colored illustrations. I've been painting digitally for almost 15 years now, but I have yet to arrive at a color style that has me going, "This is it!" You'd think, when you've been doing something for 15 years, that you would improve at it, but it still just doesn't go the way I want it to. I mean, I'm sure I have improved, but at the same time, so has my critical eye. So I'm never satisfied with my work. Of course, I do have some degree of satisfaction right when I've finished some art, but I keep going over it in my mind, thinking, "I could have colored that better. I could have made it prettier. I could have come up with a better color scheme."

Of course the only thing for it is to practice, but in the digital age, it's getting to be just as important to learn how to really use all the illustration tools. This is my weakness—I've only mastered the bare minimum of necessary tools and functions. There are a lot of tools that would probably help me get things done faster and raise the quality of my art, but I haven't figured out how to use them. I just can't learn them all. So I always end up using the same tools and the same coloring style, every time.

It's the worst when I change paint tools. I have to learn all the functions again from square one. It's awful.

Well, I'm just going to keep going at it with trial and error.

Here is my coloring tool history.

·Preschool – Middle School: colored pencil and watercolor

·High School: acrylic gouache (never got the hang of that one)

·Age 19 – Early in My Career: Copic markers (never got the hang of them)

·After that, don't remember exactly when I switched: Photoshop (never mastered it)

·Painter 6 (the tool of the gods!)

·Back to Photoshop (got a little proficient with it)

·SAI (God-like! I still use it. I feel like this is the one I'm most compatible with.)

· Clip Studio (God-like!...I think, but I haven't mastered it. I'm still practicing.)

And there you have it. I mainly use SAI and Clip Studio these days.

WELCOME TO THE NEXT INSTALLMENT OF...

(KAE SHIBATA-SAN, IBARAGI)

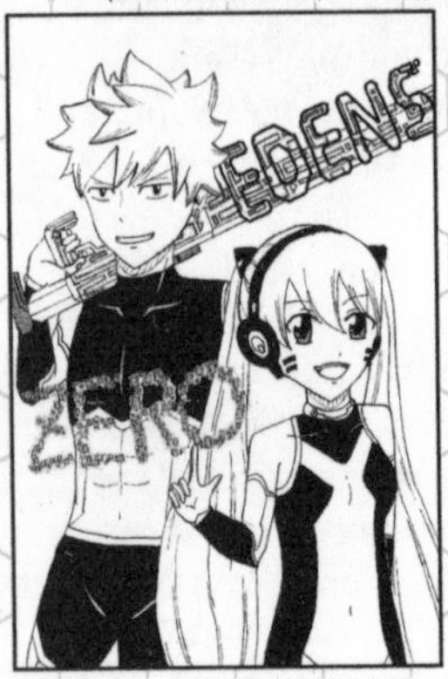
EDENS
ZERO

TWO CHARACTERS WHO ARE GOOD WITH MACHINES. I SEE THEM MAKING AN EXCELLENT TEAM.

(SHIDAKKU-SAN, AICHI)

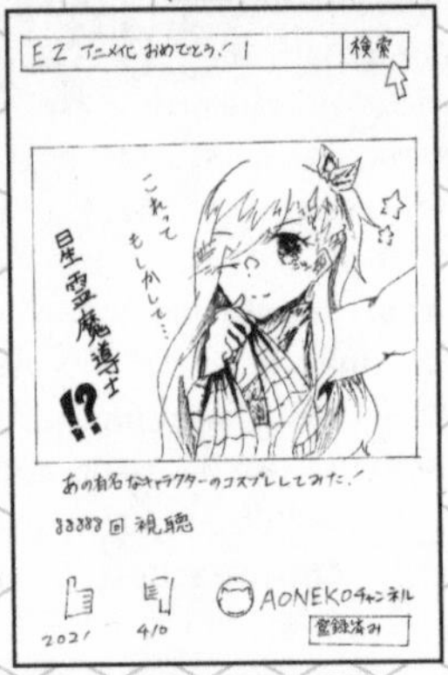
EZ アニメ化 おめでとう!
検索
これってもしかして…
星霊魔導士
!?
あの有名なキャラクターのコスプレしてみた!
88888回視聴
AONEKOチャンネル
登録済み
2021
4/10

WITH QUALITY LIKE THIS, EVEN DIEHARD LUCY FAN TAURUS WOULD BE KNOCKED OUT IN SECONDS!

(AYU TSUTSUI-SAN, KAGAWA)

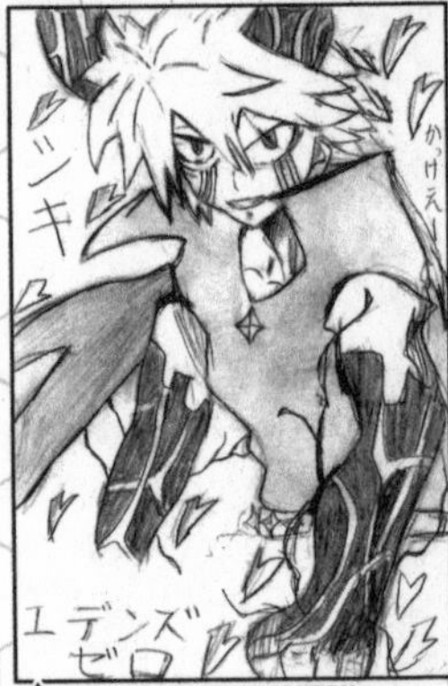
シキ
かっけえー
エデンズゼロ

▲ OVERDRIVE SHIKI IS VERY POPULAR. IS HIS UNFETTERED WILDNESS THAT APPEALING?!

(KARINA TANIGUCHI-SAN, NAGASAKI)

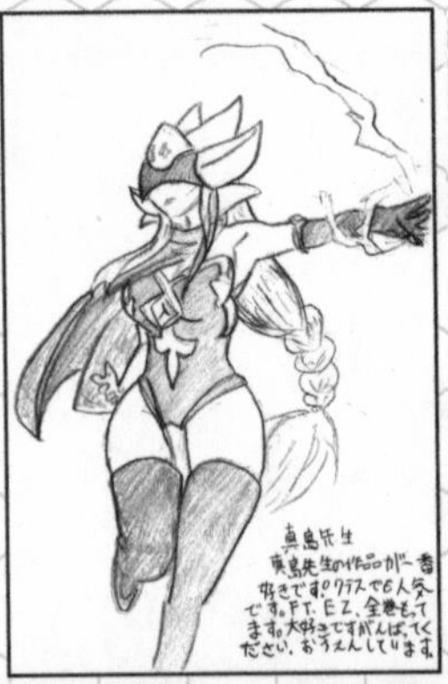

STRONG, KIND, BEAUTIFUL...AND YET, WITH A PLAYFUL SIDE.... SHE IS TRULY THE ALMIGHTY WITCH.

MASHIMA'S ONE-HIT KO

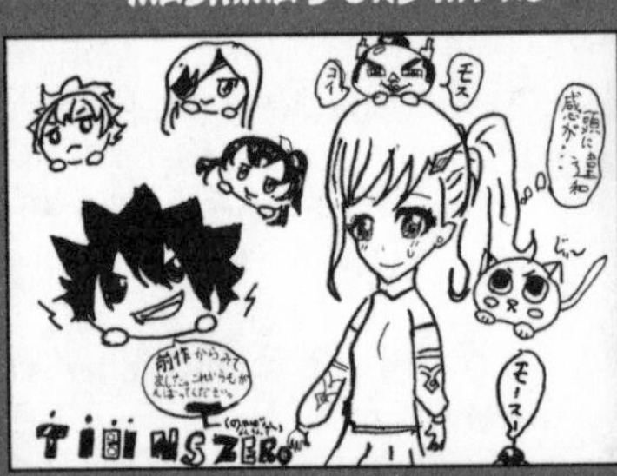
モス
モース

(MIKA MAEMURA-SAN, HOKKAIDO)

IN THIS GREAT BIG UNIVERSE, MAYBE IT'S NOT SO STRANGE TO THINK THEY COULD TURN INTO CHIBIS LIKE THIS?!

*Fan art submissions are limited to Japan-only.

E2 DRAWING

(CHIHIRO-SAN, OSAKA)

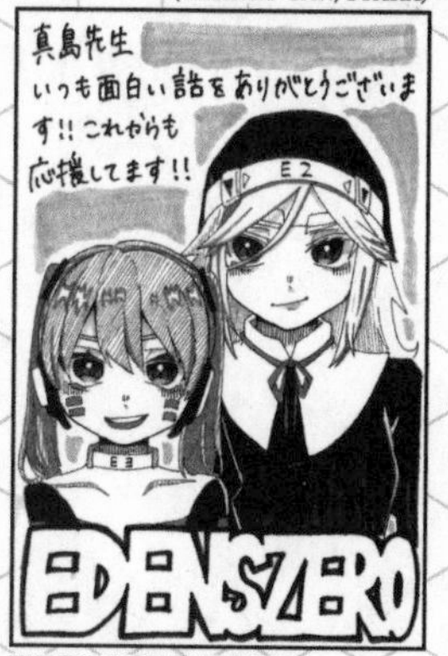
真島先生
いつも面白い話をありがとうございます!! これからも応援してます!!
EDENS ZERO

THE BIG EYES MAKE A BIG IMPRESSION FROM THE MIND AND LIFE OF EDENS. YOU CAN FEEL THEIR STRONG BOND.

(MAKI SATODA-SAN, SAITAMA)

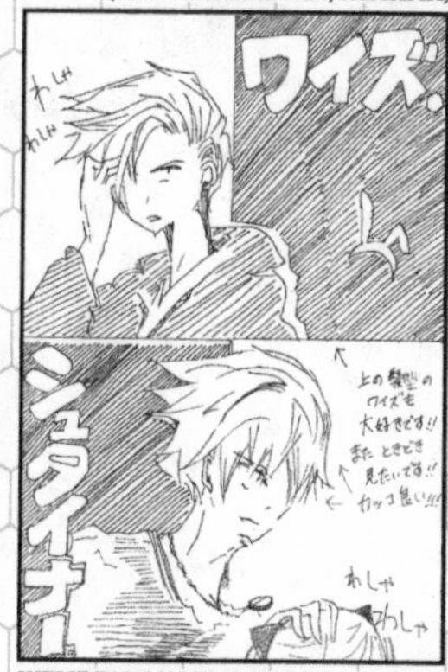
ワイズ!
シュタイナー
わしゃわしゃ
上の髪型のワイズも大好きです!! またときどき見たいです!! カッコ良い!!!

WEISZ FANS NOTICE THE CHANGES IN HIS HAIR. WHICH VERSION IS MORE POPULAR?

(SOYOKA-SAN, TOCHIGI)

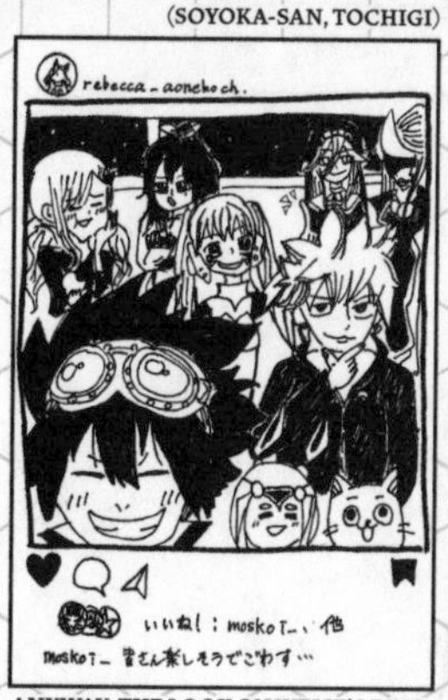
rebecca_aonekoch.
いいね!: moskoT... 他
moskoT... 皆さん楽しそうでごわす...

ANYWAY, THE LOOK ON WEISZ'S FACE IS THE BEST. MEANWHILE, WHERE IS MOSCO...?

(BAKARON-SAN, TOKYO)

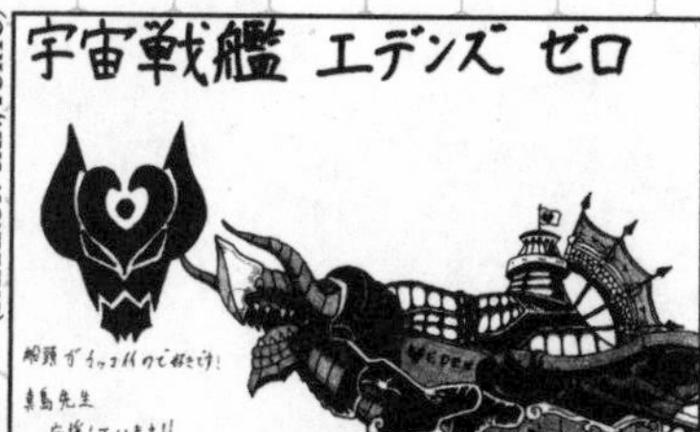
宇宙戦艦 エデンズ ゼロ
EDEN
船頭がネコっぽいので好きです!
真島先生
応援しています!!

WHOA! FIRST FAN ART OF THE SHIP! THERE AREN'T A LOT OF PEOPLE WHO LIKE DRAWING MECHA, SO THIS MAKES ME REALLY HAPPY!!

(SHOGO SHIMIZU, NAGASAKI)

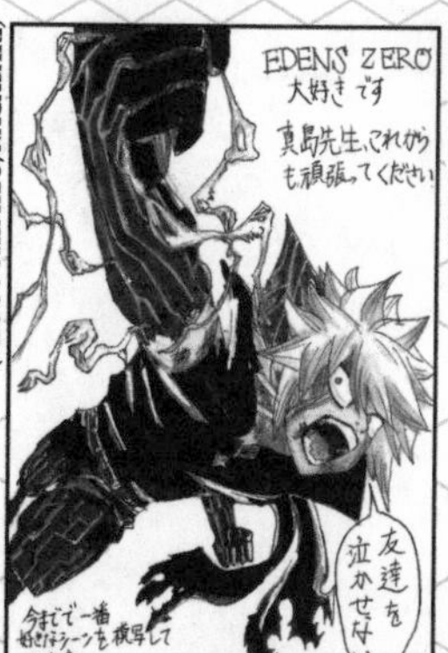
EDENS ZERO
大好きです
真島先生、これからも頑張ってください
友達を泣かせない
今までで一番好きなシーンを模写してみました。

THIS IS FROM THE CLIMAX OF THE DRAKKEN BATTLE. YOU CAN LOOK FORWARD TO SEEING SHIKI GET EVEN MORE POWERFUL!

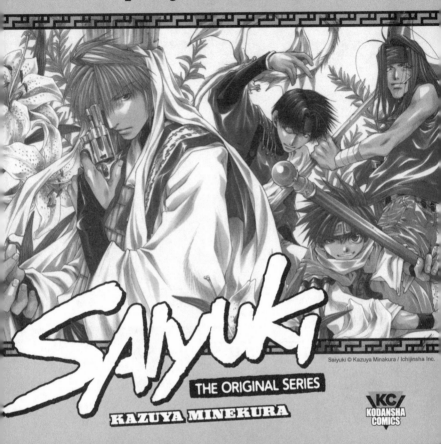

Young characters and steampunk setting, like *Howl's Moving Castle* and *Battle Angel Alita*

Beyond the Clouds © 2018 Nicke / Ki-oon

A boy with a talent for machines and a mysterious girl whose wings he's fixed will take you beyond the clouds! In the tradition of the high-flying, resonant adventure stories of Studio Ghibli comes a gorgeous tale about the longing of young hearts for adventure and friendship!

A Kodansha Comics Trade Paperback Original
EDENS ZERO 17 copyright © 2021 Hiro Mashima
English translation copyright © 2022 Hiro Mashima

All rights reserved.

Published in the United States by Kodansha Comics, an imprint of Kodansha USA Publishing, LLC, New York.

Publication rights for this English edition arranged through Kodansha Ltd., Tokyo.

First published in Japan in 2021 by Kodansha Ltd., Tokyo.

ISBN 978-1-64651-472-4

Printed in the United States of America.

www.kodansha.us

9 8 7 6 5 4 3 2 1
Translation: Alethea Nibley & Athena Nibley
Lettering: AndWorld Design
Editing: David Yoo
Kodansha Comics edition cover design by Phil Balsman

Publisher: Kiichiro Sugawara

Director of publishing services: Ben Applegate
Director of publishing operations: Dave Barrett
Associate director, publishing operations: Stephen Pakula
Publishing services managing ditors: Madison Salters, Alanna Ruse
Production managers: Emi Lotto, Angela Zurlo